D0722414

3 1

DATE DUE

M

MA

F

LIGHT ONE CANDLE

LIGHT ONE CANDLE

A *Survivor's Tale from Lithuania to Jerusalem*

Solly Ganor

KODANSHA INTERNATIONAL
New York • Tokyo • London

Kodansha America, Inc.
114 Fifth Avenue, New York, New York 10011, U.S.A.

Kodansha International Ltd.
17-14 Otowa 1-chome, Bunkyo-ku, Tokyo 112, Japan

Published in 1995 by Kodansha America, Inc.

Library of Congress Cataloging-in-Publication Data

Ganor, Solly, 1928–
Light one candle : a survivor's tale from Lithuania
to Jerusalem / Solly Ganor.
p.   cm.
ISBN 1-56836-098-3
1. Jews—Persecutions—Lithuania—Kaunas. 2. Holocaust,
Jewish (1939–1945)—Lithuania—Kaunas—Personal narratives.
3. Ganor, Solly, 1928– . 4. Kaunas (Lithuania)—Ethnic relations.
I. Title.
DS135.L52K384   1995
940.53'18'09475—dc20   95–20720

Book Design by Charles and Wendy Murphy

Printed in the United States of America

95 96 97 98 99   BER/B   10 9 8 7 6 5 4 3 2 1

For my mother Rebecca and brother Herman,
and all those who perished during the war.

For my father Chaim and sister Fanny,
and all those who helped me survive the Holocaust years.

For Chiune Sugihara, Clarence Matsumura,
and the men of the 522nd Field Artillery Battalion,
my guide and my rescuers.

For my wife Pola and children, Leora and Danny.

CONTENTS

Acknowledgments ix

Prologue xi

Part One

1 The War of Independence 3

2 The Shtrom Clan 14

3 The Soul of a Human Is the Lamp of the Lord 33

4 Schrecklichkeit 51

5 The Seventh Fort 73

6 The Ghetto 92

7 The Five Hundred Intellectuals 106

8 Aunt Leena 134

9 The Big Action 152

10 Return of a Ghost 168

11 Winter 1941 190

12 The Book Action 206

Part Two

13 The Children's Action 229

14 Evacuation of the Ghetto 249

15 Arbeit Macht Frei 261

16 Pigs 271

17   Scheherazade   283

18   Moll   291

19   The Present Is a Mighty Goddess   304

20   Christmas 1944   310

21   Vernichtung Durch Arbeit   318

22   The Death March   335

23   Liberation   344

A Remembrance   351

ACKNOWLEDGMENTS

I would like to express my gratitude to Eric Saul, Lani Silver, and the dedicated volunteers of the Holocaust Oral History Project of San Francisco, for helping me confront my past. Thanks also to Yukiko Sugihara and family, for helping restore my faith in humanity.

Grateful acknowledgment goes to my fellow survivors: Uri Chanoch, David Granat, Aba Naor, David Levine, Chaim Konwitz, Arie Ivtsan, Zwi Katz, and the many others who helped me to remember clearly the Holocaust years. Thanks to George Oiye for the valuable information on the 522nd Field Artillery Battalion and to Lea Eliash for her memories of Kaunas.

Thanks to the Japanese American National Museum of Los Angeles, the National Japanese American Historical Society of San Francisco, the Simon Wiesenthal Center, and the Museum of Tolerance for valuable information.

Thanks also to Minato Asakawa, Philip Turner, and Joshua Sitzer at Kodansha for all their help and advice. Lastly, a very special and heartfelt thanks goes to Kathy Banks for the many hours of hard work and tender care she put into helping shape this book.

Two diaries have been of invaluable help in checking facts and dates: Josef Gar's *The Holocaust of the Jewish Kovne,* published in Munich in 1948 and now out of print; and Avraham Tory's *Surviving the Holocaust: The Kovno Ghetto Diary,* edited by Martin Gilbert (Harvard University Press, 1990).

PROLOGUE

Kaunas, Lithuania, is a little-known spot on the map for most Americans. It looms large in my memory, however. It is where I spent the greater part of my childhood, and where a large part of the story that follows takes place.

In Lithuania, Kaunas has been known as the "provisional capital" of the country ever since 1920, when Poland annexed Vilnius during the Russo-Polish war. A minor war, by later standards, and only one of many struggles that have torn the Baltic states over the centuries. In Lithuania you don't have to look far for reminders of the bloody history. Kaunas itself is ringed by old forts, built around the turn of the century by a Russian Tsar. When I was about nine years old, around 1937, my friends and I were thrilled to stumble upon the skeleton of a Russian officer. He was in a cave in the woods surrounding Kalautuvas, a little resort town a few miles downriver from Kaunas. Around the earthly remains of this lonely soul, who died so far from home, we concocted a whole history full of dash and heroism and high tragedy.

By 1940 Vilnius was once again the capital of Lithuania, but Lithuanians continued to refer to Kaunas as the "provisional capital." It was a lovely city of nearly 120,000 people. More than thirty thousand Jews lived and prospered in the town, my family among them. For many years Kaunas was one of the few places in Europe where the Jews were able to live nearly autonomously, and they built a strong community. Its Yeshivas attracted students from all over Europe. Its professionals and scholars and merchants played an important role in the town's economy. Its cultural life was diverse and sophisticated. I remember being very happy there.

I was eleven years old when Hitler marched into Poland. The weeks and months that followed were fearful ones, as news of atrocities against Polish Jews reached us and refugees began streaming over the border into Lithuania. The Nazis had begun their inexorable march across the face of Europe, and would soon put our old Tsarist forts to hideous use. The next six years would turn out to be far more terrible than even the grimmest pessimists among us could foresee.

In 1939 and 1940 Kaunas became a sort of way station filled with people desperately seeking asylum from the Nazis. They sought help from any country they thought might receive them. Most of them were denied and were turned away by one government after another, including the governments of the United States and Great Britain. The one official who offered the Jews of Kaunas any hope was the representative of a government which shortly became Germany's strongest ally. That man was the Consul of Japan, Chiune Sugihara,* who risked his career, his honor, perhaps even his life, to save more than six thousand Jews.

In my memory of those years Sugihara stands out as a single light in a sea of darkness. My family, for various reasons, was not among the fortunate thousands he helped directly, but he remained an inspiration to me throughout the terrible years to come—years spent in the Slabodke ghetto and in the camps of Dachau.

How strange and wonderful it was to recognize Sugihara's ethnic features again five years after I last laid eyes on him, and at the very moment of my liberation. His eyes, and even something of his smile were in the kind face of the G.I. who brought me back from the brink of death. For it was a Japanese American, or Nisei, who lifted me from a snowbank where German SS guards had left me for dead. The Nisei soldier's name was Clarence Matsumura, and he was with the 522nd FABN—the field artillery battalion of the famous 100th/442nd Combat Team, a regimental-sized unit composed entirely of segregated units of Japanese American troops. These men came both from Hawaii and from the mainland, and many were volunteers. They served on the bloody battlefields of Italy, France, and Germany. The 100th/442nd suffered more casualties and won more medals for its length of service than any other American unit in the war.

The irony is not lost on me that even as Clarence and his kinsmen were fighting and dying for the United States, many of their families were incarcerated in American detention camps. Along with all Americans of Japanese descent living on the West Coast of the U.S. mainland, the families of nearly half of these Nisei troops had been uprooted from their homes and businesses and sent to live in tar paper barracks in desolate areas. The United States called these detention centers "relocation camps." Concentration camps under another name.

I met Clarence Matsumura on May 2, 1945. Our paths didn't cross again for thirty-six years. During those years I did not speak of my

*Sugihara's proper given name was Chiune, but I knew him as Sempo, a friendly nickname by which he was known in Lithuania.

wartime experiences with others, except among those few who survived the ghettos and camps with me. Only they could understand. I found out later that many of our rescuers could not speak of what they saw either. But then, in 1981, Clarence Matsumura walked into the National Japanese American Historical Society of San Francisco and told his story to Eric Saul, a historian who directed the Presidio Army Museum and later worked with San Francisco's Holocaust Oral History Project. Eric knew of the role that the 522nd Field Artillery Battalion played in the rescue of the infamous Death March from Dachau, but Clarence was the first to come forward and tell his personal story:

"Toward the end of the war, when we'd finally broken the Siegfried Line and the Germans were in retreat, three of my buddies and I pulled into a German village called Wasseralfingen. There was a hill there that was covered with artificial trees. These things looked like they were made of two by fours. They had painted 'em green and laid them all out over this hill, which looked like it was man-made, too. Grass was growing on it, but there were no ravines or any natural markings like that. We went around and discovered a tunnel with a great big wire fence across it. There were all kinds of people in there, staring through the fence. We were staring at them, and they were staring back at us, Orientals in U.S. Army uniforms. It took us a few minutes to realize these were not German workers, but prisoners. Polish, Bulgarian, all different nationalities. Inside the tunnel there was a railroad track, with bunk beds all lined up and down one side. Down the other side piles of all kinds of machine parts were laid out. An assembly line ran on the tracks, and it looked like they were putting together 88 millimeter artillery pieces. Antiaircraft pieces, famous for their deadly fire.

"These people in the tunnel were afraid to come out at first. We couldn't really talk to them, because nobody seemed to speak English. We more or less figured out what they were doing because we recognized the gun parts. Finally we located a few doctors and lawyers who could speak English, and they explained. The prisoners weren't starving like those we found later, but they were happy to come outside into the air. They had been in that tunnel for so long.

"We didn't know anything about slave labor camps then. We didn't know what the hell was going on.

"There were four of us driving around in a weapons transport, mostly on Hitler's autobahns and at highway speeds. Sergeant Mas Fujimoto was driving, and old man Tanaka, acting as observer, was up front, and then there was David Sugimoto, the radio operator, and me. I was there as a

repairman. We were acting as forward observers. The Germans were retreating so fast then that our infantry could hardly keep up.

"Later on we came to a really peaceful-looking town. It was called Dachau. I had never heard of it before. Right in the middle of town was what looked like a big factory, with a high fence all around and two big brick smokestacks in the middle. Before we ever reached it we noticed the odd smell. You just can't describe it, but you never forget it. The smell of decaying human flesh. There were dead corpses all piled up everywhere in there. A lot of them in striped uniforms, many of them naked. This thing is right in the middle of town, and there are dead bodies all over the doggone place. I was very shook up. I kept trying to figure out what the heck is this doggone thing?

"We went out into the town, with some men from the battery who could speak German, and started interrogating the townspeople. 'Where are the sol-daten? *The guards? Where did they go? Did you know there are all kinds of dead people in there?' Right in the middle of town, and the townspeople claimed that they didn't know anything about any of this. Then someone told us the soldiers had marched a lot of prisoners out of town several days ago. And that a day or two later the last of the soldiers came around and took all the townspeople's animals and bicycles, and just took off.*

"We took off after them, following the road the townspeople pointed out. Farther along, toward some other villages, we started finding people along the roadside. Almost all of them were wearing black and white striped uniforms. I don't know how any of them could stand on their feet. They were nothing but skin and bones. They couldn't speak. Most of them were lying on the ground, many of them unconscious. We were supposed to be chasing down the SS, but these people were starving. They were lying out on the cold ground. We said let's get them into someplace warm, get them some food. We put them into gasthauses, *we put them into barns. We got them inside and got them blankets, gave them water and food, but the rest of our guys kept bringing in more and more people. They kept finding them along the roads. Pretty soon we ran out of places. We went into the villages and got the Germans out of their houses and brought these prisoners in. We put them in their beds, on their sofas, wherever we could make them comfortable. The Germans didn't need the doggone houses. These people needed the houses.*

"The first thing we got them was water. But the thing was, a lot of them couldn't swallow. They were starving, but only the strong ones could eat or drink, and many of them had lost their teeth from scurvy. The really weak ones couldn't even swallow water. You could give it to them, but it didn't do any good because it just wouldn't go down.

"We contacted our mess crew to find out if there was any way they could make the mush they fed us in the morning. We took powdered eggs and whipped them up with water and then added more water to make them really soupy. But only the strong ones could eat it. Nothing we tried seemed to work on the others.

"I remember holding these people up and trying to feed them broth. The word came down that we shouldn't try to feed them solid food because we would only harm them. Give them broth, they said, let them drink if they can, give them mush if they can eat it. We were doing that day and night for several days. We didn't know what else to do. All we could do was clean them up, give them blankets, try to get some broth down them, spoon by spoon. The strange thing was, there were only men there. I don't think I saw any women. But unless you undressed and bathed them you couldn't really tell. They were so emaciated you couldn't tell whether they were men or women.

"Did I talk about it with my family, with the other Nisei? No, I didn't talk about it. How could anyone understand who didn't see it? It's not that easy to talk about. It affected all of us. It took us a long time to get over that doggone thing. We couldn't understand why people had to go and do things like that to other human beings. You really can't explain how it is, when you've got all these people, so many of them, and you're trying to help them and they're dying right there in your hands."

Ten years after that interview, in April of 1992, Eric Saul called me in Israel.

April is the most beautiful time of the year in Israel, just before the harsh summer heat invades the country. The orange groves are in bloom, and the sweet delicate bouquet of orange blossoms permeates the countryside. This is the month of Passover, when we celebrate the Israelites' exodus from Egypt some three thousand years ago. It is also the month of Yom Hashoa, the Day of the Holocaust, when the entire country mourns the Jewish victims of the Nazis during World War II. On that day the survivors of the Holocaust remember all their loved ones that perished during the war. For many survivors, the dead include their entire families.

That evening I was sitting on my terrace in Herzelia, listening to the waves wash ashore on the sandy beach below. It always has a calming effect on on me. Sometimes I imagine I hear a plaintive note in the constant murmur of the water, as if the sea is reminding me I wasn't true to her. For many years I was a merchant seaman, plying the oceans of the world, until I left the sea for another woman—my wife Pola.

I'd been restless the whole day. During the war I'd developed a sort of sixth sense warning me of things to come, an instinct for survival that served me well in the camps and again during Israel's War of Independence. It was an uneasy sort of feeling that something was about to happen, and when the telephone rang I didn't want to answer it. It rang several times before I finally picked up the receiver.

"May I speak to Solly Ganor?" It was a pleasant American voice. I hesitated before identifying myself.

"I am here with a group of Japanese American veterans who were among the liberators of Dachau in 1945," the man said. "I was told that you were among the survivors of the Death March from Dachau."

My instincts had been right. This man with the pleasant voice was going to stir up memories I'd kept carefully boxed off from the rest of my life for nearly fifty years.

"Do you recall the name of the place where you were liberated?" he asked. His name was Eric Saul, and he spoke quietly, with sensitivity.

I was silent for a long time, but my heart was thudding in my chest. He waited.

"I was liberated at a small village in Bavaria, called Waakirchen," I finally said.

"Do you remember seeing any Japanese American soldiers when you were liberated?"

Did I remember? Did I remember? How could I ever forget the very first face I saw, at the very moment I emerged from hell? But something within me continued to rebel against this intrusion from the past.

No one who wasn't there, no matter how sensitive or imaginative, could have any inkling of what we went through. Those who were killed in the very beginning were the lucky ones. Those who survived year after year in the ghetto and then in the slave labor camps around Dachau were ground down to less than nothing. And then in the end, with Hitler's Reich crashing around the Nazis' ears, there was the Death March. That final meaningless, grotesque, inhuman cruelty.

I survived that march, but something inside of me died. Although my body survived intact, my spirit was crippled. In my mind's eye I saw myself as the trunk of a tree that had survived a forest fire. Black and charred beyond recognition, with all my branches gone, I finally managed to sprout new branches in order to live, but the old ones never grew back, and thus I became a different, and somehow lesser, being.

"Yes, I remember the Japanese Americans," I finally said to Mr. Saul. "I remember them well. As a matter of fact, they were the first American soldiers I saw. They were my liberators."

Eric couldn't keep the excitement out of his voice. "After all these years to find you here! It's a miracle! It's a miracle!"

"Yes, it is a miracle," I thought, still wary. I was groping for denials, for excuses not to enter into this dialogue.

Eric sensed my reluctance. "Please," he said. "They have come so far, after so many years. All the way from California and Hawaii. Will you come to meet them?" Eric and Lani Silver, director of San Francisco's Holocaust Oral History Project, had organized this trip for twenty-five liberators and their families. They were being honored by Israel's Knesset.

In the end I relented. How could I not?

The next evening I found myself driving up the highway to Jerusalem. I even brought some pages I had written a few years before, about my liberation, but I was still debating the wisdom of meeting with these men.

After I left Europe for Israel in 1948, I adopted another identity. I seldom let my guard down, seldom admitted I was a Holocaust survivor. There was no uniform way survivors of the Holocaust coped with the past. Each one of us had our own ways of dealing with the terrible wounds inflicted on our psyches during the war years. I didn't believe those wounds would ever heal, even if we lived for a thousand years. What I wrote down in my diaries during the war, what I wrote down later, were private nightmares that I shared with nobody but the one or two friends who survived those days with me. In the ordinary world, in the daylight hours, I was not a survivor. I was somebody else.

Right after the war, while I was still in Europe, I went to work with a U.S. Army screening team that was hunting down members of the SS and other Nazis who were hiding among civilians in the displaced persons camps throughout Germany. I acted as an interpreter. I spoke Lithuanian, German, Russian, and Yiddish, and the rudiments of English learned during my four years in the ghetto of Kaunas.

I lived to see some of the most vicious SS guards of the Dachau camps tried and convicted by a U.S. military court, and then hanged in the same room of the Landsberg prison where Hitler wrote his infamous *Mein Kampf.*

I also lived to see the event that Jews throughout the world had prayed for and dreamed about for nearly twenty centuries—the rebirth of the State of Israel. I was actually on my way to Canada when I made the decision to go to Israel instead, to help fight off the massive Arab force which threatened to annihilate the State of Israel at the very moment of its birth. By 1948 I had a command of English, and I entered Israel with a group of Canadian volunteers. Israeli immigration assumed I was a Canadian, too. Not that anyone really cared where you came from.

Against all odds and despite the predictions of western military strategists, Israel survived the Arab onslaught. Among those who fought and died for her were many concentration camp survivors, the majority of them sole survivors whose entire families had perished in Europe.

I remember a fierce battle in the Galilee, when I came across a wounded soldier and dragged him off to safety. He had an Auschwitz tattoo on his arm. I dressed his wounds and tried to reassure him, but he only smiled. "I witnessed the two things I wanted to see—the downfall of Hitler and his Third Reich, and the establishment of the State of Israel. Now I can die in peace."

Later that evening, after the fighting was over, I spoke to the young doctor who had treated him, and discovered the soldier was already dead.

"I'll be damned if I know what he died of. His wounds weren't that serious," the doctor said.

"There was nothing you could have done for him, Doctor. He died with his family in Auschwitz a long time ago," I replied. He gave me a puzzled look, as if to say "You people are all nuts."

But I understood the dead soldier perfectly.

After fighting for Israel's defense I joined the merchant marine, and roamed the world for twelve long years. It was a kind of solitude, a way to lose myself, a kind of fugue. I also think I wanted to see if the world was as soulless and hostile as it seemed to be during all the years of the war. Why had these things happened to the Jews?

I didn't really find answers there. I did find extreme poverty, squalor, and disease in the ports and slums of Asia and Africa. I also

found people living under horrid conditions in the most enlight-
ened democratic systems of Europe and the United States—people
living in ignorance, suspicious of their fellow human beings,
resentful, bigoted, and looking for scapegoats to bear the brunt of
their anger and resentment. I saw cruelty and inhumanity among
people everywhere.

And yet, amidst all that misery, I saw love and laughter, kindness,
generosity, magnanimity of spirit, and above all, hope. The same
kind of hope that sustained me during the long darkness of the
Holocaust.

As the years passed my Canadian persona grew more comfortable.
The psychological game I played with myself was in many ways successful. I was able to compartmentalize my past, to treat it as if it
belonged to someone else. It existed in the pages I wrote over the
years at sea, but it was as if those were stories told by some third party
named Solly Genkind. I had changed my last name, as many
European Jews do when they return to Israel. I chose *Ganor* by
looking in the phone book. It was short, it started with *G,* and there
weren't many Ganors in the book. Ganor means "Garden of light." I
was now Solly Ganor.

My nightmares, however, still belonged to Solly Genkind. Many a
night I woke to the sound of my own screams, my pulse beating
wildly, my bed damp with sweat. At night the demons of the
Holocaust would come to hound me, and no daytime alter ego could
keep them at bay.

What happened in Jerusalem in the spring of 1992, when I met with
Eric Saul, Lani Silver, and the Japanese American veterans, can only
be described as a second liberation. As soon as I entered the lobby of
their hotel I noticed half a dozen Nisei in their early seventies. In
their midst stood a tall young American man in glasses—Eric Saul.
He came forward smiling, both arms extended in a gesture of
welcome, his whole being radiating kindness. I immediately liked
him. He introduced me to the group, who welcomed me warmly.
One had been with the 442nd; the rest were veterans of the 522nd
Field Artillery. I looked into their faces to see if the particular man
who lifted me from the snow so many years ago was among them. I
was sure that even after all this time I would know him. But I felt no
jolt of recognition.

Soon we were joined by others. Rudy Tokiwa, one of the leaders of the group, was from San Francisco. He was a heavyset man on crutches, a war hero decorated more than once for his valor in combat. I would later discover that the Nisei had been covered with honors.

Another man to whom I took an immediate liking was George Oiye, of Los Altos, California—another decorated veteran. He found a camera on a dead German officer, and he and Susumu Ito, another 522nd veteran, took many gruesome pictures of Dachau and its sub-camps when their unit arrived there in April of 1945.

We retired to a corner of the lobby and I began reading an account I'd written, describing where and how I met the men of their battalion. As I spoke one more man joined the group. He stood next to Eric Saul, watching me intently. He was very slim, in his early seventies, with graying hair and glasses. My heart began beating faster. Was it him? Was he my rescuer? So many years had passed—how could I be sure? The group urged me to continue reading. When I got to the part where I was lying half-buried in the snow, more dead than alive, and the four men of the 522nd drove up, I looked up again and met the eyes of the newcomer. They were filled with tears.

I stopped reading; I couldn't go on. I was gripped by such intense feelings that I was unable to speak. I struggled with them, but to no avail. After all the years of trying to suppress the unsuppressible, a tidal wave of emotion erupted inside me, and I started weeping as I had never wept before. There was no stopping me. The boy I had buried deep within me all those years had come out of hiding. It was he who was crying, while my alter ego looked on in astonishment. I couldn't believe this was happening.

During the many years since my liberation I had never cried. I couldn't. A psychiatrist once told me that the trauma of the Holocaust had dried up my tears, that I was like an emotional amputee and would probably never cry again. And there I was, sprouting new emotional branches, or perhaps reviving old ones that weren't really dead, only dormant.

Finally, with the whole group gathered around patting and comforting me, I calmed down. Everyone was surprised at what had happened. Everyone had tears in his eyes.

No one was more surprised than I at all this, and in my embarrassment I tried to explain that this was the first time since my liberation that I had been able to weep. Eric then took my hands in his and smiled at me.

"Don't be embarrassed by your tears. You are among friends here." I looked at the faces around me and saw understanding and compassion in their eyes. I suddenly felt very close to them. We seemed to have bypassed that long process of emotional attachment that usually begins new friendships, and I felt as if I had known these people all my life. I felt tremendously uplifted, as if I had taken some potent drug.

There was a moment of silence, and then suddenly everyone was talking at once, asking questions, recalling where they were at the time of my liberation. They seemed to be affected by my catharsis, as if they had been caught up in my emotional surge. Then Eric pulled me aside and introduced me to the man who had actually unleashed this flood of tears.

"Solly, this is Clarence Matsumura. We think he is the man who saved you."

Clarence, Clarence—that was his name!

We stared at each other, and then he smiled. I knew immediately that it was him. He may have aged, but his smile hadn't changed. We fell into each others' arms and it was as if the years simply melted away. I felt weak and he was holding me up, just as he did then, forty-seven years ago, by the side of a road in Bavaria.

Later, as we sat and exchanged memories of that fateful day, he showed me a snapshot of himself as a young soldier. I recognized him immediately! If I had any doubts at all, they evaporated then and there.

As I sat surrounded by my liberators, thoughts and feelings I had suppressed for years surfaced. My new friends had many of their own stories to tell. I was told that one of the men in the 522nd's medical detachment, Ichiro Imamura, had watched a liaison scout shoot the chain off of one of the gates of Dachau. I heard that several men in Charlie Battery—Minabe Hirasaki, Shiro Takeshita, and Raymond Kunemura—had "liberated" a German chicken farm near Waakirchen and made a lot of chicken soup to feed recently liberated prisoners. We talked far into the night, until one of the group reminded us that we were to attend an international press conference that morning. I was to be included. Reluctantly I said good night to my new friends and went to the room they had reserved for me. I was gripped by a tremendous excitement and apprehension.

The idea that I would have to appear before so many people and in front of cameras was terrifying. I remembered the previous year, when I accompanied my friend and fellow survivor Uri Chanoch to speak to a group of young Israeli soldiers about our experiences in Hitler's camps. As soon as I got up to the podium my stomach was tied in a knot and the blood pounded in my ears. I developed a splitting headache and felt quite ill. I vowed I would never again attempt such a thing.

The next day I was completely surprised by my sense of calm. I answered endless questions that morning, and gave long video interviews that afternoon to CNN, ABC, CBS, AP, and God knows how many other reporters. And I actually enjoyed it. It was then that I realized how greatly I had been affected by this second meeting with my liberators. I felt that a new person had emerged, and taken over the reins of my life.

The story of my reunion with Clarence sprouted wings. Few people knew the story of these Nisei and their role in the liberation of the camps, and many press agents and reporters interviewed us during the eight days the group remained in Israel. Since then I have been reunited with Clarence and others from his unit more than once, in Israel, Germany, and the United States. I'm grateful for the time I've been able to spend with them, and especially for the hours I had with Clarence, who passed away in May of 1995, to my enduring sorrow.

Each time I have met with these brave men new memories and recognitions and feelings have surfaced. Each time I have learned more about my rescuers. I often wonder if their experiences in the internment camps, and with American prejudice in general, didn't create in Clarence and his kinsmen some extra spark of understanding and compassion for those they rescued during the spring of 1945. Was there some special bond between the Nisei and the Jews they rescued? I don't know. I do know that my own sense of kinship with the Nisei and the Japanese is strong. This book is dedicated not only to the memory of those loved ones who perished at the hands of the Nazis, but equally, and with enormous gratitude, to Clarence and all the brave men of the 522nd Field Artillery Battalion of the famed 100th/442nd Combat Team, as well as to Chiune Sugihara, whose shining moral example guided me through the darkest years of the Holocaust.

PART ONE

1

The War of Independence

ISRAEL, EARLY SEPTEMBER 1948

The midday sun was a murky yellow, so dim you could almost look straight at it. A hot easterly wind had stirred up an enormous sandstorm that blasted the sky and drove grit into everything. Sand needled our faces, filled our ears, and grated between our teeth. Worst of all was what it did to our eyes. Three days after arriving on the hill they were so puffed up that we could barely see.

The *hamsin* blew in the first day we occupied the location. The only vegetation on the hill were patches of dry, thorny scrub. When we tried to escape the sun in their scanty shade we were cut by sharp thorns and invaded by swarms of tiny biting insects.

Below us, not twenty feet away, lay a dozen corpses. Some of these soldiers had been killed the first morning, and in the torrid heat their bellies had swollen like balloons. The stench was suffocating. The second day we tried to roll the bodies downhill, but enemy snipers quickly picked off another of our men. The platoon was down to six. The rest were either dead or passed out from their wounds and the thirst that plagued us all. We had drained the last of our meager water rations twelve hours earlier. It wouldn't be long before we all joined the dead below us. My tongue felt like a piece of dry wood in my mouth, and the only thing that kept me from choking was the pebble I sucked on, as Sergeant Smith taught me to do. He had learned such tricks fighting with Monty in the Libyan desert. Like many in my platoon, Smith was a British veteran who had volunteered for the Israeli Defense Forces when the British army pulled out of Palestine. He was married to an Israeli girl.

Lieutenant Feldman, our commanding officer, had been the only Israeli officer in our unit. He was killed the day before. Sergeant Harold Smith, a tall, bony Welshman with sandy hair and hard blue eyes, was now in command.

It all began about ten days earlier. Our battalion, the 72nd, was one of three that made up the 7th Armored Brigade. It was the task of the 7th to capture the areas of the upper Galilee still under Arab control. Most of the officers and men of the 7th Brigade were English-speaking volunteers from all over the world. I enlisted with a group of Canadian volunteers I met in Marseille, France. I was about to emigrate to Canada when I made the decision to come to Israel. Now I was registered as a Canadian along with the other men in my group. That suited me just fine.

We received our orders on the sixth or seventh day of the Galilee campaign, after the battalion had captured the villages of Miron and Gush Halav, or as the Arabs called it, Jish. The hill that was my company's objective was strategic and, according to intelligence, unoccupied. It was "a blessedly easy assignment," as our captain described it. The rest of the battalion was to fight its way to Malkiya, a kibbutz near the Lebanese border.

The night we set out it was moonless and dark, but our guide lived in a nearby settlement and knew the area well. By the time we reached the shoulder of the hill, around midnight, the first indications of the *hamsin* were already in the air. We radioed headquarters that we had reached our objective, and camped for the night, awaiting further orders.

The next day, at dawn, we were attacked by a battalion of Senegalese troops, part of the allied Arab forces. They came up quietly on rubber-soled boots, and suddenly there they were, charging us with fixed bayonets and shouting "Allah Akbar," their French helmets with the curious stripe gleaming in the morning sun. It is in moments like this that experience and proper leadership counts, for Sergeant Smith was the first to regain his wits. Shouting "Fire! Fire! Fire!" he sprayed the attackers with his Sten gun. Benny, another British veteran, swept our attackers with the machine gun while I fed in the ammunition belts. The Spandau was the fastest light machine gun of World War II, and we had two of them.

Our firepower, especially the Spandaus, had a devastating effect on the Senegalese. Many of the enemy fell dead. The rest retreated down the hill, carrying their wounded with them. We could see the dead lying beyond the bushes in grotesque positions. We had three dead and five wounded. Among the dead were the Israeli guide, one young man from South Africa, and an Englishman who carried our radio. The Englishman had pink cheeks and a crewcut, and couldn't have been more than seventeen years old. He had joined our company only a few days before and was very excited about his first battle. Our radio was knocked out by the same bullets that killed him.

We were cut off from battalion headquarters. Worse yet, before he died, our Israeli guide confessed to Sergeant Smith that he brought us to the wrong hill. We were hopelessly lost somewhere inside Lebanon, and no one knew where we were.

Sergeant Smith ordered us to withdraw farther up and regroup in a circle. We dragged our casualties with us, and our medic, a short dark fellow from Austria, bandaged the wounded. Benny too had been wounded, and couldn't handle the Spandau anymore. We switched positions and now I was the one looking down the barrel of that Nazi weapon, while Benny fed in the ammunition belt.

The second attack came from the west, and we knew we were surrounded. Just at sunset they moved up the slope without a sound. Many of them had submachine guns, and the bullets buzzed around our heads like angry hornets.

Several of the enemy bore down on my position. I could see their faces clearly. They were very young and very dark, the whites of their frightened eyes clearly visible. It was the first time I had seen enemy forces up this close.

At that moment, a totally unexpected feeling awakened inside me. I had seen my people victimized for so long in Europe, I had seen so many Jews murdered, that I believed I would be able to kill our enemies without a second thought. Now I found that I couldn't squeeze the trigger. The idea of killing these young men filled me with loathing. Thou shalt not kill. That conviction, instilled in me by generations of Jewish teachings, surfaced at this most critical moment. In the face of these youths bearing down on me with fixed bayonets, I simply couldn't squeeze the trigger. Death was almost upon me, but trying to squeeze that trigger was like trying to lift a house with my bare hands. My whole body trembled with the effort, and I think I must have blanked out for a second, because I have no idea when I actually began to fire. I only know that I was screaming at the top of my lungs and the machine gun was rattling in my hands like some beast with a life of its own.

Two men caught in the fire were propelled backward, their arms spread wide like scarecrows. For a moment they just hung there, as if suspended in midair; then they crumpled to the ground like marionettes whose strings had been cut. In that moment I realized I had crossed a line.

We'd successfully barricaded ourselves behind the rocks, and except for a few cuts and scratches from ricochets we took no casualties. Again our machine guns were decisive. When half a dozen of their number had fallen, the rest turned and fled.

The only water we had was what we brought in our canteens, and we used more than half of it for the wounded. In the heat water was crucial. And we were clearly outnumbered. Our only hope of survival was that the battalion would search us out when they failed to receive any of our scheduled field reports. But during the night we heard explosions and machine-gun fire in the distance, and we knew our comrades were busy fighting their own battles.

The Senegalese attacked again early the next morning. Our observers saw them coming this time. We were running low on ammunition, and Sergeant Smith ordered us to use hand grenades and spare the bullets. I was to shoot only short bursts.

When they were about a hundred feet away we lobbed about ten grenades down the hill and they exploded almost simultaneously. The explosion was deafening, showering small rocks and pebbles back over our position. We could hear some of our attackers crying out in pain, and when their sergeant was hit the rest retreated.

By evening our water rations were completely gone. The thirst was devastating. I tried to remember if I had ever felt this bad. Although we were constantly plagued by hunger in the concentration camps, we never really experienced thirst. There was always plenty of water in Europe.

By morning there were only six of us left to defend the position. Many had passed out from loss of blood or heat stroke. It was obvious we couldn't last. If the persistent Senegalese didn't finish us off, the heat and dehydration surely would.

The heat, the stench, the sleepless nights were taking their toll. My mind began to wander, drifting back to Lithuania where I was born and spent my childhood. I began to have maddening visions of green meadows and pastures, where placid cows stood knee-deep in green grass, slowly chewing their cuds. I could see the tops of the trees swaying gently in the breeze and watch the fleecy clouds sail by in an azure sky, as I lay in my hammock, suspended between heaven and earth. I could even feel the cool waters of the river enfolding me when I jumped from the little jetty near our summer house in Kalautuvas.

But then another vision superimposed itself on the first one. The cows were still there slowly chewing the grass, but the river changed to a pond where a group of naked people stood before a motley firing squad, their bare skin shockingly white, their expressions frozen in terror.

"Prepare for an attack!" I heard Sergeant Smith's hoarse voice shouting somewhere far away in the future, on a barren hill in a country called Israel. Deep in my heart I knew that the scene at the pond had in some way predestined my presence here.

The shimmering heat rising from the rocks made it hard to focus. As if in a haze, I could see the Arab forces running up the hill, zigzagging through the bushes, stumbling on the rocks. It was their fourth or fifth attack in three days. I cocked the Spandau and made sure the bullet belt was folded properly in the box. The Spandau had a small swastika engraved in front of the sights. It must have belonged to a truly dedicated fanatic. Who else would have gone to the trouble of engraving this thing by hand? None of the other guns in our unit had such markings. Ironic that the Czechs would send us arms surrendered by German soldiers. Ironic that I should be killing people with a Nazi gun. Every time I took aim I saw that damned swastika in front of my eyes and wondered how many Jews had fallen before it.

I looked at my watch. It was twelve o'clock. The sun had reached its zenith and seemed to have stopped there. The heat enveloped us like a thick blanket. I sucked on the pebble as hard as I could, but it didn't do much good anymore. My thinking became muddled. It was hard to concentrate.

Sergeant Smith crawled over to my position. Benny had passed out and was barely breathing. His wounded arm had swollen and started to stink.

"How many bullet belts do you have left, Solly?" Smith asked hoarsely, looking into the ammunition box.

"Just one belt."

"That's it then."

"I guess you could say that." I tried to mimic the Englishman's sangfroid.

"You seem to be doing pretty well." His grin was more of a grimace as he gestured to those who had passed out.

"I'm doing my best, Sergeant. I guess it must be the pebble."

"The pebble?"

"You know, the pebble you told me to suck."

His smile broadened. "It's a good trick. Remember it in the future—assuming we have a future."

Then he became serious again. "When they attack, you better shoot only single bullets."

I nodded in agreement. There was nothing else to do.

"Well, I have to get back. So long."

We looked at each other. So that was that. The end.

During the years of the Holocaust, death was my constant companion, but I never got used to it.

"Sergeant."

"Yes?"

"I just wanted to tell you that I am not a Canadian. I was born in Lithuania and am a survivor of Dachau."

"I see." He was quiet for a moment. "It doesn't really matter, does it? You've done well. Perhaps you knew what you were fighting for. But why Canadian?"

"It's a long story."

"I see."

The wind had died down and our voices carried far in the stillness. Smith seemed reluctant to go.

"When I land in hell," he said, "the first thing I will ask for is a glass of water."

And then they were swarming up the hill again. Smith ran to his position while I threw myself down behind the Spandau. There seemed to be hundreds of them. The Senegalese must have been joined by reinforcements. If only I could get a drink of water before I died. . . .

The Arabs began shooting while they were still some distance away.

When they got a little closer I jammed the gun against my bruised shoulder and squeezed the trigger. The gun went off in a long burst, the smell of burned cordite filling my nostrils. A few of them fell, but the others came on, and I had no more bullets. I had forgotten to put the gun on single shot. Not that it mattered very much. Bullets were hitting the rocks above my head and ricocheting everywhere. I was pinned down and helpless, but damned if I was going to fall into the hands of the Arabs alive, not after being in the hands of the Germans for four years. I decided to stand up with the machine gun in my hands and have it over with.

Deciding to commit suicide is one thing; carrying it out is something else. Again my body seemed to resist my will. I told myself to stand, that the Arabs would be on me any second, but I might as well have been paralyzed.

Suddenly I felt a dull pain in my back. For a moment I thought that I was hit by a stone, since I felt little pain; then I realized, dimly, that a bullet must have ricocheted. Machine guns seemed to be going off all around me. Dreamily I heard someone giving commands in English. Someone called for a medic. Our battalion had finally come to the rescue, but it was probably too late for me.

I vaguely remember being dragged from my position. I tried to hold on to the Spandau, but my hands felt like rubber. The last thing I saw was that damned swastika on the gun barrel.

I don't know how long I was out. When consciousness began seeping back I had the eerie sensation that I was floating above my body.

"What are his chances, Doc?"

I was in a long whitewashed barracks. Sergeant Smith was talking to a little man with a large head of wiry gray hair, dressed in an old British uniform that hung on him like a sack.

"What are his chances Doc, what are his chances Doc!" the little doctor parroted in irritation. "Who do you think I am? God? What are *your* chances? What are *my* chances in this flea-bitten pest hole? For this I escaped Berlin and the Warsaw Ghetto? I must have been crazy. We all are crazy to fight for this pile of stones as if it were a lost paradise!"

Sergeant Smith looked abashed.

The doctor sighed. "I apologize, Sergeant. It's just that I'm terribly frustrated. I'm running out of medications. I don't even have anymore aspirin," he gestured helplessly at the wounded who lay all around.

"Your friend's wound is not serious, but I am afraid it is infected and he is running a high fever. Without antibiotics, all we can hope is that his natural resistance is strong enough to pull him through."

I heard Sergeant Smith murmur something in response. I was slipping away again, into sleep and fevered dreams. Even under this roof the heat was terrible. My stepmother had warned me about the heat. Why are we never able to learn from others? How in hell did I end up here anyway?

I had not been raised a Zionist. Although the movement was strong in Lithuania and Russia, and many among our friends and relatives were ardent about the cause, my parents were never among them. My father believed that nationalism was at the root of most of the world's ills. Yet it was his new wife, Ethel, who was most upset about my decision to join the war for an Israeli homeland. Ethel Ostry was a Canadian from Winnipeg. She was working for a United Nations relief organization in Munich when she met my father. During the two years after the Allied victory in Europe, she helped me with my English, continuing the lessons I began in the ghetto. She got me a job as an interpreter with the U.S. Army Counterintelligence Corps, which was searching for Nazis in the displaced persons camps. I was fluent in Russian, Lithuanian, German, and Yiddish, and I was rapidly learning English.

Ethel secured my entry into a good Canadian university, and was helping me study for the entrance examinations. I was ready to emigrate to Canada with her and my father when the new State of Israel declared independence on May 14, 1948. Over the previous four years I had sworn to myself, more than once, that I would never again live in a place where I couldn't defend myself. There was no doubt in my mind that if the State of Israel had existed in the 1930s, the Jews of Europe would have been saved. Before the war started, Hitler was willing to let the Jews leave, but no country was willing to accept them. It was hard to trust the Western world after that.

A few days before we were to leave for Canada I confronted them with my decision. Both Father and Ethel were astounded. Ethel was distraught.

"I can't believe it! Are you going to let him go to Israel to get killed, just like that? He is just a boy, a nineteen-year-old boy who has gone through the worst ordeal in our history!" She was staring at my father.

"He is more like a thousand-year-old boy, after what he went through in the war," my father answered quietly.

"Oh no, Chaim, no! For Solly to get killed now, after all you managed to survive? And to get killed for a lost cause! It is just stupid! Look! Look at any news report. Israel hasn't a ghost of a chance. Five Arab armies against the Haganah. They will be defeated in a week. They don't even have weapons to fight with, for God's sake!"

I had never seen Ethel so agitated. She was usually a very calm and soft-spoken person. I was very touched, and took both her hands in mine. She pulled away impatiently and stamped her foot.

"What is it with this family?" She was almost shouting. "Haven't you learned anything? In 1939 you had papers. You even had *tickets* for the United States. Yet you chose to stay in Lithuania, for reasons I'll never comprehend. And now you, Solly, with your whole future ahead of you, you are deliberately walking into that trap called Palestine, or Israel, or whatever you call it.

"Wasn't it miracle enough you survived the Nazis? Do you have to tempt fate twice? Let others do the fighting now. You deserve a normal life in a civilized country. Please, please, Solly!"

Her eyes bored into mine, as if she was trying to assess what was going through my head. She took a breath as if to continue, then stopped. She had a pained look in her eyes when she spoke again.

"Look, I was there in a kibbutz for a while," she said quietly, "in the twenties. I too dreamed of a Jewish homeland. I lasted six months. You can't imagine the terrible conditions there. The back-breaking work in the stony fields, the swamps, the mosquitoes and the diseases they brought with them. We were all sick. Some of us contracted malaria. The food was indigestible. The drinking water was muddy. You worked in the fields, day in and day out, and at night you had a hard straw mattress in some broken-down shack. You tried to sleep, but the mosquitoes wouldn't let you. At five in the morning you were awakened to go into the fields again, but you couldn't see because your eyes were swollen shut from mosquito bites.

"And for what? To prove to the world that after two thousand years Jews could become farmers again? The only thing they proved was that they were crazy! Doctors, lawyers, architects, brilliant writers, they all came with their pale soft hands to work that hostile pile of rock and sand. What a waste of brains and talent."

She had a faraway look in her eyes, as if she were talking more to herself than to us. There was pain in her voice, a trace of regret perhaps.

"And the heat. . . . You can't imagine that terrible summer heat. It was devastating."

She lapsed into silence. I looked at my father and could see the pain in his face. For most of his life, Father's favorite saying was: "If religion is the opium of the masses, as Lenin claimed, then nationalism is its poison." He abhorred nationalism in any form. He believed in the international brotherhood of man, and he raised me in that belief. After our liberation from Dachau, however, he amended his opinion a bit.

"I still believe that nationalism is a disaster, but I do not believe the holocaust of the Jews would have occurred if we'd had a country of our own." I felt the same. In fact I'd become convinced that if we didn't regain our ancient homeland, we were bound to face another cataclysm in the future. The conviction that I should go to Israel and help fight in its war for independence had grown with every passing day.

I asked my father a simple question: "If you were in my place, nineteen years old and unattached, would you go?"

He looked at me for a long time without saying a word. We were more than father and son. We had become friends in suffering. We saved each other's lives more than once during the dark days of the war, and now I was going to leave him for Israel, where my chances of survival in the coming conflict were slim. But we were always honest with each other, and he wasn't going to lie to me now. All he could do, however, was nod. He couldn't speak.

I remembered the first time I had heard him speak on the subject of Zionism, an eternity ago. We were in a large hall, and I stood next to my mother, holding her hand. It was a debate between the Zionists advocating the creation of a Jewish state in Palestine, and "The Bund," a Jewish organization that advocated socialism among nations. My father stood at the podium, dark, handsome, and dashing in his well-cut suit and soft wide tie. Several hundred people were waiting intently to hear what he had to say.

"Nationalism is poison. Nationalism is egoism. Nationalism breeds hatred among nations. Nationalism has been at the root of more wars than any other cause, with the exception of religion. We Jews should have only one cause, the universal brotherhood of man." He said it with so much emotion that it ingrained itself in my mind forever.

I was only five years old. The year was 1933. Adolf Hitler had just come into power in Germany.

2
The Shtrom Clan

I was born in Heydekrug, Lithuania, on May 18, 1928, the youngest of three children. My sister Fanny was twelve years old when I was born, and my brother Herman was seven.

Heydekrug was not far from the East Prussian capital of Koenigsberg, and close to the Lithuanian port town of Klaipeda, or as the Germans called it, Memel, on the Baltic Sea. The area was populated mostly by Germans. German was the first language I spoke.

I have vague memories of a very clean place, with well-paved streets, white houses, and red tiled roofs. I especially remember the gardens surrounding the houses. Roses and a variety of other flowers were planted in orderly rows, and all kinds of berry vines scrambled over white fences.

In those days paddle steamers plied the Niemunas River, moving east and west all the way from Memel to Kaunas and back, stopping at various towns along the way. My earliest recollection is probably of a ferry trip to Memel in 1932, and a ride on a beautiful carousel. I was not yet four and was terrified at first, but quickly became so enamored of my horse that I refused to dismount. My father allowed me to ride the carousel twice more, until my head began to spin.

That excursion is tied up with memories of my fourth birthday a few months later. I remember wearing a paper hat with shiny silver stars on it, and gathering around a birthday cake with pink icing and four candles. Next to me was Hansi Miller, my best friend. Around us were my sister Fanny, my brother Herman, and Hansi's parents.

Mommy was waiting for my daddy to return from the factory before she cut the cake.

I always got excited when I heard Daddy's car pull up in the drive, and the crunch of his footsteps in the gravel pathway. This time I was more excited than usual. I knew he would come bearing a gift. Herman ran to open the door, and there was Daddy lugging a huge oddly shaped package wrapped in brown paper. Fanny put her hands over my eyes and I sat very still, my heart racing, listening to the rustle of the paper as Daddy unwrapped my present. It seemed to me that he was deliberately taking his time, just to tease me. Then there was a big "Ohhhh!" and applause, and I tore Fanny's hands away from my eyes. Before me was an unforgettable sight—a magnificent wooden rocking horse the size of a small pony. Every minute detail, from nostrils to hoofs, was intricately carved. It was a glossy dark brown with shiny black eyes and a mane that flared as if blown by the wind. Its white teeth clenched a metal bit, and its bridle and reins were made of real leather. I stood before this apparition for a moment, in awe, before flinging myself on it. It was the most beautiful thing I had ever seen.

My father had been so impressed with my passion for the carousel horse that he had vowed to get me a horse of my own, something equally splendid. As beautiful as the carousel horse was, my rocking horse was more beautiful. Father had contracted with a master carver for it, and it cost a small fortune.

I think that my friend Hansi may have loved that horse even more than I did. He refused to go home after the party. Because it was my birthday, our parents allowed him to stay until supper. The whole afternoon we rode the horse, sometimes both of us at once, since it was quite big enough for two; otherwise we took turns. Hansi would pretend that he was a Teutonic knight charging into battle against the Lithuanian heathens during the Middle Ages, while I pretended to be Judah Maccabee charging the enemies of Israel. Each one of us had his own fantasy, his own bedtime stories to fire the imagination.

It was well into the evening when we drowsed off together on the back of my wooden steed. That extraordinary day deeply imprinted itself on my memory. The time would come when that horse would save my life.

• • •

On January 30, 1933, Adolf Hitler was sworn in as Chancellor of Germany, and the Germans were on the march again. The German population of Heydekrug, who had generally been friendly toward the Jews, began to cool toward us. Both Heydekrug and Memel were part of East Prussia before World War I, and had only been awarded to Lithuania by the Allies in 1923. Recovering that Baltic corridor was surely one of Hitler's immediate goals in his dream of *lebensraum* (living space), and soon men with swastika armbands began to appear in the streets. German gentiles who'd had good relationships with their Jewish neighbors were being threatened. So were Hansi's parents, the Millers, who came over one night and told us that Nazis from the Fatherland were visiting the area and organizing the locals. They were very embarrassed, but they asked my parents not to visit them anymore. They said it was too dangerous for them. They advised us to leave Heydekrug, saying that the situation would only get worse.

Hansi was forbidden to visit me, but the two of us were devoted to each other and he would sneak over quite often to play.

The switch from open friendliness to open hostility in Heydekrug was extraordinary, the climate changing so quickly that my parents soon decided to sell the soap factory and move back to Kaunas.

The day we were to leave, Hansi came running over to our house. Mrs. Miller threw open a window and shouted for him to come back home, but Hansi wouldn't listen. He rushed through our door with tears running down his cheeks. Throwing his arms around me, he sobbed, "Don't go, Solly, please don't go. I won't let you go! Stay here with me!"

I was flooded with the tenderest feelings toward him at that moment. I was terribly upset myself, and couldn't understand why we had to leave, why I had to part with my best friend. I felt an overpowering urge to make some grand gesture, some supreme sacrifice to that friendship.

Most of our belongings were already packed onto the truck, but there was one precious thing still waiting to be loaded.

I grabbed Hansi by the hand and presented him with my horse, telling him that it now belonged to him forever.

I still remember Hansi's tearful, astonished face. From the corner of my eye I also caught a glimpse of my father, whose face showed equal surprise. I could see that he was about to intervene. It was, after all, his birthday gift to me, lovingly planned and purchased at great expense. I closed my eyes. Everything in me revolted against this stupid impulse. I would never be able to ride that horse again. I was torn by conflict—dread that my father would interfere, dread that he would not.

At that moment my mother put a restraining hand on my father's arm. She knelt down before me and asked gently, "Are you sure you want to give your horse to Hansi?"

I nodded quickly. My heart was seized with terrible misgivings. I had given away the thing I loved most, and I couldn't trust myself to speak.

Such impulses would get me into trouble more than once. I still remember the look on my father's face when he presented me with that beautiful toy, the pleasure it gave him to give such an extravagant gift. Yet Father often scolded Mother for her impulsive generosity, saying that it would be the ruin of us, and I suspect he believed I inherited that weakness from her. But in truth, my love of the grand gesture, and certainly my broad romantic streak, were as much his legacy as they were hers. Indeed, my mother and father might never have met if he hadn't dived into the Niemunas River and saved her from drowning, nearly drowning himself in the process. They certainly wouldn't have met if Father hadn't gotten involved in the earliest rumblings of the Russian Revolution in Minsk, at the tender age of thirteen. He exposed himself and his family to so much danger that they smuggled him over the Lithuanian border into Kaunas until things cooled off.

My mother's family lived in Kaunas, and it was to Kaunas that we returned early in the year 1934.

The move to Kaunas caused a great upheaval in my life. As soon as we moved into our new apartment, we were besieged by dozens of relatives and friends of my parents. There were my grandparents Getzel and Esther Shtrom, and an endless stream of uncles, aunts, and cousins, and I hardly understood a word they said. I mostly spoke German, and suddenly I was in a place where a babble of languages was spoken: Yiddish, Lithuanian, Russian. Most of the family spoke German as well, and they would address me in German, but the conversation among the adults and among my various cousins was completely lost on me.

I missed my friend Hansi, and I felt left out, sad, and bewildered by the huge sprawling town we had moved to. My sister Fanny, on the other hand, was delighted. She had spent her early school years in Kaunas, and was very unhappy with our move to Heydekrug, for she left behind many friends. Now she was the happiest girl in the world. Even Herman, who was quite young when my family moved to Heydekrug, seemed to make friends quickly among his schoolmates and our cousins. Only I knew no one.

It was Fanny who came to my rescue. She was nearly eighteen then, and in many ways she was like a second mother to me. With Mother spending so much time working by Father's side, Fanny often had to care for me. One Saturday she took me on my first real tour of the town. She clearly loved the place.

Our first exploration was of the town's main street, a wide boulevard called Laisves Aleya. Even though I would walk it many times in later years, to this day I can close my eyes and see that street the way I saw it the first time. It was divided by a broad pedestrian promenade, where tall chestnut trees grew in rows as far as my eyes could see. Modern buildings with elegant shops stood on both sides of the street, and at the end, shimmering in the sun, was the huge cupola of the Russian Orthodox church known as the "Sobor."

And the people! I have never seen so many people in one place. A kaleidoscope of men, women, and children, all dressed up, were milling about, chatting, laughing, calling out to each other. I held onto my sister with all my strength, afraid I would be swept away and lost in the crowd. When I asked Fanny if Kaunas was the biggest city in the world, I could hardly believe it when she laughed and told me that there were cities in the world many times its size.

After buying me a huge ice cream cone, she took me to the banks of the Niemunas, which flowed along one edge of the town. It was so wide I could hardly see the other side. This was the river Napoleon crossed on his way to conquer Russia in 1812. Fanny said that the Tsar built forts all around the town later on, during the years when Lithuania was a Russian territory.

From the river we went to the Town Garden, where the opera house stood, and then on to a movie house called "the Forum," where I saw my first full-length movie, a Laurel and Hardy film. By the time we emerged, it was getting dark, and my sister rushed us home. It was an unforgettable day, the beginning of my own love affair with the place, and ultimately with the whole Shtrom family.

● ● ●

The first Shtrom in Kaunas was my mother's grandfather, Zelig Shtrom, who came from a small village called Zhemaitkemis. He had four sons. I never knew much about him except that he sold firewood for a living, was kindhearted, very religious, and rigorously honest.

After the end of World War I, Zelig's son Getzel, my grandfather, became very religious and spent most of his time learning the Torah. He was not an ordained rabbi, but because of his broad studies he had a number of followers, friends and relatives who sought his advice on a whole range of religious and secular matters. Between the Torah and holding court among these people, he had very little time for anything else. And so it fell to my grandmother Esther to run the wholesale dairy business that was the family's means of support. Grandmother Esther was a tiny, bright-eyed, smiling woman who was enormously energetic. She came from a small town near Minsk, the same area my father was from, but I know very little about her background. All her family in Russia were killed by the Nazis in the early stages of the war.

My grandparents, two great uncles and their wives, five sets of aunts and uncles, and more cousins than I could count all lived in Kaunas. I discovered the true dimensions of the Shtrom clan, as my father called them, at Passover that first year, when my mother decided to invite the whole family to our house for the seder.

I remember how our big apartment bustled with activity that entire week. Tradesmen came and went, bringing produce that was all critically inspected by my mother. There were fruits and vegetables, fishes, meats, and chickens. Mother was helped by our old cook Sarah, who had worked for us before my parents left Kaunas.

The day before the seder, Mother took a bunch of keys from her secret drawer, and I followed her to the little storage room under the steps where she hid her black trunk. I had often wondered what that black trunk contained, imagining that it hid all kinds of secret treasures and perhaps even Aladdin's magic lamp. It was always locked with two big padlocks and hidden from sight. In breathless anticipation I watched her carefully lift the lid and fold the large linen towel spread out over the top. But there was nothing very mysterious under the towel, as I discovered when she began taking out her Rosenthal china, a large boxful of heavy Danish silver, and many crystal wine glasses. She laughed when she saw my disappointment, saying, "I suppose you thought we had a flying carpet from Baghdad hidden in here." Mother was often uncannily close to the mark.

The seder was laid out on four long tables arranged in a square. They were covered with snowy white tablecloths and arranged with all of Mother's finery from the trunk.

That was the first time I saw the whole family, or almost the whole family, gathered together at once. Three of the four Shtrom sons were there: my grandfather Getzel, and his brothers Abraham and Ichiel, along with their wives. Then there were all their children and their children's spouses, and all the grandchildren—three generations of Shtroms. Getzel alone had three sons and four daughters, and each of them had from three to five children. There must have been forty people there.

Unlike Grandfather Getzel, Abraham and Ichiel had ventured out into the modern world, abandoning the traditional paths of Jewish life. Both got secular educations and became successful businessmen. Abraham, the oldest, had completely abandoned religion and didn't even go to synagogue on Saturdays. He had two daughters and a son. Ichiel had two sons and a daughter, all of whom made the leap from traditional religious study to university educations. Ichiel was the youngest and the most successful of the brothers.

My grandfather Getzel, however, had the honor of being the most respected of the three: In those days, helping the poor and learning the Torah still commanded more respect than any other activity in Jewish life.

So it was my grandfather, in his brand new suit and black skullcap, who sat at the head of the table to conduct the seder. Seeing me at the other end, where I sat with the other young cousins, he winked at me and motioned for me to come and sit beside him.

It was quite a scene from my vantage point, at not quite six years of age. Two large crystal chandeliers lit up the room and cast reflections on the china and silver. Everything looked sparkling and warm. Everywhere I looked there were smiling faces. After those early feelings of estrangement in Kaunas, suddenly I was part of a group that took me into its warm embrace and made me feel that I belonged. I had never felt so secure.

The colorful Passover *Haggadoth* were distributed among the guests, and we all chanted the familiar story of the Exodus from Egypt. As Grandfather Getzel and I had rehearsed, I stood on a chair and with a thumping heart asked the first question of the *Haggadah* (the liturgy used at the seder): "Mah nishtana halaila hazeh, mikol haleilot?" "How does this night differ from every other night?"

I recited all four questions with so much gusto that everyone at the table applauded and Grandfather gave me a kiss. I still remember how thrilled I was with all that attention. I certainly had no doubts about how this night differed from any other. It was the best night of my young life.

Later, when we reached the sentence: "From generation to generation our enemies want to destroy us," my grandfather paused. Looking around at the gathered family he said, "Let us all pray that the new Haman from Austria will never reach the sanctity of our homes, and that soon he will succumb to a terrible and unnatural death." We all said Amen.

Night fell, and through the window I could see fat snowflakes floating slowly to the ground. Inside the house, the large glazed tile oven was spreading a pleasant warmth, and delicious odors wafted from the kitchen—chicken soup, traditional matzoh balls, and roast meats. My mouth was watering, and even Grandfather Getzel seemed to speed up the reading of the *Haggadah* in order to get to the meal.

As a child I was not much of an eater, but that evening I ate everything that was put on my plate. Everything tasted wonderful, not just because Sarah cooked it, but because I sensed in the event the sanctity of a three-thousand-year-old tradition.

The conversation of the adults kept straying to the political situation in Europe. Some voiced grave concerns about what might happen with the rise of Hitler and his Nazi party. Others believed differently.

"The Allies will never allow Germany to rebuild their military power. Besides, when the Germans took over Lithuania during the Great War they treated the Jewish population decently. Surely the whole German nation couldn't change that much in one generation."

These were the sorts of things they said to each other, and they were probably echoed at all the seder tables throughout Kaunas that evening. For centuries the Jews in Europe had survived on hope and prayer, and as the decade of the thirties advanced they clung to hope and prayer still.

With the exception of one cousin, I never really knew my father's side of the family. Father was born in 1892 in Minsk, White Russia, where most of the Genkinds lived. A few emigrated to the United States after World War I; the rest, like Grandmother Esther's family, did not survive World War II.

In 1905, on the night before his bar mitzvah, Father was caught putting up posters on the walls of the Minsk town hall. Russia's war against Japan wasn't going very well. Hundreds of wounded and crippled soldiers were arriving from the front lines, and there were rumors of heavy losses and sunken fleets in the Pacific. Every day the crowds in the streets became more numerous, and the mood more ugly. The socialist underground was doing its utmost to incite unrest against the incompetent and rapacious Tsar.

Father's older sister Malkah and her boyfriend Vladimir Greenberg were heavily involved in one of the socialist cells. It was Greenberg who fired my father's imagination with revolutionary talk, and eventually took him to his first meeting. From that day forward Father was an enthusiastic convert.

His parents, Jacob and Esther Genkind, were prosperous wood merchants, and although they were deeply religious, they were liberal people who didn't force their children along the same path. As the Tsarist regime grew more corrupt, and its instigations against the Jews more deadly, many children of pious Jews, who only a generation ago spent their time studying the Torah, became ardent revolutionaries. Father fell in with the movement that called itself social democrats, which later evolved into the Menshevik party.

Father, who was not yet thirteen, was primarily employed in distributing leaflets and hanging posters. All such activities were, of course, forbidden. Although he and his friend Noah were often chased, the imperial guards were burdened with heavy gear and were usually no match for youngsters on foot who could easily dodge into narrow alleys or lose themselves in a crowd.

On the eve of his bar mitzvah, Father and Noah were sent out with a sheaf of posters portraying the Tsar as an octopus sucking the blood of the Russian people. The Guards, tired of being outrun by such young gangs, lay in wait in various parts of the city, and no sooner did the boys begin their work on the town hall than a Cossack thundered out of a dark passageway. He broadsided Father with the flat of his sword, throwing him off his feet and knocking all the air out of him. Had the guard turned his sword the other way, Father would have been cut in half. Noah ran.

The police questioned Father for two days, withholding food and beating him regularly, trying to discover who he was associated with. For two days Father resisted.

Within hours of his disappearance, Father's family was in a state of total alarm, but a full day passed before young Noah screwed up the courage to admit what happened. Malkah and the rest of the cell immediately went into hiding, assuming that a thirteen-year-old boy would quickly break down and reveal their identities.

It took elaborate negotiations with various authorities, and a great deal of money in bribes, but Father was finally released. Days passed, and no one else was arrested. Malkah's cell finally believed he hadn't given anything away, and Chaim Genkind became a local hero. It soon became apparent, however, that the police were keeping him under surveillance. Fearing further trouble, his family quietly smuggled Father over the border to his Aunt Raya in Kaunas. Although Lithuania was under Russian rule, the Genkinds were not known there, and the Jewish population of Kaunas was large, diverse, and easy to melt into.

Father hated leaving. His ordeal had only strengthened his commitment to the cause. He now believed with all his heart that the only thing that would save Russia, and especially Russia's Jews, was the overthrow of the Tsar. And how could a thirteen-year-old fail to enjoy his local celebrity?

Kaunas, however, delighted him. Nearly a third of its one hundred thousand residents were Jewish. For decades it had been a favored asylum for all sorts of political refugees. It was a bit like some small Eastern European version of Beirut or Casablanca, with its Nordic gentiles, its Poles and Russians, its Germans and Jews, in a place forever on the border of the next war. The Jewish community was diverse, and Jewish cultural activities were highly developed. There were schools conducted in Hebrew and Yiddish, Jewish newspapers and theaters. It was ironic that the Russians permitted these activities, but forbade teaching or publishing in Lithuanian. Here the Jews were much less restricted than they were in Russia, and for whatever reasons Lithuanian Jews were never really assimilated, as they were in other parts of Europe. The native Lithuanian gentiles were mainly Catholic, agrarian, and largely anti-Semitic, but for them as well as for the Jews, Imperial Russia was the oppressor. From 1910 to the early twenties, the Jewish population was largely left in peace, and lived nearly autonomously. Although there were many poor Jews living in the outskirts, many others prospered within the town. They were scholars, professionals, businessmen, many of them quite well to do, and they were an important part of the town's economic life.

It was here that Father came into contact with young people who were preparing themselves to go to Palestine. At Hebrew school he made friends among a Zionist circle called "Hovevei Zion." Father was too ardent a socialist to embrace Zionism, which seemed to him to be too narrow in its focus. His ideals embraced the whole of humanity. Besides, Palestine was ruled by the Ottoman Empire, and the idea of settling there seemed to be a pipe dream at best. Nevertheless, among the Zionist circles in Kaunas he found an intellectual liveliness and camaraderie that were altogether to his liking. As the weeks and then months went by, his Aunt Raya and Uncle Baruch became almost a second family.

Within six months or less, the situation had cooled enough for Father to return to Minsk, but he continued to come to Kaunas through his teens when things got too hot at home, and sometimes just for vacations. He was eighteen when he met Rebecca Shtrom, my mother. How they met was one of the family's favorite stories.

It was actually in Kalautuvas, a favorite summer watering hole for the Jewish population, that they had their big encounter. Kalautuvas was a lovely little resort town on the Niemunas, about thirty kilometers west of Kaunas. Father's aunt and uncle owned a small cottage there, and the summer he turned eighteen my father came for a visit. He was spending an afternoon on the beach when Rebecca Shtrom caught his eye. She was a year or two younger than he, and so lovely he could hardly keep his eyes off her, especially since she had also noticed him and gave him some encouraging smiles. She was a strong and graceful swimmer, and would swim out into the river, well beyond the safety markers, with Father watching in open admiration. That afternoon he finally got up the courage to speak to her when she was in the water, away from the crowd and out of earshot of their families. He had waded out knee-deep when he realized she was beginning to struggle. She was far beyond the buoys, in a dangerous part of the river. Even as Father shouted a warning she slipped under and didn't resurface.

Father was a powerful swimmer himself, and he soon reached the spot where he saw her disappear. He dove under, but saw nothing. The undercurrent was very strong there, and he had to fight to return to the surface for air. He dove again, and again could see nothing. He dove several times before he spotted a flash of something in the dark water. He had barely surfaced for another gulp of air when something powerful gripped his right ankle, squeezing it as if in a vise, and dragged him down. Below him he could see the girl's distorted face. She had clamped one hand around his ankle and held it in an astonishing grip. He barely made it to the surface again for a breath before she dragged him down once more. It was next to impossible to maneuver with one leg so immobilized. She dragged him down again. And then again.

Father was on the verge of panic when she began to lose consciousness, and her grip relaxed. He twisted down and managed to hoist her by the hair, then grabbed her arm. It took enormous effort to free himself from the whirlpool, towing her along, and by the time he reached calmer water they were several hundred feet farther from the beach. He was halfway back to the riverbank and almost completely exhausted before friends and family finally spotted them and dragged them both to safety.

After this nearly fatal encounter, Chaim and Rebecca were inseparable. Neither the Shtroms nor the Genkinds quite approved of their love affair at first, chiefly because young Rebecca's politics were as radical and enthusiastic as my father's were, and both sides saw nothing but trouble ahead with the two young socialists egging each other on. In truth, Grandfather Getzel was more likely afraid that their amateur zeal would expose others to danger, for as my father would eventually discover, his sweetheart's quiet, scholarly father was also up to his neck in the revolutionary movement. He remained so until the Bolsheviks' early purges broke his heart, and he turned to religion for solace. In the end, both sides of the family accepted the inevitable, and Father would probably have remained in Kaunas had he not been urgently called back to Minsk. His mother, a mainstay in the family business, became quite ill that fall. Father remained in Minsk for two years, helping his father, until the Tsar's army called him up for the draft in 1912. My father refused to become cannon fodder for the hated Tsar. Once again he made his way back to Kaunas, where Rebecca waited.

Even considering what he knew of the Shtroms by then, he was astonished by the size of their engagement party, where he counted no less than ninety people, including friends and business acquaintances. All the younger people there wanted to see the marks my mother left on my father's ankle. Her drowning grip had left great welts on his flesh, and although they faded over time, strangely enough they never entirely disappeared.

The couple settled happily in Kaunas and made a good beginning. But Europe was stumbling toward World War I, and by the time it broke out in 1914 there was great unrest both in Russia and among its European satellites. The Tsar ordered all Jews to evacuate sensitive border areas, Kaunas among them. Father and Mother returned to Minsk, by separate routes, as it turned out. Father's was the more dangerous, for Getzel Shtrom had enlisted him to smuggle a load of gold out of Lithuania and into neutral Sweden, telling him it was the Shtrom family fortune. In truth it was all tied up with the socialist underground, which was busy trying to fund a revolt. It was only in the midst of this game that Father began to guess the true extent of Getzel Shtrom's involvement in revolutionary activities. Father actually made it across the Russian border and into Minsk through the machinations of the Bolsheviks, traveling part of the way in the company of none other than Lev Davidovich Bronstein, known to the world as Leon Trotsky.

By the revolution of March 1917, Father was deeply involved in the Menshevik party, and actually served as some kind of deputy cultural minister in Kerensky's short-lived government. Ever after that experience, Mother and others close to him would tease Father by calling him "Minister."

Toward the end of World War I, Father and the family once again fled back across the border to Kaunas. He no longer had anything to fear from the Tsar's agents. Now it was the Bolsheviks who wanted his head.

Spring always arrived late in Lithuania, and was nearly always interrupted. The first green shoots and blossoms of April would be covered over in snow more than once, and on occasion snow would even invade the month of May. We always greeted the hot days of our short summer with great enthusiasm. Just about all the Jews in Kaunas who could afford it flocked to Kalautuvas and other resorts on the river for the season. My family was no exception. Around the first of June my mother would pack the family belongings, our luggage, linens, and provisions, and Father would drive us to the cottage we rented each summer. On Monday he would return to Kaunas to tend to his restaurant supply business, coming back to spend weekends with us when he could. If the need arose during the week, we would take the paddle ferry to Kaunas and back.

In my mind's eye Kalautuvas remains a beautiful place. Dozens of summer cottages and a few little shops nestled along the river and stretched up a gentle meadowed slope with scattered patches of woods. Behind this rose higher hills which were deeply wooded with pine and hardwoods, thick with undergrowth. The cottages were very rustic, most of them built of heavy peeled logs like typical Russian *dachas*. Our cottage had electricity, but no running water. We pumped water from a well, used an outhouse out back, and bathed in the Niemunas. My parents' dangerous entanglement with the river had in no way dampened the family's enthusiasm for swimming.

The Niemunas was even broader at Kalautuvas than it was at Kaunas, and on the resort side it had a lovely little sandy beach. As I grew older this was where Fanny and especially my brother Herman taught me to swim. Herman had been frail as a small child, and our family doctor advised that he take up swimming as exercise. He took to it like a duck, and as a teenager even trained for the junior Lithuanian championship. He was the one who taught me how to extricate myself from the tricky undercurrents of the Niemunas, how to swim at right angles to the current instead of against it. I can still hear him saying "Kick out, Solly. Kick out hard."

By the time he was seventeen, Herman was six feet tall, with wide shoulders and an athletic build. He had an elongated face, black eyes, a strong chin, and prominent cheekbones. His friends called him "Tarzan" because of his striking resemblance to Johnny Weissmuller, who played Tarzan in the movies. He clearly relished the nickname, and even combed his black hair straight back, just like Weissmuller did.

He had little appetite for school, and for this he was constantly at odds with Father. Routine studies bored him to death, although he did well in languages, as all of us did. Herman was intelligent and did well enough in his studies until he started going A.W.O.L. from class, sometimes for days at a time. This was a terrible disappointment for

Father, who had entertained hopes of sending him abroad to study upon his graduation from gymnasium.

His exceptional strength, coupled with a short temper, got him into other kinds of trouble. By the late thirties anti-Semitism was becoming virulent in Lithuania. There were frequent brawls as gangs of Lithuanian hooligans roamed about beating up Jewish boys. Herman was never averse to a good fight, and many of our younger acquaintances began to depend on him to come to the rescue when a Jewish boy was assaulted.

As much as Fanny was a second mother to me, Herman was my hero. He taught me to swim, he taught me to dive. He also introduced me to my first real novel, Jules Verne's *The Mysterious Island*, which so captivated me that I eagerly searched out and read all Verne's books, and reread *The Mysterious Island* many times over.

In the fall of 1938 Herman got into a terrible brawl with a gang of Lithuanians. They robbed and beat an elderly Jewish woman in broad daylight. Herman and some of his friends tracked down the ruffians, and a bloody fight broke out. In the end Herman beat one of the gang so badly that he arrived at the hospital barely alive. It was a very serious business, and the police came around looking for Herman that same afternoon. Father sent Herman away to stay with relatives in Memel until things cooled off.

The event aroused great consternation among the family. The Lithuanian boy remained unconscious for several days, and everyone feared reprisals against the Jewish population. Fortunately, the injured boy came out of his coma and slowly recovered, but Father had to bribe some high police officials in order to assure that our family came to no harm. For the entire autumn none of us laid eyes on our Herman.

Chanukah at our house was always special, and the Chanukah of 1938 was especially magical. I remember waking in my grandparents' house on the first morning. School was off somewhere in the distant future, and I could stay ten full days with my grandparents and Aunt Anushka, my favorite aunt.

First there was breakfast downstairs with Anushka, Grandpa, and Grandma. Red Ida, the cook, served my favorite morning meal— freshly baked rolls with strawberry preserves, a mushroom omelette, and a big mug of hot chocolate, extra sweet. After I finished I thanked them, and slowly got up from the table without betraying my anxiety to run outside. Dressed in my new sheepskin coat and warm boots, I pretended there was no haste and proceeded to the front door with all the dignity of Grandfather himself. Aunt Anushka was always amused by this show. "Run, child, run," she cried, laughing. "They are waiting for you."

I closed the door quietly behind me, then took off at breakneck speed, my newly varnished sled bouncing along behind me in the fresh snow.

They were all there—Michael, Itamar, the Gladzookes twins, Izia and Vova, my cousins, Arik and Mulie, and most importantly, Lena Greenblat. I blushed just looking at her. A few days before, when we were skating, she had fallen on the ice. I helped her up, quickly removing my glove to hold her hand. The mere touch of her skin thrilled me. I had been in love with her ever since I could remember.

The snowman was half finished, and they all laughed at my tardiness. "This time we forgive you," Itamar said, "—that is if you didn't forget to bring the carrot for the snowman's nose!"

We added his features and set his hat on his head at a rakish angle, making adjustments here and there until we were satisfied that he was the tallest, most handsome snowman on the hill. When we were finished we stood together in silence, admiring him. I think in that moment we shared a sense of closeness that all of us knew was special.

Itamar was the first to break the spell. He grabbed the rope on his sled and a moment later was flying down the hill, scattering snow behind him.

Lena stood beside me, waiting to be invited for a ride. Her light chestnut hair fell to her shoulders from beneath her blue woolen cap. Her almond-shaped eyes, brown and warm, were set in a perfect oval face. She was astoundingly beautiful, with a full mouth and a small, well-shaped chin. Only her rounded cheeks betrayed her youth.

Maneuvering with all my skill, I flew down the hill with Lena holding on behind and shrieking in delight. I could smell the scent of the orange soap she used. At the bottom we hit a bump and rolled off into a snowbank. As we scrambled to our feet, laughing and out of breath, I drew close and kissed her on the cheek. She looked up at me, her eyes sparkling, and I would have dared another kiss if the

Gladzookes twins had not swept down the hill behind us and landed at our feet.

I wanted the day to go on forever, and by the time I left the hill the sun was setting. A last confused look, a swift touch of hands, and Lena and I parted. I ran all the way home in a dizzy state of happiness.

That night there was a big family dinner at my grandparent's house, and I was late. My father's car was already parked outside, among a cluster of cars belonging to various aunts and uncles. I entered through the kitchen, as I was supposed to do when my boots were wet, and went upstairs to clean up. I had just gotten into my suit when Aunt Anushka knocked and entered the room, wearing a pink dress with a lace collar and looking radiant. "Where have you been, child? Come downstairs. Everyone is waiting."

Gathered in the parlor were all of my aunts, uncles, and cousins. A tall man in a brown suit stood behind my father. It wasn't until he turned that I realized it was Herman. His face broke into a huge grin as I let out a great whoop and charged across the room. When I threw myself on him he grabbed me in his usual tackle and rumpled my hair, something I allowed no one else to do.

"Hello, sport," he said, laughing. "What's this I hear about a girl named *Leeena?*"

Today, nearly sixty years later, when I close my eyes I can still see all our family sitting around the Chanukah table. There was my wonderful Aunt Anushka, my Uncle Itzhak with his bashful wife Sonia, and their five children. There was Aunt Mere with her husband Moshe and their three daughters.

To my grandfather's right sat his older brother Abraham with his wife and their large family. Next came Great Uncle Ichiel with his wife Malka and their daughter and sons and grandchildren. And of course there were Fanny and Herman and my father and mother.

Father's favorite niece, also named Sonia, the only member of his family in Kaunas, was also there. She was only a few years younger than Father, and was happily married to a local architect called Jasha. They had two boys. Arik was a year younger than I, and a good friend of mine; little Ronnie was five.

Most children don't realize they're lucky until they're grown, but looking around at those people I think I knew even then what I had: a happy childhood.

My Uncle Jochil was there with his wife Dobbe, a heavyset woman with a red neck and sharp blue eyes. She made no secret of who was the boss in the family. They had a daughter named Miriam who had her mother's blue eyes and her plump physique as well. Their son Fima was a year or two older than I and had become very active in the Zionist youth movement. He was always trying to get me to come to the meetings.

Then there was Uncle Jacob, Grandfather's youngest son. He was a bachelor until his late thirties. The family had almost given up hope he would ever marry when he met, and soon after married, a pretty widow named Leena. Jacob was considered shy by the others, but I think this was only because his two brothers were so vociferous.

Uncle Jochil and Uncle Itzhak were irrepressible pranksters who would go to any lengths to play tricks on each other or on anyone else within reach. They were both bright and lively, and would argue endlessly about nothing and everything. In the heat of a passionate argument Uncle Jochil would gesticulate wildly, shaking his head and rolling his eyes, while Itzhak would sit there calmly, making subtle deprecating gestures and repeating only two words: "Nonsense . . . Rubbish . . . Nonsense . . . Rubbish." This would drive Uncle Jochil crazy, and he would begin to scream and tear his hair out. At this point Uncle Itzhak, his eyes glistening with mirth, would smile and concede a point or two. They both had endless tales to tell, and we children loved to be in their company.

In March of 1939 Germany demanded that Lithuania return Memel to the Germans, which came as no surprise, especially after the Anschluss in Austria the previous year. But the British and French had signed their peace pacts with Germany, and Lithuania, along with the other Baltic states, strengthened its defensive alliances with Russia.

We continued to pursue our lives as usual, returning to Kalautuvas that July. I was looking forward to seeing my friend Petras Munkaitis, with whom I often went fishing. He was one of my few gentile friends, and so gentle and polite that my parents overlooked the vile anti-Semitism of his father.

I had rehearsed several Yiddish songs for Petras to learn. He had a great ear for languages, and could imitate accents to perfection. He also had a great voice. To the Jewish vacation crowd he was a marvel. Here was a blond Christian boy singing songs in perfect Yiddish, charming everyone around, reaching into their hearts and also their purses. His family was not very well off, and it was a good way for Petras to make some money.

When we were not swimming we explored the place, or had footraces in the meadow. For years Fanny had played a game with me: we would be coming back from swimming, or headed for the little ferry, and she would suddenly say "Ready, set, GO!" Then both of us would tear off toward our destination as fast as our legs could carry us. The older and faster I got, the faster Fanny seemed to get. I loved the game, however, and would often be the one to shout "Ready, set, GO!" Eventually I was even able to give Fanny a run for her money.

Across the river from Kalautuvas were orchards where one could buy a bucket of berries or early apples or, as Petras and I sometimes did, steal a few apples from the trees. One reached the other side by way of an odd, hand-propelled ferry run by a man named Kazys. The ferry was no more than a crude sort of barge made of empty barrels lashed together and topped with a wooden platform surrounded by railings. The passengers paid a small fee, and Kazys hauled the barge hand over hand, by means of a thick metal cable strung across the river at a calm spot down from the beach.

Kazys himself was an odd man, a local peasant who had never accepted the coming of the machine age. He despised automobiles and hated all internal combustion machines. That year, on the last day of our vacation, Petras and I set off for the orchard with instructions to buy a supply of fruit to take home to Kaunas. We were already aboard Kazys's ferry when a Lithuanian soldier on a motorcycle roared up in a cloud of dust. He dismounted his machine and wheeled it over the dock toward the ferry. Kazys, who was a fearless, barrel-chested old man, demanded that he retreat. The soldier came ahead. He had an important message to deliver, he yelled, and he had to cross the river. Kazys screamed at him to take that stinking machine off his boat, at which point the soldier actually drew his gun. "Stand aside, old man," he screamed back, brandishing the pistol under Kazys's nose. "Don't you know there's a war on?"

3

The Soul of a Human
Is the Lamp of the Lord

Hitler's army invaded Poland on September 1, 1939. Two days later Britain and France declared war on Germany. Virtually all of Europe was now at war.

The Nazis smashed through Poland with astonishing speed, and soon refugees were showing up on our streets. By late fall much of the community was involved in helping the Polish Jews streaming into Kaunas, most of them destitute. My mother and my aunt Anushka were on one of the committees formed to help the refugees, and we often had several of them at a time for meals. None of these people seemed to consider Lithuania anything more than a way station.

Early that December Uncle Jochil, who had a refugee family staying at his home, brought two refugees to our house. He was a Polish Jew named Rosenblat, a middle-aged man with frightened eyes. His daughter Lea was a plump little girl of eight with rosy cheeks and smiling blue eyes. Our family agreed to put them up for a while.

I had to give up my room and double up with Herman, an idea I wasn't crazy about. In fact I was quite annoyed. Rosenblat was a small, nervous fellow, always furtively looking over his shoulder, and seemed almost shifty-eyed to me. I wasn't very taken with him.

The title of this chapter is from Proverbs 20:27.

My resentment probably showed, for Mother soon took me aside and explained that many Jewish families were taking in Polish refugees, and that we all had to make some sacrifices for these poor people who had lost their homes, their livelihood—everything they owned. I felt guilty and promised to make amends.

It was Chanukah again, the festival of lights, and I was eleven years old. As usual, relatives and family friends gave the children Chanukah money, or *gelt,* and I had collected the handsome sum of ten *lit.* I suppose I was still feeling a little ashamed of myself over Rosenblat when a group of ladies showed up at our house, asking for donations to help the refugees; on impulse I gave them all my *gelt.* I immediately regretted it, but the ladies were quite impressed, and assured me that the money would mean a visa and escape for some deserving person.

The next day a new Laurel and Hardy movie was showing at the Metropolitan. I was dying to see it, but now my pockets were empty. Mother felt sorry for me and would have lent me the money, but Father put his foot down.

"You must stick to principles," he declared. "Giving away all your money was a noble sacrifice, but not when you come whining to us for reimbursement." He had that note of finality in his voice that I knew only too well. Knowing that he was right only frustrated me more. Giving away that horse in Heydekrug had become a little Waterloo in the short history of my life.

I had one hope left, my Aunt Anushka.

Anushka was then in her late thirties. There was a certain glamour about her in my eyes. When she was in her twenties she'd had a passionate attachment to a married man, and never quite got over it. She remained unmarried, what some people thought of as an old maid, but she hardly fit the mold. She ran an elegant shop of imported and gourmet foods, and led a lively social life among a diverse group of friends. She had a large Christian clientele who were among the richest families in Kaunas. If you wanted Beluga caviar, French champagne, or fancy Swiss chocolates, you went to Anushka's shop. She also catered to foreign embassies, who placed standing orders for specific imported foods available nowhere else.

My indulgent Aunt Anushka knew how crazy I was about Laurel and Hardy, and I was counting on her mercy. I made a date for the matinee the next day with my friends, Vova and Izia.

It was cold when I set out that afternoon, but I was dressed warmly. The snow felt crisp under my boots and shimmered white in the afternoon sun. It was the fifth day of Chanukah, and all along the streets menorahs shimmered in the windows of Jewish houses, and Christmas trees glowed in the homes of the Christians. Aunt Anushka's shop window was decorated with a string of colored bulbs, and a contraption attached to her door played a merry tune when you opened it. It was a gift from some inventor friend of hers.

When I walked in she was serving an elegantly dressed gentleman.

"Ah, my dear nephew came for his Chanukah money I bet," she said in Russian, smiling at me. She'd either forgotten that she'd already given me my *gelt*, or she wanted to save me the humiliation of asking for a second donation. Perhaps she heard about my encounter with the committee ladies. Whatever the reason, I wasn't going to give her any argument.

"Come here and meet his excellency, the consul of Japan, Mr. Sugihara," she added. I suppose I was staring at him. He had the most interesting slanted eyes. I approached him slowly, and extended my hand.

"How do you do, Sir," I said politely.

He solemnly shook my hand, returning my open scrutiny, and then smiled. There was humor and kindness in those strange eyes, and I immediately warmed to him. I was reminded of what my grandfather once told me: "Remember, the eyes are the windows to a person's soul. If you look close enough you may see what is behind them." At the time I had taken this as another of Grandfather's inscrutable proverbs, but looking up into the consul's face I thought perhaps he was right.

"You want to go to the movies," Aunt Anushka said affectionately, "and you need a *lit*, right?"

So she knew. I nodded quickly, still glancing shyly up at Mr. Sugihara. When Anushka turned to the cash register, he took a shiny *lit* from his pocket.

"Since this is Chanukah, please consider me your uncle," he said, extending the coin. I hesitated for a moment. I was eager for the *lit*, but it seemed awfully forward to take it, perhaps even unprincipled. But then principles stood little chance against Laurel and Hardy.

"You should come to our Chanukah party on Saturday," I blurted out as I plucked the coin from his hand. "The whole family will be there. Seeing as how you are my uncle," I added. I was suddenly flustered. I don't know how such an idea entered my head.

Anushka had returned from the cash register and heard it all. She was fairly gaping.

Mr. Sugihara's eyes twinkled. "I have never been to a Chanukah party," he declared. "I would gladly come, but don't you think you should ask your parents first?"

Aunt Anushka recovered herself. "I'm sure that his excellency must be very busy," she said with some embarrassment, and I could feel my own face redden. "But . . . but if you're free and would like to come, you are most certainly welcome."

Mr. Sugihara bowed.

"Please, you and your wife are most cordially invited," Anushka added warmly.

"Then it's done," he answered. "I gratefully accept your kind invitation."

Then he turned to me and shook my hand once more. "I shall see you on Saturday," his excellency said. I was more or less rooted to the spot at this point, until I remembered with a start that the movie was starting in just a few minutes. If I wanted to make it I had to run. I took my leave as politely as I could, leaving Aunt Anushka to make the arrangements.

My aunt preceded me home that evening. When I entered the house Mother stared at me expectantly, hands on hips, and Aunt Anushka was grinning. I realized that I was supposed to explain my outlandish behavior at her shop.

I felt uncomfortable and rather guilty in front of Father, especially since I'd gone behind his back for the movie money. I was searching my wits for an explanation when Father held up his hand. "It's all right, Solly," he said kindly. "If you feel like inviting someone to our party, I think it's more than all right. You should never feel guilty about extending hospitality to strangers."

That evening at dinner Mr. Rosenblat began telling us the terrible things they endured when the Nazis attacked Warsaw. A bomb demolished their house, killing his wife and older daughter. He and Lea, who were in another part of the house, were trapped under the rubble. They were barely alive when rescuers found them three days later.

That was just the beginning of their troubles, for with the German occupation began the systematic persecution of the Jews. A few days after he and Lea moved in with relatives, two soldiers came in and announced that they were confiscating the house for the German army. When Rosenblat's cousin asked for a few days grace until they found another place to live, one of the Germans pulled out his pistol and shot the poor man right in front of his wife and children.

Rosenblat told us how Jews were being rounded up and sent to German labor camps, how black-clad soldiers known as the SS were terrorizing villages. "You are crazy to stay here," he said bluntly. "You are sitting on a volcano which is about to erupt, and you are all behaving as if you were living in America. I am getting out of here as soon as I get a visa, and I don't care if we end up living with cannibals as long as it's far away from the Nazis."

Many believed that the Polish Jews exaggerated their stories to gain greater sympathy from their Lithuanian hosts, and in fact my sympathy for this man's family was at war with the notion that he was embroidering his tale. Surely the sorts of persecutions he described couldn't happen in the twentieth century! In any event, these were the sorts of horror stories that belonged to another place, that happened to other people.

This is not to say that the exploits of the German army were unknown. The lightning moves of the Wehrmacht were becoming a fixture in newsreels at the Forum and the Metropolitan, and in some ways their victories had about them the air of a fictional thriller, bound up in my mind with the Hollywood plots that followed them on screen. The Germans had meticulously filmed their great *blitzkrieg* on Poland, and footage appeared in the movie houses almost as regularly as accounts appeared in the newspapers. The German army had swept through Poland with a speed that astonished the world, and their swift Panzers and diving Stukas became fixtures in my imagination. I had long been a fan of military history, and the strength and discipline of the German army inspired a certain dreadful awe in me. On screen and in print they were like something out of H.G. Wells or Jules Verne.

Saturday morning Mother finished preparations for the Chanukah party. Once again she jokingly complained about my rash behavior in inviting the Japanese consul. We had to add all the leaves to the big mahogany table and take out her best tablecloth and cutlery. But she was clearly intrigued by the exotic Mr. Sugihara, and both she and

Aunt Anushka were curious to meet his wife. They told the rest of the family that a special guest would be coming, but refused to disclose who it was.

The candle-lighting was set for six in the evening. Anushka arrived with Mr. Sugihara and his wife Yukiko precisely at six. Mrs. Sugihara was dressed in a very elegant black dress, and Mr. Sugihara wore a formal striped suit. Both looked very distinguished, and their appearance with Aunt Anushka was a total surprise to the rest of the guests. The last thing they expected was this elegant Japanese couple. Mr. and Mrs. Sugihara both spoke German and Russian, so they were able to communicate freely with the other guests.

To make our refugee, Mr. Rosenblat, feel at home, Father chose his daughter Lea to light the candles. Lea was very bashful in front of all the people, but she did it gracefully, taking the shammes and lighting the candles one by one. I helped her say the prayer. *Praised are you, Lord our God, Ruler of the universe, who performed miracles for our ancestors, in those days, in this season . . . It is You who light my lamp; the Lord, my God, light up my darkness. . . .* Afterward Uncle Jacob took out his harmonica, and we all sang Chanukah songs.

While Lea lit the candles, Mr. Sugihara stood near me and watched very attentively. Later he told me that they had a similar candle-lighting ceremony in Japan. He wanted to know more about the tradition, about the historical background of the festival.

I told him the story of how Judah Maccabee led his men into war against the powerful Greeks, who had defiled the temple, and how their tiny force defeated the much greater armies of Antiochus. Judah and his followers liberated Jerusalem, and set about rededicating the temple, but when they went to light the lamps they could find only enough oil to burn for one day. Keeping the faith, they used the one small cruse they had, and God made the oil burn for eight full days. This is how Chanukah became the festival of lights. Each evening the shammes, the one candle used to light all the others, was used to light one more candle, until on the eighth day all eight candles were burning.

The tables were laden with the best of food and drinks, including some Japanese food which Anushka supplied from her shop. We also had veal with small roasted potatoes, roast duck in orange sauce, and many other wonderful things.

Mr. Sugihara also asked me about our family life and my hobbies. When I told him that I collected stamps, he invited me to come and visit him at the consulate. He said he would give me some stamps from Japan.

After everyone had eaten, Father rang a little servant's bell and asked for everyone's attention. "I want you to meet Mr. Rosenblat and his daughter Lea, who recently escaped from Poland. Mr. Rosenblat wants to say a few words."

Mr. Rosenblat looked nervous, and a bit out of place in the elegantly dressed crowd. Father had given him one of his suits, but it was too big and he looked waifish in it.

Mr. Rosenblat spoke in German, hesitantly at the beginning, but as he warmed to his subject a hush fell over those present. He became so emotional describing what was happening to the Jews in Poland that he broke down and cried. Mr. Sugihara listened attentively, a look of dismay on his face.

After everyone rose from the table, Mr. Rosenblat cornered our guest. Mr. Sugihara asked Rosenblat for other details about conditions in Poland under the Nazis, which Rosenblat eagerly supplied. I guess it was part of the consul's job to get firsthand information on the German occupation of Europe. Rosenblat implored Sugihara to issue him a Japanese visa, but the consul sadly shook his head, explaining that his government had refused permission to issue such visas, not even transit visas.

Father was distressed to see Rosenblat hounding our guest, but he said nothing, and Sugihara seemed sympathetic enough. He invited Rosenblat to visit him at the consulate. He was pessimistic, but he would see if there was any way he could help him.

To my astonishment, Father then told Sugihara that he had visas for the United States and had been seeking a buyer for his business. Father had a brother and sister in the U.S., and I knew there had been talk of going there, but this was the first I'd heard of any definite steps toward leaving.

Mr. Sugihara studied Father for a minute before answering. Choosing his words very carefully, he said, "If I were you I wouldn't worry too much about the business."

My father seemed quite disturbed by this response, but we would all come to wish he had taken that advice more seriously.

Outside, fat flakes of snow were slowly drifting to the ground. A somber mood had fallen over our party since Rosenblat's speech, but Father, Mother, and Anushka, as proper hosts, did their best to dispel it. Sugihara himself, with his diplomatic training, was good at shifting the conversation to happier topics, and the other guests were relieved to follow his lead. Things were, after all, relatively quiet on the western front. Russia had sealed a pact with Germany, much to the world's surprise, and everyone was certain that Hitler would not affront the Soviets with further incursions into Stalin's backyard. In any event, Lithuania had already handed over to Hitler its one real plum, the Baltic port of Memel.

At the end of the evening Mr. Sugihara came up to me and shook my hand good-bye.

"I thank you very much for your invitation. I would have been sorry to miss our conversation about the Maccabees and the miracle of the lights.

"I'm especially happy to have had the opportunity to get to know your charming family," he went on. "It is the first time I've had the pleasure of visiting a Jewish home, and I hope it won't be the last," he smiled. Again I felt a great warmth toward this man. He spoke to me as an equal, rather than as a child, and I liked the feeling.

At the door he added, "Don't forget to visit me at the consulate. I believe you may find some of the Japanese stamps quite interesting."

As we entered the new decade and the early spring sun began to thaw the ground, more and more refugees streamed into Kaunas, bringing with them more horrifying stories. The refugees besieged the embassies in town for visas, but the only ones able to emigrate were those who had a lot of money, and not many did. Mr. Rosenblat petitioned many consulates, and continued to return to the Japanese consul seeking help. But Mr. Sugihara had received strict instructions from his government not to issue any visas to refugees.

Rosenblat couldn't understand how we could be so apparently indifferent to what was going on around us. However, beneath my parents' apparent calm I sensed a growing uneasiness. There were too many refugees flooding our country not to be apprehensive about what drove them over the borders with little more than the clothes on their backs. Occasionally Father would hear about someone who might be interested in buying his restaurant supply business, but nothing ever came of it. Outside of what we read and saw in the newsreels, and the many new strangers in the streets, life went on more or less as usual.

That spring I visited Mr. Sugihara, as he had suggested, to collect the Japanese stamps he promised me. He received me graciously, and gave me a full envelope of them, all different sizes and colors. Most of them bore the Japanese emperor's face.

He wanted to know whether Mr. Rosenblat had obtained his visa, and when I told him no, he shook his head.

"Things are bad. Very bad," he said quietly. "Something should really be done."

Before I left he asked me to take a message to my father. It was short. He said, "Tell him the time to leave is now."

Then he looked at me sadly and there was compassion in his eyes. Again I was struck by his unusual kindness.

"I hope that he'll take this advice, for your sake," he said.

When I returned home I gave Father Mr. Sugihara's message. He was visibly shaken, and that night he had a long discussion with Mother, who had great reservations about leaving Lithuania. Father was clearly very worried, and although he argued with Mother's inclination to stay on, he had doubts as well. "What will I do in America? How will I earn a living? I don't know the language, and at my age I would never get a job. I'm ready to sell the business at any price, but no one seems to be in the market."

Mother, whose entire family was in Kaunas, abhorred the idea of moving to the United States. The fact that we would arrive there penniless, unless we sold the business, only strengthened her resolve to stay put. She was certain that the Nazis wouldn't risk confronting the Russians over Lithuania, but the idea of Russian intervention hardly assuaged my father's concerns. He had nearly as many trepidations about the Russians as he did about the Germans. The Bolsheviks had long since put a price on his head.

Mother scoffed at his concern. "That was twenty years ago, and the country was in utter chaos. Your position under Kerensky was a fairly minor post. You weren't a big shot. You can't believe that the Russian government has kept track of you all these years?"

Father always relented a little in the face of Mother's apparent logic. "Nevertheless we're leaving as soon as I can unload the business. Once things calm down a little, I'm sure I'll find a buyer."

I often thought that things would have turned out differently if my father had gotten Mr. Sugihara's message firsthand. He might have sensed the consul's urgency.

As the first crocuses popped out of the ground and the trees began to bud we began to think of Kalautuvas, and as usual made plans to spend the summer there. We invited Mr. Rosenblat to join us. He thought we were insane.

By the end of March thousands of Polish refugees were in Lithuania, frantically trying to find a way out. With few exceptions, none of the western countries were willing to grant them asylum. We continued to give groups of them meals, as did other Jews in the community, and I remember them sitting in our parlor talking in the curious dialect that was so different from the Yiddish spoken in Lithuania. It was only gradually, as refugee children showed up in my classes that spring, that I began to catch on to it. Even the schoolboys spoke of nothing but visas and how to escape from Lithuania. They seemed like people possessed, like people from a different planet.

Then Denmark fell, and Norway. More and more of the Jewish community of Kaunas was catching the "escape fever" from the refugees. Our visas to the United States were burning in my father's pocket, and he made desperate efforts to get rid of his restaurant supply business, asking only enough to secure our passage through neutral Sweden and give us a modest nest egg.

Then the letters from Father's family in the States turned into urgent phone calls, asking us not to delay any longer. Father was finally convinced, and Mother gave in too. We were just going to walk away from the business. Finally, the very day Father was to go out and purchase tickets, he received an offer.

It was from a man named Fisher, who had worked with Father some years back. He had recently returned to Kaunas looking to start a new enterprise. Father couldn't believe his good luck. He sat up with Fisher half the night going over the books. Fisher seemed to think that the local panic was just that—panic. There had been Jews in Lithuania for the last five hundred years, he said, and they would be here for another five hundred. He was so confident and convincing that Father almost had second thoughts.

He would receive only twenty percent of what the business was worth, but it was more than he expected. There was a small catch, however. Mr. Fisher wouldn't have the money until the end of June—six weeks away.

Father's hopes were completely dashed. Under the circumstances it was a terribly long wait.

Meanwhile, however, there were rumors that the Nazis were trying to negotiate with the French and the British. The Russians had occupied eastern Poland, and there was apparent peace between Hitler and Stalin. Perhaps the dreaded invasion of Lithuania would be a long time coming, my parents said. Having that money in the States would give us a decent start, a fighting chance at a new life. As soon as we collected it we would leave the country immediately.

It was the worst decision my parents ever made.

We decided to spend the last weeks before our departure in Kalautuvas. A few days after we arrived at the cottage, however, new rumors began to circulate: Soviet troops were supposedly taking up bases in Lithuania. Although the Lithuanian government, headed by President Antanas Smetona, continued to tell the population that we would remain independent, Lithuania's long history with Russia suggested otherwise.

Father was very upset at this turn of events, given his old score with the Russians. But Smetona continued to reassure the population, and again my parents waited. "Another four weeks and we are off," they said.

Then the western front erupted like a volcano. The Nazi armies attacked Holland, occupied Belgium without resistance, and smashed their way into France, scoffing at the supposedly impregnable Maginot line.

Paris fell on June 14, 1940. The next day the Soviet army marched into Lithuania. We were trapped.

Despite Father's fears, nothing much happened the first few weeks of the occupation. Like my mother, most of the Jewish population was more relieved than apprehensive. As bad as the Russians were, they were more or less a known quantity and they didn't single out the Jews for persecution as the Nazis did.

The Soviets took over all government institutions, and nationalized large corporations and factories, but otherwise they allowed the population to go about their business. Father began to calm down a little, but with the Soviet takeover the deal with Mr. Fisher fell through. Since Father dealt in food commodities, he soon found himself doing business with the Russian army, which was happy to deal with someone fluent in their language.

After a while life settled into a new routine. People began to relax a little, and they began to think that all the stories of Soviet terrorism were exaggerated. Many in the Jewish community began going out again to coffee shops, movies, and the theater.

As the days passed, Father's fears about his Menshevik past abated. Perhaps the Soviet secret service was not as efficient as their reputation suggested. But then the Russians began massive deportations. They assembled their lists of "undesirables," including a large number of prominent citizens—men in government and business, Christians and Jews, as well as Zionists and other "counter-revolutionary" elements in the Jewish community. Without prior notice, without trials or sentencing, people were rousted from their beds in the middle of the night and barely given time to dress and pack a few belongings before they were put on trains bound for Siberia. Among the gentiles were former government officials, members of rightist parties, and known anti-Russian elements. Although it was eventually established that a greater percentage of the deportees were actually Jewish, the Christian population would later claim that it was "Bolshevik Jews" who had sent Lithuanian Christians to Siberia.

Father now decided that we would leave Lithuania no matter what. His inquiries became more and more desperate, but leaving Soviet-occupied territory was as difficult and complicated as he had feared. Since the occupation, the only route out of Lithuania was through Russia. We had to have a transit visa in addition to our United States entry visas which were now useless. They were stamped in our Lithuanian passports, which the Russians had declared invalid.

Other foreign nationals, the Poles included, managed to get visas to various destinations in Africa and South America, but it was too late for us. My parents now faced the appalling fact that Sugihara had been dead right. Delaying our departure on account of Father's business had been a colossal blunder.

Despite the apparent hopelessness of the situation, Father joined the long lines of people desperately seeking assistance from any consulate that might help.

One day Mr. Rosenblat came to our house with a young student from the famous Telzer Yeshiva. Rosenblat was very excited. It turned out that the boy was a Dutch citizen, one of many boys from Holland and western Europe who had been sent to study in the Hebrew schools of Kaunas. Now the Nazis occupied their homelands, and the boys were trapped.

On behalf of the students, the Dutch consul made inquiries and discovered that two Dutch colonies in the Caribbean, Surinam and Curaçao, didn't require visas for immigration. Permission to enter was granted at the discretion of the Dutch governor. A putative "end visa" for these colonies, from the Dutch consul of Kaunas, would be a start. In fact, the consul agreed to issue visas to these colonies to anyone who asked for them.

That left the problem of the transit visa. There was only one consulate that might help. With a transit visa from the Japanese, Rosenblat said, the Soviets might allow the refugees to pass through Russian territory.

"And that's where you come in. You know Mr. Sugihara. You should go and explain to him our desperate situation. Perhaps he will give us transit visas now. He is our only hope."

Father was exasperated. The whole business sounded terribly complicated and far-fetched, and Mr. Sugihara had already told us that the Japanese government was adamant in refusing to issue visas. Why should that have changed?

Ordinarily I would never interrupt such a conversation, but I piped up. "Surely if anyone might take pity on us it would be Mr. Sugihara. I'm sure if there is any way he can help, he will," I said.

It was worth a try, at least, and Father agreed to visit Mr. Sugihara the next day.

Other Polish refugees also came by, pressing Father to intervene with the Japanese consul. One of them told Father he might be able to buy Polish passports for us. They would be costly, but he thought he could get them.

Father was encouraged by this news, and promised to do his best to persuade Mr. Sugihara. Suddenly there was hope for us again.

Early the next morning, Father and I, Mr. Rosenblat and his daughter, and the Dutch boy all went to the Japanese consulate.

Mr. Sugihara looked weary, but he greeted us cordially. He had even saved some stamps for me. He had just returned from seeing the Soviet authorities. They had extended his stay, so the consulate would remain open another three weeks.

Father told him of the terrible danger we were all in, that our only hope of escape was through him. Then he showed him the visa to Curaçao in the Dutch boy's passport. Would that be sufficient for a transit visa?

As it turned out, Mr. Sugihara had already made his decision. Since the Soviets took power he had received many delegations of refugees. For days they had gathered outside the consulate—families with children, women with infants in their arms. The Japanese government continued to refuse permission to issue visas, but he and his wife discussed the situation, and agreed that his humanitarian duty was clear. It overrode the policies of governments, Mr. Sugihara said. He would issue visas despite the instructions of his superiors.

"But first we must find out whether the Russians will honor a Japanese transit visa. The Soviet consul promised me an answer today," he said. And with that he excused himself and went to the telephone at his desk.

All of us held our breath, our eyes fixed on Sugihara's face, as he spoke into the phone. Many lives hung in the balance. Suddenly his face lit up with a radiant smile, and he raised a triumphant fist in the air.

Mr. Rosenblat's eyes were brimming as Mr. Sugihara rang off. Without further ceremony, the consul ushered us into his office and stamped all of our passports.

Tears streaming down his cheeks, Rosenblat grabbed the consul's hand and began kissing it before Mr. Sugihara could pull away. It was a deeply emotional moment, and Father too had tears in his eyes when he shook Mr. Sugihara's hand.

"I am honored and privileged to stand in front of a true humanitarian, who considered the interests of others before his own. God bless you," he said. It was the shortest formal speech Father ever made, but I knew it came straight from his heart.

Mr. Sugihara looked at Father sadly and told him that his visa would not do us much good, because the Soviets were issuing exit permits for foreign nationals only. Father didn't want to mention anything about the promised Polish passports, not until they were in our hands.

Before we left he gave me an envelope with stamps and shook my hand. Again I felt a bond with him. He looked at me a moment and then said, *"Vaya con Dios."* I didn't understand what the words meant, but somehow I felt their intent, and during all the years of the war I remembered them.

Vaya con Dios. Go with God. I don't know why he said it in Spanish, but the words were from the heart, and to this day those three words invoke deep feelings in me.

Even while we were saying our good-byes to Mr. Sugihara and his wife, the Yeshiva boy was waving his hat out the window at someone below. When we came downstairs there were dozens of boys, all in their black coats and hats, converging at the gate.

At home another crowd of refugees was waiting, and when we told them the news they all rushed off to the Dutch consul to get their visas to Curaçao. The next day all hell broke lose as throngs of people crowded before the Dutch and Japanese consulates, some of them standing in line all night.

Father was disappointed, but not really surprised, when the man who promised to sell us Polish passports never showed up. Now he knew that the man had only promised the documents so we would go to Sugihara. He didn't know that Father would have done it for him anyway.

Others told us about the continuing scene at Mr. Sugihara's office. Day after day he sat in his shirt sleeves, signing visas, barely able to keep his eyes open, he was so weary. Long lines of people stood for hours and even days outside the gate. During the three-week period before he left for his next posting in Berlin, he signed more than six thousand visas. It was rumored that even as the train departed he was still signing visas and handing them out the window. In the end he gave one of the refugees the visa stamp, so they could forge visas for each other.

I passed the consulate once during those last weeks and saw Mr. Sugihara leaning wearily against a windowsill, taking a break. He spotted me, and waved. It was the last time I ever saw him.

It was many years before I learned the fate of Sempo Sugihara and his wife. From Kaunas they went on to represent Japan in Berlin. The end of the war found them in Prague, where they were arrested by the Russians as enemy aliens. From there they were deported to Siberia, where they spent a year and a half in a prison camp. It was only in 1947 that they were able to return to

Japan, where they were disgraced for defying the Japanese government's orders and saving thousands of Jews.

In 1985 Sempo Sugihara was recognized as "Righteous Among the Nations" by the Yad Vashem institute of Jerusalem. He died the same year. Several years after his death, the Japanese government finally apologized formally to his widow and son, and Sugihara was posthumously awarded the Nagasaki Peace Prize.

I will never forget the man with the kind eyes whom I met the winter of 1939. Vaya con Dios, Sempo Sugihara. I am sure that you have a prominent place in paradise.

Months passed. Chanukah of 1940 was a somber affair. The prayers at the lighting of the Menorah had an air of desperation about them. It appeared that 1941 would be a dismal year. Grandfather Getzel had died shortly after the Soviets took over, and Grandmother followed soon after. The remaining family—uncles, aunts, cousins—often gathered together to comfort each other. That spring I came down with terrible stomach pains, which were diagnosed as appendicitis. I had an appendectomy and was hospitalized for a miserable week.

Late in May events took a darker turn.

Not long after the Soviets entered Lithuania, my brother Herman became friendly with a young Russian captain. It turned out that he was an officer in Soviet intelligence. My brother was twenty years old at the time, and a prime candidate for the military draft. He was handsome, charming, and streetwise and when the captain found out that he was fluent in Russian, German, and Lithuanian, he assigned him to his intelligence unit.

Herman never told my parents exactly what he did, but he would frequently disappear from home for days at a time.

Then one Saturday, toward the end of May 1941, Herman appeared at our door. A number of the Shtroms had joined us for the traditional Saturday meal of *cholent*, but Herman seldom joined such family gatherings. When father looked at him questioningly, Herman said, "I think this is the last time we will ever see all the family together under one roof."

He admitted that he had seen Father's name on a list for deportation months before. He kept this to himself because he didn't want to worry us, and he convinced the captain to hold off the arrest order. Herman and the captain postponed Father's arrest for the better part of a year before the captain's superiors found out about it. The captain was immediately transferred to Uzbekistan, and Herman was dismissed and put on the rolls to be drafted into the infantry.

My father received this stunning news with a certain sober gravity, perhaps because he'd felt it looming for so long. He may well have been in a mild state of shock. Mother, however, was distraught and immediately rushed to telephone her cousin George Shtrom, begging him to intervene.

George was a businessman, one of Ichiel Shtrom's successful sons. Despite his affluence, and perhaps because of his liberal upbringing, he was a supporter of the socialists and communists, and among his friends he was known as a champion of the underdog.

During the presidential reign of Antanas Smetona, the communists of Lithuania had not fared well. They were suppressed and many of them were arrested on flimsy pretexts. Some simply disappeared, never to be seen again. George helped these people in many ways, and spent large sums of money helping the families of those sent to prison.

Thus he became a close friend of Shnieckus, a first secretary of the Communist Party who rose to power when the Soviets occupied the Baltics. George Shtrom immediately appealed to Shnieckus, who promised to look into the matter of Father's deportation.

Aunt Anushka's birthday that June was a far cry from the festive parties usually thrown by our family and friends. My cousins and I had the whole birthday cake to ourselves, for none of the adults seemed interested in eating that night. Mother didn't touch her dinner, and every few minutes my father would look at his watch. Cousin George telephoned to say that we should start without him. When he finally arrived we knew that the news was not good. He barely kissed and congratulated Aunt Anushka before he took my father into the adjoining room. With a thumping heart, I slipped behind a curtain and eavesdropped.

George came straight to the point. "I am terribly sorry, Chaim, but there is nothing anyone can do. You are on the list as a counter-revolutionary and an enemy of the Soviet Union. The party bosses are furious that you are still at large. Even Shnieckus was reprimanded for trying to interfere. I wish I could have done more, but the orders are going to go through."

He put his hands on my father's shoulders. Father's face was ashen, and his voice was hardly recognizable. "My God. I've been such a fool, clinging to this fool's paradise for so long, and now everything is lost."

George took my father's hands in his own, and said forcefully, "Chaim, listen. All is not lost. There is a chance they will send you to the southern regions, to a village where your family can stay together. The climate and conditions there are much better than in the gulags. I am sure you will all weather this. Just don't give up! Never give up!"

Then he added, more quietly, "Where there is life there is hope."

How many times in the years to come would I hear that phrase repeated!

A silence fell in the room when George and my father returned. That same evening we packed knapsacks and small bags with items we would need for immediate survival: food that wouldn't spoil, warm underwear, hats and gloves, an extra pair of comfortable shoes. Father and Herman lined their clothes with rubles.

We said little to each other. My mother was silent and pale as a ghost all that night. From time to time she would wipe her eyes as Herman sat with her, holding her hand. My sister Fanny gathered together a few sentimental things to pass on to her friends, and left the house to call on them one by one.

Only my father sat alone in a corner, stoically reading a book. It was after midnight when Fanny returned, and Father announced that we should all get some sleep. We didn't undress. We just took off our shoes. When they came for us, we would be ready.

4
Schrecklichkeit

I

JUNE 22, 1941

It was hot that night, even with the window near my bed thrown wide open. I thought I'd slept only minutes before something woke me in the dark. It was my neighbor's pigeon, Queenie, perched on the sill, cooing and flapping and making all sorts of racket to attract my attention. I wondered what made her come so early. Usually Queenie showed up around seven; it was not yet five. I didn't mind. The night had passed, and the Russian police had not come.

I found the bag of bread crumbs I kept in my room and spread the bits in the little wooden feeder beneath my window. I spent a lot of time at that window. I had the attic room, and if I stood on tiptoe I could see all the way to the river.

The sky was turning a wan gray, as it does just before sunrise. A fine mist rising from the river spread slowly over the roofs below.

I knew and loved every nook and cranny of this town. Slowly its familiar details emerged from the darkness. The golden cupola of the Chor Shoul, our loveliest synagogue, took shape in the distance. Then Niemuno and Vilnius Streets, and Rotushes Square, lined with its

Schrecklichkeit, or "frightfulness," was the Nazi policy of terrorizing the civilian population so that they jammed the roads and highways and helped block the movements of enemy troops.

massive stone houses which had probably seen Napoleon on his march to Moscow. Further west I could see the crooked cobblestone streets of the old town and the Fish Market, and in the distance the ruins of the old castle where the ancient kings of Lithuania once resided.

The first rays of the rising sun spilled on the Alexotas hills, painting them pink and orange. The town began to stir from its slumber. I took a deep breath of morning air. It was going to be another scorcher.

Then I noticed something strange above the airport in Alexotas—a dozen or more silvery dots swarming in the air, as if silver butterflies were performing some early morning mating dance. I watched dreamily as black puffs of smoke mushroomed around them. Then from the distance came sharp cracking sounds, like guns.

All at once the craft dove one after another, emitting shrill whines that sounded like metal being torn apart. German Stukas! I had read about them often enough, and seen them in newsreels.

Deep rumbling explosions followed each dive, rattling all the windows in the house, and a thick column of black smoke rose over the airport, spreading slowly over Alexotas.

It had finally happened; the war had caught up with us.

Another wave of planes screamed down, followed by heavy explosions. Antiaircraft guns were now going full blast. Some shrapnel suddenly fell on a neighboring roof, sending roof tiles flying in all directions.

I jumped back from the window in alarm. Suddenly the war was very near and very real. I ran downstairs to discover my family already gathered around the radio.

Molotov was making an angry speech. It was June 22, 1941. The Germans had begun "Operation Barbarossa," as they called their campaign against the Russians, in flagrant violation of the treaty Ribbentrop and Molotov had signed less than a year before. The two worst butchers ever known to man, Hitler and Stalin, were now locked in a bloody struggle.

Berlin gave brief and factual reports of the German armies' rapid advance into Lithuania on one side and Belorussia on the other. From London, the B.B.C. more or less confirmed the German account.

How ironic that the Nazis had saved us from deportation to Siberia.

Over breakfast Father held a family conference. We all agreed that it was too dangerous to remain in Kaunas. As frightening as the Russian police were, the Nazis were scarier. And no one had much confidence in the Soviet forces. We had heard plenty about the German *blitzkrieg*, and seen the Russian army for ourselves. In Kaunas, the Soviets' lumbering pre-war tanks had been dubbed "tanks of fifty." It took one man to steer, we joked, and forty-nine to push.

It was decided. We would make a run for the Russian border. The Soviets had long since confiscated all private automobiles, so we would have to find transportation, but even if we ended up in Siberia, it would surely be better than life under the Nazis.

The phone was dead. Father and Herman went down the street to speak to Uncle Itzhak. They returned with grim news. The Russian army was evacuating the town full speed, jamming the outgoing trains. Even if we managed to get on, the Germans were bombing the tracks, and the chances of getting through were slim. There was no other public transport. We would have to reach the border on foot.

There was even worse news—a new threat from an unexpected quarter. Even with huge numbers of Soviet troops still in Kaunas, gangs of Lithuanians armed with rifles and revolvers were roaming the streets. They called themselves "Siauliai," or "Patriots," and although they occasionally fought the Russians, for the most part they were robbing and beating up Jews. Our neighbors had turned against us, and the Germans hadn't even arrived.

With this urgency upon us, we had a last, strange family meal at home. Mother behaved very oddly, insisting upon her best china. She moved stiffly about the room, setting the table and switching on the crystal chandelier. The Rosenthal dishes gleamed under its sparkling lights. Father stopped his protests when he saw my mother's tucked-in chin, a sure sign that nothing he said would move her. What was she thinking? We sat around the big mahogany table in silence, surrounded by the heavy blue drapes, the family pictures and paintings, the knickknacks and embroidered pillows—all the secure, familiar things that were part of our lives. It all felt eerily unreal to me, and sad, like the last meal of the condemned. Mother even served wine.

I remember going to my room to take a last look at all I was leaving, and slipping my beloved copy of *The Mysterious Island* into my knapsack.

A series of distant explosions brought all of us back to reality. Downstairs we assembled our bags and were about to leave the house when Uncle Itzhak arrived, red in the face and breathing heavily. He had recently developed heart trouble. How would he ever be able to walk all the way to Russia?

This time the news was good. Uncle Itzhak knew a man named Leizer who owned a horse and wagon. Leizer was willing to allow a few of us to ride with his family, though he wanted a lot of money.

After some bargaining, the men made a deal. Three of us would be permitted in the wagon with Leizer's family. The rest would have to walk. Mother was afraid my appendectomy incisions might open up under stress, so I was to ride in the wagon with her and Uncle Itzhak. Father, Fanny, and Herman would walk, as would Aunt Sonia and our cousins. We all agreed on a rendezvous: a bakery in Janeve, which was about thirty kilometers northeast of Kaunas. Leizer's brother-in-law Jankle owned it. Father and Uncle Itzhak knew the place. We would meet there if we were separated.

The narrow road leading toward Ukmerge and the Latvian border was choked with refugees and retreating Soviet troops. An endless variety of vehicles, horse-drawn wagons, motorcycles, and bicycles threaded their way through a huge swarm of people on foot. Although ragged columns of Soviet soldiers mingled among them, most of those on foot were civilians, and most of them were Jews.

Almost as soon as we got out of Kaunas, the Luftwaffe attacked the road, apparently intent on machine-gunning everything that moved. Everyone dove for the ditches. I lay face down in the dirt, trembling, as bullets thudded around us, raising clouds of dust. Luckily, no one around us was hurt, not even Leizer's horse, which stood off in a field shivering. But as the crowds pushed back onto the road, we realized that in the confusion Aunt Sonia and my five cousins had disappeared.

Uncle Itzhak was terribly upset, but Leizer insisted we move on, and there was nothing we could do. "I'm sure they are all right," Father kept saying. "We'll see them in Janeve."

We made very little progress that day. In many places the road was blocked with broken-down army vehicles. Some had simply run out of gas. Others had been hit by bombs and were no more than piles of smoking debris.

Hitler's surprise had been complete, and as the day wore on the whole Soviet Baltic Army turned into a disorganized mob struggling toward the border. Here and there an enterprising colonel or general tried to organize his troops by sending out messengers on horses or bicycles, or simply on foot, but the slow river of civilian refugees simply swallowed them up.

Schrecklichkeit had worked in Poland, and it was working here.

Late in the afternoon, as a column of Soviet tanks and ammunition trucks made their way past us, we heard again the shrill whistle of diving Stukas. Again the screaming civilians ran in all directions, while a few Russian soldiers took shots at the aircraft with their rifles.

"Into the ditch!" my father shouted, waving us toward a gully by the road.

In the distance the first bombs exploded sending flames and pillars of earth spurting into the sky. I remember watching the bombs advance in a neat pattern, like a tailor taking stitches, when suddenly I was lifted off my feet. A tremendous explosion shook the earth, sucking the air out of my lungs. I found myself up in the air, my feet flying up behind me and my eyes, strangely, wide open. It must have taken a mere second or two, yet time seemed suspended. I saw a truck on the road exploding in flames and a body rising into the air in pieces, the severed head flying past me, its eyes bulging. My mind registered every horrid detail.

Then I was on the ground, half-conscious, with clods of dirt and rocks falling on me. All around me people were crying for help. A Russian officer galloped by on a white stallion, his face grim and bloody under his officer's cap.

I must be hallucinating, I thought. Everything seemed to be in slow motion. From far away I heard my father's voice, "Are you all right, Solly? Are you all right?"

Slowly I sat up. Father, Herman, the whole family was coated from head to toe with dirt, but alive and unharmed. Bomb craters were all around us, and the wounded lay everywhere, moaning pitifully. An elderly man stumbled along the road, his right arm missing below the elbow. The dead lay about like broken dolls.

A tank that must have received a direct hit lay in a smoldering ruin, twisted pieces of metal pointing toward the sky. Another headless corpse hung out of the turret, spilling blood over the wreckage.

How did all this happen? Only hours earlier I had been in my room, dreamily watching tiny silver planes flutter over Alexotas.

A huge Soviet tank came clanking down the road, followed by a truck towing a long cannon. A dozen figures were clinging to the barrel, all so covered with dust that man and machine seemed one.

The officer on the white stallion came galloping back, waving his arms wildly for the tank to stop. It came to a grinding halt, and the truck towing the cannon rammed into it. The dust-covered soldiers tumbled off the cannon, and rained curses on the officer as they struggled back to their feet.

The officer ignored them. "Push these wrecks off the road," he said to the man in the tank, "and proceed to Janeve. Report to the MPs at the gate for supplies."

Suddenly my father leaped out of the ditch and stood in the horse's path.

"Comrade colonel," Father called up, "can you advise us on the situation? Can we proceed to the Russian border?"

From his mount, the surprised officer looked down at my father's grimy face. Pulling impatiently on his cap, he reined his horse around, then turned back in his saddle. "If you want to make it," he said, "you'd better move fast. The Germans are advancing on Kaunas and Vilnius both."

Before my father had a chance to thank him, he was galloping off. I looked at my father admiringly, a bit surprised at his boldness. When we located the others, Herman and Fanny were busy tying bandages on the wounded and helping people to their feet. Only my mother remained sitting on the ground, deathly pale and staring into space. As Father approached her, she covered her face with her hands and began to sob.

"Please pull yourself together, Rebecca," Father said gently. "We have to get out of here, and we don't have a minute to spare."

Now we discovered that Uncle Itzhak had disappeared, and so had Leizer's family and the wagon. We examined the wreckage and dead horses along the road, but they weren't to be found.

Again Father reassured everyone. "They've gone ahead to Janeve. We will meet up with them at the rendezvous." But he didn't sound very convincing.

I was still in shock, and my legs trembled as we set off on foot. My mother worried aloud about my incisions, but it couldn't be helped.

The Luftwaffe continued its strafings, and the farther we proceeded the more thickly the road was strewn with corpses. After one attack we encountered a young Jewish girl whom Fanny had tutored in Hebrew before the occupation. Her name was Dvora, and she had become separated from her family. It was not long after she attached herself to us that a single Stuka passed overhead, machine-gunning the crowd. As usual we dove off the road, but when the attack was over Dvora didn't get up. A shell had ripped through her back as she lay in the ditch, and she was moaning pitifully. Father and Herman tried to stop the bleeding.

My father pointed to a thicket a short distance across a field. "There's a pond there," he told me. "Go and get some water."

The bushes surrounding the pond were thick and tangled, and I had to thread my way through, my head down to protect my face. I glanced up as I neared the edge, then froze in my tracks. A group of naked people, their skin horribly white, was standing in the water at the other end. The wind made ripples on the surface of the water and blew the women's hair. Most of them were dark-haired, except for one tall blond woman whom I recognized, with a shock, to be my history teacher. Next to her stood her husband, a middle-aged man in glasses whom I had met a few times at school.

My teacher's five-year-old daughter, thumb in mouth, clung to her mother's leg. Before them, dressed in old Lithuanian uniforms, stood a group of *Siauliai* with rifles.

One of the men yelled *Fire!* and they opened up. I saw the shocked faces of their victims as they fell into the water. Only the little girl stood unharmed. She seemed frozen there, her thumb still in her mouth, the other hand vaguely extended as if reaching for the woman who had fallen beside her.

"Shoot her!" the officer shouted again, but no one fired. They just stood there looking embarrassed. Then the leader, an older man, calmly went up to the girl and hit her over the head with his revolver. Blood spilled down her face, but she made no sound as she fell.

For some moments I continued to crouch there, barely breathing. It took all my will power just to keep my wits together.

Then I was on my feet and running.

I couldn't believe what my eyes had seen. The retreating Soviet army was only a few hundred yards away, and the Lithuanians were murdering Jews under their very noses. I rushed onto the road and tried to rouse a Russian crew who were refueling their tank from jerry cans. The lieutenant in command gave me a tired look and told me that he expected nothing less of the Lithuanian swine. But he had his orders, he said. Besides, they were the army not the police, and this was obviously a police matter. I tried other soldiers, and they too shrugged me off. Finally, in desperation, I located an MP who was directing traffic, and grabbed him by the sleeve.

"They are murdering civilians down by that pond! Please, please, come and help us!" I cried, the tears beginning to run down my face. He looked down at me. I could see he was taking in my dirty swarthy skin, my dark eyes and black hair. His gray Slavic eyes first registered recognition, then hostility. I had seen that look before, and would see it many times again.

"Are they Jews?" he asked coldly.

I lowered my eyes. I knew he wouldn't help even if he could. When I located my family, my mind in complete turmoil, my father turned to me in anger. "And here you show up, empty-handed! The child is already dead. Where have you been?"

I'd completely forgotten the wounded girl, and the water. As if it could have saved her life, I thought. But I could see that Father was very upset. I had never seen him cry before.

Dvora was lying in the grass, a surprised look on her face. Her white dress was soaked with blood, and her eyes stared unseeing at the blue sky.

It was nearly dark when we came across a camouflaged truck on a side road. A Russian sergeant was working under the hood. He was a short, broad-shouldered man, with blond hair and prominent cheekbones. The truck was full of artillery shells and ammunition.

Father offered him money to give us a lift to Janeve.

"Sure, hop aboard, but I must warn you this truck is not the safest place in the world," he said, smiling wryly. He refused to take the two hundred rubles Father offered him. He then shook Father's hand and introduced himself. His name was Sasha Illitch Rodenko, and he was from Novosibirsk, Siberia.

We'd seen what happened to loads of ammunition when they were hit in air attacks, but we were so tired we decided to risk it. We hadn't driven five kilometers before the Stukas appeared again.

Sasha stopped the truck and we all ran for the nearest clump of trees. Within seconds the now-familiar heavy machine-gun shells ripped into the road ahead of us. Bombs exploded not too far away. I looked up at the sky and saw a plane with black swastikas painted on the fuselage skimming the trees, its guns blazing. Then it was gone.

I was about to get up when Sasha, who was lying next to me, jerked me back.

"Stay down! They usually come in pairs."

No sooner had he said it than the shrill whistle of a falling bomb made me bury my face in the soft moss beneath us. A tremendous explosion shook the ground, then all hell broke loose.

Above the din Sasha shouted, "Stay down! They must have hit my truck!"

The shells in the truck were exploding in all directions, sending shrapnel and bullets whizzing about like angry bees, chopping off branches and thudding into tree trunks over our heads. I buried my face in the ground, wishing I could crawl into the very earth.

When the inferno finally subsided there was nothing left of the truck but a ragged pile of charred metal.

My ears were ringing as we set out again on foot. Sasha was going to go his own way, but when my mother asked him to join us he consented. He had taken a liking to her. She reminded him of his own mother, he said.

It was well past midnight when we finally reached the outskirts of Janeve. Sasha suggested we try to get off the congested highway and find a side road in.

We were footsore and dead tired by then and decided to recoup a little before proceeding. Sasha picked a spot on a hill a few hundred meters from the road, beneath a giant oak. We wearily sank to the ground, and Father divided some black bread, cheese, and sausage among us. It was our second night on the road, and we had to conserve supplies. Sasha, who had run out of rations some time ago, accepted the food gratefully. He confessed that his mother was Jewish. He preferred to keep it a secret, because even as a child he knew that among the anti-Semitic Russians there was no percentage in being a Jew. In both name and appearance he was thoroughly Slavic, so he had no trouble hiding his identity. He was a sergeant in a supply company, he told us, and had been sent to Lithuania two weeks before.

As we ate and listened to Sasha's story an eerie sight spread before our eyes. In the moonlight, wave upon wave of Soviet military vehicles, heavy and light artillery, ambulances and trucks were inching their way into town. Thousands of people on foot were also trying to gain entrance. At the first intersection a white-haired officer stood on an oil drum, shouting orders. Thousands of weary soldiers and a hodgepodge of officers were digging in around the town, while tanks, howitzers, and heavy machine guns took up strategic positions.

"I think they are stopping all stragglers and lost units to fight a rear guard action. They're covering their retreat," Sasha said. "Once the German Panzers start rolling, everyone you see here will be dead." He seemed quite calm about it.

"What do you suggest we do, Sasha?" Father asked wearily. He sounded as if he expected orders from him.

"We'd be well-advised to clear out, my friend." Sasha answered. "I personally am not going to commit suicide by staying, not for the Soviet army or the 'Great Stalin' himself. I need some civilian clothing. Do you have any that would fit me?"

My father stared at him. The man spoke of desertion as if he were about to walk out of a movie he didn't care for.

"You're one cool customer," my father said, shaking his head. "But I'm afraid we have nothing extra."

"All right," Sasha said. "You wait here. I'm sure I'll find someone who won't be needing his clothes anymore. I'll also try to find a better route in," he said, gesturing at the highway below. "Don't worry, I won't be long."

With that he hefted his submachine gun and walked off into the darkness.

In the distance several heavy explosions shook the night. Artillery shells rumbled over our heads, exploding seconds later inside Janeve and painting the sky dark red and orange.

Half an hour passed, and Father began to look worried. We had grown to depend on Sasha in the brief time we'd been with him.

"We'll just have to go on without him," Herman said aloud.

At this Fanny began to cry quietly. "Oh dear," Mother sighed. "I wish he would come back. He's such a likable young man and so helpful." These were the first normal, complete sentences she had spoken in two days.

"I think we should give him another ten minutes," Father said. He was saying something about finding another road into town when the terrifying whistle of Stukas drowned him out. I thought they were coming straight at us until bombs began exploding in town, sending shock waves back over us.

When we finally dared to sit up, Sasha was standing quietly by the tree, looking at the wan sky to the east. He wore a funny little hat and a gray civilian suit. Just under the breast pocket of the jacket was a dark hole stained with blood.

"The Germans will probably mount their attack at dawn. We'd better push on," he said.

"Should we go through the town?" Father asked anxiously. "It seems to be coming under heavy fire."

As if confirming his words a barrage of heavy shells passed overhead again, sounding like trains passing through the sky. Here and there we could see the dull glow of fires in town. A faint smell of smoke drifted in the air.

"Unfortunately, we have no choice. I nearly stumbled on a German patrol out there, and their main force is probably not far behind. I would rather risk the bombs than tangle with that.

"One more thing. If we are stopped by the MPs, I'm your brother-in-law and we left Kaunas together. O.K.?"

We all agreed to that, though I wondered what would happen if the Russians caught us with a deserter. Death seemed to lurk everywhere.

The noise of artillery barrages intensified. A broken-down fuel truck was blocking the road and an armored vehicle was trying to push it into a gully. Suddenly, from somewhere behind us, a machine gun began to chatter, sending tracer bullets over our heads.

"My God!" shouted Sasha. "Run!"

When Herman saw that my mother could barely walk, he grabbed her in his arms and jogged off after Sasha. We all followed him down the hill, running as fast as our legs could carry us.

Thousands of panicked soldiers were now abandoning their vehicles and rushing into town on foot. I stumbled and nearly fell as I looked back to the hill where we had rested only minutes before. Over the crest rose a dark phalanx of Panzer tanks. The Germans were already upon us.

II

To this day I don't quite know how we escaped Janeve. We were swept into town by a wildly running mob of soldiers and civilians. Shells exploded all around us, and every other building seemed to be in flames.

Somehow Father managed to find Jankle's bakery, which was just off the main street. Incendiary bombs seemed to be raining all around us, and the bakery was enveloped in flames. "There's no way we'll be able to find anyone in this inferno," Sasha shouted as we stared in anguish at the burning building. Even as we stood there, the sign over the door let go and crashed in flames at our feet.

The sight of Jankle's bakery brought Mother to her knees, sobbing. "I can't go any farther. I just can't."

"We all must rest, Matushka," Sasha said, "but it is suicide to stop here." (Matushka is a Russian diminutive meaning "Little Mother.") Sasha had clearly taken control of our group, and no one was going to dispute him.

A tremendous explosion staggered us as another shell hit nearby, raining rubble down around us. Suddenly, from a side street, a horse and carriage came charging in our direction and almost ran us down. Miraculously, it was Leizer and his family.

Once again Mother and I were handed up into the wagon. Leizer agreed to allow the two of us back on, but the rest had to walk. The horse was simply exhausted and couldn't handle more.

The main road was still jammed, but Leizer, who was born in Janeve, quickly turned off onto a narrow side street, and after several turns we were on a relatively quiet road that led out of town. The horse picked up its pace.

Leizer had been wounded by shrapnel in one of the raids, and had a large bloody rag tied around his head. Weeping, he told us that his brother-in-law Jankle and his whole family were dead. Uncle Itzhak and his family never showed up at the meeting place. Itzhak, after a long wait, had hitched a ride on a Russian truck. We wouldn't see him again for the duration of the war.

I felt guilty that I was riding in the wagon. Father was too heavy to keep up with the horse for any length of time, and my sister Fanny also showed signs of exhaustion, but Leizer was unwilling to slow down for them. Once again he promised to wait for them if we got separated. The next town was Ukmerge: we would wait for them there. Herman, who had no problem keeping up with the horse, was to accompany us. Sasha would stay with Father and Fanny.

But fate would have it otherwise. Just outside of Janeve a group of *Siauliai* rose up beside the road, their rifles raised. Mother screamed as one grabbed Leizer's horse by the bridle. Another ordered us down from the wagon.

At that moment Sasha, who was twenty paces behind us, dropped to the ground, rolled over and opened fire with his submachine gun. Some of the surprised Lithuanians simply froze, gaping as he mowed them down, but the rest jumped back into the ditch beside the road and began returning fire. A bullet whistled past my ear and I pushed Mother down into the straw at the bottom of the wagon. Then I heard Leizer cry out in pain. His wife, Hanna, started crying and begged Leizer to stop the wagon, but instead he used his whip to urge the horse on.

"Go, go, GO!" shouted Sasha, continuing to fire. He shoved Herman forward, too. "You can't help. Go," he shouted again. "I'll meet you in Ukmerge."

"To Ukmerge!" he shouted once more as we rounded a bend in the road. Those were his last words to us.

Spurred on by Leizer, the horse took off at a trot. We could still hear rifle fire and the short burps of Sasha's gun. The scare had given Father and Fanny a spurt of energy, and they kept up with the wagon fairly well. Leizer was slumped in his seat, but wouldn't let go of the reins. He was losing blood, and finally Hanna made him stop long enough to apply a bandage.

Soon the side road turned and merged into the main highway to Ukmerge. Again we encountered a stream of civilians and retreating Russians, and again we came under German fire. Each time we scattered into nearby bushes and trees, and after several strafings Father and Fanny were lost in the surging crowds. Herman, who kept very close, managed to stay with us all the way.

About five miles before Ukmerge we came under fire again, with explosions so close they deafened us. We climbed back up onto the road, blood running from our ears and noses, only to discover Leizer's horse lying dead in the ditch.

We collected the few things we still had on the wagon, and decided we would wait there for Father and Fanny. There was a clump of trees about fifty yards off and we gratefully sprawled under their cover. Leizer and his family quickly disappeared into the stream of refugees and soldiers passing before us. That was the last time we ever saw them.

We still had a few bits of bread and sausage, which we devoured, all the while watching the road for Father and Fanny. Fanny wore a distinct red coat which we hoped to recognize her by, but two or three hours passed with no sign of them. We came under air attack several more times, and were forced to retreat farther from the road. Dusk was falling, and we knew we'd never be able to spot them in the crowd, certainly not in the dark. There was a small farm not too far across the field, and Herman suggested we try to find shelter there.

Mother could barely walk, so Herman carried her almost all the way. The farm looked serenely peaceful as the melee on the road faded behind us, but when we arrived at the gate a black dog ran out snarling and baring his teeth.

A tall man with a walrus mustache and steel-rimmed spectacles came out of the house and called him off. After our encounters with the *Siauliai* we were very apprehensive about our reception here.

Our clothing was torn and covered with dust, and our faces smeared with soot from the fires in Janeve, but the farmer merely looked us over and calmly bid us good evening. We were in luck—he was ready to help his fellow human beings. He demanded exorbitant sums for the food and lodging he provided, but we didn't argue.

Like the ferryman at Kalautuvas, the farmer's name was Kazys, a common name among Lithuanians. He led us to a large barn where about six Jewish families were already bedded down. Most had three or four children. Three of the men were wounded and in great pain. Except for a young couple who were from Slabodke, a suburb of Kaunas, most of them were from Janeve and the surrounding small villages. Mother knew the young woman from Slabodke, whose name was Rachel. She told us tearfully that her parents had refused to evacuate, and they had been forced to leave them behind. They too had been driven off the road by the constant bombings and were anxious to know if the Russians were holding out. We told them what we knew. Some of the group still thought the Russians would push the Germans back. Surprisingly, Kazys thought so too.

Otherwise he might not have given us shelter.

Kazys showed us a water trough where we could wash up, and his wife brought out food—a large round loaf of black bread, a slab of butter, and a liter of milk. She was a chunky woman with kind blue eyes and a shy smile. She crossed herself at every possible opportunity.

The milk, still warm, must have come straight from the cow. Suddenly I discovered how ravenously hungry I was. The bread, the fresh butter, and the warm milk were the best meal I had ever had.

That night we slept soundly in spite of the moans of the wounded and the explosions coming from the direction of the road. It was very early when Herman woke us, the sky barely paling in the east, the barn still quite dark. Mother was very tired and wanted to go back to sleep, but Herman wouldn't let her.

"Listen, listen," he whispered.

"I hear nothing," Mother said tiredly.

"That's what I'm afraid of."

Indeed there was an unusual silence. No explosions, no shooting, not even the jarring noise of the tanks as they moved on their tracks. "I don't like it," Herman said nervously. "What if we are already behind the German lines?"

We gathered our few things and went outside, where it was just getting light. A faint breeze rustled the poplar trees overhead. Suddenly we heard voices around front, and Herman moved us quickly behind a stand of trees with heavy undergrowth.

A group of armed Lithuanians emerged around the side of the house and beat on Kazys's door. He emerged, still in his white nightshirt.

"We heard you're hiding Jews here. Where are they?" one of the *Siauliai* demanded. Before Kazys could say a word he was knocked to the ground. As he tried to rise he was hit again, and a gout of blood spurted from his nose and splattered down his chest. He remained on his knees, begging them not to hit him again.

"The Jews. Where are the Jews, you swine! Show us where they are or we'll kill you," their leader demanded.

Kazys pointed a trembling finger at the barn.

"All right, you can go back to bed now old man," one of them laughed. Then the whole group, about eight men, crossed the yard. As they passed by the bushes, I realized that two of them were dressed in gray uniforms and coal-scuttle helmets.

"They are Germans!" my mother whispered in a horrified voice, and Herman put his hand over her mouth.

From inside the barn we could hear shouting and crying and then several shots were fired. I squeezed my eyes shut and put my hands over my ears, and as Herman put a comforting hand on my head I opened my eyes again to see Rachel and the others being led outside. To our horror, they were marched in our direction and came to a halt only a few meters from our hiding place. My heart was pounding so loud I was afraid the murderers would hear it.

It was horrible. Some of the men were attempting to reason with their captors; others just whimpered. The children seemed to be too frightened even to cry. Several of the people were bleeding and had torn clothes.

Rachel was the nearest to us. She was slumped over her husband, whose body had been unceremoniously dumped outside. He was one of two who had apparently been shot in the barn. Rachel's face was starting to swell, and her mouth was a bloody gap. They had knocked out her teeth. From time to time she straightened up, spreading her arms in the air as if crying out to heaven, but no sound came from her mouth. I felt sick, my stomach convulsing, and I had to swallow back bitter bile.

Several of the Lithuanians disappeared and returned with some spades. They handed them over to the Jewish men and told them to dig their graves.

Besides the wounded there were four men in the group. One of them, an elderly man with glasses, froze in terror. The taller of the Germans went up and put the barrel of his gun to his chest.

"Pick up that shovel and start digging," he said coldly. When the man did not respond, he shot him. The force of the bullet at such close range spun him around. His wife let out a terrible wail and threw herself on his body. Their five children stood around them, gaping in disbelief. It happened so fast.

My mother was so shocked that she cried out loud. Luckily the condemned Jews cried out at the same time so no one heard her. She struggled to rise, but Herman forced her down.

The other three men began hastily digging into the sandy soil as if their life depended on it, which it did, if only for a few more minutes. The Lithuanians were passing around a bottle of vodka and jeering at the Jews, who were unused to menial work and awkward with the shovels. "Well, you lazy Jews, you are finally doing an honest day's work. Too bad it will be your last!" The two Germans stood aside and smoked, quite aloof, and refused when the Lithuanians offered them the bottle.

"Perhaps when you land in your Jewish paradise they will let you inside the gates if you show them your fresh calluses," another Lithuanian piped up, and the others joined in laughter.

When they were satisfied that the grave was large enough, they told the Jews to undress. Realizing that their last hour had arrived they began to cry, some begging for mercy, some praying. A few loudly repeated the "Shma Israel." Then the taller German stepped up again and shot one of the diggers, and the rest hastily removed their clothes. We could smell sweat, urine, and feces. We were witnessing the ultimate distress of people who are about to die a violent and shameful death.

When they were down to their underwear, the German told them to line up in front of the pit, but the Lithuanians wanted them to strip, especially the women.

"No. They will stay in their underwear," the tall German said.

"Let the men have their fun. They've earned it," the Lithuanian officer persisted, smiling at the German. He spoke German quite well.

"I said no!" the German snapped. "I know what I'm doing. It's psychologically undesirable for the men to see them naked, especially the children. Many good men simply lose their nerve. Better to leave these *untermenschlich* in their ridiculous underwear. You understand me?"

The Lithuanian looked doubtful, but didn't argue the point.

I will never forget the German's little lecture. He had enunciated clearly, as if giving a speech, and I heard every word. It gave me my first insight into the Nazi killing machine.

They shot Rachel first. She was still seated at her husband's side, performing her strange ritual, bending down to her husband's body, then lifting her arms up to heaven in a silent cry.

The shorter German came up behind her, and at the exact moment she raised her arms he deftly brought up his Luger and shot her in the neck. There wasn't a single wasted motion in the execution. The Lithuanians gave him a respectful look.

Then the rest began shooting. I closed my eyes and covered my ears, but the terrified screams of the victims, especially those of the children, still haunt my nightmares. It was intolerable. I was about to bolt, but Herman held me down, hissing in my ear not to make a sound. Mother had passed out entirely.

When they were finished they hauled the trembling farmer from his house and told him to cover the grave with earth. "Make sure they don't walk away," the officer laughed. Then he added sternly, "Next time you try to hide Jews we'll bury you with them. Understand?"

"Yes sir, yes sir. I'll never hide Jews again as long as I live," Kazys answered, crossing himself several times.

After they left he fearfully approached the ditch and looked down at the bloody bodies. We could see the shock spreading over his face. Then he put a hand to his mouth and retched.

The massacre of these people at such close range, where we could see, hear, and smell every minute of it, went through me like a branding iron. I was a normal thirteen-year-old boy brought up in a sheltered environment, and suddenly I was plunged into a world where anyone who felt like it could hunt me down and kill me.

When the farmer finally recovered he picked up a shovel and began tossing dirt into the grave.

Herman rose from behind the bushes holding out a calming hand toward Kazys, who let out a piercing yell and dropped his shovel.

"Please, please don't be frightened. We hid when the Germans came."

The farmer, backing away, began to cry, "Get out of here! Get out of here, now!"

"Please help us," Herman pleaded. "We'll pay you well. Here, we'll give you all our money," he said, thrusting out a fistful of currency.

"No, no, no!" the man cried. "If they find you here they'll kill us! Just leave, or I'll call them back!" His voice had risen almost to a scream, and he was shaking his fist.

Suddenly we heard a muted cry. It sounded like a baby. Both Herman and the farmer turned toward the open grave, their faces registering astonished disbelief.

In spite of Herman's warning to stay down, I jumped up and ran to his side. Kazys hardly noticed me as all three of us stared down into that pit. To my dying day I will never forget that scene. About thirty bodies lay pell-mell in the grave, most of them children, most of their faces frozen in expressions of terror. Others, who were shot point-blank, were a bloody unrecognizable mess.

The baby cried again, and Herman and Kazys climbed down and shifted the body of a large red-headed woman. Beneath her was a tiny child with carroty red hair and lots of freckles. She couldn't have been more than two, and although there was a bleeding cut on her scalp she was very much alive. Her mother must have shielded her with her own body.

"Oh my God, oh my God, what terrible times. Just a baby! Oh my God . . ." Kazys moaned, wringing his hands irresolutely. Then as the child's cries increased he scooped her up and ran to the house without giving us another glance.

We returned to my mother, and Herman began rubbing her wrists and patting her face. For some moments she looked bewildered, and kept asking where we were. As she regained full consciousness, an expression of loathing passed over her face. We helped her back to the barn, where bales of straw lay scattered about. Herman hastily kicked straw over two large bloodstains on the earthen floor. I was trembling, and Mother looked as if she had aged ten years.

We settled her comfortably in some straw and sat quietly for a few minutes, holding hands. "I think," Herman said quietly, "that we have no choice but to try to return home. The Germans are probably all the way to the border by now. The farmer may let us stay for a while, but the Siauliai will probably come back."

At that moment the farmer entered the barn, carrying the baby. Both of them were freshly bandaged.

"I want you to take the baby and go," he said grimly. "It is a Jewish baby and your responsibility. I don't want to have anything to do with it. You understand?!"

His wife Magda, however, was right on his heels. Even as she crossed herself she began cursing her husband.

"You shameless ape," she cried, taking the baby from his arms. "Why are you so scared of dying? You'll be dead soon enough, and if you don't give these poor people shelter, you will rot in hell!"

Kazys was about to retort, but she silenced him.

"You've said enough for the day! Now get out of my way."

With that she led us back to the house, where she made up a cot for the child and then brought us some food. We hadn't eaten since the evening before, and again she served home-baked bread, butter, and milk. Kazys lapsed into a miserable silence, but after a few minutes he rose and fetched a piece of smoked pork.

"I know you people don't eat pig, but you may need your strength, and there is nothing like pork to give you strength," he said apologetically, not looking Herman in the eyes. His wife's reprimand seemed to have cut him to the core.

Later Kazys, Herman, and I went out and covered the mass grave with earth. I tried not to look down, but I couldn't help it, and with every shovelful I could feel my gorge rise.

That evening Kazys apologized to us.

"I was so afraid! I didn't know what to do. They broke my nose!" he said, pointing at his bandage and the blackening flesh around his eyes.

"But, as my wife said, you only die once and it's the Christian way to help people in need, even Jews."

What followed was a peculiar conversation. Herman asked Kazys if there were any Jewish people in the area.

"I've been trading with Jews from Ukmerge all my life. To be truthful, I always found them fair and honest. But, you are so different from us. . . .

"You look different, you dress different . . . And what we hear in church . . . I am not a very religious person, like my wife here, but you did crucify our Lord Jesus Christ, there is no denying that fact."

When Herman pointed out to him that Jesus was born a Jew, he looked almost outraged. "He was not! He was born a Christian! He was the first Christian!" he said vehemently, and looked over to his wife for confirmation.

"He was born a Jew," Magda said tartly. "If you ever bothered to read the Bible you would know this. All your life you go around hating people and you don't even know the facts." She sounded as if she had lost her patience. Kazys looked at her as if she had uttered some profound new truth.

When Herman told them about our plans to start out for Kaunas the next day, Magda suggested we wait. She said she would go to the neighboring village and find out what was happening.

Then, as if sensing our worry about the child, she told us she would keep her until her relatives claimed her. In spite of the cut in her scalp, she was remarkably quiet. Magda had washed her wound and applied some herbal ointment.

"I never had a girl," she said quietly. "I had four boys. Two died young during the diphtheria epidemic. The other two, God knows where they are now. The younger was mobilized by the Russians, and the older joined the *Siauliai*." At the mention of this name she crossed herself several times. I almost crossed myself too.

We spent the night in Kazys's apple cellar. It was just large enough for us to lie down and it smelled sweetly of apples. The tension of the day had exhausted us, and I was asleep within seconds.

We were awakened by loud banging on the front door of the house.

Above us Magda began to shout. "Who is it? What do you want? It's the middle of the night!"

"Open up, goddamnit. It's me, Vytas!"

"Vytas!" Magda cried. "Go and sleep in the barn, you drunken lout!" She sounded furious.

The banging only increased in volume. "Are you gonna make me stand out here all night? I'll break the door down, you hear?" Vytas must have been using his rifle butt, because the din was earsplitting.

Then, abruptly, it stopped and we heard the sound of boots over our heads. "Get that gun out of my sight," Magda said angrily, and Vytas dropped it with a clatter.

"I haven't slept for two nights. I need a drink. Please Mother, I need a drink," he said in a completely different voice. He sounded as if he were on the verge of weeping.

"For two days now we have been rounding up Jews. All the Jews in Ukmerge. I never liked the bastards, but this was horrible. Shooting women and children. . . ."

My hair stood on end.

"Heavenly Father," we heard Magda say in anguish. "I told you not to join those hooligans. Now you'll have to live with your crimes for the rest of your life." Then she said something else too low to hear, and we heard her footsteps. Their voices began to drop, Magda making soothing sounds and telling Vytas to get some sleep. Then all was silent.

In the darkness Mother began to weep, and it was a long time before I fell asleep again.

Magda must have gotten Vytas good and drunk, for the next morning when she lifted the trapdoor above us, he was still passed out somewhere. "You must go quickly, before my son wakes up." Her voice was thick, as if she too had been crying. Seeing our faces, she said, "I'm sorry. I'm very sorry you heard all that. He was always a good little boy, but he fell into bad company. I pray for him," she said, crossing herself. Her eyes were brimming with tears.

"My husband will take you back to Kaunas. He is hitching up the horse now. But before you go you must change those city clothes. They'll be looking for Jews, and you look too conspicuous." She shoved some old work clothes at us, and we quickly obeyed.

We knew that Magda and Kazys were risking their lives for us, and we were very grateful. Magda handed us a bundle of food at the door, and Mother was so touched that she kissed Magda on both cheeks.

Our disguises were not very convincing. The clothes fit badly, and our features and dark coloring weren't typical of Lithuanian peasants, who were generally Nordic types. But none of that could be helped.

5

The Seventh Fort

The sun was just rising when we set out in Kazys's wagon. In the
beginning we took a narrow country road used only by a few
farmers, but as we approached the main tributary we began to hear
the noise of heavy traffic. We emerged from a clump of woods to see
scores of tanks and heavy trucks lumbering along the highway. The
German Wehrmacht was moving east in orderly formations, unlike
the Russian convoys we last saw on this road. Then we realized that
there was no civilian traffic at all.

Mother and I were lying on the straw in the back of the wagon.
Herman sat next to Kazys in front. The old hat Magda had given him
covered his face to some extent, but his faded khaki shirt was much
too small. It stretched across his shoulders and rode up the small of
his back. Kazys wore a similar hat and old clothing. An unlit pipe was
stuck in his mouth, and from time to time he would take it out and
give a short piercing whistle to his horse.

As we approached the highway, a German MP signaled us to turn
back. Kazys, trying to look casual, took his time turning the horse,
but he was clearly frightened. Without uttering a word he pulled over
at the nearest wooded area, climbed down from the wagon, and
hung a sack of grain on the horse's neck. Then he stuffed some
tobacco into his pipe and had a smoke. We waited. There was
nothing to be said. We were people without rights, and our fate was
in his hands.

Finally Kazys knocked out his pipe. "We'll take the side roads in. It
will take much longer, but we'll get you there."

Herman and Mother thanked him quietly, but he just made a deprecating movement with his hand.

To this day I wonder what made this man act the way he did, especially given his prejudices. I remember promising myself never to judge people at face value. It was not an easy promise to keep.

For four days we traveled on small, unmarked roads, and more than once we were stopped by *Siauliai*. Somehow Kazys always convinced them to let us go. These "patriots" were now rounding up all the Jews straggling back to Kaunas on foot. We met many such groups on the way. Few of them made it home.

Once as we were traveling parallel to the main highway, we heard German soldiers shouting from their trucks, "Jude, der Weg nach Jerusalem ist frei! (Jews, the road to Jerusalem is free!)"

We froze with fright, thinking we had been discovered, but they were shouting at a group of Jews being led across a field by the *Siauliai*. They lined them up and shot them down while the Germans watched, some of them taking photographs.

Kazys quickly turned the horse away from the scene, but I was overwhelmed with despair. Everywhere we went they were slaughtering Jews. What was the sense of continuing to Kaunas? Everyone there was probably dead. Sobbing quietly, Mother lay down and covered herself with straw. Herman sat next to Kazys not uttering a word.

At night we would hide out in the woods. Kazys knew the area well and always found a good spot.

We finally reached the outskirts of town about the fifth of July. Kazys picked the Janeve Street entrance, near the Vilija River.

Here and there a German lorry would pass, but the drivers paid us little attention. Mother and I lay low in the straw, pretending to sleep. We were almost halfway into town and beginning to hope we would make it when we suddenly heard the dreaded shout. "Halt! Identify yourselves!"

There was a large chestnut tree by the road, and two Lithuanian guards emerged from its shadow, one of them waving a rifle.

"We are just farmers sir, going to town for some supplies," Kazys said, taking off his hat.

One guard wore thick glasses. He looked at Kazys suspiciously, and Kazys gave him a submissive smile. He still had the plaster on his swollen nose and looked a bit comical.

"Who broke your nose, old man?" the one with glasses wanted to know.

"It was my wife, Sir. She hit me with a tankard. I drank all the beer and didn't leave her any."

The two men found that very funny and laughed heartily. "Proceed," one of them finally said.

Anxious to get away, Kazys lashed his horse with a whip. The horse shied. He was accustomed to Kazys's whistle. Desperately, Kazys used the whip again, and the horse lurched forward just as one of the men shouted, "Hold it! Stop there!"

Kazys pretended not to hear, urging the horse on until a warning shot was fired over his head. He pulled up just at the foot of a little bridge, cursing under his breath.

"You're in a hell of a hurry," one of the guards said when he caught up. "What have you got here?"

Both men now leaned against the wagon bed, looking down on us. Mother and I hid our faces, pretending to sleep, but it was a foolish ruse, since a gun had just gone off at close range. When we both sat up the game was over.

"So, you are trying to smuggle in Jews are you? Well, well, well," the one with the thick glasses grinned.

"I don't know if they are Jews or not," Kazys said indignantly. "They paid me to take them to Kaunas, and that is what I am doing."

"We'll see, we'll see," they said, and telling Kazys they would deal with him later they ordered us to move under the bridge. A small stream flowed under it. We stared in horror at the half a dozen corpses lying in the water.

"You Jews, stand there with your comrades," the one with the glasses said, pointing a pistol at us.

At that moment, a black Mercedes stopped on the bridge and two German officers in SS uniforms stepped out. They heard the shot and wanted to know who fired it. When they saw the corpses under the bridge and us with our hands raised, they wanted to know who gave the Lithuanians permission to hold executions here. The Lithuanians, who couldn't understand a word the Germans said, just gaped at them.

At that moment Herman stepped forward and addressed the officers in perfect German. The surprised *Siauliai* took aim at his back as he climbed the embankment, but one of the Germans drew a pistol and angrily waved them off.

We couldn't hear what Herman said to the SS men, but one of the Germans motioned for the guard with glasses to come up and join them.

For some minutes they carried on a discussion, Herman apparently acting as an interpreter. The Lithuanian kept shaking his head and pointing toward the chestnut tree. Finally the SS officer grabbed him by the tunic and practically lifted him off his feet.

"You will listen to my orders, you understand? You dumb ox!" he shouted, shaking the Lithuanian so hard his glasses fell off.

After that there was no more argument from the *Siauliai*. We were ordered back onto the wagon, and the Lithuanian with the thick glasses joined Kazys up front.

Herman climbed into the black Mercedes with the Germans, and soon the car disappeared on a narrow road leading up the mountain. We followed the car.

The Lithuanian with us kept turning around in his seat and hissing at us through clenched teeth. Behind the glasses his eyes were malevolent.

"You Jews will soon get what is coming to you. Wait and see!"

All this time Kazys never said a word, and I felt sure he regretted ever getting involved with us. A few times he looked at us with serious eyes, as if he was studying our faces.

Because of its proximity to the German border and its situation between the Niemunas and Vilija rivers, the Russians long considered Kaunas to be strategic. Late in the nineteenth century the Tsarist regime surrounded the area with forts, originally housing heavy artillery to defend the town, but after the First World War their strategic importance diminished. One fort was turned into a prison; most fell into disuse.

The Seventh Fort was enormous, perhaps the largest of the group. When we reached its thick stone walls, we were met by an SS corporal in leather gear, straddling a heavy motorcycle. He seemed to be expecting us. He ordered us to wait inside the gate, then started his engine and roared off. Kazys pulled the wagon into a large courtyard.

Before us rose another massive stone wall that encircled an inner compound. From behind these walls we heard shots being fired.

Half an hour passed as we sat in the wagon, waiting. The firing behind the walls would die off, then begin again, and we could hear screams. Chills were going down my spine, and Mother began nervously talking to the Lithuanian guard. We had been peaceful neighbors for many generations, she said. What was going on? What had we ever done to them to deserve this? This only incensed the guard, and he began shouting at her to shut up.

"You bloodsuckers took the bread out of our poor peoples' mouths, and now you are going to get what is coming to you. All of you, *kaput*, you understand?" And he made a slash across his throat with his forefinger.

A small gate opened up in the inner wall and three Lithuanians in uniform staggered out.

"Hey, what do we have here! Some privileged Jews?" one called. "Why are they lounging about out here? Why don't they join the party inside?"

Our guard told them the German's orders, but they only laughed. They were clearly drunk.

"Hey, hey, this is Lithuania, not Germany," one said.

"It is our country, we fought the Russians for it. We don't have to take any shit from the Germans," another chimed in. He was swaying from side to side, barely able to stand.

Suddenly a tremendous volley of shots echoed inside. "Let's give these Jews the welcome they deserve," the first Lithuanian cried, and with that he yanked my mother to the ground. The other two grabbed me by the neck, and with our guard yelling in protest they dragged us toward the inner gate.

Inside the gate a vision of hell spread before our eyes. It was a huge compound. The yard sloped from the walls down to a long ravine, with what seemed to be thousands of men massed at the bottom. On the slopes above them stood scores of Lithuanians, many in civilian clothes, taking aim at those below. Yellow flashes spurted from their gun muzzles, and everywhere blue cordite smoke rose into the air. Below us people were trying to dodge bullets, screaming and running in a frenzy from one side to another. Bodies of the dead and wounded lay everywhere. It was a monstrous shooting gallery, the groans and cries of the victims terrible in our ears. That scene burns in my mind to this day.

My legs were giving way beneath me when behind us someone bellowed, "Let go of those Jews!"

Our captors turned. Standing at the gate was one of the two SS officers from the Mercedes. With him was our guard and another man in a Lithuanian officer's uniform.

"Let go of those two Jews!" the officer bellowed again. The three startled drunks suddenly let go, and my mother and I fell to the ground.

When the gate swung shut behind us, I noticed for the first time the green trees and shrubs growing in the fort's outer yard. The sky seemed especially blue. The fleecy clouds looked like small sheep. The world suddenly looked so beautiful.

It was several years before we found out that between eight and twelve thousand Jewish men were murdered at the Seventh Fort. Using documents and the testimony of a few survivors, the Jewish historian Josef Gar described the Seventh Fort massacre in a book published shortly after the war:

> In the beginning of July 1941 there were mass arrests among the Jewish population of Kaunas. Ten to twelve thousand people, most of them men but including a number of women and children, were brought to the Seventh Fort.
>
> The weather was unusually hot, and the men were kept for days in the open yard of the fort, under the burning sun, without a drop of water. They were not allowed to make a move. The patrolling Lithuanians opened murderous fire on anyone caught raising his head or changing his position or speaking to his neighbor.
>
> The Lithuanians were given ample beer and vodka so that they stayed drunk. This made them even more sadistic in the burning heat.
>
> Especially gruesome was the fate of the young women who were locked up in the fort's underground barracks. During the night drunken Lithuanians would drag them out in groups, rape them, and then shoot them. This went on for many nights.
>
> The panic among the poor women was terrible. Many of them simply lost their wits as the Lithuanians staged wild orgies, raping dozens at a time. Some women smeared their faces with dirt, but that didn't help. In many cases mothers and daughters were raped at the same time.
>
> During this time, in Kaunas, the Germans had a basketball match with the Lithuanians. The Lithuanians had a championship team before the war, and they had no difficulty defeating the Germans. As a

"reward" each of the Lithuanian players was allowed to come and shoot a dozen Jews at the Seventh Fort.

The seven to eight thousand men who survived the first days at the fort were later shot and buried in mass graves dug by Soviet P.O.W.'s. *

What happened to Mother and me that day seemed nothing short of a miracle. We were ordered back onto the wagon, and I swear I heard the German tell the Lithuanian officer that he'd given his word to let us go. We were even sent home with an escort. The Lithuanian with the thick glasses was ordered to ride with Kazys and make sure nothing happened to us on the way.

What Herman said to the Germans and how he obtained their promise to release us will remain a mystery forever.

As the wagon descended from the Seventh Fort and entered the city, my heart contracted with pain. At the bakeries and food shops there were long lines, but almost everything else looked the same: the same tree-lined streets, the same shops, the same sun-filled gardens. But before the war the Jewish community had been a third of the town's population. Now there was not a Jew anywhere to be seen.

It took a good hour for Kazys to get to our building on Kalviu Street. We were stopped several times by Lithuanians, but our guard explained his orders and they let us proceed. At our gate he took a small notebook and pencil from his pocket and told Mother to write and sign a statement, in German, that he had delivered us safely. With a trembling hand my mother obeyed. Then he turned and walked away without giving us a second glance.

By then dusk was falling, and the sky in the west was turning a purplish red. There were only a few people out. One was a neighbor who crossed herself when she saw us, then quickly walked away.

We stood fearfully at the entrance, not knowing what to expect inside. Perhaps more Lithuanians were behind the door. Perhaps the Germans had confiscated the apartments of the Jews, as they did in Poland.

Kazys had gone through the trials of the past week with us and had witnessed the atrocities of his own kinsmen. He understood our fear, and told us he would wait in the street until we found out what

* *The Holocaust of the Jewish Kovne* was written in Yiddish and published in Munich around 1948. My father, a friend of Gar's, passed the book on to me before he died, and asked me to pass it on to my children.

awaited us. We had become his charges, and when we were released from the Seventh Fort his eyes had filled with tears.

We lived on the top two floors of a five-story building. The elevator wasn't working, so we slowly climbed the steps. We were terribly tired and hungry. The apartments in the house were occupied mostly by Jews, and we could hear no sounds within the building. Where was everyone? The Rogols, the Greenblats, the Friedlands, the Roms?

Finally we stood before the door of our apartment. It was locked. I put my ear to the door, but could hear nothing. With trembling hands my mother inserted her key and slowly turned it. I pushed the handle down and swung the door open.

We found ourselves staring into the frightened faces of my father and my sister Fanny.

How can I describe our joy? The four of us fell into each others' arms, hugging, kissing, crying, and talking all at the same time. We were sure they were dead, and they were sure we were; they thought they were about to be arrested when they heard us at the door. Our reunion was marred only by Herman's absence.

Suddenly we remembered that Kazys was still waiting for us downstairs. Father gave me a bundle of money for him. There was no other way we could express our gratitude.

I ran down the steps two at a time and found Kazys dozing on the wagon bench. The horse was slowly munching grain, and as I approached he turned his head and looked at me over the edge of his feed bag. Perhaps I was imagining it, but I felt a certain sympathy in his brown eyes.

I went up to him, put my arms around his neck, and kissed his forehead. When I turned around Kazys was looking at me with tears in his eyes. He was apparently touched by my sentiment. He nodded and said quietly, "The good creatures of this earth are not the human ones."

For a moment we looked at each other in silence. It seemed like an eternity had passed since that evening we walked into his yard, and Kazys did not seem like the same man. The horrors we witnessed together, the long journey to Kaunas—he had risked his life for us, and stood by us until the very end. Those were the acts of a good man.

I told him that we had found my father and sister in the apartment. "Thank the Lord," he said, a great smile breaking over his face.

When I tried to give him the money, he pushed my hand away.

"In the days ahead you will need it more than I will," he said. Then he gave me a large loaf of bread and a piece of cheese from his bag. The bread was stale, but it smelled delicious. I realized that I hadn't eaten since the day before.

"I wish I had more to give you. You will probably find it difficult to buy food in town," he said. I thanked him.

In the gathering darkness I watched Kazys's wagon until it disappeared at the end of the street. I felt a great sadness. Kazys and his horse were among the few kind creatures we had encountered since we started our journey home.

Once our initial joy was over, Father, Fanny, Mother, and I all wept again, this time in anguish. We mourned the loss of Herman. We knew in our hearts that his chances were remote. Mother kept wringing her hands and saying that Herman had sacrificed himself for us, that he made a bargain with the two SS men, his life for ours, and no matter what we said she kept on repeating the same sentence.

The few cans of food we had in the house and the food Kazys gave us didn't last long. We had to go out and find food. We waited as long as we could, hoping things would calm down, but the sounds of gunfire could be heard from some quarter of town every day. From my window I could occasionally see Nazis and *Siauliai* moving about in gangs. Our experience en route made it clear that Jewish men in particular were targets. It was thus out of the question for Father to go out, and Mother seemed to be in a state of shock. She frequently wept over Herman and became more withdrawn every day.

That left Fanny and me. When the last morsel of bread and can of sardines were consumed, Fanny and I went out to buy food. Fanny bleached her hair with peroxide and became a blond. I covered my black hair with a big cap. We decided our chances would be better if we split up.

I chose a shop that had been run by Jews before the war began. There was a long line in front. I stood at the end, hoping that no one would recognize me, but I was soon discovered by neighbors who began to shout, "Jew, Jew out of here!"

Two boys whom I vaguely knew came toward me brandishing sticks, and without looking back I took off. I heard them running after me, shouting, "Stop the Jew! Don't let him get away!"

An elderly man coming from the other direction tried to trip me, but I avoided him and ran for the fish market, where I quickly slipped in among the crowd. My heart was pounding in my chest as if it would take off, and I had difficulty breathing. It was quite a while before I calmed down.

The streets were still too dangerous for us to walk. I headed straight for home, but when I reached Kalviu Street, I slowed down. There were still four hungry people to feed, and no food in the house.

I gathered my courage, pulled the cap deeper over my forehead, and headed for Vilnius Street. Perhaps no one there would recognize me. Eventually I found an open bakery, and another long line waiting for bread. Keeping a few paces back, I carefully walked down the line, scanning it to see if I recognized anyone.

In the middle of the line I saw a familiar face. With a shock I realized he was a Jewish boy named David I'd gone to school with. When he saw me, he looked away. We didn't dare greet each other.

The line inched forward. I kept my head down until a hubbub at the corner caused me to look up. A gang of half a dozen Hitler Youth was coming down the street. I recognized their brown uniforms, the red and black swastikas on their armbands.

They stopped in front of the bakery. In German, the leader said loudly, "I bet you there are Jews in this line too. Miller, you're an expert at smelling out Jews. Let's see how you do it."

Obediently the boy went to the head of the line and began scrutinizing people one by one. He was a bit taller than me, with a short blond crew cut and light blue eyes. There was something familiar about his face, but I couldn't quite place him.

I peered around trying to spot an escape, but the rest of the Hitler Youths were watching us carefully. They would jump me if I bolted, and I didn't want to gamble on outrunning all of them. There was nothing to do but sweat it out.

Then my heart sank. Miller collared David and told him to look him in the eyes. Unlike me, David didn't "look Jewish" at all. He was dark blond, with gray eyes and a small straight nose. When David did as he was told, the boy grabbed him by the neck and pulled him out on the street.

"He is a Jew, all right. Hold onto him until I finish with the line."

"But he doesn't look Jewish at all! How do you know he is a Jew?" the others demanded.

"Well, these stupid Lithuanians don't understand a word of German. This little Jewish scholar does. He should have played dumb—I might have given him the benefit of the doubt."

While Miller continued screening the line, the rest of them attacked David. Soon he was lying on the street trying to cover his head with his arms while they kicked him in the back, the ribs, the stomach. Then the leader of the gang raised his boot and viciously stomped on David's face. He did it again, and then again, until David lay still.

A pool of blood formed around his head, but the hoodlums didn't let up until they were flushed and perspiring with effort. There was an expression of sadistic satisfaction on their young faces. I averted my gaze, my heart racing like crazy. Miller continued to move down the line. My end was at hand.

The boy took one look at me and a smile of satisfaction spread across his face. At that moment I realized who he was.

My heart twisted in my chest, but I managed a smile and said quietly, "Hansi, how is my wooden horse doing?"

He lifted his arm as if to strike, then his confused look turned to shock. For a long moment we stared at each other, then he abruptly turned and walked away. The other Hitler Youth noticed our exchange and began to protest.

"Surely this one is a Jew! Why did you let him go?"

"No! No. I know him. His father is Italian, that's why he looks so dark."

Their leader gave me a doubtful look, then put his arm around Hansi. *"Schon gut,* Hansi, *schon gut.* We don't have to kill all the Jews, you know. We have to leave some for the Gestapo and the SS. I see that this one means something to you. Right?"

Hansi's face hardened. He realized that he was being tested. Shaking off the leader's arm, he said stiffly: "No. I know the family. He is not Jewish. I told you he is Italian."

Hansi never looked back as he turned to walk away. The leader looked me up and down as the others drifted off, and suddenly said: "Come sta?"

Although my heart was beating wildly, I answered with a smile "Grazie, bene."

He gave me a surprised look, then waved. I waved back, still smiling. The gang departed, leaving David in a pool of his own blood. He didn't move. Some Lithuanian women in the line began crossing themselves. I thanked God that I had learned that one Italian phrase from Uncle George.

I realized that I was shaking all over, but I was as baffled as I was frightened. Under normal circumstances I would have started crying, but these were not normal circumstances, and unless I controlled myself I would soon lie next to David on the cobblestones. What evil power had turned my beloved Hansi into a murderous thug? What was he doing in Kaunas?

When my turn in line finally came I bought two loaves of bread, the maximum allowed for a family. On the wall there was a notice stating that as of the next day, bread would be rationed and only sold to those with ration coupons. I asked the baker where one could get these coupons, and he gave me the address. Then he bent over the counter and said quietly, "Watch it, Jew boy, or you'll end up dead like the other one." I left quickly, panic rising in my chest. How would we ever survive this?

My parents were overjoyed to see me. They had been terribly worried by my long absence. Fanny too had returned safely, and with a bag full of food. We were delighted as she took the things out one by one, exhibiting each item like some small treasure. She had half a pound of butter, half a pound of cheese, a piece of pork, a bag of sugar, barley, tea, salt, and two large beets. Each thing was precious.

She displayed the pork with some reluctance. Although we were not religious in the Orthodox sense, Mother had always kept a kosher house. But we had already eaten pork under Kazys's roof, and we decided that under the circumstances God would forgive us this sin.

That night, as I lay in my bed with a reasonably full stomach, I thought about Hansi and my strange encounter with him after so many years. How could my dearest friend in Heydekrug have come to this? Yet if it had been any other German I surely would not have lived through the day.

After the war I discovered that Hansi was killed defending Hitler's bunker in Berlin. He remained a Nazi fanatic until the end. I was sorry to hear that he died so young. He had saved my life.

For the rest of the month, Fanny and I went out every few days for food. She would go to the vegetable market, while I would line up for bread. Several times we were accosted by the Lithuanians, who cursed us and landed a few blows when they could, but we usually managed to get something, even if it was only a few beets or potatoes. I witnessed some merciless beatings, but I soon learned how to smell and escape danger. The minute I saw a group of young Lithuanians approaching the bread line, I would run at top speed in the other direction. After a short chase, they would give up on me and beat up the slow ones. I was grateful for all those footraces Fanny and I had in Kalautuvas.

We had very little contact with the other Jewish families who lived near us. I had no idea what happened to Lena Greenblat and her family. Nobody answered when I knocked on her door. Nor did we know what had become of my beloved Aunt Anushka or any of the rest of our family. The telephone was dead, and had been since the invasion. Our only contact with other Jews were furtive conversations in the street when we ran into someone we knew. At the fish market we were told that most of our family, like us, had fled Kaunas when the Germans attacked. What had happened to Sonia and Jasha? Where were Jochil and Jacob and Aunt Mere and all my cousins? Were they all dead?

As the days wore on it became more and more difficult to obtain food. One day Fanny and I split up as usual. I had no luck, and was glumly returning home when I spotted my sister being led into a side street by a gang of Lithuanians. One of them had a thick rope around her neck and pulled her along like an animal. Her dress was torn and she was bleeding from the nose. They were drinking and laughing and boasting about how they were going to rape her one by one, and how she was going to enjoy it.

Without giving myself time to think I ran at the Lithuanian pulling the rope and rammed my head into his stomach with all my strength. He gasped and dropped the rope. I scooped it up and shouted, "Ready, set, GO!"

We took off in a burst of speed, leaving the startled Lithuanians momentarily confused. Thanks God, they were too drunk to run very far. Fanny pulled off the rope after a couple of blocks, and once we reached a quiet side street we were able to slow down a bit. I covered her with my jacket and we made it home safely, but the incident seemed to rob her of all her spirit. The next day she refused to leave the apartment and she wouldn't even eat. As the days passed she grew more and more despondent, and seemed to be wasting away before our eyes.

One afternoon my mother, who had not stopped mourning for my brother Herman since our return, suddenly seemed to recognize that

Fanny was in grave trouble. This stirred her out of her lethargy, and the same evening, not heeding our protests, she wrapped herself in a peasant's shawl and gathered a few rubles and items for barter. Scarce material goods were becoming more valuable than currency. Father wanted to go with her, but we stopped him. The streets were still particularly dangerous for Jewish men.

It was more than an hour before she returned, and we had begun to fear the worst. Then came our prearranged signal, three short knocks followed by two more. We quickly opened the door and there she stood with two baskets full of vegetables. It was the first time I'd seen her smile since we lost Herman.

She had been extremely lucky. She met a farmer she had known for many years who had been happy to trade vegetables and a bit of pork for the garments she offered. That evening we filled ourselves with a thick vegetable soup laced with meat. It was the first time since we left Kaunas I'd felt that full.

Mother also brought news that all Jews were to leave their homes and move to Slabodke, where a ghetto was to be established. Slabodke was a poor suburb inhabited by workers and small craftsmen. The Lithuanians called the district Vilijampole; the Jews called it Slabodke after the world-famous Slabodker Yeshiva, which had graduated generations of distinguished rabbis. But the streets were unpaved and most of the houses were small and run-down. About five thousand people lived there in overcrowded and unsanitary conditions before the war.

For the Jews, it had become a slaughtering ground. On the night of June 25, just three days after the Nazi's surprise attack, the Lithuanians staged their first massacre there. In the darkness a large group of civilians armed with axes, guns, and knives converged on the Jewish section. The light of morning revealed a gruesome scene: men, women, and children hacked to pieces, the walls and floors of their homes splattered with blood. It was said that some of the drunker Lithuanians played soccer with the heads of their victims. Who could have believed that our Lithuanian neighbors, with whom we lived in peace for centuries, could turn into such bloodthirsty monsters? I thought of Hansi. I thought of how little I understood.

More than seven hundred Jews lost their lives during that night. It was a prelude to the thousands massacred at the Seventh Fort. It was only after the German civilian and military administration became organized that such mass attacks against the Jews abated somewhat. Some of the Germans frowned on such methods. They were too messy.

On July 10, the German authorities issued an official proclamation that was posted on nearly every building in town. All persons of Jewish origin were ordered to move to Slabodke no later than August 15, 1941. Any Jew found outside the ghetto after that date would be shot.

We were now faced with the task of moving our household to Slabodke within a month. The ghetto was across the Vilijampole Bridge, over the Vilija River, to the northeast of town. It was quite a distance from where we lived, and we had no idea how we would get ourselves and our belongings there safely. Then there was the question of lodging.

Several days passed, bringing us nearer to the deadline. It was getting harder to find food. One day I ventured out as far as the road leading to the Vilijampole Bridge. Many Jewish families were already evacuating, moving along the road carrying bundles in their arms or pushing improvised carts and baby carriages. A few had horse-drawn wagons. Lithuanians stood on both sides of the street, watching in silence as their Jewish neighbors abandoned their homes. Some of the youngsters jeered and baited the Jews; many simply went up and helped themselves to anything they liked. The Jews didn't dare object.

I ran back home and told my family the news. Unless we did something soon we would end up in the ghetto with neither shelter nor belongings. That night I went to bed feeling jittery and exhausted. We hadn't eaten so much as a morsel of bread all day.

The next morning we were startled by a loud knock on the door. It was extremely early, and we feared the worst. Father immediately hid inside the wardrobe, and I asked cautiously who it was.

To my surprise and delight it was my friend Petras! Tears sprang to our eyes and we threw our arms around each other.

I had not seen him since Kalautuvas, the summer before, when I taught him all those Yiddish songs. He had grown since then, and was somewhat taller than I, but it was the same old Petras with his laughing blue eyes and white blond hair. To our great joy he brought a bag full of food.

There was food we hadn't seen since the Soviet invasion: bread, butter, two types of cheese, pork and sausage, and a bag full of white cherries. A rare delicacy indeed!

It couldn't have come at a more opportune moment. We carefully divided the food to last us for several days, then devoured the day's portion as Petras sat sadly looking on.

It was certainly a reversal of fortune. In his childhood he was quite often hungry, and it was we who fed him. I couldn't help feeling a pang of resentment. I remembered all too well his father's anti-Semitic outbursts when he was drunk, even though most of his customers were Jews. Suddenly I realized how condescending my feelings for Petras had been. As if sensing my thoughts, he put an arm around my shoulder and smiled reassuringly. I felt ashamed.

Petras didn't just bring us food. He brought us the solution to our most worrisome problem. It seemed that during the Soviet rule his father, who was a poor tradesman, was offered an apartment in Slabodke where they paid a very low rent. Petras suggested that if we had no other place to go, we could exchange apartments. He realized that there was no comparison between the luxury of our four-bedroom flat and the one he offered us, but if we needed a place . . .

"What about your father? Does he agree to this arrangement?" Mother asked him.

Petras avoided Mother's eyes.

"Father joined the Lithuanian army," Petras finally said with a sigh. As if sensing our thoughts he hastily added, "He was wounded by a Soviet sniper when they withdrew, right at the beginning of the war. He hasn't moved around much since." He paused, and then added, "His friends consider him somewhat of a hero. He knocked out a Soviet tank before their sniper got him. He was actually awarded a medal by the provisional Lithuanian government." There was a note of pride in his voice at this.

"Since then the patriots have provided us with food and money. We lack nothing," he said, unobtrusively looking at the food he had brought.

Mother, who had just put a cherry in her mouth, spat it out. We all stared at Petras in horror. He looked at us uncomprehendingly.

"Petras, don't you know what your father's friends have been doing to the Jews?" Mother asked him gently.

Petras blushed. "I know that they beat up some Jews in Vilijampole, and we heard all kind of rumors, but these were the actions of a few drunks. The majority of the army only fought the Soviets. Actually, Father told me that he helped some Jews escape from the hands of the Germans," Petras said defensively.

"Your father?" Father asked incredulously.

"I don't think you know my father very well, Mr. Genkind," Petras said, lowering his gaze. "It's true, he has been a drinker and a violent man. It is also true that he is an anti-Semite, but all the Lithuanians are anti-Semites in that sense. We are taught that you have murdered God. And what could be worse than murdering God?

"But my father, believe it or not, reads the Bible. He told me that you are the chosen people. You see, in his way, he is a religious man. I believe what he says about helping those Jews escape. As a matter of fact, I'm here with his consent."

That was the longest speech I ever heard Petras make. He was surprisingly articulate, and seemed a bit resentful that my father doubted his words.

Father was about to respond, but Mother gracefully interrupted him.

"You're right, Petras. We don't know your father very well, and I'm sure that he's done exactly as you say. Besides, you have come to us like an angel from heaven at our most difficult hour," Mother said tearfully. Impulsively she came over to Petras and kissed him on the cheek.

Petras, who was a good soul, was immediately mollified.

We made an agreement. Petras would bring his uncle's horse and wagon, and two of his cousins would help us load our belongings. Naturally, we wanted to move as soon as possible, but his cousins couldn't come earlier than August 7. That was only a week before the closing date, but we didn't have much choice. We trusted Petras to do his best for us. He and Father then drew up a simple agreement for exchanging our homes.

True to his word, Petras and his cousins pulled up to our door just after dawn on the seventh of August.

We left them most of our heavy furniture and only took the bare necessities with us: the beds, two small wardrobes, a small woodstove, a kitchen table and chairs, dishes and cookware. The one luxury we took was a large wooden library commode full of books, which Mother insisted on. She loved her books and spent years collecting them. She had a formidable collection of classical writers—Russian, German, Yiddish, as well as French and English authors in Russian translations.

With everything else piled on the wagon, however, there was simply no room for the commode. Mother was terribly saddened. Petras promised he would bring it before the ghetto closed, but none of us thought we would ever see those books again.

We waited until late in the morning before we set off, at Petras's older cousin's suggestion. Most of the Lithuanians would be at work by then, and we would be less likely to encounter violence.

We were watching the clock when the telephone shrilled and made us all jump. We looked at it in disbelief. It had been dead for weeks.

On the line was my uncle Jochil. They had been trying to contact us since their return a week earlier.

They managed to elude the *Siauliai* all the way home, thanks God, only to discover that a drunken party had commandeered their apartment. This lot held them captive the better part of a day, subjecting them to abuses that Jochil now described in exhaustive detail. Aunt Dobbe—who was so large Fanny and I referred to her as "Dobbe the Grobbe," which in Yiddish means "Dobbe the fat one"—had been particularly tormented.

They managed to escape and were staying with Aunt Anushka, who had hidden in her attic when the Lithuanians made their raids. But they were left with nothing. They were practically naked, Uncle Jochil said—the only thing they owned were the filthy garments they'd worn since they fled for Russia.

All of this Uncle Jochil told Mother in a torrent of words, sobbing so loudly that all of us could hear him. I pictured him tearing his hair out, like he did during arguments with Uncle Itzhak.

"Oh Rebecca, what's to be done? We have to move to the ghetto soon and we have no shelter. We have no clothing, no beds, nothing! How are we going to survive? What will we do, what will we do?"

Mother had hardly been able to get a word in, and there was a growing fury in her eyes. "Will you stop your whining one second," she cried, "and let me say something?" There was a sudden silence on the line.

"We have lost our Herman and barely managed to survive ourselves," she told him. "Your whole family survived, so be grateful for that. As for a place to stay in the ghetto, you can move in with us until you find something better."

Then Aunt Anushka got on the line and there was a lot of crying and more talk. I too insisted on saying hello. I was so happy to hear Anushka's voice!

It was settled that she would move in with us as well.

Petras, who was discreetly listening, kept shaking his head in astonishment. When Mother looked at him questioningly, he spread his hands.

"I explained that we have only two rooms, and they are pretty small at that. How are you going to fit so many people in?"

For a moment she looked at him grimly. Then she said softly, "We'll manage, Petras, we'll manage."

6

The Ghetto

On August 7, the same day we set off for the ghetto, Lithuanian partisans arrested Jewish men all over Kaunas, for reasons that were never disclosed. Perhaps they decided to have a last bash at the Jews before the Germans locked them up. All the Jews still in Kaunas dropped what they were doing and tried to hide. The families who lost their menfolk converged on the Central Prison and begged the Lithuanian authorities to let them out. After long negotiations, where money and gold exchanged hands, about a hundred and fifty men, many of them elderly, were allowed to rejoin their families. The remainder were never seen again. We later found out that several days after their arrest, over a thousand men were taken to an unknown destination and shot. This action against the Jewish men became known in the annals of the ghetto as "The action of the famous Thursday." We were unaware of any of it when we departed Kaunas with Petras's wagon.

To our surprise there weren't too many Jews moving to the ghetto that day, only a group here and there converging toward the Vilijampole Bridge.

Later, we found out that most people were afraid to stay behind until that close to the expiration date, and many found themselves in the same predicament as Uncle Jochil and his family when they returned from the road: turned out of their apartments by Lithuanians or Germans and left with nothing.

Most of the people on the street went about their business, but from time to time someone would curse us. "You Jew bastards, your end is near!" or "Christ killers, soon you will rot in hell!"

At one point a small group of youths tried to rob us, but Petras and his cousins defended us and sent the gang packing.

Otherwise the town seemed quieter than it had been for some time—perhaps because of the German military units that patrolled the streets leading to the ghetto. I thought to myself, My God, has it come to this, that the Nazis have to protect us from our own neighbors?

At the Vilijampole Bridge a mixed patrol of Germans and Lithuanian partisans in uniform lounged at the railing, smoking. We couldn't hear the remarks they made to each other, but I noticed that the Germans and the Lithuanians looked at us differently. While the Germans showed contempt and indifference, the Lithuanians looked sullen and there was hatred in their eyes.

I felt terribly vulnerable walking this gauntlet. I expected any minute to be attacked and murdered in the middle of the street.

Although it was a warm day, I huddled in my jacket and shivered. My parents walked close to the wagon, their heads bent, not daring to look up at the passersby. Only my sister Fanny held her head up high, looking defiant. Petras's cousins looked very uneasy, and tried to hurry the horse.

Midway across the bridge we were stopped. One Lithuanian held the horse while another approached the wagon. "What are you, some kind of Jew lovers?" he asked the cousins threateningly. Both of them paled, but Petras stepped forward and took a square of newspaper from his pocket. "I am the son of Sergeant Munkaitis, who single-handedly knocked out a Soviet tank. Look for yourself. He is one of our heroes."

The Lithuanians looked confused, but obediently took the clipping from Petras's hand.

"My father instructed us to take Mr. Genkind and his family to the ghetto. He fought the Bolsheviks and was imprisoned by them for a long time. These people are not to be harmed!"

Here Father suddenly straightened up, eyes forward, and clicked his heels German fashion. Standing there straight as a ramrod, his gaunt face twitching with fear, he looked ridiculous. My heart went out to him in his humiliation.

The *Siauliai* gaped, then burst out laughing.

"Okay, you big anti-Bolshevik. We won't shoot you this time. We'll let the Germans have you," the leader said. The other two laughed again.

Then he turned to Petras and said, "I'm surprised that Munkaitis would bother with these Jewish maggots. Last I heard he wasn't exactly a Jew lover. But I guess each one has his own Jew. Okay, get out of here."

I cannot describe my dread as we crossed that bridge, expecting at any moment to be set upon again. Finally, after what seemed an eternity, we reached the ghetto gate. Men with a yellow Star of David attached to their garments were busy working on the fence, stretching and nailing barbed wire between tall posts that were being raised from Krisciukaicio Street to the river.

We had to traverse the entire ghetto to get to our new home. Krisciukaicio Street was the longest street in the ghetto, and most of the Christians who lived there had already moved out. The street was unpaved, and the houses were dilapidated wooden structures with crooked windows and doors. Here and there, on the newer structures, one could still see some traces of paint.

To my surprise I felt a wave of relief. Through the windows we could see families unpacking their bundles of clothing and arranging furniture. The street was full of noisy kids playing in the dirt, and many of them called out greetings in Yiddish. We had left the hostile Christian world behind us. I thought of what my grandfather used to say: "Whatever destiny has prepared for all of Israel will include us as individuals." After what we had gone through, this looked like heaven.

A few children, seeing Petras and his blond cousins on the wagon bench, dispersed in panic. Petras looked at me and lowered his head in shame.

The ghetto had the opposite effect on Petras's cousins that it had on us. The further we got into it, the more nervous they became. They beat the horse to get it to move faster, but it was difficult for it to drag the wagon over the soft ruts in the road. Petras tried to calm the boys down, but that only irritated them more. At one point, when the wagon got completely mired, they were ready to dump our stuff in the street and take off.

Petras finally convinced them to stick to the original agreement, and with our combined effort we managed to pull the wagon out of the sand. It took half an hour to get to Gimbuto Street, where Petras lived.

Old man Munkaitis was standing in the middle of the street in front of their house, waving his walking stick. His hair was much whiter than I remembered, and he had grown a Hitler-style mustache. He was drunk and in a foul mood.

"Where the hell have you been?! I've been waiting for hours! Let's get out of here before the goddamned Germans come in and start shooting. We're the last goddamned ones to leave!" he shouted, limping about on his wounded leg. He didn't even look in our direction. To him we were already dead.

Petras blushed to the roots of his white blond hair. He avoided looking at us. His two cousins also showed signs of embarrassment and quickly began unloading our stuff. Old Munkaitis paced up and down, nervously scanning the street. From time to time he pulled a small bottle of vodka from his back pocket and took a drink.

The Lithuanian hero who knocked out a Soviet tank single-handedly, I thought bitterly. I wondered how much of it was true.

It took about fifteen minutes to unload our belongings, and about five minutes to load their shabby things. I was thinking about our beautiful mahogany wardrobes, the rosewood tables, and the massive leather chairs that we left behind for this drunk anti-Semite.

But then I remembered that Petras would also enjoy our things, and it made me feel better. Petras promised to bring us food from time to time, in exchange for the belongings we left behind. He also promised to return the commode before the closing date. After that we were going to meet regularly once a month, by the old movie house "Lithuania," which was somehow included in the ghetto—he on the Christian side of the fence and I on the Jewish.

The flat vacated by Munkaitis was part of a wooden structure containing several apartments. It had a bedroom and a living room. There was no kitchen, no bathroom or toilet, no running water. In the corner of the living room stood a small wood-burning stove for cooking. The water had to be brought from an artesian well down the block, and the toilet was an outhouse, used by all the neighbors. The complex was new and considered luxurious compared to most of the dilapidated structures in Slabodke.

Even before we unpacked, Mother sent Father and me with two pails to fetch water from the nearby well. Father hadn't spoken a word since the incident on the bridge. I think he felt embarrassed. Father was always careful of his dignity. His charade in front of the family, though it may have saved his life, had deeply humiliated him. He wouldn't even look at me as we walked to the well. I tried to say something to him, but he only motioned for me to be quiet.

It took us a while to clean up all the dirt the Munkaitises left behind. When we had finally moved all our belongings inside, we found to our dismay that our three beds took up most of the room. By the time we finished squeezing in the rest of the furniture, the apartment was jammed.

"Where are we going to put Jochil's family and Anushka?" Mother exclaimed.

We all looked at each other, suddenly feeling guilty that we had forgotten all about them. But what were we going to do? We looked around the tiny apartment, trying to visualize where we could put five more people and their belongings.

"Well, Mother, since you so magnanimously invited them to live with us, you will have to share your bed with 'Dobbe the Grobbe,'" Fanny said, straight-faced.

Aunt Dobbe was almost as pompous and unpleasant as she was wide, and Mother's expression registered so much horror at this idea that we all started laughing. Even Father burst out laughing. The more we laughed, the more comical Mother's expression became, until we all had tears running down our faces. At the end we were all lying on the floor laughing hysterically. After the tension of the last few weeks, it was an extraordinary catharsis.

But we still had a big problem. Aunt Anushka and Uncle Jochil and his family were supposed to join us the next day, assuming they made it safely past the partisans. It took us most of the evening to arrange our belongings to make enough space.

That night Mother cooked us a reasonably satisfying meal, and after dinner I took a short walk along Gimbuto Street. The sky was deepening to purple, and people were emerging from their houses to sit on their front steps. They all politely returned my greetings. It was our first day in the ghetto, and perhaps because I was not suffering hunger pangs, or because the hazy summer sun was setting so peacefully behind the hills, I felt secure.

The next day I went out to get better acquainted with our new surroundings. Gimbuto was a short street boxed in between Varniu and Naslaiciu Streets. Varniu was the second longest street in the ghetto, running from the river Vilija to Paneriu Street, which formed the northern boundary of the large ghetto. The low wooden flats where we lived were on one side of Gimbuto and on the other side there were small individual houses. Each block was served by several outhouses which stood behind the living quarters. The artesian well, where we all got our water was across the street. Surprisingly, the water was excellent and cool, even in the summer.

At the end of Gimbuto I saw a girl about my age standing and talking to a smaller boy. She looked familiar, but for the life of me I couldn't remember where I might have met her. She had raven black hair, dark brown eyes, and a straight nose. And if it weren't for her overly long chin she would have been very pretty. When she saw me her eyes widened, and she blushed.

"Excuse me. Don't I know you from somewhere?" I said, looking straight into her eyes. Before the war I wouldn't have been able to approach a strange girl and speak to her this way if my life depended on it. A great deal had changed since then.

She was confused for a moment, then found her tongue. "Yes, we met at Lena Greenblat's Chanukah party. Don't you remember?" She sounded a little hurt.

"But of course! I do remember. You were standing next to Lena and you helped her light the Chanukah candles."

The scene that suddenly sprang into my mind was so vivid that it gave me a painful twist in the stomach. It was a big party; all the neighbors were there and the food was incredible. There were even oranges from Jaffa. It was the first time I had gotten up the courage to try to kiss Lena on the lips, but I never could get her apart from the others. In fact, it was this very girl who always seemed to be at Lena's side. Her name was Aviva. Once I managed to sneak a hasty kiss on Lena's cheek, and Lena squeezed my hand. This exchange of affection was not lost on Aviva. She gave me an amused smile, which only accentuated her chin. No matter how hard I tried that evening, I couldn't separate her from Lena, and by the end of the party I hated that girl.

Now Aviva stood in front of me, somewhat older, a little taller. Under her wool sweater I could see that her breasts had begun to develop. We shook hands awkwardly. I saw the wistful look in her eyes. She was trying to fight back tears, and suddenly I too had a lump in my throat. How little we appreciated our happy childhood days. Then I realized with a start that "those happy childhood days" were only a few months ago.

I asked Aviva if she had heard anything from Lena since the invasion. It was little more than an attempt at conversation; no one I had spoken to had any idea what had happened to the Greenblats.

"But they're here in the ghetto! Didn't you know?" she exclaimed in surprise.

"Where? How? No one seems to know what happened to them. Do you know were they live?" I asked excitedly.

"I've only seen her once. She told me that when the war started they got a lift from the Russians. They got all the way to the border only to be turned back by Soviet guards.

"They were afraid to go home because they heard that anyone who had tried to run away would be shot when they returned. They ended up hiding with Lena's uncle. They're living with him now, in the ghetto. I think he's a policeman."

"Yes, yes, but where are they? Do you have her address?" I asked impatiently.

"Somewhere on Linkuvos Street, I think."

It was almost dark before I returned home. Mother was angry that I stayed away so long, and I promised her I wouldn't do it again. Both of my parents were very nervous about the coming arrival of Aunt Anushka and Uncle Jochil and his family. My father kept admonishing my mother for her impulsive generosity, complaining that someday it would lead us to ruin.

Personally I didn't mind that they were coming. I adored my Aunt Anushka, and I loved Uncle Jochil's funny stories. I was also eager to see my cousin Fima.

I didn't even mind "Dobbe the Grobbe," who was always nice to me, or my chubby cousin Miriam, who was physically an exact replica of her mother. She was very studious, and like me always had her head in a book.

That night our supper consisted of thin cabbage soup and a slice of bread with some bacon fat. It was the last night that I had a bed of my own, but I had a hard time going to sleep. I still felt hungry. I tried to divert my thoughts by thinking about Lena. Lena was alive and here in the ghetto! I tried to imagine our meeting, how I would hold her close to me and kiss her lips. Should I press them hard or just barely touch them? I drifted off between thoughts of her and thoughts of food.

Early the next morning we rushed to answer a knock on the door. It was Aunt Anushka! Behind her stood Uncle Jochil, Aunt Dobbe, and my cousins Fima and Miriam. Everyone had lost a lot of weight since the invasion, which made Uncle Jochil look wan, but the women looked much better for it, although their faces showed strain. Even Fima looked different; somewhat older and somewhat sadder, but when he saw me he smiled, and that hadn't changed.

We started hugging and kissing each other, and we all spoke at the same time, trying to recount all that had happened since we saw each other last. In the end we were all crying. I went over and kissed Anushka, who patted my head and made soothing noises.

By the time we brought in their belongings, there was not an inch of space anywhere, but we were happy to be together.

Anushka had managed to hide some canned food, and it was a welcome addition to our meager rations. To celebrate our reunion, we opened some canned meat and ate it with boiled potatoes.

That night, since there weren't enough beds for everyone, we all paired up. Fima and I were given pallets on the floor. It was hot inside, and Uncle Jochil snored. I hardly slept at all, and it wasn't because I was hungry.

The next day, at dawn, a man came to our house and delivered a message to my father. He was to report immediately to the "Committee of the Elders," or *Aeltestenrat* as the Germans called it. We simply called it "Der Yiddisher Kommitet"—The Jewish Committee. It was headed by Dr. Elchanan Elkes, a man Father respected.

Father quickly dressed in his best suit. Although he was told they were calling him for a job, we were nevertheless apprehensive, and gathered solemnly at the door to say good-bye.

We felt an enormous sense of relief when he returned late that evening. I knew immediately that something positive had happened to him. His whole posture had changed, and some of his color had returned. He had that aura about him, of a man in charge, that he used to have before the war.

Stretching our curiosity to the limit, he first ate the soup Mother had prepared and then settled down to tell us the news.

The German in charge of the ghetto was S.A. Hauptsturmfuehrer Jordan, a man who was born and lived in Lithuania but was of German origin. He ordered the *Aeltestenrat* to organize the ghetto and begin sending workers to various institutions in town.

"The more use we get out of you Jews, the better your chances of staying alive. If you don't like the job and we have to do it for you, believe me, your Jews will be much worse off," Jordan informed Dr. Elkes.

Understanding very well Jordan's threat, Dr. Elkes and his committee began to establish the various organizations necessary to run the ghetto. The Germans decided to give the *Aeltestenrat* a certain autonomy.

The Jewish Committee was given a two-story house on Varniu Street for their administrative offices. Right from the start they had their hands full. It was up to them to take care of the thirty thousand Jews who now lived in the ghetto. They had already established a housing committee, and begun establishing a police force, labor, medical, and other departments, but they urgently needed capable administrative staff. Father, who'd had experience in the food business, was assigned to food supply. An old friend of Father's by the name of Rapoport was in charge of the department; he had recommended Father for the job.

Father was pleased with his assignment. It was work he understood, and it meant he wouldn't be consigned to hard labor. He was forty-nine when we entered the ghetto, and he had never done any physical work in his life.

That night I felt better about our situation than I had in a long time, and the rest of the family seemed cheered as well. We had tried to arrange some makeshift curtains in the house so that we could dress and bathe privately, but I couldn't help seeing the women changing into their night gowns. I even caught a glimpse of my cousin Miriam in the nude. She was all pink and fleshy and the sight of her provoked strong erotic feelings in me. I felt ashamed that I should feel that way about Miriam, but that didn't prevent me from hanging around every time she was dressing or undressing.

The first day Father reported for work, shipments of food began to arrive in the ghetto, and he was assigned to supervise their distribution. We didn't have to stand in long lines to receive our rations, as others did, since Father brought them home to us. Except for an occasional kilo of rotten potatoes, he never brought home anything more than our allotment. He had many opportunities to obtain more, but when Mother gently asked him about it he said he would never "stoop so low as to steal other people's food." My father had always been an idealist, and he remained one even under these trying circumstances.

The same evening he brought a list of our weekly rations and our hearts sank. How were we to survive?

Each person would receive, per week, less than a kilo of bread (about 700 grams), 125 grams of horse meat, 122 grams of flour, 75 grams of coffee substitute, and 50 grams of salt. From time to time we would get a few kilos of potatoes.

These were starvation rations, pure and simple, and unless we found other sources of food we would never survive.

Ever since she made the "Dobbe the Grobbe" joke, my sister Fanny seemed to have returned to her old self, the same Fanny who had almost been a second mother to me. She was twenty-seven years old when we moved to the ghetto, and a determined young woman. "The only way we can get extra food is from the Lithuanian Christians," Fanny said. "Soon the Germans will be sending us out to work. I am going to try to get a job where I can trade with the Lithuanians." Fima and Miriam agreed with Fanny. The next day all three of them went to the administration building to find out if there were any requests for workers in town.

They arrived to find thousands of people gathered around the building. Some were looking for work, and although there were rumors that the Germans were demanding workers for their institutions, no one knew anything definite. Most of the people there still didn't have a roof over their heads. Hundreds of Jews from the surrounding small towns and *shtetls* who somehow managed to escape slaughter had arrived in the ghetto looking for shelter, but most houses and apartments were already occupied by families like ourselves who had arranged exchanges with the Lithuanians. The Committee had to find space for all of them.

Our first week in the ghetto we began to make contact with the rest of our family. Uncle Itzhak had not been seen since he disappeared with the Russian troops evacuating Janeve, but his wife and all but one of his children had returned to Kaunas and were living in the old part of the ghetto. His son Arik had been killed during one of the Luftwaffe's strafings.

Sonia and Jasha Temkin and their youngest son Ronnie also made it safely to the ghetto. Father had been very upset about leaving Kaunas without Sonia, his favorite niece, but the Temkins' oldest son was away in Palengen, and they refused to leave Lithuania without him. Sonia, Jasha, and Ronnie hid in a village about ten kilometers away from Kaunas, where they were given refuge by a young Lithuanian woman named Maria. For years she had been the Temkin childrens' nanny, and had become like one of the family. Maria rescued them from almost certain death, for all the Jews who returned to the Temkins' apartment building were seized and taken to the hellish shooting gallery that Mother and I witnessed at the Seventh Fort.

When we discovered that Aunt Leena and Uncle Jacob had also arrived safely and were living near the hospital in what was called the small ghetto, Mother and Anushka put their arms around each other and cried. Jacob was Mother's youngest brother, the one who didn't marry until he was in his late thirties. His wife Leena was a quiet, sensitive woman who never said much, but it was a successful match, and the two were devoted to each other. Before the invasion, Leena worked as a nurse in the Jewish hospital, and she was considered to be one of the most dedicated nurses there. She cared for me when I had my appendix removed, and seemed to be at my bedside ten times a day. Aunt Anushka, who adored Leena, said that she always thought of others before she thought of herself.

On August 14 the first demand for workers came from an unexpected source. We all thought the Germans would be the ones to demand labor, but instead Kaminskas, the Lithuanian adviser on Jewish affairs assigned to the German commissioner, came forward with a demand for five hundred "learned workers." He specifically asked for men from the intelligentsia. Kaminskas tended to treat Jewish representatives with open contempt, but in this instance he sounded quite reasonable and persuaded the Committee that five hundred educated men were needed to work on the archives of the town hall, which were in a state of neglect. It was an opportunity for our scholars and professionals to enjoy suitable jobs. Kaminskas promised that they would be treated decently. They would work under favorable conditions and be fed three times a day. They were to appear at the ghetto gate on August 18, 1941. So the labor office of the *Aeltestenrat* sent out orders to lawyers, doctors, bookkeepers, engineers, teachers and the like to join the newly formed "learned brigade."

Father brought the news when he returned from work on the fourteenth. No one in our household was instructed to appear, but Fima thought it was a great opportunity—a job that could determine his whole future in the ghetto.

Fima was only sixteen, but looked much older. He had managed to grow a respectable mustache, and with his thin metal-framed glasses he had an intellectual look. He also spoke both Lithuanian and German very well.

Jochil tried to talk him out of it. "I learned one thing when I served in the army: never volunteer. Besides you are much too young. You could get into trouble if they find out that you lied to them."

But his mother and sister sided with Fima, and so did Fanny.

That night Sonia appeared at our door with little Ronnie. She was crying bitterly. The next day the ghetto would close, and Maria was going back to her village. She had stuck by the family until the last minute, and now she was trying to talk Sonia into letting her take Ronnie back to the village with her. Maria was close to the whole family, and loved Ronnie like her own son, but Sonia wouldn't hear of it. She wasn't going to give up her little boy, come what may.

But the Lithuanian guards and other hooligans continued to take potshots into the ghetto, and the day before, a stray bullet almost hit Ronnie. "Uncle, what am I going to do? He almost got killed!" Sonia cried. "I just can't bear this. How can I give up my child? Maria is wonderful, but she is not his mother . . . I can't, I just can't," she kept repeating between sobs.

I could see that Ronnie was getting very upset about the whole conversation, so I took him to the other room where we played his favorite game. We had given him a globe on his last birthday, and he'd been thrilled. I never could understand how a six-year-old boy could be so crazy about a boring subject like geography, but he was. The game consisted of naming countries, towns, rivers, and mountains around the world. The first person names a country or town, then the next person has to think of a place that begins with the last letter of the first place. For instance, if he said Japan I would say Norway. He could play this game for hours.

Just when I was stuck on the outlandish name of some South American river, Ronnie looked at me, his blue eyes expressing fear.

"Do you think I should leave with Maria, or stay with my parents?"

I looked him straight in the eyes and said, "You should leave with

Maria. You'll be much safer with her than in the ghetto."

"I don't see you in such a hurry to leave your parents." Again that serious, skeptical look.

"If I had a Maria like you do, I would leave too," I answered him as honestly as possible. In my heart I wasn't quite so sure.

"I'll miss you, Solly," he said with tears in his eyes.

"I'll miss you too, Ronnie," I said, giving him a big hug.

Sonia and Father came into the room, and from the resigned look on Sonia's face I realized that she had come to a decision. My parents and Anushka persuaded her that she shouldn't forego an opportunity to save her son.

The next day the ghetto gates would close, and Maria was coming to say good-bye in the hope that Sonia would change her mind. Lithuanian thugs continued to raid the ghetto plundering Jewish households, and there was a lot of shooting still going on around the fence. Returning to the ghetto was a brave thing for Maria to do, but we had yet to discover just how daring she could be.

During the night Sonia washed Ronnie's hair with peroxide and it turned almost white. She packed his clothing and a few toys in a backpack and dressed him to look the part of a local village boy.

Getting him past the guards was the biggest problem. Almost all the Christian families had left weeks ago. If Maria were to appear at the gate with Ronnie and his backpack, the guards would immediately become suspicious.

The next day we were very much surprised when Petras showed up with his uncle's horse and wagon, bringing Mother's commode full of books, as he had promised. None of us believed we would see those books again. Underneath the commode he smuggled in some food, including five large loaves of home-baked bread.

Here was our solution. After some hesitation, Petras agreed to take Maria and Ronnie with him. It was risky, but there was at least a fair chance of success. Ronnie would pose as Petras's little brother. Luckily, Ronnie's bleached hair was nearly the same color as Petras's. Maria also looked unmistakably Christian, so we were hopeful.

Petras and Maria sat up front, while Ronnie curled up in the wagon bed and pretended to sleep.

That evening the ghetto gates officially closed, locking us in like helpless sheep. Even so, we had books, we had bread, and God willing, we had gotten Ronnie safely out of the ghetto.

• • •

It was a month before we knew how Petras, Maria, and Ronnie had fared. Petras described it to me when we had our first rendezvous, at the fence near the old "Lithuania" movie house.

Two Lithuanians and one German policeman were guarding the ghetto gate that evening. Petras presented his I.D. card and told the Lithuanians who his father was. He explained that they exchanged apartments with some Jews and he had delivered some of their furniture as part of the deal.

Maria's papers were in order as well, but the Lithuanians became suspicious of her presence. She told them that she was curious about how the damn Jews lived, so she'd come along for the ride. When they looked inside the wagon and saw Ronnie, their suspicions grew. It didn't help that Petras told them he was his brother. Now they looked at Petras with suspicion, too.

"Anyone can falsify papers and your hair is too blond. Peroxide is cheap," they said.

"What are you trying to do, woman? You want to smuggle these Jewish kids out of the ghetto?" one of them said to Maria, waiting for her reaction.

"The two of you, let me see your peckers!" the other Lithuanian said.

Petras quickly jumped off the wagon and let his pants down. While the German policeman stood aside enjoying the spectacle, the Lithuanians bent down and with serious faces inspected his penis.

"I guess you are all right," they admitted.

"Do you want to see my brother's, too?" Petras asked and put his arms around Ronnie as if to lift him out of the wagon.

"Ah, forget it. Just get on out of here if you know what's good for you."

7

The Five Hundred
Intellectuals

AUGUST 18, 1941

Fima rose early the next morning. He was going to try to get into the brigade of "learned men," and I decided to accompany him to the gate. I had to promise Mother I would return before we got within reach of the guards at the gate.

On Varniu Street we met quite a few acquaintances, all headed in the same direction. Among them were many leaders of the Jewish community in Kaunas. Suddenly I noticed a tall familiar figure striding ahead of us.

"Mr. Greenblat!" I exclaimed in astonishment. It was Lena's father. I barely recognized him. In the short time since I'd last seen him his face had aged greatly.

He looked at me puzzled, and then smiled.

"It's you, young Genkind! How is the family, are they all right?" He had great respect for my father, and always called me "young Genkind." He believed socialism represented the epitome of man's ideals, and he was a committed member of the Bund. He knew of my father's participation in the Revolution, and whenever he met my father he would politely tip his hat.

I told him about Herman and he expressed his regrets.

"Please convey my condolences to your family. But now I must be off. I don't want to miss this working party. The whole ghetto will probably try to get in on it."

He took off almost at a run, as if he wanted to make up the time he lost talking to me.

"Mr. Greenblat, wait!" I cried after him. "Where do you live? What is your address? I want to visit Lena!"

"Thirty-six Linkuvos. Come and visit us," he shouted back, waving.

In the distance we could see the ghetto gate and hundreds of people already assembled there. Fima promised my mother to send me back before we got there, and he now urged me to turn back.

"I'll see you in the evening," he said, but as I turned away a group of Lithuanian partisans swooped down from a side street, dragging with them dozens of young men.

Before I knew what was happening more groups converged from other streets, and I was swept up into a growing mob. I saw Fima making frantic signals for me to run, but it was too late. The Lithuanians were clubbing anyone who wasn't moving to the gate quickly enough, and I was right in the middle with *Siauliai* surrounding me from all sides.

For a moment I thought I saw Lena's father's ashen face, but then he disappeared from view. We were all herded toward the gate and surrounded by Lithuanian and German soldiers. Fima pushed through the crowd until he stood next to me.

"Something is wrong here. We must get away," he whispered in alarm.

Among the Jewish policemen standing next to the gate I noticed a friend of Fanny's. His name was Ika Grinberg. I called out to him and waved, and his eyes widened in surprise. He made his way over to us and quietly asked me what the hell I was doing there.

Then he saw Fima and told us to stand aside. He made his way up to the German in charge and spoke to him, at one point turning and pointing at us. The German glanced up briefly and they continued to talk.

Then Ika was back at our sides. "All right, you two jokers," he said loudly. "What are you trying to do, grow up in a hurry? You're too young for this job." Then he roughly pushed us past the Lithuanian guards toward a side street. "Run home now," he said under his breath. "You understand?"

We didn't need further encouragement, and took off at breakneck speed. We could hear the laughter of the Lithuanians behind us. Later we found out that the German who let us go was none other than Rauca, the man who later would come to be known as the butcher of the ghetto.

We ran all the way home and arrived completely out of breath.

"What happened, what happened?" they all wanted to know. But we had no answer. We just told them how the *Siauliai* were herding people off the streets and beating them.

"I doubt we'll see those people again. It was just a Nazi trick. And to think that I fell for it," Fima said angrily.

"You don't know that! They've been beating Jews since the war started. There is nothing new in that," Dobbe said sharply, her neck and face reddening as she looked at my mother. She sounded defensive.

"Then why did they collect all kinds of men from the streets? They certainly weren't all doctors and scholars. They weren't selecting candidates for some high-flown job," Fima replied.

Mother, who looked distraught, had said little during this exchange, but suddenly she crossed the room and slapped me in the face.

"Next time you will listen to me. I told you to stay away from the gate, but in your childish stupidity you didn't obey. I lost one son and I don't intend to lose another. You understand?"

That slap stung like a whip and I had tears in my eyes, but more than anything, I was completely astonished at my mother's reaction. I think it was the first time she had ever slapped me.

The others were clearly just as astonished. It was completely out of character for Mother to do something like this.

As if suddenly realizing what she had done, she hugged me and then kissed me on my burning cheek. She used to do this when I was a child and hurt myself—she would kiss the place where it hurt.

It took all of us a while to calm down, but I hadn't forgotten Lena's address. That afternoon I went to Linkuvos Street to look for her. If our fears about the "learned brigade" were true, she would need some moral support.

Thirty-six Linkuvos Street was an old but sturdy-looking wooden structure. It even had a small fence in front, and a few flowers growing by the steps. For a while I stood there looking at the house, trying to feel Lena's presence. Suddenly the door opened and a slim girl emerged. She wore a short checked dress with straps that exposed her shoulders. Her hair was disheveled and she looked as if she was crying. With a shock I realized it was Lena. My heart beat faster as she ran down the steps and passed me without even giving me a second glance. Then Mrs. Greenblat appeared in the doorway calling after her. She too had aged in a short time, but she still sounded as energetic as ever. She noticed me immediately.

"Solly, don't just stand there like a dumb ox! Run after her!" she shouted at me, as if she had seen me only yesterday, as if the last few weeks hadn't opened a chasm between the present and the past.

I didn't need another summons and began running after Lena, catching her easily. I wrapped my arms around her.

Her stricken expression turned to astonishment, and then her eyes lit up. "Solly, Solly, it's you. I thought you were dead. They told us that you were all killed at the Seventh Fort!"

I held on tight and she hugged back, but then she began to weep. "My father . . . he went this morning with the others. He was so optimistic. . . . He thought he had found a good job, but they are going to kill them, I know it. . . ." She broke down in sobs again, burying her face in my shoulder. I could feel her tears through my thin shirt and I thought my heart would break. I too started crying. Standing there with my sweet Lena, I felt the whole of our calamity engulf me. I cried for my brother Herman. I cried for my history teacher and her little blond girl who lay dead in the pond. I cried for the redheaded woman and her little redheaded baby and all the others shot at Kazys's farm. And I cried for all of us here in the ghetto, condemned to certain death.

It seemed we stood together crying like that for a long time. Lena clung to me, and I could feel her breasts against my body. When our sobs subsided I kissed her on the forehead, but she pulled my head down and gave me a long passionate kiss that took my breath away. I never suspected shy little Lena to act that way, and I ascribed it to her overwrought state, for the next minute she was crying again.

"He's dead, he's dead, I know it. I love him so much, and I'll never see him again, never."

I wanted desperately to rekindle some hope in her. "But Lena, you don't know that! Why would the Germans use such tricks if they just wanted to kill them? All those people killed at the Seventh Fort—

they were just taken off the street, dragged out of their houses.

"If they wanted to kill five hundred people they didn't have to pretend they wanted them for work. They can kill as many as they feel like, any time. You will see, your father will come home tonight and all your fears will turn out to be baseless."

Then, as if to reinforce the argument, I told her that I had seen her father by the gate. I left out the part about the brutal beatings, and told her that they'd turned down Fima and me because we were too young.

"You saw my father? You are not just saying this to cheer me up?" she asked doubtfully, looking me in the eyes.

I had to swear several times that I really saw her father and even spoke to him. "How do you think I found you? He gave me your address!" This finally convinced her. I thought with guilty sadness how easily people cling to hope; as if my seeing him had anything to do with his fate.

"Let's go back and tell Mother," Lena said almost cheerfully, taking me by the hand.

When we entered the house I was warmly embraced by her brother Vova and her older sister Rachel. Again I was struck by how much the whole family had changed.

When we sat down and I repeated my story, Mrs. Greenblat gave me a hug too. Somehow I had rekindled the spark of hope they needed.

We exchanged stories of our experiences on the road to Russia, and what had happened to us since the beginning of the war.

Rachel told their story, with Vova and Lena interrupting from time to time to add some forgotten detail. The family had managed to get a ride with some Russians that Mr. Greenblat became friendly with. They were high-ranking party officials and were given a truck to evacuate Kaunas. The Greenblats were put on top of their belongings. They were strafed and bombed all the way to the Russian border, but all of them managed to escape injury.

"You can imagine our terror when the Russian border guards took us off the truck and wouldn't let us into Russia. We couldn't believe it was happening. Only Soviet citizens with proper papers were allowed in. The truck entered without us."

The Germans were approaching with alarming speed and it was too dangerous to stay at the border. The family made a final attempt to get across, but they were shot at by the Russian guards. They had little choice but to return to Kaunas.

"And you know," Rachel said sadly, "had we waited a few more hours we would have gotten across. Back in Kaunas we found out that at the last minute the Russians opened the border to everyone."

Rachel had been an excitable, vivacious girl, and as the firstborn she was rather spoiled, but she told their story of horrors calmly and without histrionics. I was struck by the way she seemed to have matured.

They tell you that you can't possibly have deep emotions at the age of thirteen, that love, as we know it at maturity, cannot be felt by a boy that age. But when I think back to that time, I know what I felt for Lena was love, perhaps even purer and sweeter than what we know as adults. I could hardly take my eyes off her.

It was almost noon when I remembered my promise to my mother and rose to leave. Mrs. Greenblat took four small slices of bread from a tin box, carefully spread a thin layer of margarine on top, and handed each one of us a slice. I began to protest, but she shut me up.

"Be quiet. You deserve it. You brought us hope. Perhaps it's false hope, but that remains to be seen."

As I ate the tiny sliver of bread savoring every crumb, I couldn't help remembering the quantities of food we ate at their Chanukah parties. Now, even when my belly felt more or less full, I never felt sated.

When I returned home and told Mother about the Greenblats, her eyes filled with tears. Although they were never really close friends, she liked them. She also knew how I felt about Lena and never teased me about her like Father and Herman did. She said she remembered feeling that way about a classmate of hers when she was my age. I asked her permission to go to the ghetto gate that evening with Lena. I wanted to be with the Greenblats when Mr. Greenblat and the brigade of five hundred returned from work, if they returned. I prayed for Lena's sake that they would.

Mother didn't answer for several minutes. I could see the inner struggle taking place in her mind. She was desperate for a reason to refuse me, but in the end her clear-mindedness and compassion for her fellow man won out. She nodded her head.

The families of the five hundred, or rather five hundred and thirty-four to be precise, began to gather at the gate early in the afternoon to wait for their loved ones. Many of them were crying. I stood with the Greenblats, and Lena held my hand. As time passed and the brigade did not return, she pressed it harder and harder. Finally a Jewish policeman arrived with a message. The Germans had informed the Committee that the brigade would not be coming back that evening because they had been detained for additional work in town.

Many of the families were relieved. "Since when did the Germans make up excuses for killing Jews?" they said. "If they went to the trouble of informing us, it must be true."

But Mrs. Greenblat's face had fallen. She obviously didn't believe the Germans. Lena, on the other hand, felt encouraged by the message. So did Rachel and Vova. When I said good-bye, Lena kissed me in front of the whole family. I felt embarrassed at her boldness. She certainly had matured in a short time, and I wasn't quite sure whether it was to my liking. How could I be bold if she was always a step ahead of me?

For a week the Greenblats went to the ghetto gate every evening. Each night the men did not return; each night the Germans stubbornly insisted that the men were alive and well and working somewhere in Lithuania.

Hunger was the problem the rest of us faced every day. There was only one thing that could temporarily make me forget my hunger, and that was a good book. At least we weren't short of books. There were Mother's books, Aunt Anushka's, Father's, Fanny's, and some of Herman's. Even Uncle Jochil's family managed to bring some books.

Miriam was an avid reader, but she tended to read books of philosophy, which were too heavy for my liking. I still preferred Dumas, Jules Verne, and Sir Walter Scott, although I didn't mind Gogol and Tolstoy. I loved *War and Peace,* and couldn't understand why Mother thought it wouldn't interest me. I thought Tolstoy was a great storyteller.

Sometimes I would revert to *Emil and the Detectives,* or even the fairy tales of the Brothers Grimm. Fanny used to read those stories to me in German, when I was very small. In the beginning I preferred books in German and Lithuanian, but soon, because we had so many books in Russian and Yiddish, I began reading more in those two languages.

The next few days I worked with Father at the supply depot. The Germans had sent in two truckloads of rotting potatoes and we were supposed to save as much as possible of the shipment. I was promised a kilo of potatoes for my work. By the time we were finished, more than half of the shipment had to be buried, as they stank to high heaven. So did I. The man in charge of the depot gave me my kilo of potatoes and added another kilo for the half-spoiled ones. I smelled like a skunk, and Mother spent an hour helping me scrub the smell off my skin, but I felt proud that I brought food into the house.

Fanny, in the meantime, got a job as a cook for a brigade that unloaded goods at the railway station. The work was hard and the Germans considered it important, so the workers were given extra rations and a daily bowl of soup. Fanny made the soup, and she was a good cook. She was also pretty, good humored, and spoke perfect German, all of which endeared her to the German who ran the station. He would call her "Die schwarze Sarah" (The black Sarah). Within days Fanny managed to become friendly with the Lithuanian employees at the station, and she would trade clothing with them for food. In the beginning she brought home some bread and a few potatoes, but later she would bring pork, flour, and sometimes even sugar and butter, which were true luxuries. Her role as provider of the family suddenly promoted her to a new status. She insisted that everyone should get an equal share.

Although Fanny made light of her trading with the Lithuanians, we knew that it was extremely dangerous. We all worried about her safety, especially Mother, who kept begging her not to take such chances.

I was very proud of my sister for being so fair-minded, but dividing the food nine ways made the individual portions very small. I was hungry most of the time.

Fima and I decided to go to work ourselves and bring additional rations. That meant working outside the ghetto. Father heard that a brigade of youths was going to work at the large vegetable fields in Alexotas, which had become neglected during the hostilities.

It was backbreaking work. The fields were badly overgrown with weeds, and we had to kneel among the rows of carrots and cabbage the whole day, digging out the weeds with our bare hands.

There were about thirty of us, mostly around my age, some younger. We were warned not to steal anything. If we were caught with a single carrot in our pockets, we would be shot. Nevertheless I managed to eat about ten carrots that day—straight out of the ground with the sand grating between my teeth. Once, when I saw the Lithuanian supervisor approaching, I had to swallow a big chunk, which stuck like a rock halfway down. For lunch they gave us some watery cabbage soup, which tasted vile, but at least I managed to wash down that carrot stuck in my gullet.

We were given a half hour break for lunch and I found a spot near a chestnut tree that provided some shade against the midday sun. I was glad I could stretch my back a little.

In the distance I could see the blue waters of the river shimmering in the sun, and a cool breeze coming from the river played in my hair and cooled my face. I thought of Kalautuvas, and swimming in the river. Its source was the snowy hills of Russia, and I remembered how cool the water was, how fresh and sweet. I had a place in the sun then.

The wind stirred the branches and rustled the leaves over my head. I closed my eyes and visualized that world. "Oh God! If you will only make this nightmare go away, I will bless your wondrous creation every day of my life. I will kiss every tree and praise every flower. I will spend my life serving the poor. I'll help every stray dog and cat that crosses my path. Please, God. . . ."

A sharp kick in my ribs brought me back to my miserable reality. The Lithuanian supervisor stood over me.

"I didn't bring you here to sleep under trees, you good for nothing lazy Jew swine," he shouted, giving me another kick in the ribs. I must have dozed off wishing for my miracle. I jumped up and ran all the way to my place in the carrot patch and started jerking up weeds as fast as I could. I didn't want the supervisor to single me out. He had spent the morning brutalizing two small boys who weren't quick enough for him, kicking them every time he passed their row.

Fima, who had sneaked off during the lunch break to find someone to trade with, returned without accomplishing anything. He looked disappointed and tired. We brought some small items for barter with us, but except for the supervisors we never came into contact with any Lithuanians.

When evening came I could barely stand up. My back hurt terribly and the kicks in the ribs didn't help much either. I thought I would never make it back to the ghetto, which was about a two-hour walk from the fields. Both of us were tired and discouraged, and every step I took was sheer agony. I simply wasn't used to physical labor.

Just before we got to the Alexotas Bridge Fima slipped down a side street and disappeared. None of the guards, thanks God, noticed.

We were walking four in a row, and I began falling back to see if Fima returned. The boys behind me cursed as one in each row had to move up to take my place. When I finally reached the last row I found Fima there all sweaty and red in the face. His freckles stood out like yellow spots, and his curly hair was all disheveled, but he was smiling from ear to ear.

"I got half a loaf of bread and ten potatoes for that stupid neckerchief. Would you believe it!"

"If they had caught you, they would have stretched your neck with that neckerchief! You were crazy to take such a risk," I told him angrily.

I didn't want to admit it, but I was jealous of his success. It would be humiliating to come home empty-handed while Fima brought food. As if sensing my thoughts, Fima gave me the bread to hide in my backpack.

"This way it will be less risky if they search us at the gate. I'll tell them at home that we did it together," he grinned at me.

It was dark by the time we got to the ghetto. A spotlight illuminated the gate area, and the guards were searching everyone who had a bundle. A few boys who had stolen vegetables from the fields were beaten mercilessly. We were in the last row, and Fima managed to throw away the potatoes, but I impulsively stuck the bread under my shirt. When our turn came we both showed the guards our empty packs. They apparently had enough fun beating up the other boys, and let us through.

Two small boys not more than ten years old stood at the gate with swollen faces and bleeding noses. Each one had a large carrot stuck in his mouth, much to the amusement of the guards. They were to remain standing like this the whole night.

"In the morning we'll decide whether to shoot you or send you to your mothers," one of the guards laughed. The next day we heard that the guards released them that morning, after receiving bribes.

On the way home I gave the loaf of bread back to Fima. At first he didn't want to take it, but when I insisted he sheepishly put it into his knapsack.

"Hiding that loaf of bread was courageous, but stupid. You saw what they did to the other boys. What possessed you to do it?" Fima admonished me. I guess he felt guilty that he had thrown away the potatoes.

That evening Fanny came back from work crying. A Lithuanian guard caught her trading and took the food away. Then he slapped her in the face until it was all swollen. She said she didn't mind the beating so much, she just felt terrible that they took the food.

"What are we going to eat?" she sobbed, crying in Aunt Anushka's arms.

Anushka wiped her tears. "We'll manage. You don't have to feel that you're responsible for feeding the whole family," she said, stroking Fanny's hair.

That evening we ate a watery vegetable soup prepared from leftovers. Father brought back our rations of bread and tiny pieces of margarine, and Aunt Anushka opened a can of beans from our emergency supplies.

Mother divided the bread Fima brought into thin slices with a barely visible film of margarine on top. Fima called them "jam sandwiches," because they were no more than two pieces of bread jammed together.

That evening we debated on strategies for feeding the family. Uncle Jochil would go with Father to see if he could find work at the supply department. Mother and Aunt Anushka decided to go to the Committee to see if they could find some work there. Aunt Dobbe and cousin Miriam decided to wait until Mother and Anushka came back with news.

That night I went to bed hungry and sore. There were blisters on my feet and a stabbing pain in my lower back, and my ribs felt as if they were cracked. I was going to take my usual place on the floor, but Fanny let me curl up next to her.

"Tonight you sleep with the working folks." Her eyes were all puffed up, but her smile was still sweet.

I fell asleep as soon as I put my head on the pillow. It seemed to me that I had hardly closed my eyes when it was time to go to work again.

It was five in the morning and still dark outside. I tried to get out of bed but I couldn't straighten up, and my ribs hurt so much I could barely breathe.

"You can't go to work in this condition," Mother declared, and everyone agreed, although Fima was disappointed. He didn't want to go back to the field alone, but he had arranged to meet his Lithuanian contact again and he was anxious to do some more trading.

Boys my age weren't actually required to work at that point, and in fact there were many more boys volunteering than there were jobs, so I stayed in bed. As soon as everyone left, I fell asleep again.

I was awakened by a loud banging on the door. Before Aunt Dobbe had a chance to open it, it sprang open and four German policemen entered, demanding to know why we didn't open up sooner.

I ducked under the blanket, hoping they wouldn't notice me and wishing I had gone to work with Fima. But the next minute the blanket was ripped off me and I found myself staring at a broad fleshy face with cruel gray eyes. A huge hand reached out and grabbed me by the scruff of the neck. The German was about forty years old and had a sergeant's stripes on his sleeve. His wide nose must have been broken at some point. He looked like a boxer. I still see that face in my dreams.

"I see you are the man of the house, you little Jew bastard," he growled. "So you better tell us where you're hiding the gold and the jewelry, or I'll break your scrawny neck." He squeezed my neck so hard I couldn't breathe.

Miriam leapt up from her chair. "He's only a boy. He doesn't know anything," she said loudly. The policeman looked round at her in surprise, then unceremoniously dumped me on the floor.

"All right, *you* tell us where you've hidden your gold, or we'll kill all of you," he said.

The other three were opening the wardrobes and drawers and dumping everything on the floor.

Miriam quickly removed a gold necklace and Aunt Dobbe pulled off her wedding band. The others were gathering up some family silver that belonged to Aunt Anushka. They also took the women's fur coats.

"You look like the kind of Jews who would hoard gold. I know you have jewelry and money somewhere, and so far you've given us nothing. You better not trifle with us, or you'll regret it," the man with the boxer face told us.

When Miriam didn't answer he changed his tactic. "What's your name, girl," he asked her almost in a conversational tone.

"Miriam, Sir."

"Ah, Mary. Like Mary mother of Jesus," boxer-face laughed. "For the last time, where are you hiding the gold?"

"We don't have anything else, Sir. The Lithuanians took everything we had in the first days of the war."

"Oh really," he replied. "And just what might you two fatties have under your skirts? Take them off."

When they didn't respond, he hit Miriam across the face with his stick. "Get undressed!" he thundered. A big red welt appeared on Miriam's cheek, and tears began streaming from her eyes. Still she hesitated, and boxer-face hit her again. Then both women hastily shed their outer garments. That didn't satisfy the Germans, who ripped at their underwear until both stood completely naked. Aunt Dobbe had lost a lot of weight, and the skin hung loosely on her body, her triangular breasts almost reaching her belly.

Her face had turned so red she looked almost purple. She was crying bitterly and begging the Germans not to harm them.

Miriam was still chubby, but she had a glowing pink look and her breasts were round and firm. Her pubic triangle was almost carrot red and she tried to hide it with her hands.

I felt deeply ashamed that I was sexually aroused by her nakedness.

"Now bend over. You are probably hiding gold pieces in your cunts."

Aunt Dobbe fell to her knees and redoubled her pleas, sobbing uncontrollably. But boxer-face beat her with his stick until she and Miriam finally bent over a table. Then to my horror boxer-face came up behind Aunt Dobbe and rammed his stick into her vagina. She let out a terrible scream and collapsed on the floor. He then approached Miriam and began playing the stick between her legs.

Shaking like a leaf, Miriam said in a trembling voice, "Please, Sir, don't. I am still a virgin."

"Well, well, the Virgin Mary," boxer-face said. "Are you going to bring us another Jesus? Eh? I think the first one is more than enough for me. Isn't that so boys?" And he laughed obscenely.

They decided to take our mahogany wardrobe and mother's book commode, first dumping all the contents on the floor.

"You have until tomorrow to produce the valuables. If not we'll be back to finish your virginity," boxer-face grinned, making a sudden lunge at Miriam with his stick.

Miriam leaped back in fright. She had managed to cover herself and throw a blanket over her mother, who was still lying on the floor half-conscious.

After they left I remained crouched in the corner where boxer-face had dropped me, unable to move or say a word.

I was so shocked and disgusted that I felt sick to my stomach, and I was terribly angry at myself for not doing something to help Miriam and her mother. I felt so ashamed, so helpless in the hands of these repulsive brutes. For the first time I realized what the Nazis meant when they called us subhuman. To use a wooden stick on Miriam and Aunt Dobbe as if they were cattle or swine, or not even living creatures but something insensible. Somehow I felt that if they had actually raped them I would have felt less anguish.

After the Germans left, we revived Aunt Dobbe and helped her to bed. She was in pain and moaning piteously. Miriam begged me not to tell the family what I'd witnessed. I was especially not to tell her father or Fima.

"They must not know, you understand?" she said fiercely.

I didn't have the courage to look at her. I just nodded miserably, tears running down my face. Then she did a strange thing. She smiled at me and kissed my cheek. She was indeed a strong and courageous girl.

It was late in the afternoon before Mother and Aunt Anushka returned. Some Germans dragooned them outside the administration building and forced them to clean their headquarters. In spite of Miriam's protests, Aunt Dobbe couldn't hold back and told them what had happened.

Anushka immediately wanted to take Aunt Dobbe to a gynecologist who lived not far from us in the "Big Blocks." But Aunt Dobbe refused. All she could think about was what would happen when boxer-face returned.

"What are we going to do, what are we going to do . . . if we don't give them what they want they'll kill us," she cried, wringing her hands.

I had begun to recover my composure, and wasn't in pain, but Mother examined the bruises on my throat and neck, hugging and kissing me, grateful I had come to no serious harm.

"Clearly the man wasn't making empty threats. They've already killed people over this," Aunt Anushka said. "We have no choice but to dig it all up and hand it over. Otherwise we can expect the worst."

Miriam and I both gasped in surprise. I had no idea we had any gold, let alone that we'd buried it.

"You mean we could have avoided all that? Mother's injury, and that humiliation? Mother, did you know about this?!" Miriam cried, her face contorted with fury.

"Miriam please, darling, you don't understand . . ." Aunt Dobbe began saying in a sorrowful voice.

"Oh, yes! I understand very well! Your gold is more important to you than anything! Our dignity, our integrity, even our lives! If I live a thousand years I will never be able to overcome the humiliation, the disgust, of that beast touching me!"

"Miriam please!" Anushka broke in. "We all sympathize with you. It was dreadful, horrible, but none of us could have foreseen such a thing. We thought the valuables might keep us from starving. That's why we hid them."

Miriam stared at Aunt Anushka, then lowered her gaze and mumbled an apology.

During all this turmoil I began to worry about Lena. The Germans had apparently made raids all over the ghetto. I was terrified that she might have been subjected to the same treatment as Dobbe and Miriam. Every time I thought about it, I broke out in a sweat.

I felt guilty sneaking off during such a crisis, but I couldn't stand the thought of anyone doing that to Lena. I had to make sure she was all right.

I ran all the way to Linkuvos Street and arrived there completely out of breath. To my great surprise the Germans hadn't been there at all. The Greenblats heard about the searches, however, and knew some people had been shot. They were quite relieved when I showed up unharmed, and bombarded me with questions. Lena looked thin and haggard, and her hair was untidy. She put her head on my shoulder, and began to cry.

For many days the Germans continued to insist that the five hundred "learned men" were alive and working. To this day no one understands why the Germans kept up that lie. Jews who worked in town were told by the Lithuanians that the five hundred were taken that same day to the Fourth Fort, which was situated near Panemune, and shot. Sturmfuehrer Jordan later admitted to the Committee that the five hundred had been killed. He claimed it was punishment for an act of sabotage committed by some Jewish workers, who allegedly poured water on some sacks of sugar destined for the Wehrmacht.

Lena was still mourning her father, and her mother told me that her mind was wandering.

"I'm terribly worried about her, Solly. She's not eating at all. Even the little food we get she doesn't eat. You seem to be a good influence on her, please speak to her," her mother begged me.

I felt guilty that I hadn't visited them lately, and explained that I had worked at Alexotas the previous day. Then I warned them about the Germans' searches, without going into any details about Aunt Dobbe and Miriam.

Later we went out and sat on the steps. I tried to tell Lena that she must eat, that life must go on.

"What's the use?" she said. "They've taken Father, and he was everything to me. He was so strong. He thought he could do anything. He got us all the way to Russia safely, he got us all the way back, he did everything right until the day he decided to join that death brigade. He was so confident, so convinced he knew what he was doing, and with all his cleverness he walked straight into a trap. Don't you understand? It's all for nothing. The sky has fallen."

"You must think of your mother, little Vova, and Rachel. They are your family and they love you," I pleaded.

"And what about you? Do you love me?" she asked sharply.

"You know that I love you. I've always loved you," I said, softly stroking her hair. She shook my hand off impatiently.

"Then prove that you love me. Marry me," she said in a completely altered voice. Seeing my shocked expression, she laughed.

"What's the matter? You think we are too young? I am sure we won't get much older. We'll all be dead before the year is out, if not sooner. So let's at least enjoy the little time we have left. Do you want to die a virgin?"

Then her expression softened again. "If only we could go back in time. . . . You know where I would want to be? Remember the day we built that really big snowman? You had forgotten to bring the carrot for his nose and Itamar made you go back and get one?"

I nodded miserably.

"You looked so handsome in your sheepskin coat. And then you kissed me. It was the sweetest, gentlest kiss. . . . That was the happiest day of my life," she said dreamily.

Then her face darkened. "Do you believe in reincarnation? I sometimes have the feeling that I lived before. Perhaps the next time around I will be granted all the years that I am going to miss. Would you like to meet me in our next life? If you promise that you will kiss me again the way you kissed me on 'Snowman's Hill,' I will spend my next life with you."

She shuddered and leaned against me. I tried to kiss her, but she pulled away and began to weep again. It was impossible to calm her. Finally Mrs. Greenblat came to the door and I looked up at her help-lessly. She put a soothing hand on my shoulder and led Lena back inside.

When I returned home it was dark and I expected my mother to scold me, but she only gave me a confused look. Father and Jochil sat at the table, looking grim. Miriam sat red-faced, reading a book, and Aunt Dobbe lay on her bed crying. Fanny, Fima, and Aunt Anushka hadn't returned. There was a heavy silence in the room and I wasn't about to interrupt it.

I sat down next to Father, and Mother served me a bowl of barley soup, which contained more water than barley. A small piece of pink pork fat floated on top of it. It was the last piece of pork that Fanny had brought from work. I greedily fished it out and ate all of it, even the hard brown rind. It tasted like a delicacy to my fat-starved body.

When I finished I felt hungrier than before. I sat next to Miriam in the dim light of a single bulb and read a detective story by Edgar Wallace. I tried to lose myself in the book, but I couldn't stop thinking about the next day. I could still feel boxer-face's iron grip on my neck.

Then Fanny came back from work with Aunt Anushka carrying her backpack. I guess Anushka went to the gate to meet her. From the way she looked at Miriam I realized Anushka had told her what hap-pened. A few minutes later Fima walked in. It seemed that the guards didn't check the incoming brigades very carefully, and they both managed to bring some food.

When Fima saw his father he came over and hugged him. He heard that the ghetto was raided during the day and that many men were shot.

Miriam and Aunt Dobbe were quiet, and Uncle Jochil remained grimly silent. They let Anushka explain the events of the day to Fima. She left out the details of Miriam and Aunt Dobbe's mistreatment. She didn't want to upset him.

It seemed that neither Fanny nor Fima knew about the buried valuables, either. Before they could become indignant, Aunt Anushka explained that they didn't tell us because they feared what would happen if we were questioned by the Germans. The less we knew, the safer we would be.

The big question was what to do next. Anushka was all for digging up the hoard and giving it to the Germans.

"Of what good would the gold be to us if they kill us," Aunt Dobbe put in. Everyone agreed except Miriam, of all people.

"No, we shouldn't give our valuables to the swine. Besides what guarantee do we have that they'll let us live even then? For all you know, they may say that we lied to them yesterday, and kill us for *that*. I think we should stick to our story. There must be many families who truly don't have anything hidden. What are they going to do, kill us all?"

"But darling," Aunt Dobbe began, but Miriam gave her a look that hushed her up immediately. Since the incident my voluble Aunt Dobbe had become greatly subdued. Secretly, I admired her guts. I would never have believed that she knew about the valuables and didn't tell the Germans.

The logic of Miriam's argument was very convincing. For a while the adults discussed whether we should all leave the house and disperse among friends, but they dismissed the idea. The Germans were going from door to door. Why would we be better off in some other Jew's house?

Since they only seemed to be killing the men, it was decided that I would go back to the vegetable patch with Fima. Jochil had gotten a temporary job through Father, and would go with him.

I was relieved that I didn't have to stay and confront boxer-face again, but I felt like a coward abandoning the women like that. I was especially worried about Mother.

As the adults continued talking, Fima and I slipped out and sat on the steps, which were becoming our favorite spot. We watched falling stars streaking through the sky and listened to the random rifle shots echoing from the ghetto perimeter.

"You know, Jabotinsky was right," Fima said. "There is only one way the Jews can survive in this Christian world. They have to arm themselves and live in their own country. Only when we fight back will they have respect for us. It is the way of force. That is the only language they understand."

I knew Fima's obsession with the Zionist cause, but I was not raised that way. In spite of everything, there was a big humanity out there in the world, and deep in my heart I believed the forces of good would eventually destroy the world of evil Hitler had created.

"Our way has been the way of the Torah and learning for too long," Fima insisted. "We have forgotten how to fight for our rights the way our forefathers did. Look at the Maccabees! They defeated enemies much more powerful than themselves. We have relied on God to help us for too long. God has been away on vacation for about two thousand years, leaving us to fend for ourselves.

"Let's make a promise. If by some miracle we survive this hell, we will go to Palestine. All right?"

My father had taught me well. The idea of Zionism was synonymous with nationalism in my mind, and nationalism was a constant source of strife and war. Besides, why should we retreat to a tiny strip of desert? It would be like a voluntary ghetto, as far as I was concerned.

But, to please Fima, I promised. We sat for a long time in silence, Fima thinking about Israel, me about Lena, each of us tortured by longing.

The next morning Fima and I left early. He told me that there were many boys who volunteered for the weeding brigade and we'd better be among the first. But when we arrived at the gate there were already twice as many as they needed.

First they picked those who worked there yesterday, including Fima, and then they added a few more of the older boys. I was left behind. Fima was very sorry that I couldn't come along, and even debated whether he shouldn't stay behind with me, but I talked him out of it.

Among the rejected workers I noticed a boy I'd known before the war. His name was Cooky Kopelman and he was about my age. He was a lanky boy with dark blond hair, a long neck, and intense blue eyes. He tended to stoop a little. Our parents knew each other, and his family once spent a week at our summer house in Kalautuvas. We got to know each other well then. His mother, Vera Shore, was a famous violinist, and his father was a well-known chess champion. Cooky took after them both. He was a junior champion in chess, a gifted violinist, and also a very good tap dancer. He was considered to be a child prodigy, and at the age of six was already earning quite a bit of money.

The summer the Kopelmans visited Kalautuvas, Cooky even taught Petras how to tap dance, so that Petras had both Yiddish songs and tap dancing in his repertoire.

I seldom saw Cooky after that, but he was something of a local celebrity and we often heard about him. There was even talk that Cooky had signed with a Hollywood producer.

Because his father was from Berlin and his mother was from Moscow, his parents constantly quarreled about which school Cooky should attend, and he attended many. He was as mixed-up as I was in this regard, and, like me, spoke several languages. For some reason we spoke Lithuanian to each other. Somehow it seemed the most natural.

I dreaded returning home to confront boxer-face again, and asked Cooky if he knew of some hiding place. Cooky suggested we go to his house. His father had improvised a hideout in the attic.

The Kopelmans shared the house with a young couple, some distant relatives, but everyone was at work that day. The house had a small kitchen and two tiny rooms that were barely furnished. The Lithuanian with whom they exchanged houses insisted that they leave everything behind, and he, in his magnanimity, left them his broken-down old furniture.

Behind one room was a narrow passage with a wooden ladder that led up to an opening in the ceiling. Cooky's father had moved a heavy wardrobe over the passage, and fixed the back panel of the wardrobe so that it could be easily removed and replaced. We tried it a few times, and managed to get in and hide in less than a minute. It was a makeshift hideaway, but it was better than nothing. We kept a sharp lookout for the Germans, as they usually came early in the morning.

I discovered, to my delight, that among the scanty belongings they managed to bring to the ghetto was an enormous box full of books. Cooky was apparently as crazy about books as I was. I even found two books that I had been seeking for a long time. They were the sequels to *The Mysterious Island*—*Captain Nemo* and *The Children of Captain Grant*.

I soon found myself completely absorbed in *Captain Nemo*. I was back in the last century, in a much friendlier place than the ghetto, and among the friends who inhabited the book and the wonderful mysterious island. After a while I was so oblivious that I didn't even hear the Germans shouting and cursing next door. Cooky nearly had to push me off the bench to rouse me.

We barely managed to get up to the attic when the Germans burst into the house. In our hurry to hide we got so nervous that we couldn't get the back panel of the wardrobe completely back into place. A small gap showed, but there was nothing we could do about it. All we could do was pray they didn't notice it.

The ceiling was constructed of wooden planks which were not completely even, and we could see the Germans through the cracks. We were so scared that we didn't dare even breathe. We were even afraid that they could hear our wildly beating hearts. To my great horror I recognized boxer-face among them, and on closer inspection I realized that these were the same four Germans who'd paid us a visit yesterday. I couldn't understand why they were in this part of the ghetto.

The Germans turned the place upside down, looking everywhere for hidden valuables. When one opened the doors of the wardrobe, we held our breath again.

The German pulled out some boxes and clothing and threw them on the floor. Then he began feeling around the shelves and tapping the walls. I knew that our final hour had struck.

Oddly enough it was boxer-face who saved us.

"We're wasting our time. There's nothing worth taking here. Let's go find some rich ones," he said, and stomped out of the house.

The one searching the wardrobe hesitated, but the other three were already out the door. He tossed something back into the wardrobe and followed the others out.

We stayed glued to the boards without moving or saying anything for a long time. We had taken an awful chance. We were only boys, and we might have been all right had we stuck it out downstairs. But if they found us hiding I'm sure they would have shot us.

We crouched there for what seemed like hours, straining to hear every noise. It was worse than the day before. There were threats, screams, shots fired, at first nearby, then farther away. We didn't dare move. Eventually, in the semidarkness of the attic, we dozed off. When we woke up it was dark outside. The Germans must have left the ghetto, because it was awfully quiet. We crept down the stairs, slid the panel aside, and slipped out. The house was a wreck. I helped Cooky put the few pieces of furniture back in place and we swept up some broken crockery before I left. As we said our good-byes Cooky gave me the two books by Jules Verne. I promised to bring him some of my books. We also agreed we would try to get into the weeding brigade again the next morning.

When I returned home I was astounded to learn that the Germans never showed up at our house. What a relief that Mother didn't have to go through what Miriam and Aunt Dobbe did.

I managed to get into the weeding brigade nearly every day for a week, and worked next to Fima. Many of the younger boys couldn't keep up with the hard labor in the fields and were left behind, making room for us older ones. Because of his slight build, Cooky never managed to get selected, although he came to the gate every day.

At the end of the first week boxer-face and his three goons showed up at our house again, but fortunately Miriam was out working at the airport and only Dobbe, Anushka, and my mother were there. They took some more porcelain and silver pieces that the women had deliberately put aside for them, so they wouldn't feel they had come for nothing. They slapped Mother and Anushka a few times, and gave Dobbe a black eye. Perhaps they were finally convinced that there was nothing more in the house, or perhaps boxer-face had raided so many houses by then he'd forgotten which was which. In any event they didn't come again. Not everyone fared as well.

I continued to visit the Greenblats when I could, but Lena seemed more wraithlike each time I saw her. It was as if some fever was burning her away from the inside. One evening as we sat on her steps she told me about her grandmother's death.

"She was ninety-two years old. I was five. I recall every little detail of the scene," Lena said softly. "She was lying in her big brass bed propped up by a pile of white pillows. We were all standing around her bed, the whole family. That was her last request, that all of us come. Her face was as white as the pillowcase, but her eyes were alive and she was smiling. She called everyone by name. When she called my name I started crying. I loved her so much. I didn't want her to die.

"'Don't cry little Lena,' she said to me. 'Don't cry. I am dying, but I am a lucky woman. I have all my loved ones around my bed and I feel no fear. I am dying contented.'

"Then tears came into her eyes too, and she said, 'I hope when your time comes you will be as lucky as I am now.'

"At the time I didn't understand what she meant. I was only five years old, for God's sake. . . ." Lena fell silent and stared up the darkened street for a moment. In the dim light from the house she looked gaunt.

"Perhaps the dying have the ability to foresee the future," she continued. "I certainly know what she meant now. We won't be dying with all our loved ones around a big brass bed. They'll shoot us down like rabid dogs.

"I don't want to die, Solly! Death is horrible . . . I feel it coming like a faceless evil, creeping up on us from the unknown. I wish I could be a believer. But all I see is a bottomless black pit." Her voice was rising as she spoke.

"Blackness, just blackness—I'll never feel the warmth of the sun again. I'll never hold my own baby in my arms. No more singing, no more dancing, no more sun, no more moon. . . ."

Then she jumped up and stretching her arms towards the sky she screamed, "I want to live. I want to live. Oh my God how much I want to live!"

Lena's desperate outburst released a flood of similar emotions in me. I felt that if I let go, I would do the same, just stand up and scream at the sky: "Hey God! Wake up there! Look what they are doing to your chosen people. They are murdering us, and you do nothing! Where are you? God of Abraham and Isaac, where are you?!"

But I remained where I sat, staring up at Lena in the gathering twilight. She was right. We were doomed. Yet a spark of hope must have glowed somewhere in my soul. It was irrational, against all odds, but it was there. Lena yearned for life with all her being, but that spark of hope had died in the mass grave of the five hundred intellectuals, somewhere near Panemune.

My eyes stayed dry, only my heart felt a terrible pain, a terrible loss. My Lena was slipping away.

The Germans continued their search for gold, terrorizing the ghetto, beating up women and children and murdering many men. They would show up in one part of the ghetto, and then suddenly in another, surprising the residents and leaving them paralyzed with fear. It went on for two weeks.

In the beginning the people tried to hide their valuables, but when the dead and wounded began to mount in numbers, many decided to get rid of them, just to end the nightmare. Many, however, clung to the idea that their future might depend upon having something of value and hid whatever they could.

The Germans were not satisfied with the money and valuables they managed to plunder, so Jordan, the ghetto commandant, issued a proclamation. The ghetto inmates were to bring all their money, gold, and jewels to a collection place by sunset the next day. Anyone who failed to do so would be shot, along with their families. But then he added another sentence: The neighbors of the offenders would be shot as well. This statement had a stunning effect.

It induced the fear of neighbor against neighbor. Many who had cooperated with each other and even hidden their valuables together now advised each other not to hide anything. Innocent people might be killed because of it. Some even threatened their neighbors with exposure if they didn't comply.

But most were conscientious people who were unwilling to put their families or neighbors at risk on their account. We were no exception.

Our first week in the ghetto, without the rest of us noticing, Father and Jochil had buried all our valuables beneath the house. The wooden structure stood on short stilts, so it was easy enough to crawl under there. Now we had to dig it all up again.

That night one could see many shadowy figures digging in various parts of the ghetto.

Our work in the weeding brigade was over, so I helped carry our things to the assembly point the next day. Except for a few items of sentimental value, Mother and Anushka were indifferent about the loss of all our possessions. Aunt Dobbe, however, cried when she had to part with her jewelry, which she had carried safely all the way to the Russian border and back. Miriam too was furious. She couldn't forget the shameful way she and her mother were treated.

Some of these things had been in the family for generations, handed down from mother to daughter, and from father to son. But two weeks of terror had turned them into a burden that we were anxious to be rid of.

It was the beginning of September, and the first signs of autumn were making their appearance. Hundreds of families were coming to the assembly points with their possessions. We saw gold and silver objects, jewelry and fur coats, works of art and foreign currency. Some people cried bitterly when they had to part with things given to them by their loved ones, many of whom were murdered by the Nazis. In the end, with very few exceptions, the whole Jewish population of the ghetto became destitute.

During these two weeks I went to the Greenblats several times to see how they were doing and to cheer up Lena, but she was getting more and more morose. We would sit on the steps and she wouldn't say a word. I tried my best to get her out of this mood, and once even suggested that I take her up on her offer and marry her. First she looked at me startled, then she finally smiled. It was the first time I'd seen her smile in the ghetto.

"It was a stupid idea, forget it. We're too young, although we may die soon. Anyway, the way I feel I wouldn't be good to you or anybody else."

We had both grown up in that short time. Before me was not the round-faced, cuddly, lovely young girl of my memory, but a gaunt, wild-eyed young woman. Perhaps she was even more beautiful in an adult sense, but the sense of adoration, the feeling of tender love I had for her had given way, changed as she had changed. When I looked at her now, what I felt was the deep and painful loss of my childhood.

One day I brought Cooky over. I thought since he wasn't working, perhaps he could spend some time with Lena. Mrs. Greenblat was afraid to leave her alone. Cooky put on his best charm for Lena. He even tap danced, to the great amusement of the rest of the family.

For the first time since her father was murdered I saw Lena show a flicker of interest. She liked Cooky, and in truth I felt a bit jealous because he did something for her that I couldn't do. But as she slowly began to stir from her lethargy, my jealousy was displaced by gratitude. I didn't even mind when I started finding him there every time I came to visit. He lived around the corner from their house, and since he wasn't able to get into the weeding brigade he spent a lot of time with her. He tried to interest her in books and told her jokes and stories about his family.

Once when the Germans shot one of their neighbors, Cooky got the whole family into his attic hideout. That evening Mrs. Greenblat gave me a kiss for bringing Cooky to them.

"The boy is a blessing, a true noble soul. Look how Lena has improved since he started coming here." And indeed, there was an improvement in Lena's behavior. She even ate all the carrots I brought her from Alexotas.

Then one day Cooky confessed to me that he had fallen in love with her. Of course, he assured me, there was nothing going on between them. He hadn't even kissed her. But he wanted me to know how he felt. To my surprise I was relieved. Lena was no longer the same girl who had been my childhood sweetheart.

I had just read Erich Maria Remarque's *Three Comrades,* in which two men and a woman were the greatest of friends. It was a wonderful book, and I loved the characters. The woman in the novel came to a tragic end, and I cried bitterly when I read that part. I felt that the newly formed emotional triangle between Lena, Cooky, and myself was like that of the characters in the novel.

I made both of them read the book, and Lena, Cooky, and I became the three comrades. At first, Lena was hurt at my suggestion. She felt that I was distancing myself from her by allowing Cooky into our relationship. But under Cooky's adoring influence she began to relent. We started reading passages of the book aloud, and playing out the parts. It brought Lena out of that terrible mood she was in and she even lost some of that haunted look.

One day I brought Lena's school friend Aviva with me. Lena was very happy to see her, but once again she showed signs of jealousy.

"Is she your girl now? You brought Cooky to me so you'd be free to take up with someone else?" she asked when we had a few minutes alone. She sounded very possessive.

"No, she is not my girlfriend. I thought you'd be glad to see her again, that's why I brought her," I said, annoyed.

Aviva, unexpectedly, turned out to be a great source for books. Her grandfather, who lived near them, owned many. Before the war he owned a foreign language bookstore in Kaunas, and when he moved to the ghetto, he brought some of his best stock. When Aviva told him about our "obsession" with books, he invited us to his room, a tiny attic that was crowded from floor to ceiling with books. He barely had space for a bed. He was a short man with a huge forehead, snow-white hair, and kind humorous eyes. Besides the classics we knew about, he had books by authors we had never heard of. There were books by Stefan Zweig, Jakov Wasserman, Kafka, Thomas Mann, and many others. He let us look at all of them, but told us to handle them very carefully.

His name was Chaim, and it was he who taught us how to really appreciate literature.

In the beginning he didn't quite trust us with his precious books, and would only allow us to read in his room, but when he grew to know us a little he would allow us to take them home for brief periods. After we'd all read something, he would explain and analyze the characters, the background, the hidden meanings and nuances, and every possible aspect of the book. His lectures were fascinating. It was as if all these years I'd been looking at a two-dimensional picture, and suddenly someone came along and showed me that it was actually three-dimensional.

Later he began giving us lectures on other subjects such as history, geography, political science, and Judaism. He loved to lecture, and in us he found an enthusiastic audience. Whenever the ghetto was shaken by a new trauma, he would patiently give us lessons from history or philosophy, trying to put things into perspective.

When endless stories of German victories in Russia threatened to destroy our morale, he gave us an account of Napoleon's Russian campaign. He described the humiliating defeat of the French forces in the vast lands and cruel winters there, and predicted a similar defeat for the Nazis. It was he who gave us hope that one day the loathsome Nazi empire would crumble into dust. When I came home and told my family his predictions, they would all shake their heads and call him a dreamer.

Things settled down a little after the valuables were turned over. Our food situation even improved somewhat. Fanny would bring in more food and so would Fima, who had gotten into a small brigade that worked in town. One of the brigade had been caught at the ghetto gate with a bag of potatoes and was so severely beaten that he couldn't work for a while. Fima took his place.

Uncle Jochil worked with Father in the supply department, and Aunt Anushka got a job with the Jewish Committee making up a list of available workers in the ghetto.

By the middle of September we had begun to settle into a regular routine. It seemed that at last the Germans might leave us alone. But on the fifteenth of the month Father came back from work very despondent.

He silently removed four pieces of paper from his pocket and handed them over to Mother. "I just received these certificates from the Committee. They will probably save our lives. They only issued five thousand of these certificates to the whole ghetto population!" he said bitterly.

As the significance of what he said sank in, a tremor ran through my body. I looked at the four certificates in awe.

Each said that the bearer of this certificate was a Jewish craftsman. They were signed by S.A. Hauptsturmfuehrer Jordan. The implications were stupefying. The five thousand bearers of these certificates were protected, but there were nearly thirty thousand Jews in the ghetto.

Then it struck me that Father only had four certificates. What about the others? Aunt Dobbe and Miriam looked deathly pale, but Father reassured them that Jochil also received four of the certificates. At that moment Aunt Anushka walked in, looking wan.

I realized that even though she now worked for the Jewish Committee, she didn't get a certificate from them. My heart contracted with grief. Unable to hold back, I fell into her arms, crying bitterly. Dear God, my beloved aunt was now condemned to death, and there was nothing we could do about it. For a moment I entertained the idea of offering her my certificate, but in truth I was terribly afraid of dying. I knew, too, that Anushka would never accept such a sacrifice.

She told us that a large mob broke into the Committee office demanding certificates, but all of them were already gone. I had no idea how Father obtained them for the four of us, but I felt terribly guilty. These certificates were issued for craftsmen, which none of us were.

Later that month we were given proof that the Jordan certificates could save lives.

8

Aunt Leena

SEPTEMBER 26–OCTOBER 4, 1941

The days went by, and the first signs of autumn appeared. We had a big scare when the Germans rounded up nearly all the people in what we called the small ghetto—a section across Paneriu Street. My Aunt Leena was among those put in trucks and sent off to the Ninth Fort. Inexplicably, the Germans then brought everyone back. Aunt Leena returned in a terrible state, but whenever anyone asked her what had taken place at the Ninth Fort, she denied she had ever been there. She seemed to have erased the whole experience from her mind.

Gradually everyone relaxed, and many concluded that we were needed by the Germans and were too valuable as slave labor to be destroyed.

Those without Jordan Passes felt more vulnerable than the rest. I felt less pressure than Cooky did. He, Lena, and Chaim had no passes, and Cooky always seemed to be looking for a job. I was driven more by hunger than by an immediate sense of threat. From time to time, when shipments of potatoes would arrive in the ghetto, Father would get me a job sorting them out. My wages were paid in potatoes, which were a welcome addition to our household food supply.

Such jobs were only temporary, however, and not very frequent. I spent a great deal of time reading books or meeting with Cooky and Lena.

I also met with Petras, who showed up as promised at the

"Lithuania," which was less closely guarded than most of the perimeter. We scheduled our meetings in the evening, at twilight. The Germans would only light the lamps along the fence when it was completely dark, apparently to save electricity. I used an iron ladder that led up to the roof of the cinema; from there I had a much better view of the area. When I gave a low whistle as an all-clear, Petras emerged from the shadows and darted to the fence. I climbed down and we crouched together against the wall of the theatre. Petras brought a bundle of food, which he shoved through the wires of the fence.

After he left I remained huddled in the shadows for a moment, watching him scuttle down the road in the gathering dusk, headed toward our old apartment and freedom. Once again I envied him, but it was envy tempered by admiration. He placed himself at risk for our sakes. I giggled when I thought of Petras dropping his pants in front of the stupid Lithuanian guards. He had saved Father when we moved into the ghetto, and his quick wits had saved Ronnie as well.

Toward the end of the month Cooky and I decided to visit Lena. We had to get back a book that she borrowed from Chaim. Chaim was fussy about his books, and very strict about the number of days he would allow us to keep them. Lena had kept the book two days longer than he permitted, and he was very annoyed.

Cooky and I walked up Linkuvos Street where the Greenblats lived and were almost at the house when a truck full of Lithuanian guards drove up. They spread out over several blocks and barred our way to the Greenblat's house.

Mrs. Greenblat, who was standing on the steps, waved to us, but the soldiers pushed us back. Looking behind us we saw German soldiers and Lithuanians driving everyone out of their houses.

Terrified, I rushed up to a young Lithuanian guard who was standing before Lena's house. In Lithuanian I told him that we lived in this house and that Mrs. Greenblat was our mother.

When I went up to him he raised his rifle as if to hit me with the butt, but when he heard my perfect Lithuanian, he looked at us with some surprise. Cooky, who looked more Lithuanian than Jewish, began pleading with him to let us through to our home.

"Are you Jewish? You don't look like a Jew or sound like one. What the hell are you doing in the ghetto?" the guard looked at him suspiciously.

"My mother is Jewish and my father is Lithuanian, Sir. Please, please, let us through, Sir. We don't belong on this side of the ghetto, we belong on the other side," Cooky pleaded.

The Lithuanian was about eighteen years old, with a sparse blond mustache and baby blue eyes. As in so many instances our fate depended on his whims. We were to live or die at his pleasure.

"Well, if you live in this house, you really don't belong on this side, so go ahead," he mumbled, scratching his chin. Even before he ended the sentence we ran past him and slipped into Lena's house.

Before we slammed the door we heard him shout after us: "And don't you let me catch you again, you hear!"

Frightened to death, we nevertheless started laughing hysterically. How many times had we heard that sentence? How many times when we were out stealing fruit from an orchard or picking berries from along a neighbor's fence?

Mrs. Greenblat, pale as a ghost, pulled us inside the room where Rachel, Vova, and Lena sat huddled together on the sofa.

"Why are you laughing like lunatics? What's going on? Why are they after those people? Are we next in line? Perhaps we should go and hide in Cooky's hideout?" Mrs. Greenblat asked, all in one breath.

We told her we had no idea what was going on, but whatever it was, it was bad for the people on the other side of Linkuvos Street.

We thought her idea of going to Cooky's hideout was a good one, but when we opened the door ever so slightly, the Germans and Lithuanians were practically at the doorstep. There was no way we could get out of the house unseen. Hundreds of men, women, and children were being beaten and herded into the waiting trucks. There was nothing to be done. We had to wait until the action was over.

We sat in tense silence, listening to screaming women and children and the guttural orders of the Germans. From time to time a shot was fired, followed by louder screams. Every minute seemed like an eternity. Lena covered her ears and began nervously pacing the room. Suddenly we heard a rapid knocking at the window. I cautiously looked out and saw a little girl of about six looking straight at me. Lena, who was standing right behind me with a horrified look on her face, saw her too. "It's Havale, our neighbor's daughter," she whispered.

"Let me in, Lena, please let me in," Havale cried.

Before we could even rise to go to the door two Germans came after her. They were cursing her and calling her a "little Jewish bitch."

Seeing the Germans coming I dropped to the floor and dragged Lena down with me. I didn't want them to see us. I peeked over the sill and saw one of the Germans pulling Havale along the street by her hair. Then the other one took her by the arm, and swinging her over his head like a sack of potatoes, hurled her inside the truck.

In the beginning Lena fought me and begged me to let her go. She wanted to run after the Germans to get Havale back, but then she went limp in my arms and began sobbing quietly. "I can't take it anymore, I just want to die, and get it over with."

I stroked her hair and kissed her hands and tried to calm her down, but we were all crying with her.

Finally it was over. The last trucks rumbled away with their human cargo, and there was silence. The silence of the grave.

We waited a while longer and then cautiously opened the door. The street seemed deserted. We all hugged and kissed and Mrs. Greenblat said the "Gomel," a blessing said by Jews who escape sudden death.

Knowing how anxious my parents would be—by now they must have heard of the action in this part of the ghetto—I hastily said good-bye.

At the door I asked Lena for Chaim's overdue book. For a moment she looked at me in confusion, then she turned around and went to get it. When she came back she threw the book at me and screamed: "Here, take your precious book! I bet when we're all dead you'll still be around reading your damned books!"

How could I have been so insensitive to the tragedy that had just played out before our eyes? I don't know. I can't remember what Cooky said or did after Havale rapped on that window, but I remember Lena's accusation vividly.

In years to come, in the worst of times, I always remembered Lena's words. Indirectly she implied that I was insensitive, but a survivor. She made me feel guilty, but strangely, she also encouraged me to go on, against all odds. Her words would prove to be prophetic.

When I returned home Mother was already hysterical with worry. Everyone knew by then that an action was taking place in a part of the ghetto near Lena's house.

The next day the Germans informed the Jewish Committee that the action of September 26 took place as a reprisal. The Germans claimed that someone in that area—a section of Linkuvos, Messininku, and Veliunos Streets—shot at the chief of the ghetto guards. For that a thousand Jews paid with their lives. Once again, those who had a Jordan certificate were allowed to live. From that day on we all carried our Jordan certificates with us wherever we went.

The next day the entire ghetto mourned. The brigade of the five hundred "learned men" had disappeared under a veil of German lies, but this time a thousand elderly men, women, and small children had been hauled out of their homes and murdered. Many still couldn't believe that the Germans would carry out such a mass execution, so when a rumor that these people were seen at a camp somewhere in Lithuania reached the ghetto, many chose to believe it. Later we found out that spreading such rumors was a deliberate Gestapo tactic, designed to pacify the population and keep them manageable for the next liquidation.

After the incident at the Greenblats, I felt uneasy about facing Lena again and stayed away for a few days. I tried to analyze myself objectively. Were her accusations correct? But who can be objective about oneself? I had to admit that I showed a lack of sensitivity. How could I be thinking about the book so soon after seeing poor Havale thrown into the truck?

There were vague and unsatisfactory answers in my mind, but finally it was thinking about Aunt Leena that gave me some insight into my behavior. I remembered feeling an almost unbearable anguish when I saw Havale's face in the window and heard her cry for help. I felt my mind might snap. Like Aunt Leena I had to make it all disappear. I had to go back in time, back to ordinary daily life, and I said the first mundane thing that came to my mind—I asked her for the book.

The next few days I spent many hours with Chaim. Aviva and Cooky would come along and we would listen to classical music Chaim played on an old gramophone. Because of the book incident, Lena was angry with Chaim and me and stayed away.

While the music played, Chaim would sit in his old rocking chair with his eyes closed, an expression of bliss on his face. Aviva and Cooky were also enthralled.

"Music is the most enriching and rewarding of all the human arts," the old man would say, "greater even than literature. It's the only art form in which a group of human beings can achieve almost total unison."

Chaim helped me appreciate music much more than I had before. I understood what he was trying to say, but books still remained my greatest pleasure. They helped make a terror-filled world a little more bearable.

Cooky was fascinated by the old man. To him, Chaim was the epitome of wisdom, a master of the arts. He appreciated what the old man said about music, because he himself was a violinist. More and more often Cooky would come to Chaim for personal advice, and Chaim responded readily. When Cooky told him about the incident with Havale at Lena's house, tears came to Chaim's eyes. He understood my emotional state and also the reason I asked for the book.

"What you witnessed was so terrible that your conscious mind simply rejected it. You were desperate to get back to life," he said.

I was astounded that he could so easily explain something that took me days to figure out. The next day Cooky brought Lena to Chaim's house, and in my presence explained to her the reason for my seeming insensitivity.

Lena listened to him, and when he finished, she came over and gave me a hug and kiss. Then she cried a little and we hugged some more.

"So the three comrades are together again. Good," Chaim smiled.

The next morning, a Saturday, Father had some official business at the hospital, and he invited me to come along. I would get to see my Aunt Leena, and there was work I could do, helping Father, for some soup and potatoes. Since Father wanted to finish early, we left the house well before six. It was October 4, 1941. The chill in the air was the first sign of the coming winter.

When we approached the bridge into the small ghetto we heard shooting in the area. We had almost gotten used to hearing shooting from the fences, but that morning there was more than usual. Father hesitated before we crossed over.

"Perhaps you should go back. I don't like the sound of this. I have to go. You don't," he said.

"No, if you're going, I'm going too," I said firmly.

As we crossed the bridge the shooting tapered off. Everything seemed to grow quiet. Then trucks began moving down Paneriu, and

German soldiers and Lithuanian partisans fanned out around the fences. Suddenly, on the bridge behind us, two Germans carrying a heavy machine gun took up position.

We had walked into a trap. There was nothing to do but proceed to the hospital. Along the side streets we could see groups of soldiers going from house to house, chasing people out into the street.

The hospital was a group of several buildings housing surgery, maternity, and children's wards, and the unit for contagious diseases, where Aunt Leena worked. Not knowing what else to do, we headed for her building, but were stopped by a German officer. Father tried to explain to him that he came to the hospital on official business, but the German only shouted "Halt die Schnauze! (Shut your trap!)"

He then pushed us together with a group of men. Shovels were produced, and the officer told us to begin digging a trench. Father became ashen pale. We all knew what that meant. But when the German showed us the size of pit we were to dig, we realized that it was much bigger than necessary for our group of ten. For whom was this grave being prepared, we asked ourselves. The Lithuanians guarding us began shouting and beating on us to hurry us up. Father received a blow to the face, lost his glasses, and began bleeding from his nose and mouth. Without his glasses he was nearly blind.

One of the Lithuanians approached and was about to step on them, but I dove to the ground and scooped them up. For my dexterity I was kicked in the rear so hard I was almost lifted off the ground, but he let me keep the glasses.

The German officer came back and was annoyed.

"How do you expect them to finish digging if you keep beating them up?" he said to the partisans. "Perhaps you want to finish the job yourself? Eh?"

After that the Lithuanians left us alone. I gave Father his glasses and he thanked me. There were tears in his eyes.

He spoke quietly over the scraping of our shovels. "If only I had kept my mouth shut, you would have been safe. What caused me to bring you out here, for God's sake?" he kept repeating.

I bent to my work, unable to think of anything to say. I didn't want to worry him, but I was sure that they were doing the same thing in the big ghetto. Nobody was safe from these murderers.

The people being dragged from their homes were marched off to a nearby square, where they were divided into rows. Suddenly one of the soldiers encircling Leena's building began shouting at someone running toward the entrance. "Halt! No one goes in or out of this hospital!"

"My wife is in there! I want to be with my wife! Leena! Leena!" the man was shouting.

With a shock I realized that it was Uncle Jacob. When he reached the door, the German unholstered his pistol and shot him in the back. Uncle Jacob spun around, facing the soldier, and took a few steps toward him. Then his knees buckled and he collapsed on the ground.

Almost immediately the door opened and Aunt Leena came rushing out. She dropped to her knees next to Uncle Jacob's body.

"That is my husband, please, don't harm him. That is my husband!" Aunt Leena cried out in anguish. The German, who had lifted his pistol to shoot her as well, lowered it. A sarcastic grin spread across his face.

"All right, then, take your husband back into the hospital. Perhaps you can cure him there," he told her.

Aunt Leena began dragging Jacob, begging him to get up.

"Jacob, get up darling, please get up. I haven't got the strength to drag you."

The whole incident happened so fast that my brain couldn't grasp what my eyes saw. I watched it all in shock, as if it were happening to strangers.

I remember thinking, "So this is death?" One moment Uncle Jacob was an animated figure, the next he was dead. He didn't seem to feel any pain as he fell. There was no pain or horror reflected in his eyes, only surprise and confusion. At that moment, death didn't seem so terrible.

Father must have felt the same, because he suddenly stepped out of the dugout and approached the German. "Sir. May I help the lady? She is my sister-in-law."

I quickly joined Father and said, "I want to help too. She is my aunt."

The German stared at me, and then again at Father, obviously startled by our insolence. My fear was gone, and somehow I felt free. I knew that we were going to die. We might as well die with some dignity, I thought. I felt strange, almost as if I were drunk.

Father looked at me and I saw pride in his eyes. I could almost hear him saying he was proud of me, that he had raised his son well.

For a moment the German balanced his pistol in his hand, appraising us. I thought I detected a tiny spark of admiration in his eyes. The Nazis drummed it into their heads that the Jews were gutless sheep, and here were a father and son who showed courage at gunpoint.

"Go on, shoot us and get it over with," I thought to myself. Strangely enough, I felt nothing. Only a certain numbness and a sense of the unreal, as if I were already dead and observing myself from somewhere over my head.

But the German had other plans for us. He gave us a curt nod and motioned us ahead with his pistol.

Aunt Leena was still tugging at Jacob's body, talking to him, oblivious to her surroundings and our presence.

Father got hold of Jacob's legs and I took his right arm. Together we managed to lift him off the ground.

"I told him not to drink so much vodka, now we have to carry him home," Aunt Leena smiled at me. She seemed to be blushing. "But you are a good boy, Solly. You understand that sometimes a man has the right to get drunk." Her mind seemed to have snapped completely. In a way I was glad for her.

Once we got inside the doors two doctors in white coats immediately examined Uncle Jacob, but the bullet had pierced his heart. He was dead before he hit the ground, one of them said.

"At least he didn't suffer. I hope my death will be as easy," he added nervously.

We wanted to stay with Aunt Leena. Somehow it seemed safer inside. Surely, I thought, hospitals are internationally protected by the Red Cross. But the German officer ordered us back out to the pit.

After another hour of work, when we were almost hip-deep, two more officers joined the one who shot Uncle Jacob. One of them was a higher ranking officer and seemed to be in charge.

"We are behind schedule," he said, looking at his watch. "Lock the place up and burn it. We can't afford the spread of infectious diseases."

For a moment we didn't grasp the significance of the order. We thought he meant to evacuate the sick people and the personnel first. But we were shocked into reality when the Lithuanians and Germans surrounded the wooden building and began barring the doors from the outside. Several machine guns were placed around it, and the Lithuanians began pouring gasoline around the base.

Stunned, I felt barely able to move, but I kept scraping and lifting my spade, tossing out a few crumbs of earth at a time. Surely they wouldn't set the building on fire, with the sick, the doctors and nurses still inside? Surely, even the Nazis were incapable of such barbarism?

Then the officer who shot uncle Jacob came over to the trench and singled out two elderly men. He told them to come out of the trench and handed them over to several Lithuanians.

"Throw them inside. They are useless."

The two men fell to the ground and began begging for their lives, but they were only answered with blows. Then they were dragged over to the one remaining entrance, and heaved inside.

Meanwhile the German was looking the rest of us over. Except for Father and me the rest of the diggers were men in their twenties and thirties. I shook off my fright and started tearing at the earth with my spade, but it was too late. When he stopped before us, his legs spread apart, I froze again, staring at his pressed pants and glossy black boots as if hypnotized.

"The two of you, cavaliers in shining armor, it is time to join your Aunt Leena." He even remembered her name! Silently, as if in a daze, Father began climbing out of the trench. Suddenly my instinct for self-preservation came flooding back.

"Sir, please Sir, we have certificates issued by S.A. Hauptsturm-fuehrer Jordan," I cried, whipping out my paper. Father gave me a startled look. There was pity, but also hopelessness in his eyes. He thought that I was grasping for straws, and no certificates in the world were going to save us.

Again the German seemed astonished at such impudence. Then his green cat's eyes narrowed as he looked at the document. I was afraid he would tear it up, but he seemed to think better of it. Orders were orders. Where would the Nazis have been without their fanatical obedience to orders?

After looking at Father's certificate as well, he told us to remain where we were. Father fell back into the trench and crumpled to his knees, almost passing out from relief.

I remained standing, barely. My legs were trembling and my heart was beating wildly. I thought I could feel the blood surging through my whole body, and it felt good. However temporary the reprieve was, I had saved both of us from a horrible death.

Even as I thought this, and even as the Germans poured can after can of gasoline along the foundation of the building, I was telling myself that this wasn't really happening.

Several torches were lit and thrown before our horrified eyes, the gasoline exploding with loud thumps. Blue flames began to shoot up along the building's dry timbers.

At first all we heard was the roar of the flames as they ate their way through the wood. Then we began to hear the terrible shrieks and almost inhuman cries of those inside. That blood-curdling sound will remain branded in my soul forever.

Several of the doctors and nurses tried to break out through the windows, but were cut down by a hail of fire from the machine guns. They were the lucky ones.

At some point I thought I saw a figure in a white dress through one of the upper windows. I was sure that it was Aunt Leena, but soon she disappeared from view as other windows shattered and a thick black smoke poured out of every opening, enveloping the whole building. The fire spread so rapidly that soon the entire structure was a roaring torch.

The heat became so intense that we all crouched below the rim of the trench, and the Germans and the Lithuanians hastily drew back.

I thought I was inured by the murders I had already seen, but this act of barbarism shattered me completely. I covered my ears, unable to shut out the horrible screams emanating from the building, and fell to the bottom of the trench sobbing. I couldn't stop. I decided that I would not rise. I would let the Germans shoot me right then and there.

It was one of the few times during the war that I lost all hope and really wanted to die. There were many ways to die, and I knew I would rather die from a quick bullet than be burned alive.

Within a short time the beams in the building began to give way. First one section, then another collapsed with a great roar, sending waves of heat and smoke roiling across the pit. We heard no more screams, but the smell of roasted flesh began to rise from the conflagration. Many of our crew became sick.

Even the Germans and Lithuanians stood in silence. No one was laughing or talking. Many of them pulled out handkerchiefs and covered their noses. Perhaps even they realized the enormity of what they had done.

Our tribulations were not over yet. We didn't believe that this was the end of the action, and soon we saw that we were right. Long columns of Jews were marching past us on the way to the gate. Many women with children, elderly men, and handicapped people were among them. They were marched out onto the road leading to the Ninth Fort. When they realized where they were headed many tried to run, but they were beaten severely and forced to rejoin the ranks.

The diggers stood quietly by the flaming ruins of the contagious disease unit, waiting for the Germans to decide our fate. No one had any doubt that it would be our turn next.

The sun had emerged from behind the clouds, and as I watched the sky a flock of birds took off from a nearby field and flew south. I followed them with my eyes until they became mere dots and then disappeared. How I envied those birds! What I wouldn't give to be one of them.

A German messenger on a motorcycle arrived and handed the officer in charge a dispatch.

"All right, you lot! It's time for you to earn your living!" the German officer barked at us after reading the note. We were marched off toward the surgical unit. Several trucks drove up to the entrance, and we helped load many patients into the trucks. Some who were carried out on stretchers begged us to let them die in their beds. They'd recently had surgery and every movement caused them excruciating pain. It was terrible to watch them suffer. When it seemed that just about everyone had been cleared out, the doors were locked again and the trucks drove up the hill to the Ninth Fort.

Our next job was to move the elderly from the old people's home. They hardly had any strength to protest; their teeth were chattering and their eyes were full of fear. They too were loaded onto trucks and dispatched to their deaths.

The most heartbreaking job was to move the orphans out of the children's ward. Little children with shaved heads led by older ones, young boys and girls whose parents were murdered by the Nazis, holding on to each other, making strange noises. Many of them, out of fear, wet their pants, as their teachers and caretakers led them on their last walk on earth. And why and for what? What had they ever done to deserve such a fate? Even hearts of stone would melt at the pitiful sight of these children, but the hearts of the Germans and the Lithuanians were harder than stone. There were more than two hundred of them, and about ten teachers and caretakers. They were all loaded onto trucks and sent away. Our hearts were breaking and we couldn't hold back our tears as we silently handed them up.

It was late in the afternoon before the last group was sent to the Ninth Fort. By then we were physically and mentally exhausted. Father could barely move, and was helped by two young men who had worked beside us since the morning. All the houses in the small ghetto were empty now. The few Jews who had not been shipped out were now congregated near the bridge.

Finally the German officer approached our group. Because of our hard work and good behavior, he said, we would be allowed to return to the big ghetto. We could hardly believe our ears. We were reprieved! We didn't know for how long, but for the moment that was irrelevant. Until then we had no idea what was taking place in the rest of the ghetto. Now we understood that the big ghetto still existed. God willing, our loved ones were safe.

I took a final look at that German officer, the man who had orchestrated the events of that day. He stood with his hands on his hips observing us coldly as we made our way to the Paneriu Bridge.

A shudder went through my body when I remembered how he calmly pulled out his pistol and shot Uncle Jacob in the back, how unemotionally he gave the orders to set the hospital on fire, how showing him a stupid piece of paper signed by another murderer had saved our lives.

When I closed my eyes I could still see Aunt Leena standing in that window.

Finally the word was given for our release. Hundreds of people, "the chosen ones" as we were called, began pushing across the narrow bridge. Each one was eager to escape this place of death, many leaving their loved ones behind in the ashes of the hospital or among the condemned at the Ninth Fort. Behind us we heard shooting.

The bridge was too narrow to accommodate such a surge of people, and it threatened to become a stampede, but somehow our group held together as a crowd of Lithuanians descended on us with sticks.

When we finally made it across the bridge it seemed like half the ghetto was at the fence, searching for surviving relatives. There were heartrending scenes as men found out that their wives and children had been taken. I felt dazed as we turned toward home, shouldering our way through the crowd. Then we heard Mother and Fanny calling our names.

We fell into each others' arms, hugging and kissing and crying. Then Anushka and the rest of the family, who had been searching the crowd as well, joined us.

"You see, I told you they would survive," Anushka kept repeating with tears running down her face.

"So where are Jacob and Leena?" Jochil asked.

"Yes, where are they?" Anushka repeated anxiously.

I looked away, unable to meet their eyes. Father, too, remained silent, his head lowered. Mother immediately understood the meaning of our silence.

"My goodness, look at them," she said. "They must be exhausted! Are we going to keep them standing here all night? We can talk at home."

But Anushka wouldn't be put off.

"They are alive, aren't they?" she cried. "Tell us they are alive," she demanded. "Please!"

Father then reached for her, and wrapping his arms around her he broke down in terrible sobs. The accumulated tension of the day erupted in him like a volcano.

We all cried with him. A great, eerie groan seemed to go up all around us, and I realized that hundreds of people who had lost their families in the small ghetto were weeping too.

The next few days were spent in mourning. One by one we were visited by other family members as they learned of Jacob and Leena's deaths. A black despair descended over the entire ghetto. About two thousand people had been sent to their deaths. The rest of us realized it was only a matter of time before we went the same way.

We didn't tell the family the details of Leena and Jacob's death, except that Jacob died painlessly and was unaware that he was about to die. About Aunt Leena we said nothing.

"How did we ever come to this?" Cooky cried one day. We had all gathered at Chaim's to exchange some books and discuss the situation.

"How could we have provoked the wrath and hatred of all of Europe? What have we ever done to come to the point that a madman like Hitler can decide one day to annihilate us, and the whole Christian world just ignores it? It simply doesn't make any sense."

We felt we could discuss any subject on earth with Chaim and he would know the answer. "On the contrary, it makes very much sense," Chaim replied. "How does it happen that a man like Hitler and his gang hate the Jews so much? Many will tell you that we're just a convenient scapegoat, but that's not true. They really hate us, passionately and mercilessly. And it stems from the fact that endless generations of Christians were brainwashed to hate us by the Christian churches.

"From the very beginning of Christianity they saw in the Jewish religion a rival that could undermine their hold on the masses of Rome and its empire.

"Later, when the Nicaeans completed the New Testament they added hundreds of anti-Semitic passages, describing the Jews as vile and greedy creatures responsible for the death of Christ, the son of God. They identified the Jews with Judas, who sold Christ for thirty pieces of silver. This was done in the early days to discredit the Jews, so that the pagans would turn away from Judaism and adopt Christianity. Of course, if the Apostles, who were Jews themselves, had known to what their teachings would lead, I'm sure they would have turned away from that propaganda in horror."

Several days had passed since the action at the small ghetto. With the echo of the machine guns at the Ninth Fort still ringing in our ears, everyone had gone back to their daily routines. Life must go on, everyone said. Surprisingly enough, with all the widowed workers and broken families, there were hardly any suicides.

Lena was horrified. "We've turned into beasts! How can we go on living as if nothing happened? Get up in the morning, go to work, eat, drink, laugh, sing. Yes, I actually heard our neighbors laugh and sing this morning, and they lost their parents!" she said in an outraged voice.

Lena seemed to have become our voice of conscience. It seemed impossible to go on living without developing some immunity to the raw horrors around us, but she seemed to lack even the slightest ability to shield her feelings.

Chaim looked at her with compassion, and my heart went out to her.

Once again I had been insensitive. I had described everything that happened in the small ghetto, and I was sorry I had done so, especially in the presence of Lena. They were all shocked to hear the details of what happened there. Chaim, Cooky, Aviva, they all looked at me with horrified eyes, as if what I told them couldn't possibly have happened. Lena broke down and wept. Yet they'd all seen the columns of people being led to the fort and heard the distant firing of machine guns. What did they imagine was going on? It was only after I told them the details that they seemed to feel the full emotional impact of what had happened. By their horrified reactions I felt that perhaps I'd gone too far.

Another week passed, and the day approached when I was to meet Petras again. He was supposed to wait across the road from the "Lithuania" until I gave him the signal. As dusk began to fall I made my way to the cinema and climbed up to my perch on the roof. I waited there until the guard moved well away, then gave a low whistle. No answer. I held my breath as the guard headed back my way. When he was again beyond earshot, I whistled once more. Soon the lights would come on around the fence, and then it would be too dangerous to come near it.

I whistled one last time, my heart sinking. Even though things had remained quiet for a while, and the food situation had improved a little, Petras's supplies were eagerly anticipated. There was never any surplus, and no one knew what the next day might bring.

I was about to give up when I finally heard a low whistle from the other side. Petras. The guard was now at the furthest point on his beat. In the semidarkness I saw Petras streak across the street. He swung the bag of food twice around his head and let it sail over the fence, then darted back into the shadows. I carefully scanned the ground until I spotted the bag, then climbed down the ladder at full speed. In the meantime the guard had returned. I flattened myself by the theatre entrance and sweated it out.

When he reached the spot where he usually turned and marched back the other way, he lowered his rifle and groped around in his pocket, then pulled out a cigarette. Standing not far from where I was lying, he leaned against a fence post, lit his cigarette and blew a few leisurely smoke rings.

I cursed him. I cursed his family and his ancestors that he had to stop and smoke when I was about to retrieve that bag. Precious minutes passed before he finally shouldered his rifle and moved on.

When he was about halfway down his beat, I dared not wait any longer. It was dark now and the lights would come on any minute. I moved as quickly and as quietly as I could. I had the bag in my hands when the lights flared on. I froze. The guard, who must have heard something, turned around and raised his gun. I was standing right beneath the lamp, and he could see me clearly.

I didn't even have time to think of death. I just stood there unable to move, with no thought at all in my head. An eternity seemed to pass, yet the guard simply stood there with his rifle raised and me in his sights. Finally, keeping the gun pointed in my direction, he approached.

"Any cigarettes in that bag? If there are, you win your life. If there aren't, you are dead."

I closed my eyes and waited to die. I knew that there weren't any cigarettes in the bag. Why should Petras put cigarettes in that bag?

"Well? I haven't got all night." I heard the click of the safety catch. I turned the bag upside down, dumping out the contents. Three loaves of bread and some carrots fell out, but as I expected, no cigarettes. I looked at the guard helplessly.

"Looks like you won your life, boy. Hand over the cigarettes and get out of here."

I stared again at the pile on the ground to see where these cigarettes were, but there weren't any. Suddenly the guard laughed and took the pack out of his pocket.

"You see, here they are. Now get out of here before I change my mind." He shouldered his rifle, and without giving me another look returned to his rounds.

"A miracle! A decent Lithuanian partisan," I thought, quickly scooping the bread and carrots off the ground. My hands were shaking violently as I stuffed the food into the bag. It was only then that I noticed a slip of paper with the bread. A note from Petras. I shoved it in the bag, and ran.

I did not stop until I was several streets away. I had to move close to a lighted window to read Petras's note, and when I did I didn't know whether to laugh or cry.

"Solly, I'm sorry that I couldn't bring any butter or bacon. I'll try to get some for you next time. Don't worry about the guard. I know him and he said he'll 'close his eyes' when you pick up the food. I bribed him with some cigarettes."

The son of a bitch! And I thought I had discovered a decent partisan. It was all a sadistic joke. It was just a game to them. Well, if it was a game, I too would learn to play.

9

The Big Action

Shortly before the small ghetto was liquidated, the Germans stepped up their demand for workers. A thousand men from the ghetto were to report for work every day at the airport. It stood to reason that the Alexotas airfield was of particular interest to our captors. The Germans had nearly demolished it during the invasion, and now they wanted it for the Luftwaffe.

Jordan's insistence that the Jews could save themselves through work was taken to heart by nearly everyone, but work at the airport was backbreaking. Workers had to hack at the ruined tarmac with picks and shovels, and break new ground where the Germans wanted to extend the runways. The shifts went on for twelve hours, and the German overseers drove the men mercilessly. Only the young and strong could stand up under such abuse. Often the crews had to be conscripted—which meant dragging men out of the streets or from their homes—in order to fill the quotas. Despite all this, many of those without Jordan Passes viewed the airport brigade as a way to prove their value to the Germans.

Isaac Trotsky was one of those forced to show up daily for the airport brigade, and he was not holding up well. His wife Dora was my mother's cousin.

In exchange for some soup and slices of bread, I agreed to take Uncle Isaac's place at the airport one day, to give him a rest. He had been singled out by the overseer, and suffered many beatings. Aunt Dora begged me to take his place so he might recuperate. It was terrible work, much worse than the weeding brigade, and when Isaac came a second time to ask me to substitute, I was very reluctant to go. Cooky had no Jordan Pass, and he was always looking for work. Although I told him how awful the job was, he thought that the airport would be at the top of the list of German priorities. They would spare their most important laborers, he said.

It was late on a Saturday afternoon when I took Cooky to the Trotskys' to discuss the airport job. We had been at Chaim's, and since Lena lived not far from the Trotskys, we accompanied her home. She was very low, and as we walked in the gathering dusk we tried to cheer her up.

"Why the long face Lena? The three comrades should never be sad when they are together," Cooky said with forced gaiety. "Your mother has a good job, and so does Rachel," he pointed out.

Cooky gave Lena a nudge, and when she looked away he jumped in front of her and started tap dancing in the dirt. He went tumbling head over heels in the rutted road, and he looked so comical I started laughing. Lena couldn't keep a straight face either, and when she started to giggle Cooky sat up, smiling from ear to ear. Then he jumped up, grabbed Lena in his arms and planted a loud smacking kiss on her forehead.

"You're covered with sand, you beast. Look what you've done!" she cried, shoving him away. Then we both began to brush her down with our hands, patting her here and there in fun.

"Get your hands off me! I can do my own brushing, thank you!" Lena shouted, but by then she was laughing out loud. She was in a much better mood by the time we reached her house. We promised to come and see her the next evening when Cooky returned from work.

"What would I do without you, you two clowns," Lena said with a sigh, giving each one of us a kiss.

When we arrived at the Trotskys' we found out that Isaac was given a day's leave, but he pleaded for Cooky to take his place on Monday. Cooky had screwed up his courage to go the next day, and he was hungry for the rations he was to receive in payment. Now he had to wait. Then Dora produced a bowl of soup with a piece of bread as a bonus, and Cooky agreed.

In the morning I went to work with Father in the supply department. A shipment of potatoes had come in and they needed sorting. During the break Father came in and together we lined up for our soup. He seemed to be very upset, and I waited for him to tell me what was troubling him.

The harrowing experience in the small ghetto had brought us closer together. We developed a certain comradeship that we hadn't had before, and he began to consult me as an adult.

"That butcher Rauca is here and he's been inspecting the ghetto together with another high ranking officer. He brought some new orders for the *Aeltestenrat* which are very disturbing."

Rauca, the officer who let Fima and I leave the "learned brigade," was the Gestapo officer in charge of Jewish affairs. It was he who had given the orders for all the previous actions in the ghetto, and he consistently acted with duplicity and deceit.

"It looks bad," Father continued. "Rauca announced that the Germans have decided to separate the working population from the non-working one. The non-workers will be housed in the small ghetto, while the workers and their families will remain in the main ghetto. They say they want to give the workers additional food rations so that they can produce more."

I felt chilled. For us the small ghetto was synonymous with the grave.

"Rauca has demanded that the entire Jewish population assemble for roll call on Tuesday, at Demokratu Square." This was the largest field within the boundaries of the ghetto.

"It sounds very bad. I'm going over to the Committee building to talk to Dr. Elkes. I want to find out what is happening," Father said with a sigh.

He returned later in the afternoon, his face drawn. The Committee had gotten nowhere with Rauca. There were to be no exceptions, he said. Everyone, including the sick and the invalids, had to assemble at Demokratu square at six A.M., October 28. On that day no one would be allowed to leave the ghetto. All the doors of the houses were to remain open, and anyone found indoors would be shot.

The story of Rauca's visit to the Committee spread like wildfire. Everyone seemed to know the gist of his instructions before any official announcement was made. Worse yet were the recent rumors that mass graves were being prepared at the Ninth Fort.

The members of the Jewish Committee were now in a dilemma. Given Rauca's reputation and the rumors about the Ninth Fort, no

one really believed that all he wanted was to change the food distribution. The Committee feared the worst. The question was whether to
obey Rauca's instructions and inform the ghetto, or to refuse and
suffer the consequences. Dr. Elkes had no doubt that if they refused
to cooperate all the members of the Committee would be shot, but
beyond that no one could guess what action the Nazis might take.

The debate went on for quite a while, and although Father was not
a member of the Committee, he sat in on the discussion. In the end
they decided to consult the ex-Chief Rabbi of Kaunas, Abraham
Shapiro. It was an unusual step for these people to take, as so many of
them were non-observant Jews, but with the shadow of death hanging
over the ghetto, it seemed right to consult a spiritual leader.

Father had taken Talmud lessons from Rabbi Shapiro many years
before and knew him well. The members of the Committee asked
him to join them.

The rabbi was very old and ill, and the delegation got him out of his
sickbed. When he heard their question a great sigh escaped him. He
didn't give them an answer right away. He said that he had to consult
his holy books to see whether any precedent was recorded in the long
annals of suffering endured by the Jewish people. After waiting for
some hours, the Committee was told to return the next day.

Finally he came to the same conclusion as Dr. Elkes and half of the
Committee members, that obeying the Germans might save some
lives. Morally it was a bitter pill to swallow. Many felt that obeying the
Germans put the Committee in the position of collaborating with our
murderers. But disobeying them might be the end of everybody.

On Sunday afternoon Cooky and I went to see Lena. She was waiting
for us on the doorstep, and without a word we all put our arms
around each other. We stood and clung together in silence for quite
a while. At that moment words were simply meaningless. We knew
that we might soon be running through a hail of bullets at the Ninth
Fort. How could we possibly console each other?

Cooky began crying first and we soon joined him. We felt a tender-
ness for each other that only the approach of death could fully
expose. There were so many things yet to be done, books to read,
movies to watch, marriage, children, a world to explore. . . .

Finally we went in to pay our respects to Mrs. Greenblat, Rachel,
and little Vova. Lena's mother was quite calm, and seeing our tearful

eyes, she gave us a reproachful look. She and Rachel kept glancing at Vova. I suppose they didn't want to frighten him.

"Look, we don't have to panic," Mrs Greenblat said. "The instructions were that everyone should assemble in columns according to their place of work. If they want to harm us why would they give such orders? Perhaps they really do want to separate the workers from the non-workers. Anyway, we are going to stand with my brigade. They need us for the war effort."

There was some logic in what she said, but what about those mass graves being dug at the Ninth Fort? Everybody knew about them by now. Yet Mrs. Greenblat planted among us a kernel of hope, and hope like a weed can sprout under the harshest conditions.

I will always remember the quiet sorrow in Lena's face when we said good-bye, how she stood on the steps in the twilight, watching us go.

I went with Cooky to the Trotskys' and said good-bye to them. Isaac was overjoyed that Cooky was still willing to go to the airport for him. I hated that he would be so far away the day before the action. Most of us felt we should stick close by our families, but Cooky had made up his mind. Dora felt so guilty that she gave us both a bowl of soup and Cooky an extra portion of bread.

The next day I went to work with Father and Uncle Jochil. Around noon Father came in, his face gray. He told us that the orders for tomorrow's action were posted all over the ghetto.

That evening we took out all the cans still left over from Anushka's shop, and had a big supper. Some of our other relatives came over to discuss the situation. The crucial question was whom the Germans would consider important enough to live. No one doubted by then that the mass graves prepared by the Germans at the Ninth Fort were meant for us, but how many would die?

Then Cooky's mother, Vera Shore, showed up. She'd been an elegant woman before the war, and now she looked almost haggard with worry. The airport brigade had not returned from the day shift. What if they had simply been taken away and shot? she asked. What if he didn't get back in time for the roll call?

Father tried to calm her. The airport workers were important, he said. Perhaps they were being deliberately kept away from the action. Words of comfort, however, rang hollow that night. Some spoke of resisting the Germans, fighting them with our bare hands, but we all knew that would be futile.

We were instructed to assemble in groups according to the working place of the head of the family. But which group would be safest? Father and Uncle Jochil worked for the administration, Fima worked for the German Wehrmacht, and Fanny worked for the railroad brigade. After long discussions, we couldn't come to an agreement.

Father thought that if any part of the ghetto population remained intact, the Germans would need administrative workers. Fima persuaded his family that his brigade would be safer. At the last minute Anushka obtained a certificate as an airport worker, and she decided to join that group. Perhaps this way some of us would survive, they argued, and so the family split up.

We decided to retire early that night because we knew that the next day was going to be long and cold, and we would need every ounce of strength. But very few of us could sleep.

Well before dawn Anushka prepared some hot *kaffee ersatz* while we all got warmly dressed. When it was time to go we all embraced and kissed each other. We couldn't hold back our tears. I especially cried when I said good-bye to Aunt Anushka. I thought that without a Jordan Pass she had the least chance of survival, and I loved her so much. She looked me in the eyes and smiled.

"Don't worry, darling, we'll see each other tonight," she said, and gave me a big kiss.

Before we left the house I looked at the shabby room we lived in. Suddenly it seemed incredibly pleasant and cozy. If only I could curl up in my warm bed and go to sleep forever. . . . Then I noticed the book I'd been reading, Gogol's "The Overcoat," and impulsively slipped it under my sweater. I don't know why.

The streets were covered with an early morning frost and mist shrouded the fields. It was going to be a cold day. I pulled the flaps of my leather hat down to protect my ears.

Hundreds of people were emerging from the houses all around us. In the semidarkness they looked like gray ghosts. Some carried candles which cast an eerie light on their faces. Many were carrying small children in their arms, or pushing baby carriages through the sandy streets. Some supported their elderly parents, others carried invalids on stretchers. No one wanted to remain behind and be shot. I began to hear a strange humming sound. When I listened closer I realized that many were reciting psalms.

I thought about Cooky. I thought about Lena, hoping that her uncle, the policeman, would keep her safe. I also thought about my cousins Arik and little Ronnie, hiding with Maria and her relatives. Why couldn't *I* be hiding somewhere outside the ghetto, instead of marching to my death? Why didn't we get out of this horrible place when we had the chance? This and many other thoughts were going through my mind as we trudged toward Demokratu Square. One minute I was imagining myself falling into horrible pits full of dead bodies, the next I was imagining all of us back home and safe. I kept touching the Jordan Pass in my pocket, a terrible fear rising in me like the waters of a flood.

At Demokratu Square a Jewish policeman directed us to our assembly point. A man in the first row carried a banner with the words written in German: Ghetto Administration Workers. In front stood the members of the Committee and other policemen with their families. The rest of us lined up behind them. We were ordered to form rows of ten. Since there were only four of us another family joined us, a woman with two children and an old couple who were her parents. The woman worked with Father at the supply department.

"Rachel, where is your husband?" Father asked.

"He went to the airport yesterday morning and didn't come back," she told Father, looking anxiously around. Perhaps Cooky had chosen right, I thought with a pang of envy.

As the deadline neared, the mass of people pouring into the square increased. A tall man approached our assembly point and began running up and down our column. His old suit was smeared with mud.

Father was the first one to recognize him and called out "Moshe! Here!" and the man came running over and embraced Rachel.

"Thanks God I found you! We've been running all over the field looking for our families. We had to work two shifts at the airport because the night shift wasn't allowed out of the ghetto," Moshe gasped, completely out of breath. I met him once or twice at the supply department when he visited his wife, but I barely recognized him. His face was so hollow and gray he looked like an old man, and his filthy clothes smelled of sour sweat and urine.

Then I realized with horror that Cooky too must be running

around among the crowd looking for his family. And I had envied him that he managed to avoid this action! Another wave of dread left me feeling sick.

Daylight found the whole ghetto population, about twenty-eight thousand men, women, and children, standing in neat columns waiting for the German executioners to finish their breakfast.

An hour passed, and then two. A few flakes of snow drifted to the ground. The cold soon seeped into my fingers and toes, but we continued to stand and wait. Soon my legs ached as much as my hands and feet. All around us we could hear babies crying. Children begged their parents for food. Many began reciting psalms again, and that melancholy melody spread among the condemned throughout the field. Here and there some old person would buckle to the ground as their families struggled to hold them up.

Finally, at around nine in the morning, a strange new sound traveled through the square. It reminded me of the wind moving through the tops of trees. It was the sound that escaped from thousands of mouths as German and Lithuanian battalions surrounded the square. They were armed with machine guns and they looked grim. Many of the Lithuanians seemed drunk.

Then two figures resplendent in new uniforms and shiny black boots approached us. They were the ghetto Kommandant Jordan and the Gestapo man Rauca. These two were to decide our fate.

Rauca placed himself in front of our column and without any further ceremony began his bloody job.

The members of the Jewish Committee and the ghetto police were standing in front of the column. They and their families were sent to the left, to a specially assigned area. After them came all the departments of the ghetto institutions.

Many of these were sent to the left, some to the right. As the columns filed past and were divided, it appeared that there were more elderly people and women in the group to the right. There were also more children, including many boys my age.

At first Rauca seemed to pay attention to the worker's certificates, sending those families to the left, but soon he was tearing families apart, and the somber quiet that had fallen over the crowd was rent by their heartbreaking cries. Occasionally someone tried to rejoin their loved ones, but they were beaten back by the Lithuanian guards, who struck them with the butts of their rifles. A few who had been directed to the right tried to show Rauca their Jordan Passes, but he only tore them out of their hands and threw them into the mud.

My heart was beating wildly. The precious life certificate that I held in my trembling hands had become worthless before my very eyes. It had become obvious which group would live and which would die, and I could already feel the cold breath of death on my neck.

I thought that if I willed it with all my being, perhaps I could stop time and go back for a short time into the past . . . *There is the snowman on the hill . . . Here is Sugihara at our table, raising his glass in a toast . . . Here is Uncle Melech, his dark eyes laughing at me. Come, Solly my boy, come with me to Palestine. But there was my father shaking his head. A fanatical Zionist, an impractical dreamer. . . .*

Our column inched forward. I started praying. Oh, God, give us a little more time, just a little more time.

A red face, pale blue eyes, his right arm extended as if he were conducting an orchestra, Rauca stood before us.

Three rows, two rows, one row before us. . . . Left . . . right . . . left . . . I couldn't even hear the screams of the separated families anymore. My heart stopped beating. I was drowning in fright.

Then we stood before him. His eyes scanned us indifferently. He seemed bored.

He pointed at Moshe and his family and said, "You! Dreck sack, you and the rest of your garbage, off to the right."

Moshe, who stood next to me, began shaking like a leaf. Because he stood so close I could actually feel his trembling. It reverberated through my body like the death throes of an animal. It made me nauseous and I thought I would vomit my breakfast at Rauca's feet.

I stood frozen to my spot as Moshe and his family began to move off. Then Rauca's gloved hand shot out at me, and he flipped his thumb in the same direction.

"You too," he hissed. Two words that might as well have been bullets from a gun. A tremor shook my body, the same I had felt from Moshe.

Moshe, who was only a few steps away, turned around and our eyes met. He had dark brown eyes, and they looked at me with compassion.

"He is not my son. He belongs to the other family," he said quietly, pointing at my father.

Father, Mother, and Fanny, who had been as hypnotized as I, suddenly woke up, all of them speaking at once. "He is with us. He belongs to us." At the same time I whipped my mitten off my right hand and extended to Rauca my Jordan Pass. He blinked. Later I thought how easily I could have shot him if I had had a gun. Perhaps he thought the same thing.

Rauca was already busy with the row behind us. In a trance I moved to the left with my family, Fanny holding on to me with all her strength. From the corner of my eye I could see Moshe and his family being chased by the Lithuanians, and I turned and looked back. His older son, who was about my age, was looking at me, and there was reproach in that look. Perhaps he thought that his father could have saved him instead of me.

Moshe's last words will live with me until the day I die. They symbolize the nobility of mind of so many of our people, who even at the brink of death tried to save others.

All those gathered on the left stood transfixed, watching the ever-growing number of the condemned. We were the lucky ones. It didn't matter that we might die the next day or the next. The future has no meaning at such moments.

A flicker of hope was rekindled for the condemned, as well, when the partisans began to march them toward the small ghetto. Perhaps, just perhaps, they were really only going to separate the working population from the non-working. Perhaps they too still had time. But why would they send so many young and able workers there? None of it made sense.

As the afternoon wore on and the sky darkened, the square began to fill up with the bodies of the old and the sick. They simply couldn't endure the cold or the fearful wait, and gave up the ghost. If this goes on much longer, I thought, all of us will be dead.

It was not until Jordan and Rauca got word that ten thousand men, women, and children had been collected in the small ghetto that they called it a day. All of us still standing in the square, the "lucky" ones, were finally allowed to return to our homes.

When we got back to Gimbuto Street we found the house upside down. Obviously the Germans had turned the place over looking for people in hiding. They had left the doors hanging open, and it was terribly cold. With trembling hands Mother managed to light the stove and put some water on to boil. Whatever small comfort we felt soon turned to despair. Anushka did not return, nor did Jochil and his family.

We took turns anxiously watching the street. Thousands of people were still coming from Demokratu Place, and that gave us some hope. Perhaps we were among the first to return and the rest of the family would soon follow. We wondered aloud what had happened to our other relatives. What had happened to Cooky and Lena? What about those sent to the small ghetto? I felt dread in my heart.

We were gathered around the stove, nursing cups of *kaffee ersatz* and trying to console each other when the door flew open. Uncle Jochil and his family stood at the entrance, and a few seconds later, Aunt Anushka arrived. For a moment we stared at each other as if we were seeing ghosts. The same thought must have passed through their minds, that we were among the unfortunate ones. Then we fell into each other's arms and cried.

Jochil's family stood in the column of Fima's brigade. They were among the earlier groups to be selected. At that time Rauca was still patient enough to sort people out. Jochil's family of four, all relatively young and well dressed, seemed to fit the criteria by which he made his decisions. The row behind them, which included many small children, was sent to the right.

Anushka, who stood among the airport workers, didn't fare so well. Just before they filed past Rauca, a message came from the small ghetto which made him furious. Apparently he wasn't filling his quota as fast as he thought.

"'All of you shit-heads, off you go!' he screamed at us, sending row after row of airport workers and their families to the right," Anushka told us. "When our turn arrived he didn't even bother to look at us. He just kept his arm extended to the right, and before we knew what was happening we were driven by the Lithuanians with clubs and rifles toward the group headed for the small ghetto.

"Suddenly, Greenblat the policeman, you know, Lena's uncle, appeared out of nowhere like an angel from heaven. He took me by the arm and started shoving me toward the other side, giving me such a heave he almost lifted me off my feet. He was one of my customers before the invasion, and we used to play cards together. I must go and thank him. He saved my life," Anushka said with a smile that nearly broke my heart. She reached out for me and wrapped me in a big hug.

"You see, I told you we would see each other again tonight, and you wouldn't believe me."

It was a long and gruesome day for all of us, young and old, and we were dead tired, but it was hard for anyone to sleep that night. We couldn't stop thinking about the rest of the family, about our friends, about the fate of those sent to the small ghetto. Previous actions made the intent of the Germans deadly clear, but it was hard to believe they would commit murder on such a massive scale. No one even considered venturing out of the house for news. We went to sleep telling ourselves there was hope.

I woke up in the morning to the terrible screaming of my sister Fanny. I sat up in bed just in time to see her clutching at the windowsill before her knees buckled and she fell to the floor.

We all rushed to the window, Mother and Anushka kneeling and lifting Fanny up, trying to revive her. The rest of us stared through the glass. In the gray light of early morning an endless column of people moved up a distant hill toward the Ninth Fort. Miles and miles of people. It wasn't as gory as many scenes I had witnessed, yet it was a thousand times worse. In my imagination I could see these unfortunate thousands being shoved into huge graves, layer upon layer of the dead being covered with freshly dug earth.

Driven by an inexplicable force, we threw on our coats and together with thousands of others we rushed to the ghetto fence. Armed Lithuanians lined both sides of the road as far as the eye could see, ready to shoot anyone who tried to escape. It is impossible to describe the cries of people from both sides of the fence as they recognized friends and relatives, sometimes parents, brothers, and sisters. How could the heart take it in without breaking to pieces? How could the mind remain sane?

I kept trying to see if I recognized anyone on the other side. The numbers were so great that the death march lasted from dawn until noon, but we weren't able to bear it so long and stumbled away, shocked to the bone.

I couldn't bear to think of Cooky returning to Demokratu Place after that horrible twenty-four hour shift, nor could I bear to think of what happened to Lena. I knew that the one way to find out was to go to their houses and check, but the very idea was so frightening that I pushed it away.

Even as we fled that scene we couldn't help looking back. From almost every spot in the ghetto you could see the road that wound up the hill to the Ninth Fort, and the endless procession of the doomed moving slowly along it. I couldn't stop shivering. When we returned home I slipped into bed with all of my clothes on, but I was still cold. Finally I fell into a dreamless sleep. When screams woke me again I was completely befuddled, but when I joined the others at the window I understood. Although the Ninth Fort was several kilometers away, we could hear the faint but unmistakable chatter of machine guns.

The next two days were the most terrible since the war began. The surviving ghetto population ran around like a mad mob, looking for relatives and friends, covering their ears to shut out the terrible sound of machine-gun fire emanating from the Ninth Fort. The shooting, sometimes fainter, sometimes louder, continued incessantly, hour after hour, day and night. We tried to shut out the terrible sound by plugging our ears, but it didn't help much. At times I wished that I had gone off with Moshe and his family. At least this nightmare would be finished once and for all. How many of these terrible selections would we have to face? Who knew when our luck would run out?

The spirit of the people was at its ebb. If there was one belief we had clung to, it was that as long as the Nazis needed labor for their war effort, they would keep us alive. That theory collapsed when Rauca sent so many thousands of young and able workers to their deaths.

The next day no one reported for work. The Germans threatened the ghetto with dire consequences, but no one really cared. What more could these butchers do to us? When the Germans realized that the Jews would not be deceived this time, Jordan, and later Rauca, came to the Jewish Committee and tried to bring them around.

They promised that there would be no more such actions. If the Jews cooperated and worked hard, they said, their lives and those of their families would be spared. Of course, no one really believed them. They had lied too often.

There was one thing, however, that could bring us back to work. Hunger.

For two days I hoped that Lena and Cooky would come to us, but they didn't, and I knew that I would have to take the dreaded step and seek them out. The third morning Father and Uncle Jochil went to work again and I left with them. I decided to go to Lena's house first.

Aviva's street was on my route. In the terrible upheaval I had completely forgotten about her, and even about Chaim.

Their door was slightly ajar. I knocked several times, but there was no answer. With growing trepidation I cautiously pushed the door open. In the semidarkness I found Chaim sitting on Aviva's bed, staring into space. His head was bandaged with a piece of linen soaked with blood. He hadn't noticed my arrival at all and didn't move a muscle.

When I shook him a few times, he finally turned his head and gave me a strange look.

"I should have gone with them instead of hiding. Perhaps I could have saved them. At least I could have gone with them." His voice was so low that I could barely hear him.

My heart sank. I understood who he was talking about, and with a pang I realized how fond of Aviva I had become.

Chaim asked for some water. When I came back with it and he had roused himself a little, he told me what had happened.

In spite of the threats by the Germans, he refused to go to the assembly point. He had concocted a plan. He made it look as if his place had already been looted, and his bookshelves had collapsed. He piled hundreds of books and boards on the floor in one big heap, and somehow managed to bury himself in the middle. He doubted that the Germans would bother to dig through it. He was right, but what he hadn't counted on was that the Germans would simply spray the pile with their machine guns. Fortunately the books took nearly all the bullets, and he had only been grazed. Now he was alone in the world with no one to take care of him.

I assured him that we would never abandon him. Of course, by "we" I meant Lena, Cooky, and I, but now I was not at all sure that they were among the survivors. Seeing Chaim this way and discovering that Aviva and her mother had been taken filled my heart with fear. All my reluctance evaporated. I promised Chaim that I would return soon, and rushed out the door to find Lena.

When I arrived at Linkuvos Street the door of the house was closed. I stood outside with a trembling heart, trying to sense her presence inside, afraid to knock. The house looked abandoned.

Suddenly I saw some movement behind the curtain. With a cry of joy I leaped up the steps and burst into the house, expecting to throw myself into Lena's arms. Lena's aunt jumped back in alarm. Behind her Greenblat, the policeman, lay in bed with his head in a bandage.

He was pale as a ghost, but when he saw me he tried to get up. His wife gently restrained him.

"No, no darling. You must stay in bed. Doctor's orders."

He sank back with a groan. "I tried my best to save them," he blurted, and then he began to weep.

"I almost succeeded, but they knocked me down. I saved so many that day, but when it came to my own flesh and blood . . ." and his face crumpled as he broke into sobs.

My heart had stopped beating.

He controlled himself, but his face was a mask of pain. "That crazy girl. Even Rauca wanted to save her. Even that butcher recognized her beauty. 'You're much too pretty to go with the others.' I heard it with my own ears. But that crazy girl insisted on going with her family. Beautiful Lena, she could have saved herself." Again he broke down in sobs.

My head was buzzing and I thought I would collapse. Mrs. Greenblat quickly brought me a chair and a glass of water.

Then, avoiding my eyes, Mr. Greenblat said, "I have more bad news for you. Your friend Cooky was with them."

"No, no! You're mistaken!" I screamed, jumping up from the chair. "Cooky was at the airport that day. How could he be with Lena? What about his parents? He must have joined his parents!" I refused to believe what my ears were hearing.

"It was a terrible mess. The airport workers were running around looking for their families, but there were thirty thousand people on the square. Cooky must have stumbled on them when he couldn't find his parents. The day shift had been forced to work twenty-four hours, they were exhausted and filthy, and that bastard sent most of them to the fort!"

The implication of what he said hit me like a thunderbolt. Lena and her family had gone to their deaths because of Cooky's appearance. And what was even worse, Cooky was at the airport instead of me! I was the one who introduced him to the Trotskys.

Greenblat was looking at me with compassion now, and he somehow sensed what I was thinking.

"It wasn't Cooky, Solly. Rauca sent most people without a man at the head of the family to the bad side. I'm so sorry, Solly. I know how close the three of you were."

I was so wild with grief and guilt that I don't remember leaving the house, much less saying good-bye. The next thing I knew Mrs. Greenblat was stopping me in the street. She had a small portrait of Lena. "I am sure she would want you to have it, Solly," she said with tears running down her face. She gave me a hug, and I managed to mumble my thanks. It was a beautiful little portrait painted only a year or two before. Lena looked exactly as I remembered her before the invasion, a million years ago, on a different planet. I could hardly bear to look at it.

It was all my fault. If I hadn't introduced Cooky to Lena, she might still be alive. And so would Cooky if he hadn't taken my place for Isaac Trotsky. I was the one who should be at the Ninth Fort.

I knew I should go to Cooky's, but I couldn't bear the thought of facing his parents. Everywhere I went I heard the terrible lament of people who had lost their families. I felt guilty to be alive. Yet I had very little doubt that my turn would soon come. The only reason the rest of us were still alive was because they couldn't murder thirty thousand people at a time.

In one house after another I heard people saying Kaddish. The dead praying for the dead.

10
Return of a Ghost

Many of the workers in the ghetto returned to their jobs within a week of the "Big Action." What the threats of Jordan and Rauca didn't achieve, hunger did. All the brigades, especially those of the airport workers, had to be restructured because so many were missing. The supervisors expected the work to be done, whether the workers were dead or alive, and they filled out the decimated work crews by dragging people off the street.

I began working in the supply department more often, not wanting to be sent to the airport, but I barely had the energy to go about even trivial tasks. I visited Chaim almost every day and brought him food whenever I could. With Aviva and her mother gone, he lived solely on his rations and was slowly starving to death.

He was terribly saddened by the death of Aviva, and he missed Lena and Cooky almost as much as I did. From time to time we would discuss the books he lent me, but his heart wasn't in it. Now he let me keep his books as long as I wanted.

In the evenings, when everyone was asleep, I would sit in my corner wrapped in a blanket and read in the dim light of a candle that Fanny from time to time would bring from work.

One night as I sat reading I heard a tap, and then three more taps on the window near my head. My heart skipped several beats. This was the signal Cooky and I used after curfew. Either Cooky had passed on our signal to someone else, or his ghost was standing outside. No one had ever escaped the Ninth Fort.

I got out of the house without waking anyone, and there he stood in the moonlight, like an apparition from another world. He wore a huge overcoat and a crazy sheepskin hat. He looked and smelled awful, but it was Cooky all right. Even as he struggled to smile his face crumpled. We fell into each other's arms and started crying. When we both calmed down a little, a thousand questions flooded my mind at once.

"How?! How for God's sake?! What happened? How did you manage to escape?" And then with a jolt I remembered. "And . . . Lena? What about Lena?" His face contorted. All he could do was shake his head no. Both of us sank down on the steps without another word and cried our hearts out.

Finally I roused myself. "It's cold out here. Come inside."

"No!" he said quickly. "No one must see me. If the Germans find out that I escaped they'll come after me. No one must know. Not even my parents know!"

He had spent all day hiding in an abandoned shack near the edge of the ghetto. I brought out some bread and half a potato I had saved for the next day. He ate quickly and mechanically.

We decided that the safest thing would be to take him to Chaim first. The problem was how to approach his parents without giving them a heart attack, especially his mother who had a weak heart.

We made our way to Chaim's house and slipped in. When I shook him awake he stared at me in confusion. Then his eyes fell on Cooky and he sat up with a jolt.

When we all calmed down we discussed Cooky's problem. Chaim suggested that we stay the night and in the morning I could approach his parents and prepare them for the good news.

Chaim warmed up some water on his kerosene stove and we helped wash Cooky down. A strange smell seemed to permeate him and his clothing. It was a smell I would get to know too well in the years to come.

Chaim gave him some clothing that had belonged to Aviva's father. He suggested we get some sleep, but all three of us knew that sleep would be impossible until Cooky unburdened himself of his story. He looked as if a terrible load was crushing his very soul. He tried several times to begin. Clearly it was a painful struggle, and we couldn't help him. We could only sit and listen and try to share his pain.

Finally, after sitting for about ten minutes in silence, rocking back and forth as if he were trying to force an evil spirit out of his body, he began his story in a strange, low voice. It didn't sound like him at all.

"It was gray all the way back from the airport. The sky was gray, the houses were gray, even the people in our column looked gray. No one spoke a word. We were too tired to speak. Only the guards could be heard swearing at us when we moved too slowly.

"When the night shift didn't arrive to relieve us, we figured the action was already beginning. I was hopeful, in a way, thinking that perhaps we would escape whatever was going on in the ghetto. But when they marched us back and we saw that huge crowd in the square, I knew that I had made a terrible mistake. I should have stayed with my family.

"At first we didn't see a living soul. The ghetto looked deserted. But then a detachment of Germans came up and forced us to run all the way to Demokratu Square. As we rounded a corner a surreal scene, like a painting, appeared before our eyes.

"The square was covered with people, a huge horde that seemed to stretch a mile long and a mile wide, with a mist rising above their heads. Everyone stood in deathly silence, in ranks like soldiers. No one stirred, no one spoke. Everyone seemed to be staring at one spot, a group of German soldiers standing near the front. Everyone seemed to be waiting for something.

"In the beginning I tried to find my parents, but it was an impossible task. A gasp seemed to go up from the crowd, and I turned to see a group of German officers enter the square. Rauca had come. The selection was about to begin, and the guards were forcing us into the nearest groups. Finally my eyes fell on a familiar face. I couldn't believe it. Right in front of me stood Lena and her family.

"At the same time Lena turned her head and gasped in disbelief. 'Cooky, oh Cooky! You're here,' she cried out, and started to weep. But I couldn't even speak."

For a minute Cooky interrupted himself, and looked at me with tears standing in his eyes.

"She was wonderful, so wonderful. And she loved you, you know. . . ."

I felt this like a stab in my heart. I felt terribly guilty that I had withdrawn from her during those last few weeks.

"It took almost all day for our group to come before Rauca. Lena clung to one of my arms and her sister Rachel to the other.

"It had become terribly clear that the side to his right was the bad side, and in our column most of the people were sent to the right. As we approached, Rauca just kept his stick extended to the right. We were condemned to death.

"I wanted to scream that there must be some mistake, that we were young and could work, but I was only screaming in my mind.

"Then Rauca saw Lena and suddenly stopped our row. He singled her out and told her to move to the left.

"*'Du bist viel zu schön zum sterben,'* he said.

"But Lena shook her head proudly and told him that she would share her family's fate. 'Very well,' he said, annoyed, and waved her away."

Here Cooky looked at me again, the tears running down his face. "I know it sounds incredible, but I swear to you, that's what happened. We tried to push her in the direction Rauca wanted to send her, but she wouldn't listen.

"Suddenly from among the rows Lena's uncle, the policeman, appeared. He got hold of Mrs. Greenblat's arm and began moving us to the left. Only a few meters separated us from the people standing on the 'good' side.

"We were almost saved. Just a few . . . goddamned . . . meters! Then we heard the fateful command in German. 'Halt! Where are you going? Back! Take them back!' A German soldier came running over, threatening Greenblat with his pistol.

"'Please Sir, it's my family. This is my family, Sir,' Greenblat was begging the German.

"*'Halt die Schnauze, Du Schweinehund!'* the German barked at him and hit him over the head with his pistol butt. Greenblat fell to the ground, holding his head, blood streaming from between his fingers. Some other Jewish policemen carried him off. I don't know what happened to him after that.

"We came that close to being rescued . . . That close. . . ."

I told Cooky that I saw Greenblat after the action and that he was all right. "He too told me that Rauca wanted to spare Lena. I hardly believed him, it sounded so incredible. Why didn't she rescue herself? For God's sake, why?"

Cooky continued: "After we were selected by Rauca, we were surrounded by dozens of German and Lithuanian policemen. Cursing and shouting obscenities at us, they herded us toward the small ghetto at a run. People who were too sick or old to keep up were beaten and trampled before our eyes.

"In order to avoid their blows we ran as fast as we could, holding each others' hands. Some risked crossing to the 'good' side, but almost all of them paid with their lives. Only the Jewish police were able to get some of the families back over safely. The Germans saw what was going on, but for whatever reason allowed them to rescue the few. They would be replaced, anyway. It was our bad luck that our rescue did not succeed.

"As soon as we arrived in the small ghetto the guards let us loose, and everybody rushed to claim an empty house. 'They're not taking us to the fort! They're not taking us to the fort!' people began saying to each other. A spark of hope was rekindled in our hearts. Perhaps they really were only going to divide the population.

"'Quickly, let us find a place to stay,' Mrs. Greenblat said. 'I don't know how long they're going to keep us here, but I think the worst is over, children,' she said.

"Some people were so hopeful that they began quarreling about the houses they occupied. Most of them were in shambles.

"It took us about an hour to find a place near the end of the ghetto where we could put our heads down. It was a two-room house, and one of the rooms was already occupied by a large family. They were sprawled on the floor, many of them asleep. I counted five children, a baby sleeping in her mother's lap, and five adults. No one was in the other little room, and it was immediately apparent why. The window was broken and it was bitterly cold.

"No one said a word. They just stood there looking lost, and they were all looking at me. Even Mrs. Greenblat, who is rarely at a loss for words, was close to tears. They seemed to be looking for guidance, from me of all people.

"'I think we'd better stay here tonight,' I said a bit too loudly. I was trying to play my role.

"'Perhaps we can find something to cover the window with,' little Vova said. We all looked at him. He hadn't said a word since Rauca sent us to the small ghetto, and we had begun to worry about him.

"'Good idea Vova,' I said, giving him a slap on the shoulder.

"We pushed an old wardrobe against the window and stuffed rags around the edges. Then we all just lay down on the floor. The day had lasted an eternity, and we were exhausted.

"Lena lay next to me and I could feel her trembling from fear and cold. After a while she whispered and asked if I was awake. I tried to quiet her and keep her warm, but she wanted to talk.

"'Cooky, what's going to happen to us? They're going to kill us tomorrow, aren't they?'

"I told her I didn't know. 'There are so many people here,' I said, 'I don't think they can kill so many people at once.' I tried to sound convincing.

"'Why do they all hate us so much? Can you understand it?'

"I talked about what Chaim had said, but she'd heard his theories before. And what difference did it make? I tried to say some words of comfort, but I was so exhausted I think I fell asleep while Lena was still whispering in the dark.

"I don't know how long we slept. It seemed to me that I had barely closed my eyes when I heard shots being fired and screams. It sounded as if it was coming from some distance. No one else in the room stirred. 'We are going to die, now,' I thought, and my heart began beating like a drum.

"Then a woman in the next room began to wail, and Lena sat up and looked at me with terror in her eyes. The shooting and the screams were coming closer. In the other room the men began chanting psalms.

"The rest of the family woke up too. Mrs. Greenblat held little Vova close to her, while Rachel put her hands over her ears and began screaming. It was as if a great black tidal wave was towering over our heads, about to come down on us. Only Lena seemed to be calm. She even tried to smile.

"'I knew it would happen all along. I felt its presence from the very beginning,' she said, looking at me sadly. There was nowhere to run. All we could do was sit and wait for the Germans to come.

"Just before they reached us I felt almost resigned. But when they kicked in the outer door my calm completely shattered. We huddled together quaking with fear, and a strange odor suddenly filled the room. It was pure fear, the odor of death.

"They burst into our room like a bunch of wild beasts, screaming orders. We quickly rose to our feet. The hourglass was empty. I grabbed Lena by the arm and we ducked through a hail of blows out to the street.

"They were counting people off into groups of a hundred, and when our turn came Lena and I were separated from the family and sent to another group. We begged the Germans to let us rejoin them, but they only shoved us back. Lena kept screaming and trying to get to the other group, but they kept slapping her and dragging her back.

"We could see Mrs. Greenblat waving her arms and screaming and Rachel holding her hands over her ears. Only little Vova stood there quietly, looking at us with his sad eyes. Soon they were marched off while our group was held back.

"Lena had sacrificed her life to die with her family, but the bastards didn't even allow her that.

"The road to the fort was uphill all the way and a difficult climb. Lena continued to cling to me, crying pitifully for her mother. In spite of the cold I was soon wet with perspiration. In front of us a long snake of people wound up the hill, as far as the eye could see.

"We walked four or five to a row, but everyone was so tired and weak from hunger that the ranks soon broke. Taking advantage of the confusion I began falling back, dragging Lena with me. I don't know why I did it. I knew that escape was impossible, but I wanted to postpone death as long as I could. Besides, Lena's strength seemed to have left her completely and she could barely walk.

"Several times the guards hit me in the back for falling back, but I didn't even feel it. There were guards on both sides of the road, all of them armed. We'd hear shots, and then a truck would drive up and the dead would be thrown inside.

"I looked around trying to spot a familiar face, but there were only strangers. No one spoke. Even the children were very quiet. The smell of fear and death was everywhere.

"Then I found a familiar face. It was my old math teacher, Jablonsky. He was a skeleton compared to what he used to be, but his gray mustache hadn't changed. He was breathing heavily as he struggled to keep up.

"I called out to him, but he didn't even recognize me. I had to tell him who I was. He tried to smile, but didn't quite manage it.

"'Give me your hand Cooky, I'm afraid I'm at the end of my tether,' he said. Lena had calmed a little, and took his arm from one side while I tried to support him from the other.

"It was almost evening when we reached the fort. The walls were old and thick, with small barred windows. Lena was sobbing and trying to pray as they rose up in front of us. I was in turmoil. The deepest, most intrinsic, most pervasive instinct in us is the instinct for survival. No matter what poets say, when it comes to dying, everything else is forgotten.

"I heard Jablonsky say, 'Don't cry, children. Let's not give them the satisfaction. Let's die with our heads held high.'

"German and Lithuanian guards stood at the entrance with several large dogs straining at their leashes, barking and snarling furiously. We were pushed through the gates.

"Several trucks were standing inside the courtyard, their engines running. They often backfired and it sounded like shots.

"A young German officer addressed us: 'In spite of all the ridiculous rumors, you're going to be transported to working camps in the east. You will shower and then be issued working clothes. Undress and leave your clothing here.' He spoke in civil tones, and in spite of all we knew about this death factory he almost sounded convincing.

"Whatever spark of hope we felt was extinguished when we heard a long burst of machine-gun fire and distant screams. The Germans heard it too, for they raised their guns and pointed them at us.

"'Quickly you Jews! Undress and into the showers! You're just hearing the backfire of some trucks,' the officer shouted. They wanted to dispatch us at maximum speed and efficiency, I suppose. Resistance on our part might have delayed their tight schedule.

"But no one moved, no one seemed able to move a muscle. The officer calmly walked up to an elderly man who was standing near the front, drew his luger and shot him in the face. When he fell to the ground his head opened up and his brains poured out into the mud.

"Suddenly everyone was undressing. When you're about to die, even a few minutes seem precious, as if another second might bring a reprieve. Finally we all stood naked, covering our private parts with our hands and shivering in the cold. These despicable men weren't satisfied with merely killing us, they had to humiliate us even at the end. Why didn't they allow us to die with our clothes on? Did they really need our ragged old clothes?

"Lena looked so terribly thin standing naked next to me. She was terribly ashamed to stand among naked men. I tried to say something comforting, but my teeth were chattering uncontrollably. I wanted to say something meaningful to her. But what could I say? I was as terrified as she. At that moment I would have sold my soul to be able to die peacefully in bed, between clean white sheets. Anything but this.

"But we weren't given much time for reverie. What followed was a nightmare in slow motion. Every tiny detail will stay burned in my memory forever.

"On the officer's signal the Germans and Lithuanians launched themselves at us. 'Run, run, you Jew swine,' they shouted, lashing out at us with sticks and rifle butts, their dogs attacking the slow-moving ones, tearing pieces of flesh from their legs and buttocks. We started running in a wild panic with the guards and dogs after us. In that nightmare it was strange to see steam rising from all those bodies as they herded us along the wall of the fort. Then as we rounded a corner we saw dozens and dozens of machine guns mounted around an open field. They were firing long bursts into a huge pit. I could hear screaming from inside and it drove me almost mad with fright.

"I wanted to stop, to run, to escape, but a mass of stampeding naked bodies crushed around me, encircling me like a straitjacket.

"Lithuanians and Germans with rolled up sleeves and red faces were loading and firing into the mob. You could see the yellow flashes from the barrels, and a veil of blue smoke drifting over the field.

"It was a scene out of hell itself. There were hoarse shouts, and women's screams—shrill, and children and babies crying and barking dogs. It stank of sweat and urine and excrement as terrified bodies just . . . let go. I saw one bearded man standing by the pit, shaking his fists at the sky and screaming.

"'Jews! There is no God! There is a devil sitting up there!' He looked a lot like my old rabbi. Blood was streaming down him and they kept shooting at him, but he kept standing there, screaming at the sky.

"Then we were at the pit. It looked like thousands of bodies, one on top of another, screaming and writhing, begging the Germans to finish them off. A vision of hell. A vision of hell."

Cooky was almost chanting now. I thought I might go mad listening to it.

"We were right in front of the guns. Bullets were buzzing around me like angry bees, but all I felt was the crush of the mob behind me. Then I felt myself falling with Lena still clinging to my arm. She was gripping me with terrible force. There was a look of horror in her eyes, and she was trying to say something. But only a croaking sound came from her lips. A gaping hole appeared in her throat, and a stream of blood gushed out over her breast. Then I felt a weight fall on my head, knocking me into merciful oblivion."

As Cooky droned on I felt as if I had been sucked into the scene against my will, as if some force had lifted me out of my body and dumped me into that pit with him. I could see Lena's eyes and the blood pumping out of her throat. I could see naked frozen bodies tumbling slowly into a horrible maw. I couldn't breathe. I jumped up and covered my ears with my hands, trying to shut out his terrible monotone.

"No, no! I'm not going in there!" I screamed. But Cooky acted as if he didn't hear me. He gave me an unseeing look as Chaim took me by the hands and drew me down to my seat, shushing me and patting my shoulder.

Cooky continued his story. He hadn't changed his position since he started talking. He remained crouched in his seat, his hands clenched in his lap. Only his lips moved. He was in that pit and he was drawing me in with him.

"I had that terrible nightmare again," Cooky continued in his strange voice. "I was lying in my crib and a huge striped tomcat was sitting on my chest, staring into my eyes. He was so heavy, I couldn't breathe. I was suffocating. Then my mother would appear and chase the cat away. I could breathe again. I had this nightmare many times in my childhood, but this time Mother wouldn't come. I was gasping for air and she wouldn't come. I knew that this time I would have to rescue myself or choke to death. I willed myself awake, but even before I was fully awake I realized that I didn't really want to wake up.

"I tried to suck in some air, but there wasn't any. Something enormously heavy was pressing down on my head, pushing my face into something soft and cold. The return to reality was the most terrifying experience imaginable, for the reality was that I was buried alive.

"The whole scene of the massacre came back to me in every detail. I couldn't understand how I could possibly be alive. By some miracle all the bullets missed me.

"I struggled wildly to free myself, but I was pinned down by a heavy body that wouldn't move an inch, and my right foot seemed to be caught from below. 'Why me, oh Lord? Why couldn't I have a caught a bullet straight through the heart?' I thought as panic swept over me. I heaved and struggled some more but I was twisted in an awkward position, and I felt like I had no strength at all. And yet, somehow, I managed a gulp of air.

"So where was the air coming from? The darkness was the darkness of a grave, but from somewhere I was getting air. I managed to move my head an inch or two, enough to clear my mouth and nose, and there was air—cool, glorious air!

"I realized that I was wedged in among several bodies. My head was resting on what was obviously a woman's large, cold, dead breast.

"Again I thought I would lose my sanity. I started struggling wildly. The body above shifted slightly, and suddenly my right arm was free. I twisted my neck, peering around and trying to see in the darkness. That's when I saw the stars. I dared not believe my senses, and closed my eyes. When I opened them again there they were, stars in the sky. It was the most beautiful, most moving sight. . . . I was sure I was hallucinating.

"I forced myself to calm down and think clearly: 'There must be more than one body above me, or it wouldn't feel so heavy. It must be night, for I can see the stars. The grave is open, but why?'

"Then I remembered that it was almost evening when they shot us. They probably didn't have enough time to cover the pit before it got dark.

"Another wave of terror swept over me. 'Why am I the only one alive? Why was I chosen to lie here and wait until they bury me alive?' As if in answer to my question I began to hear noises that froze my blood. There was a wail as if from an infant, and from a distance I heard a man screaming. 'Murderers! Murderers! Come and finish the job!' The baby began crying in earnest, and I heard what seemed to be muffled groans.

"Dear God, how many of us would the bastards bury alive?

"Then something stirred below me, and I was able to free my other arm. Finally it dawned on me that the body pinning me down must be alive as well, because it was still warm.

"I started pushing at it with all my strength and screaming. 'Are you alive? Can you hear me?' Finally he stirred and groaned. I kept yelling and pushing at him until he spoke.

"'Where am I? What is happening?' It was Jablonsky. He had been right behind me when we were chased to the pit. He must have shielded me from the machine guns.

"I started shouting at him, begging him to answer me. Finally he responded.

"'Cooky? Cooky? Is that you? What happened? Why are we still alive?'

"'Mr. Jablonsky, can you move at all? You're on top of me and I can't breathe. I'm not even wounded.'

"I felt a slight movement, and then Jablonsky wailed 'I can't move. Cooky, I can't move!'

"'Mr. Jablonsky, please! Please try to move, for the love of God,' I begged.

"'I can't! I can't, I tell you. I can't move anything! My God, they are going to bury us alive!' There was unbearable terror in his voice.

"I was afraid he might lose his wits entirely, and I kept quiet a moment, hoping he would calm down. I could hear him panting, struggling for breath.

"Then he said in a strange voice, 'Thanks God my son got away. Thanks God he got away.'

"After another moment he said quietly, 'Cooky, if you are not wounded you must get away. You must go back. You must tell them what they are doing up here. You must warn them. It is indecent to die like this. They must put up a fight. They have nothing to lose.'

"'You must do this, Cooky. You must try to come out from under me,' he insisted, and I felt him strain his muscles, trying to move. I began pushing and heaving with all my strength, but to no avail. I lay back, trying to gather my strength again, both of us panting. Then suddenly there was a heave from below, as if the ground itself was shifting, and somewhere beneath us a man screamed.

"Then it stopped. I felt Jablonsky's body slide off a little to the side. I began groping in the darkness and felt someone's head. The face was cold and clammy, and it had long hair. It was a woman's corpse, and I hoped to God that it wasn't Lena. I pulled with all my strength and heard a strange snapping sound, as if the head was going to come off in my hands. I was filled with revulsion and such horror that all I could think of was getting out of that pit. I began frantically pulling and tugging at whatever I could reach."

These last sentences made me so sick that I ran to the window and vomited my guts out. Chaim turned white as chalk.

Cooky barely paused before he continued speaking. I knew that he wouldn't stop whether we were listening or not, until he came to the very end.

"I struggled until I was able to pull my whole body clear. The exertion made me feel faint, and I lay on top of the bodies trying to catch my breath. Millions of stars were looking down on me. It was freezing cold.

"Once again I was aware of groans and gurgling sounds coming from the pit. The mass of bodies beneath me began to feel like a living, writhing entity. I felt sure I would go insane. What was I doing here? Why was I making such an effort to free myself? I began to feel the cold biting into my naked body. I might as well lie down and freeze to death and have it over with.

"Then I heard Jablonsky's voice again, as if it were inside my own head.

"'Cooky. Go to the place we undressed. Get some warm clothing. You must make it back to the ghetto to warn them. It is your holy duty. You must go. You must go, dear child, and bear witness.' He sounded much weaker now.

"He is fooling himself, I thought. 'I'll never make it,' I cried. 'They will catch me and kill me.'

"'Hush, hush. They know that the dead don't walk out of the grave, so what is there to watch? They're all inside the fort, drinking. And what have you got to lose, child? At least if they catch you, you'll die quickly.'

"I was weeping now, but Jablonsky wouldn't let me alone.

"'You must do one more thing. Before you leave, you must kill me. I know what I ask of you is a terrible thing, but please, Cooky. Please don't let them bury me alive.'

"I gasped in horror. I begged him not to ask this of me, but he kept saying, 'You must, Cooky, you must!'

"I began grasping for straws. How was I to do this, I asked, with my bare hands? Was I supposed to search out everyone still alive there and kill them?

"For a moment he was quiet. Then he began speaking in reasonable tones, as if this were an ordinary rational conversation.

"'It would be the humane thing to put them all out of their misery, but I know it's not possible. Now what you must do is take the body above me and cover my face with it. You must press down hard. I won't last long.'

"He was silent for a moment. 'I'm ready to die now,' he said then. 'Good-bye, dear boy, and good luck.'

"It was macabre. He had calmly laid out plans for his own death. It went against every instinct in me, but how could I refuse him? How could I leave him to suffer that terrible death?

"In the end I did what he asked me to do. It was a child's body I smothered him with, the body of a child. . . .

"I don't know how long I knelt there, irresolute, but Jablonsky continued begging me to relieve him of his agony. In the end I found myself pushing the body into his face. For a minute I thought he died right away. But then he started struggling violently. I was screaming in terror and despair as I fought to hold him down.

"After that I didn't really care if I lived or died. I managed to heave myself out of the pit. I didn't stop to look for the baby. It had stopped crying and I hoped to God that it had died.

"Again I thought about just lying back and letting the cold finish me off. My mother nearly froze to death once. She told me how strangely peaceful she felt, how she didn't even feel the cold anymore, just a pleasant drifting off into eternity.

"But now the cold was making me quake, and it wasn't pleasant at all. I crept toward the wall where we had undressed, listening for guards. Nothing moved. I was especially afraid those dogs might come after me. But there were not even any dogs.

"I realized that unless I found some clothes soon I would pass out from the cold, and forced myself to run the last few hundred meters to the yard.

"Fortunately, the pile was still there. By the time I reached it my teeth were chattering uncontrollably. Most of the clothing I found belonged to grown-ups and was too big for me, but I found warm underwear, a suit, and a coat with a sheepskin lining. I padded the boots with several pairs of socks.

"And I discovered other treasures. In the pocket of the coat was a piece of bread! I didn't even bother to chew it, I just swallowed it whole. It only whetted my appetite and made me aware of how terribly hungry I was. It occurred to me that there might be more food in other pockets. Luck was with me.

"I found more bread, margarine, a small jar of jam, and joy of joys! A piece of sausage! I divided the food in two portions and ate half, hiding in the pile of clothing in case a guard turned up. But there was absolute stillness, as if I was the last man left alive on this cursed planet. I deliberately tried to crowd the terrible events of the night out of my mind.

"The choking of Jablonsky, the cry of the baby, the crunch of the woman's neck. Lena's last accusing look with the blood gushing out of her throat. If I didn't hold my thoughts at bay they would engulf me.

"'I promised Jablonsky to try and get away, I promised, I promised,' I kept repeating to myself. But how was I going to get back into the ghetto?

"Suddenly overwhelmed with self pity, I began to cry and cry and just couldn't stop. I wanted to wake in my bed in Kaunas. I wanted my mother. If only I could run to her and put my head in her lap, all my problems would be solved.

"'My Cooky is so spoiled. I just can't refuse him anything when he starts crying,' my mother used to say.

"'Mother, look at me now!' I cried out. 'Look at me, Mother. Your pampered Cooky is lying on a heap of dead people's clothing, freezing, a refugee from death. Is this cause enough for crying?' I was so overwhelmed I didn't care who heard.

"The distant barking of a dog brought me back to my senses. The Germans and Lithuanians might be back soon. I had to get away from there. To avoid going through the gate, which could be guarded, I decided to circle past the pit, around the back wall and from there through the fields to the road.

"It wasn't far, but it took half an hour. I kept stopping to listen for the guards and the dogs. Below, the ghetto loomed in darkness. Here and there a light appeared, wandering through the dark streets, probably the flashlights of the guards. From time to time I heard shots being fired from that direction, the tracer bullets leaving a bluish trail in the sky.

"As soon as I reached the road I heard the voices of Lithuanians approaching. They were marching up the road toward the Ninth Fort. I jumped into a ditch, and after they passed I started out again, but there were more of them patrolling the road toward the ghetto. Then came several trucks. I realized that I had no chance of getting into the ghetto that night. What was I to do?

"Then I remembered that Maria's village was about ten kilometers up the road from the fort. Remember the hike we took that summer?"

I nodded. We had had a picnic up in the field with Jasha, Ronnie, and Maria, and she had shown us her father's house on the other side of the village.

"I knew that Maria would help me," Cooky continued. "I knew it would endanger her and Ronnie, but what other choice did I have? It was either that or death for me. Once I made my decision I felt better. I started back toward the fort, heading north. Once an army truck full of Russian prisoners of war passed by. I could hear the German guards cursing them from my hiding place in some bushes. The truck turned toward the fort, and I realized it was probably the burial detail, sent to cover the graves.

"The first signs of dawn appeared in the east and I tried to speed up, but I'd had little sleep in two nights, and I was growing terribly weary. I realized that I would never make it to her house before daylight. I had to find a safe place to hide.

"There was a clump of birch trees and bushes across the field, and I decided it would have to do. I pulled the overcoat over my head, the sheepskin lining warming my face. I closed my eyes and drifted off into a dreamless sleep.

"I don't know how long I slept, but when I woke up it was night again. I must have slept through the whole day.

"I continued on the road, but it was slow going. My legs and body felt like wood. At one point I didn't get off the road fast enough when a truck approached, and they must have spotted my movement. The truck pulled over, and two Germans got out. A little mongrel dog had started following me the evening before, and when it emerged from the bushes where I lay the Germans laughed and threw it a piece of sausage. Then they drove away. That little dog saved my life.

"It was a terrible scare, but it gave me a shot of adrenalin and I took off at a brisk pace. I resolved that no matter how tired I was, I was not going to stop until I got to Maria's. I had to get there before daybreak.

"The road stretched on without end and seemed to lead nowhere. Again I had the feeling that I was all alone in the world and condemned to walk this road to eternity. Several times I thought about just lying down on the road, but as the sky in the east started to pale I saw the faint outlines of a village. It was Maria's. A dog barked somewhere, and then a rooster crowed, but nothing moved.

"Maria's house was at the end of the village near a small forest. To get there I either had to go through the village or make a circle around it. I was tempted to go straight through, but it was too risky.

"I have only a vague recollection of crossing the fields. I was blacking out even as I was walking. I remember seeing Maria's house as I came around the other side, and that's all I remember.

"Maria later told me that she opened the door to find me collapsed on the stoop. Once again the little dog saved me, by barking and scratching on her door. She was still half asleep, and at first had no idea who I was, but she saw the yellow Star of David sewn on my coat, which I stupidly forgot to remove, and dragged me inside.

"I must have slept a very long time. When I woke up I didn't know where I was. I was lying on a straw mattress with only a thin blanket, but I was very warm. A whitewashed ceiling was right over my head. I couldn't figure it out. Then my memory began to return, and with a start I realized I must be inside Maria's house. I was safe! An incredible feeling of peacefulness enveloped me. I rolled over in the blanket and dropped right off to sleep again. It was the first time in a long while that I slept without feeling that my life was in danger.

"I was finally awakened again by a growing hunger. I crawled forward and cautiously stuck my head out an opening.

"It was then that I realized that I was lying on the shelf by the oven. You know, the place the farmers call 'Grandma's niche,' where the grandmother sleeps in the cold winter months. I had no recollection of Maria getting me up there. Small wonder it was so warm.

"Just as I stuck my head out someone popped up from below and we almost bumped heads. A pair of familiar blue eyes regarded me excitedly. I recognized Ronnie immediately, although he had grown quite a bit since I last saw him. He recognized me too. He is such a bright kid. He remembered me from the days when the world was a safer and kinder place.

"I lowered myself from the shelf and he climbed up into my arms. Both of us started crying. It was the first time since he left the ghetto that he'd seen a face from his old world, besides Maria. And the first thing he asked about was his parents.

"I told him that I had seen them both and they were well and sent their regards."

"'Did they send you to bring me back?' Ronnie asked. I looked at him sadly. What was I to tell him, that I was a refugee from a mass grave who didn't know how to get back to the ghetto?

"Then Maria entered the house carrying a bundle of wood. She looked older and sadder than when I last saw her, but she was still as pretty as I remembered.

"The dog that was my companion came trotting in with her,

wagging its tail. I scooped it up in my arms and it licked my face. I had forgotten all about it!

"Maria dropped the wood by the oven and rushed over to greet me. She took my head between her hands and gave me a big kiss on the forehead. She smelled of fresh snow and soap and there were tears in her eyes.

"'We were worried about you. You slept so long,' she said, looking anxiously into my eyes. It was obvious that whatever news I brought, she didn't want me to tell it in front of Ronnie. She knew that it couldn't be anything good.

"Later she told me that all the villages in the vicinity knew about the thousands of Jews taken to the fort. Even in her village, ten kilometers away, they could faintly hear the sound of the machine guns. It went on day and night.

"When she found me on her doorstep she realized I must have escaped from the massacre. She hoped to God that none of the villagers had seen me.

"I tried to reassure her, telling her I came through the fields and it was still dark, but we both knew that I couldn't stay there for any length of time.

"'But what am I thinking! You must be starving! Let's sit down and have some food,' Maria exclaimed when Ronnie began asking me questions again. She had cooked a meal while I was sleeping and was now taking it out of the oven. There was a thick soup of cabbage with pork, boiled potatoes, and stew. The rich smell of the food almost made me feel faint. I'd almost forgotten food like that still existed, and I wolfed down two heaping plates of it. I've never felt so full. I guess my stomach has shrunk.

"Maria had stoked the stove with lots of logs and the house was pleasantly warm. Outside the wind was whistling in the chimney and a thick snow began to fall. We sat around the table drinking tea and remembering the days before the war. For a little while reality was far away, and only the present mattered.

"It was after ten before Ronnie fell asleep at the table and Maria carried him to his room. When she came back we sat for a while watching the fire in the stove. There was a mute question in her eyes. She didn't want to prod me, but she was clearly waiting for me to speak.

"In the beginning I tried to hold back on the gruesome details, but it was as if my tongue had a life of its own. I poured out the horrors before her like some poisonous brew. I just couldn't help myself. Once I started I couldn't hold it back.

"When I finished we both wept. Taking me in her arms she rocked me back and forth, stroking my hair as if I were a child. She kept whispering, 'Why, sweet Jesus, are they murdering these gentle people who have never harmed anyone, why, why?'

"Later on she told me that things weren't going so well for her either.

"When she brought Ronnie back from the ghetto, she pretended that he was her son. Her father had been ashamed that she worked for Jews, and had invented a husband for her in Kaunas who was a high-ranking officer in the Lithuanian army. When Maria returned to the village with Ronnie, she told them that her husband was away with the Germans, fighting on the Russian front, and that was why she and Ronnie had returned to live for a while in her father's house. But her father had died, and she was without protection. People in the village were suspicious of her. There was one troublemaker, an old school-teacher of hers who had once tried to rape her. Her father gave him a royal beating, and he had never forgiven him or Maria. Now he was snooping around again, asking why Ronnie wasn't in school. Maria called Ronnie 'Vacius,' and pretended that he was retarded.

"Maria said she was afraid she had made a deadly enemy of this man Krakauskas, because she continued to resist his advances, and once even threw him out of her house, threatening him with the wrath of her husband and his brothers. It was all a big ruse, and she didn't know how much longer it would work. That's why she was so worried that someone had seen me. She was already being watched.

"And Ronnie too was giving her a lot of trouble. He was terribly lonely and missed his parents. 'He is cooped up here with me all the time with nothing to do,' she said. 'Lately he has grown very silent and hardly talks to me. At night I can hear him crying.'

"I told her I was sorry I had exposed her to such danger. I felt I should leave as soon as possible, so I told her I had to get back to the ghetto. 'My parents think that I'm dead,' I said. 'Perhaps I should leave tonight.'

"'That's out of the question!' she insisted. 'You can't leave in this terrible weather. Besides, I think I have a plan that will get you into the ghetto safely.'

"'I have an uncle here in the village that we can trust. He goes twice a week to Kaunas carrying vegetables for the Germans. He can drop you off at the ghetto gate when the brigades return from town and you can join them. In the darkness the guards won't notice you.'

"I wondered how and when she cooked all this up. Seeing the surprise on my face she smiled.

"'I have been planning for some time to pay Sonia and Jasha a visit, and I've done some research. Tomorrow morning I will talk to my uncle and we'll decide when to take you. I still intend to pay them a visit, you will have to tell them that. Krakauskas may put Ronnie's life in danger, and I may have to find a way to get him away from here.'

"I slept well that night. Ironically, knowing that I would be in the ghetto soon made me feel good. When I woke up Maria was already back from seeing her uncle. It was all arranged. He would take me early in the morning when all the night shifts were returning to the ghetto.

"I spent the whole day playing with Ronnie. I hated to tell him that I was leaving the next day. Maria told me that Ronnie had become a different boy since my arrival, and she hated to see me go.

"That night she prepared a lavish meal with a pudding for dessert. I wondered if it would be the last time I ever ate such a meal. She also packed me a parcel of food for the road.

"When I said good-bye to Ronnie, he didn't cry. He just looked at me sadly and asked me to tell his parents to come and get him. 'Tell them that I miss them too much and I can't hold out any longer.' Then he put his arms around me and held me tight. 'I love you, Cooky. I wish you didn't have to go.'

"It was still dark when old Karolius came for me. He had a wrinkled face and gnarled hands. His wagon was full of vegetables piled on a bed of straw. Maria gave me a last hug and helped to hide me beneath the straw. We drove off without another word.

"I wrapped myself in my sheepskin coat and went back to sleep, only waking when Karolius shook me. A familiar noise reached my ears. It was a thousand pairs of feet trampling through the snow: the airport brigade arriving from the night shift. I didn't even have a chance to thank Karolius for risking his life for me before he drove away.

"It was still dark. The workers shuffled along with their heads lowered, a mass of them pouring in through the gate. Just my luck, there seemed to be more guards than usual around.

"I hid behind a fence near the gate waiting for an opportunity to merge with the crowd, but every time I started out another guard appeared and I had to duck back behind the fence. Down the road I could see the end of the column. I was growing desperate. It was almost as if the Germans were expecting me. At the last moment, one of the guards dropped back to light a cigarette and while the match flashed in his face I jumped out and joined the brigade. One bored German stood by the gate counting the incoming workers. There was no way to trade for food at the airport, so nobody bothered to check the workers' pockets. If they counted an extra worker returning, perhaps they'd assume they'd made a mistake. They were concerned that no one should escape. Why would they worry about an extra person returning?

"You can't imagine what it felt like as I walked the streets of the ghetto again. I could have kissed every crooked house and every dirty cobblestone. It was good to be back home, no matter how humble."

When he finished his story, we sat for a long time in silence. I was certain of one thing: none of us would ever be the same again.

The question was what to do next. We knew that if the Germans ever found out about Cooky's escape they would hunt him down and kill him. All those he came in contact with would share the same fate. At first Chaim suggested that Cooky go to the Committee and have them record his story, but we realized that it would be too dangerous to talk to people about it.

Chaim then suggested that we record it in our ghetto diaries. I had started mine the day the Soviets entered Lithuania. It was not a daily diary, but I wrote in it at least once a week and sometimes twice. Chaim, as an amateur historian, kept a journal for years. Cooky too kept some sort of a diary, although he liked reading much more than writing. We promised each other that whoever survived would see that all three diaries were published.

It was my task to go to Cooky's parents and prepare them for the good news. We also decided to tell everyone who thought Cooky perished in the "Big Action" that he had hidden for a few days with my friend Petras. It seemed important that no one know he had survived the Ninth Fort.

Cooky's parents were both working outside the ghetto, so I headed to their house toward evening and waited outside for them to arrive. I came up and said hello as they were about to go in the door. All my prepared speeches suddenly leaked away, and we just stood there smiling sadly at each other. They looked so old and unhappy.

"There are some books here that I am sure Cooky would want you to have," his mother finally said.

I just nodded my head and waited until we got safely inside. "I have some news . . . for you," I stammered, "but s-sit down first, please." They looked at me as if I had lost my senses. What kind of news could I bring that would matter to them?

"Cooky is alive," I blurted. "He is alive." At my words they both jumped up in the air.

"If this is some kind of cruel joke, I suggest that you get out of here now!" Mr. Kopelman yelled.

"No! No! He is alive! He is alive! He didn't want to scare you that's why he sent me first!" I yelled back.

Cooky's mother let out a deep sigh and fainted. We both caught her before she fell to the floor.

"How? What? Where is he?" Cooky's father began questioning me fiercely even as he lifted Mrs. Kopelman up and began patting her face with a cloth to revive her.

"He is just outside waiting for my signal. And one more thing, for God's sake, no one is to know that he was at the fort, or we are all dead."

"Yes, yes. I understand. Just tell him to come home!" he yelled.

When I left they were all crying in each others' arms. I was unable to control my own tears, and quickly slipped away. It was one of the few times in the ghetto that I cried out of happiness.

The next few days I felt like I was walking around in a dream, I was so happy that Cooky was alive and well. But I had horrible nightmares. I wish Cooky hadn't told me about the pit, and how Lena died. It would have saved me many sleepless nights.

11
Winter 1941

*T*he morning of December 7, 1941, a Japanese armada of thirty warships, including two battleships, two heavy cruisers, and six aircraft carriers mounting 423 aircraft, cruised toward Oahu. Diplomatic tensions between Japan and the United States had reached an impasse over Japan's military expansion into China, and despite warnings of a possible attack in the Pacific islands, the American fleet lay quietly at anchor in Pearl Harbor. It was a brilliantly sunny Sunday morning. About a third of the crews were on shore leave, and many officers and enlisted men had spent a typical Saturday night at parties and clubs in town. The surprise was complete. Local church bells were ringing when the first bombs fell.

Air raid sirens sounded too late in Honolulu, but when word of the attack reached the U.S. mainland, sirens sounded up and down the West Coast. In Hollywood, California, twenty-year-old Clarence Matsumura was walking home from his job at a food market when he heard the news.

Like other second-generation Japanese or Nisei, Cal Matsumura gave little thought to the fact that the United States now considered the Japanese to be belligerent. He was an American, born and raised in Wyoming. He was a member of the local Congregational Church. He had graduated from John Marshall High School in Hollywood. Some of the Disney kids and other children of movie moguls and actors were his classmates. He was attending Los Angeles Trade Technical Junior College, working toward a license in the burgeoning field of radio and telecommunications. Like most American boys, he wanted a car of his own, and was holding down two part-time jobs—one at the food market, the other as a repairman at a large radio wholesaler—to earn the money. What did Pearl Harbor have to do with him?

The next evening Franklin Delano Roosevelt announced that the United States had declared war on Japan. The day after that Cal's boss at Radio Products Sales Company called him and two other Nisei employees into his office. He had no complaints, he said, but if he did receive any complaints from customers about the Nisei working there, Clarence and his friends might have to be let go.

The West Coast was designated Defense Zone One, and was soon effectively under martial law. Rumors flew. A submarine had been captured off Santa Barbara. There were rumors of sabotage in local industries. Clarence's parents and other Issei, or first-generation immigrants, were questioned by the FBI. Clarence's apartment was searched for transmitters. He had no idea how the government knew he had radio equipment.

Irony of ironies, the same fear of sabotage in Hawaii had helped assure the near total destruction of American defenses there. The local command had been more worried about sabotage by Hawaiians of Japanese descent than about an attack from Japan itself. Ammunition aboard American ships in the harbor was stored in padlocked steel chests which frantic sailors had to crack open with hammers and crowbars. Aircraft at Wheeler field were lined up in tidy rows, under guard. They were perfect targets. Their ammunition belts had been removed and stored in hangars. The four Japanese planes that were destroyed in the first wave of the attack were brought down not by ack-ack, but by American soldiers firing Browning automatic rifles and machine guns at the low-flying Zekes.

As devastating as the attack on Pearl Harbor was, it was in many ways a strategic error for the Axis. It ended forever America's isolationist tendencies and its ambivalence about the war overseas. That night hundreds of angry young Americans flooded recruiting stations all over the country. Some stations set up cots in the halls, where the would-be recruits grew weary waiting to sign up. Those who didn't fall out talked of "dirty little Japs" and "monkeys without tails." Anti-Japanese sentiment grew throughout the mainland. In downtown Los Angeles, which had a large Japanese American population, rocks were thrown through their storefront windows, and crosses were burned in front of their homes.

Adolf Hitler may have rejoiced that the American Navy had been dealt a crippling blow, but most of Germany received the news with great foreboding. No one had forgotten the effects of American intervention in the First World War. Equally depressing news arrived from the eastern front on the same day. Hitler's offensive in Russia had been predicated on the quick dispatch of the

*enemy before winter set in, but the assault was now struggling against stiff-
ened defenses outside Moscow. On December 8 the temperature dropped to forty
degrees below zero. The German troops were still dressed in their summer uniforms, with no hope of being re-equipped.*

In the Kaunas ghetto the snow and cold that made its appearance on
October 26 deepened in November. Those inmates who had survived
the "Big Action" fell into a mood of total despair. Nearly everyone
had lost some family member, and it was quite clear that our useful-
ness as workers would not save us.

In November of 1941 even the news from the front lines was bad.
According to the Germans, the war against the Soviets was just about
won. Leningrad was besieged, and the Germans were within twenty-
five miles of Moscow. The Wehrmacht had inflicted three million
casualties on the Russians in one of the greatest sustained offensives
in military history. We were certain that we were all marked for death.
Even Father and Aunt Anushka, the optimists in the family, seemed
to think our situation was hopeless.

Isaac Trotsky came around again. His foreman at the airport had
taken a distinct dislike to him, and his last beating had left him with a
broken nose and blackened eyes. He looked terrible, and was practically in tears when he begged me to replace him in the brigade for a
few days. Despite myself I blamed him for what happened to Cooky,
and I loathed the idea of going to the airport. Working in the cold
and wet was hell, and the long march to the airport and back was
equally terrible. But how could I refuse him?

Father came to the rescue. He told Isaac that so many of the
airport workers had been killed during the "Big Action" that the
labor department was in total confusion. No one had a list of who was
dead and who was alive, and many workers were simply hiding out. At
this point, even the Council and the Jewish police didn't give a damn.

"What more can they do than kill us? They are doing that anyway,
so why worry?" Father said. Trotsky was convinced, and decided just
to take off for a few days. Before he left he took me aside and told me
how terribly sorry he was about Cooky.

"I feel rotten about it. Several times I was on my way to the
Kopelmans to express my condolences, but every time I turned back.
I just couldn't face them."

He looked so miserable that I decided to tell him the story we had concocted. Sooner or later Isaac would find out that Cooky was alive anyway, so I told him that he had escaped the small ghetto and hidden with my friend Petras.

He was very angry that I hadn't told him sooner, and he didn't believe the story. He insisted that I tell him the truth. I had to admit that Cooky had actually escaped the Ninth Fort. In the end Isaac understood why were keeping Cooky's story a secret. "He'd better stay in hiding," he said nervously. "If he's seen, word will get around, and some informer is bound to tell the Gestapo."

The same evening I went to the Kopelmans, hoping that Cooky hadn't shown himself in the open, but I needn't have worried. He was hiding out in the attic, where his parents had made up a bed and provided a big stack of books.

Later that evening Father told us that the Germans were starting to threaten the Council about the work details.

"Less than half of the airport brigade showed up and there was pandemonium at the gate," Father said. "The guards started grabbing anyone they could lay their hands on to fill the quota.

"Later the butcher Rauca and Jordan himself showed up at the Committee and began to threaten Dr. Elkes and the others. But when they realized their threats wouldn't work this time, they changed their tack, assuring the Committee that there would be no further actions against the ghetto. From now on, they said, if everyone carried out orders and worked hard, we would be left alone. He even produced a modest payment to be distributed among the airport brigade, and promised more rations for all the workers."

No one really took these assurances seriously, but not going into town meant not being able to trade for extra food, and not working meant our rations would be cut. Under those circumstances everyone would starve.

Around the middle of November, on a Sunday, Petras met me again at the fence and brought bread, carrots, and cabbage. His note apologized for not bringing any meat or butter, and promised some next time. The second part of the note was disturbing. He said that many foreign Jews were coming through Kaunas and being marched to the Ninth Fort.

When I got back to the house Fanny was in the middle of telling the family that hundreds of Austrian Jews had arrived at the railroad station. Several told her they were coming to our ghetto to join the workforce.

Father also heard that Jews from Western Europe were being brought in to replace the workers killed during the liquidation of the small ghetto.

"They will replace no one," I announced grimly. I didn't want to sound harsh, but I was dismayed at how gullible we continued to be.

A sudden silence fell in the room. They were all looking at me.

"What makes you say that?" Father asked, annoyed at my tone.

"Because right now they are being marched to the fort. Petras saw them," I said, showing them the note.

Not even the welcome supplies from Petras could dispel our gloom that night. Few words were spoken as we gathered at the table for our soup, which tasted vile because we had run out of salt.

"Lies, lies, nothing but lies! Hardly a week has gone by since Jordan and Rauca made all their promises, and already they are murdering Jews again!" Father said bitterly.

For the rest of the month Fanny reported that thousands of Jews from various parts of Europe were arriving at the station and being sent to the Ninth Fort. Although they marched them at night to avoid creating a panic among the ghetto population, everyone could hear the faint but steady machine-gun fire echoing from the fort, and once again we were plunged into despair. The Germans desperately needed manpower at the airport, and healthy young workers were being mowed down at the Ninth Fort. It didn't make sense.

December of 1941 brought one of the worst winters we ever experienced. It became so cold that lying fully clothed under the blankets didn't do any good. I lay shivering the whole night, unable to warm up. Fanny and Fima would bring a little wood from town, but it was barely enough to cook the evening meal. As temperatures began dropping to four below zero Fahrenheit, our situation became intolerable. Fima and Fanny came back from work so frozen that it took hours of massaging their hands and feet to get the blood circulating again. Many people in the ghetto suffered terrible frostbite. Some lost whole limbs.

One night I dressed as warmly as I could and went out hunting for wood. I decided that I'd rather be shot than freeze to death. I didn't tell anyone that I was going, because I was sure that the family would never allow it.

A couple of streets over there was a block of houses with wooden fences between them. Many planks were already missing, and I decided I'd better get to work before the rest disappeared. It was so cold that I had difficulty breathing, but within half an hour I had removed about twenty planks and dragged them home. No one bothered me. I went back several times until I had taken down more than half of the planks. The rest were hard to remove and I made some noise trying to knock them off.

Someone inside the next house began to shout at me and I ran all the way home, certain that their screams would bring the guards. I made a commotion bringing the precious loot inside, and soon the whole family was awake and yelling that I'd bring disaster down on us, destroying ghetto property this way. But I didn't care. Fima and I stoked the stove until it glowed red, and we all huddled around it. It was an incredible pleasure to feel warm for a change. The next day dozens of people were at the fences tearing down planks. We managed to get a few more boards, but not many. With careful rationing, however, our hoard would last a couple of weeks.

Although we were suffering terribly from it, the unusually cold weather brought us a ray of hope from the eastern front. The Nazis' victorious sweep over the Soviet forces had stalled in the frozen vastness of Russia, in one of the severest winters of the century. Fanny brought us the news that whole trainloads of German soldiers with frozen limbs were coming through the railway station, headed back to Germany.

We all prayed that Hitler's army would go the way of Napoleon's, but we knew that this would be a painfully slow process at best, and most likely we wouldn't be around to see it.

Whenever I heard any encouraging news I went to Cooky and shared it with him. He had slipped into a terrible depression, and hiding out in the attic all the time wasn't helping. Every time he heard the slightest noise he would tremble with fear, sure that the Germans were coming to get him. When I tried to distract him with some anecdote, he looked at me accusingly. And when I suggested that we go to Jasha and bring him Maria's message, he looked at me as if I had lost my mind.

"Are you crazy?! If I tell him where I have been the whole world will know about it. You want to kill me?" he shouted.

Then he gave me a suspicious look. "You didn't tell anybody about me, did you? Swear it! Swear it!" he screamed, grabbing me by the shoulders. I had to swear. I dared not tell him about Isaac Trotsky.

I began to think that Cooky's experience at the Ninth Fort had permanently damaged him. I was afraid that if he stayed cooped up in that attic he would lose his mind entirely. No one had any illusions about the killings at the Ninth Fort. He wasn't privy to some big Nazi secret anymore.

"Surely enough time has passed that it's safe now," I insisted. "Everyone in the ghetto has too many troubles of their own to be thinking about who was and who wasn't sent to the wrong side." But Cooky refused to listen.

I hadn't seen Jasha since the "Big Action," and Maria's message was weighing on my conscience. Almost two months had passed since Cooky's return, and I thought I should tell Jasha in spite of Cooky's paranoid fears. So when Jasha showed up at our house one day I took him aside where no one could hear us.

"Look, a message arrived from Maria, and please don't ask me how I got it. She has problems in her village and may have to leave. But wherever she goes she will take Ronnie with her. So you don't have to worry about him," I blurted out.

Jasha gave me an incredulous look and then demanded to know what the hell I was talking about. When I started to repeat the message, he interrupted me.

"I heard you the first time. What I want to know is where did you get this message? Who gave it to you? We are talking about the safety of my son. Speak up!"

I could see that he was getting pretty excited. When I tried to evade him, he became very loud and attracted everyone's attention. That was the last thing I wanted. I realized that I would have to tell him in spite of Cooky's objections.

We went outside and I told him Cooky's story. At first he had a hard time believing that someone had escaped the fort alive, but in the end he accepted it. He shook his head sadly and was about to ask something. I could see that he was struggling.

"I must talk to Cooky, Solly. I want to know how Ronnie is doing and why Maria has to leave the village. I will wait a little while until he feels better, but I will go to him soon. Tell him that he doesn't have to be afraid. His secret is safe with me."

The end of 1941 found us cold, hungry, and disheartened. To us it was an accursed year, probably the worst in the history of the Jewish people. Nobody celebrated New Years of 1941 in the ghetto. Our only satisfaction was that our Nazi torturers were now freezing in the vast muddy wastes of Russia. And there was an even better piece of news. Word had filtered into the ghetto that the United States was now involved in the war.

But about the plight of the Jews the Western world was silent. It was obvious that Hitler and his henchmen intended to rid the world of the Jews, and Europe would do nothing to stop him. The Germans even boasted that they had gotten approval from the Vatican.

Nevertheless, perhaps out of habit, we all sat until midnight waiting for the arrival of 1942. No one went to sleep. We decided to warm up the house a little, and Mother cooked a large pot of soup, thick with potatoes, barley, and sausage that Fanny had managed to bring from town. The grown-ups began reminiscing about past New Years and how they celebrated. In the end we all ended up crying. At midnight we listened for the church bells in Kaunas, but instead we heard a barrage of rifle fire from the guards around the fence. Thus they heralded the Christian New Year.

When Cooky found out that I told Jasha about his escape, he was furious. I reminded him that he owed Maria his life, and Jasha had a right to get her message, but Cooky just screamed that I was endangering his life and had no right to do it. His paranoid outbursts had become too much for me, and for a long time I stayed away from him. When I wasn't working I would sit and read, wearing woolen gloves and pulling a blanket over my head. We burned the wood from the fences sparingly. It was only January, and winter would be with us for a while.

Around the middle of the month Father brought us the news that a new outfit would be in charge of the ghetto. It was called the National Sozialistisch Kraftfahr Korps (National Socialist Vehicle Corps), or N.S.K.K. No one had any idea who they were. The name gave us no indication of who we were dealing with except that it sounded blandly professional. Perhaps, God willing, they would be less strict than the German police.

The next day I was supposed to meet Petras at the fence and I was looking forward to it. I hoped that his cigarette friend would be on that beat again. He had frightened me to death, and I had daydreams about somehow getting him back. The idea sent my pulse racing. I was beginning to enjoy a certain element of danger. I had even made myself a sort of robe out of an old white sheet to wear over my coat. Snow camouflage, like the brave soldiers of Norway wore.

Again I told no one about my appointment at the fence. I left the house late in the afternoon, and at the prearranged time was sitting on the roof of the cinema waiting for Petras's signal. A light snow began to fall. About ten minutes passed and still no sign of him. It was getting dark, and I was getting anxious about the lights coming on. Knowing that the guard was bought was of some comfort, but the guard patrolling the fence wore a winter hat with flaps over his ears, and there was no way I could recognize him for sure. From time to time he would slap his arms and jump up and down to warm himself. When he was about fifty meters away I finally heard Petras's signal. Once again he ran across the street and sent the parcel flying through the air, landing it neatly inside the ghetto. Fortunately it didn't fall too close to the fence. I scrambled down from the roof and ran straight for the bag, not even bothering to check where the guard was. I was keyed up and full of adrenalin, my heart racing like the pistons of an engine. I wasn't even very alarmed when the guard said "Hey!"

"Halt or I shoot," he yelled. But it was in German. He wasn't a Lithuanian at all, he was a German!

I didn't have much time to contemplate my situation. If I stopped as ordered I would be dead. Not letting go of the bag, I straightened up facing him, then spun around and took off, running in zig-zags away from the fence.

My sudden move probably surprised him for an instant. Then he started shooting. I heard a deafening boom, and the reloading of the rifle, followed by another shot. Something hot touched my right shoulder. The corner of the cinema wall loomed in front of me. I knew that if he had enough time to cock and shoot again he would get me.

With all my strength I launched myself into the air and leaped for the wall. As I hit the ground the third shot exploded and the bullet smacked into the wall above my head, but I was safe. I had such a feeling of triumph that I let out a whoop of joy. I don't know what got into me then, but I turned around and screamed "You missed me, you German asshole!"

I regretted it instantly, knowing how many innocent people might be shot because of me. But it was too late for regrets. I heard his furious shouts for me to stop, and several more shots in my direction, but I had the bulk of the cinema at my back. I ran through the narrow streets of the ghetto as I had never run in my life.

As I neared our street and my panic subsided, I noticed something sticky on my right hand. I looked down and realized it was blood. Then I remembered the sensation of heat touching my shoulder and I realized that I was wounded. Obviously it wasn't a very serious wound, but if I returned home bleeding my mother would probably faint.

As we so often did when one of us was in trouble, I headed for Chaim's.

He was, as usual, very glad to see me, although he was dismayed when he saw the blood. Fortunately, it was a flesh wound and not too deep at that.

But my coat had a hole in it where the bullet had penetrated, and my undergarments were bloody. Chaim gave me a clean jersey, but there was nothing to be done about the bullet hole in the coat. I would just have to hide it from my parents.

When I entered the house the family was in an uproar. I hadn't realized how much time had passed since I left. I dropped the bag on the table for all to see and stood there to be admired, but they just stared at me angrily.

"You were at the fence today? Today of all days?!" Father exploded at me. "Haven't you heard that the new guards shoot people just because they don't take their hats off fast enough? What are you, some kind of suicidal maniac?!" he shouted, lifting his hand as if to strike. I looked him in the eyes without flinching. I had faced a German guard with a rifle, so Father wasn't about to scare me, especially since I knew that he wouldn't slap me anyway. He stood there furious, his hand still raised, not knowing what to do.

"Are you going to bless me or slap me? Make up your mind," I finally said, giving him a wink. That confused him even more, but he quickly lowered his hand. Miriam was the one who appreciated my humor and burst out laughing, while Anushka and Uncle Jochil tried to hide their smiles. Mother, however, grew indignant.

"Don't you speak to your father like that, young man! You deserve a real spanking!" she said in an angry voice. Then Fanny came to my defense.

"He obviously didn't know about the change of guards or the shooting, otherwise he wouldn't have gone. Besides, he came back unharmed and brought some food home, so let's be thankful for that."

Taking the cue from my sister I started removing things from the bag. There were three loaves of bread and some lard. There were also two white cheeses and a big piece of bacon, and when I produced these everyone sucked in their breath. The ice was broken. That evening we had a fine supper, and everyone congratulated me on my coup. But I was not to go anywhere near the fence again, my parents declared, not until the situation with the new outfit was clarified.

It soon became evident that our new masters were more fanatical than the previous ones. During the first week they searched every person returning from town, and anyone trying to smuggle in food or firewood was severely beaten. Several men were shot to death. They meant business, and if this kept up the ghetto would soon be starving again.

Fortunately it wasn't long before the Committee arranged some handsome bribes, just as they'd done with the previous crew. Soon the workers were able to bring in small quantities of food again, and the situation more or less returned to normal. In one respect it worsened. The new German administrators set up a station inside the ghetto, and guards began patrolling the fences inside the perimeter as well as outside. The Germans had declared the fence to be a "death zone," and anyone caught within three meters on either side of it would be shot. They also threatened to shoot anyone out after the nine P.M. curfew.

My next meeting with Petras was set for the middle of February and I didn't know what to do. Many of the Lithuanians were brought back to guard the fences, and I hoped that Petras's friend would be among them. In the end I wrote him a letter explaining the new situation, which Fanny delivered through a friend at the railroad station. It would be a shame to give up the extra food we so desperately needed.

• • •

One evening I heard Cooky's signal outside the house. It had been more than two weeks since I'd laid eyes on him. In the light of a full moon he looked like a ghost. His hair was matted and he smelled like he hadn't washed for ages. He wore the oversized coat and boots he had brought back from the fort.

"You were right. I was going out of my mind in that attic. Since you wouldn't come to me, I decided to come to you. Besides, what else can they do to me except shoot me?" he said with his old crooked smile.

"Friends?" he asked, extending his hand. "Friends," I answered, putting my hand in his, "But not until you take a bath. You stink to high heaven!" Both of us started laughing. I was glad to have my friend back.

Our next stop was Chaim's place, and he received Cooky very warmly. We sat and talked as we had in the old times. I could almost feel the spirits of Lena and Aviva in the room. Part of my mind rebelled against this "normal" behavior. I could imagine Lena's reproaches. How could we smile and laugh after losing our friends? We should be tearing our hair out and putting ashes on our heads.

Around the first of February Father returned from work with more bad news. After a too-brief period of calm, Jordan had demanded that the Jewish Committee provide five hundred able-bodied workers to be sent to a camp near Riga, in Latvia. Once more the ghetto was gripped in a wave of fear. We all remembered what had happened to the squad of five hundred "learned men."

No one was about to volunteer. Even if the Germans really did want laborers, no one wanted to leave the ghetto. The Committee was forced to decide who would go. Fanny, Miriam, and Fima felt that they would be likely candidates, since they were young and single. Fima suggested that they go into hiding for a while, but no one knew exactly when these people were to be delivered.

Several days passed. All three went back to work. They didn't want to lose their jobs. Miriam had started working in town too, for the Gestapo brigade. A Jew by the name of Benno Lipzer was in charge of it. Strangely enough that brigade was considered a good place to work, because Lipzer had the ear of the Gestapo chiefs. He was becoming a very powerful figure in the ghetto.

Finally, the Germans set February 6 as the date when the five hundred were to be delivered. The evening before, groups of Jewish policemen, accompanied by Germans, spread out through the ghetto. They had lists of the people who were to be deported. Most of them were single women or elderly men without families. These unfortunate people cursed and denounced the Jewish police for doing the German's dirty work. They had to be forcibly dragged to the assembly place. When they were delivered to the railway station the Germans in charge stopped the whole shipment. They had only rounded up 180 people, and most of them were unfit to work. All were returned to the ghetto the same night. Needless to say, most of them went into hiding immediately.

Although it was the middle of the night, the news that the deported had returned to the ghetto reached every house. We all knew there would be hell to pay. We decided that the safest place for us to be was at work. No one wanted to be found hanging around at home.

The next day Jordan showed up at the Jewish administration office in a rage, cursing the Committee and accusing them of incompetence. He ordered everyone still within the confines of the ghetto, including the workers in the various ghetto institutions, to assemble at noon on Demokratu Square.

Since my parents worked for the Council itself, they decided their best course of action was to obey. Uncle Jochil, Aunt Dobbe, and Anushka also reported to the assembly point. Fanny, Miriam, and Fima went to their workplaces in town. Cooky's parents also worked in town, and Cooky and I decided to hide in his attic.

Around four in the afternoon the Germans crashed through Cooky's front door. We trembled as we heard their heavy boots below, but they left without discovering us. It was bitterly cold in the attic, but we stayed up there for the rest of the day.

About an hour after dark the door opened again, and Cooky's mother called out. We quickly descended and she told us what had happened. It seemed that Jordan, not finding any younger men assembled at the square, began conscripting anyone, including some important ghetto officials. Even then he couldn't fill the quota. The next step was obvious. He began selections from the returning town brigades. Cooky's mother barely escaped selection herself. She was now very worried about her husband, who usually returned from work about the same time as she.

I said good-bye to them and rushed home. I was scared to death that Fanny, Fima, and Miriam had been taken. Somehow I was not worried about the adults.

No one was home. It was dark and cold in the house when I entered. The unusual silence made me feel terribly abandoned. I waited until I felt the very walls were closing in on me. Finally I rushed out into the street, thinking the neighbors might be able to tell me something. I noticed a light on in the Krokin's window next door. I knocked a few times, but no one answered. I had already turned to leave when Mrs. Krokin suddenly opened the door and shouted, "Your uncle Jochil and his wife were sent to Riga. Your parents and your cousins went to the Committee to try and get them back." I gaped at her, and she stared back, then emitted a high-pitched laugh as if trying to demonstrate that she was quite mad. Then she slammed the door in my face. I had no idea whether to believe her or not.

I thought perhaps I should go to the Committee myself, but it was close to curfew, and if what she said was true they would soon be home.

I tried to imagine what life would be like without Jochil and Dobbe. I loved Uncle Jochil, and had even grown fond of Aunt Dobbe. Contrary to what we all expected, living together in such close proximity, being in each other's way, and never having any privacy, only brought us closer together.

It was bitterly cold in the house. I lit the stove to warm it up a little, and put on the pot of soup Mother had prepared the previous evening. Still they didn't come. I feared they had all been sent to Riga, or perhaps even to the Ninth Fort. When my spirits were at their lowest ebb I finally heard their voices outside. Fanny and Anushka, thanks God, were with them. I could hear Miriam weeping and my mother trying to calm her. So it was true. Uncle Jochil and Aunt Dobbe wouldn't be coming back.

At least my parents were not sent away. I was ashamed at the relief I felt at that moment. Grief came later. After supper we sat together and cried until late at night. Miriam blamed herself for being hard on her mother. Father was accusing himself of stupidity. Why did we go to the assembly? he kept repeating. How could we still be so gullible? Since they started working together he and Uncle Jochil had become very close.

Most of the people who showed up at the square were either members of the administration or elderly people who believed that since the Germans wanted young, able workers, they wouldn't be touched. Jordan appeared with a group of German guards around midday, and began sorting the crowd.

"When our turn came, Jordan simply divided our row in half and sent Jochil and Dobbe to the group destined for Riga. I knew Jordan from his occasional visits to our department, and begged him to release Jochil and Dobbe. He didn't even give me a second glance. Even then he didn't have the five hundred people he wanted."

"I know," Fanny said. "At the gate they took about ten men from our brigade. But everyone said they were actually going to Riga," she added, trying to console Miriam.

But Fima and Miriam were inconsolable.

The next day Father and Fima went to the Jewish Committee to try once more to free Jochil and Dobbe. There were rumors that certain Committee members selected by Jordan were actually brought back to the ghetto, due to the intervention of Dr. Elkes and other influential persons.

More than a thousand people were there, clamoring for the Committee to help free their husbands and fathers. Father managed to speak to Dr. Elkes, who sat ashen-faced in his office, but it was too late. No one could bring them back anymore.

One of the lucky ones was Cooky's father, who was sent back to the ghetto with the few Committee officials the Germans decided to let go.

A few weeks later someone smuggled in messages from the deported people. All were well. They were actually in Riga, and working. The work was terrible, but they were alive. This message had a calming influence on the ghetto, although the deportations still had tragic consequences for the many families who lost their breadwinners. Nevertheless everyone was heartened that the workers were alive. Fima and Miriam actually jumped for joy.

All our other family members had eluded Jordan's clutches, and many came to console Miriam and Fima. Uncle Itzhak Shtrom, his wife Sonia, and my cousins Milie, Zunie, Frieda, and Miriam (another Miriam) all gathered at our house that night.

Milie and Zunie, who were twenty-four and twenty-one years old, spoke of organizing an armed resistance. Zunie had served a year with the Soviet army, and was especially eager. "What have we got to lose? We might as well die fighting."

"But where would we get weapons? The Lithuanians are our enemies, as we well know. And even if we did get weapons, it would be suicide to fight the German army here," Fima said.

"I'm not talking about an uprising. No, our method of fighting would be sneak attacks, probably from the woods. We cannot attack the Germans from the ghetto or they would murder the whole population," Zunie answered.

The idea of fighting the Germans with weapons in our hands excited my imagination. I could see myself standing, flag in hand, firing an automatic weapon into the enemy, just as they showed in Soviet movies before the war.

"You can count me in!" I cried, jumping out of my chair and straightening myself to my full height. They all looked at me standing there as if at attention, and burst out laughing. I was thirteen years old, and rather small for my age. Malnutrition didn't exactly improve my appearance. I guess I was hurt by their laughter and showed it, because my older cousin Milie came over and clasped my shoulder. He was one of the kindest men I knew.

"Your turn will come too. When we get organized we will be able to use you as a runner. But you mustn't say a word of what you have heard here. Right now it is just talk, but it will mean a death sentence if the Germans find out that we are entertaining such ideas."

The discussions of armed resistance bolstered Fima and Miriam's morale, even though they knew that Milie and Zunie probably raised the subject specifically for that purpose. It still felt like a breakthrough. It was the first time anyone in our family openly contemplated organized resistance against the Germans. It was a dream that had already taken hold of others in the ghetto.

12

The Book Action

By the end of 1941 thousands of frozen German soldiers were being transported by rail back into Germany. Although the campaign had inflicted staggering casualties on the Soviets, it had also taken an enormous toll on the Wehrmacht, which lost some 800,000 men. The Russian offensive had been halted, however temporarily, by "General Mud" and "General Winter." German supply lines were stretched to the breaking point.

But somehow the Wehrmacht had to be supplied and supported. On January 20, 1942, Reinhard Heydrich, the "blond beast," chaired the Wannsee Conference on the Final Solution of the Jewish question. There he proposed to a group of top Nazi officials that the Jews of Europe be worked to death building roads into Russia.

In the occupied territories the Germans pressed local industries into service. Few Jews had any illusions about their fate after the "Big Action," but remaining useful to the Germans seemed to be our only hope for survival. The Jewish Council organized ghetto workshops, which produced necessary goods for the Germans in exchange for food and erratic token payments.

Unlike the Jewish councils and capos in most ghettos and camps, the Kaunas Council and its Jewish police force managed to hold the community together, opening vocational training schools in carpentry and other basic skills for the youth. The classes provided effective cover for more traditional education and for the operations of Zionist youth organizations. Through these and other clandestine means, the Council and the ghetto inmates struggled to keep some remnants of civilization alive.

● ● ●

The deportations to Riga on February 6 were soon followed by more sad news. Late that month the Germans ordered all books in the ghetto to be turned over to the authorities. Anyone caught with books after the deadline would be executed. The people of the book, as we had been known throughout the ages, were to be separated from our ancient companions.

Earlier in the year the Germans ordered an area about a block from where we lived to be evacuated, and that part of the ghetto remained abandoned. There were strict orders not to enter it, but it wasn't long before Cooky and I were sneaking in to look for scraps of firewood or whatever else could be salvaged from the place. It was risky, but it was clear to me that unless I took a few risks my chances for survival were nil. I figured I didn't really have anything to lose.

After several such "raids" we discovered the best of all treasures— an attic with some old books in it. It could be reached only through an opening in the ceiling, and after some scavenging we managed to put together a rope ladder we could haul up behind us. It became another good hiding place, and it was perfect for what we came to call "operation library."

When Cooky joked that we could probably hide half the books in the ghetto in our new attic, he immediately regretted it. He knew exactly what I was thinking, and he didn't like it. Even though he had regained some of his old vitality since his visit to the Ninth Fort, he no longer had any nerve. I had to push him.

Nearly everyone complied with the order and began delivering their precious books to the assembly point.

It snowed the night before the deadline and the ghetto was covered by a thick white blanket the next morning. My mother had tears in her eyes as she helped me load her beloved books into my homemade sled. The final load consisted of ten volumes of Russia's best authors, all bound in red leather with gold embossed lettering. Tolstoy, Lermontov, Dostoyevsky, Turgenev, Pushkin, Gogol—the thoughts, passions, ideals, and feelings of literary giants were in those books. The set was a wedding gift from Jochil.

I felt a deep compassion for my mother. She had never quite recovered from Herman's disappearance behind the walls of the Seventh Fort, and now her brother Jochil had been deported to Riga, perhaps never to be seen again. Mother rarely laughed or smiled these days.

Like me, she escaped from her grief by reading. She would sit almost motionless for hours, only moving two fingers to flip the pages. Nothing else existed when she read. Not even food interested her. And now they were even taking her books away.

"Keep them, Mommy," I wanted to tell her. "We are all going to be killed anyway. You might as well enjoy your books while you can." But I kept my silence. Mother found it difficult enough keeping in touch with our terrible new reality.

"Make sure you take these books straight to the German storage center," she said to me sadly, and as if sensing my thoughts she added in a stern voice, "Don't even think of hiding them, you hear me? It isn't worth getting shot on account of books."

I quickly averted my eyes. My mother could always sense my thoughts when she looked into my eyes.

Cooky waited for me on the corner of Gimbuto. He also had a sled loaded with books, and he looked jittery.

"Let's go," I said firmly. I knew he hated this idea, but I also knew he would follow me. We quickly crossed the road leading to the forbidden quarter, and within half an hour we had hauled all the books into the attic.

The same day we brought four more loads of books given to us by neighbors who had no sleds and were glad that someone would take them away.

But I wasn't satisfied, and I had an idea. Cooky put up a bigger protest this time, but in the end he went along. I got both of us work sorting the books brought to the assembly point. The man in charge, Mr. Grodnik, was sorting the books by language and subject matter, and he was glad to let us carry the sorted stacks from the first floor to the second. When I reported for work the next day, I announced that Cooky was at home sick. He was actually waiting behind the house, below a small window in the stairwell. All day I ran up the stairs with a load of books under each arm. As I rounded the first landing, I dropped the stack under my left arm out the window into the snow below, where Cooky waited, then continued up the stairs and deposited the remainder in stacks as instructed. After about an hour I could almost do this without breaking stride.

It was risky business, and despite the cold I was soon dripping with sweat. After two or three days of this Cooky was caught by a German guard. He gave the guard the story we had concocted, that he was delivering books and looking for the entrance to the building, and the German believed him, giving him only a kick for his stupidity. Cooky wet his pants in fright that day, and refused to go on with the scheme. By then, however, we had accumulated quite a stash. A few ghetto inmates saw us trundling the books to our hiding place, but they paid us no mind. As it turned out, others in the ghetto were doing the same thing we were.

I sneaked books back to the house only one at a time, and kept them hidden from the family. But it weighed on my conscience. Here we were with this rich collection of literature, and we only used it for our own selfish ends. Soon Cooky and I began giving out books, first to our closest friends and relatives, later to more and more people who became "customers." The word got around.

Cooky and I both began attending trade school, in carpentry. One day I was approached by Mr. Edelstein, our instructor, who taught mathematics before the war and tried to instruct us in math when we weren't pounding nails. He asked me point-blank if I could get hold of any textbooks, especially in mathematics. I first denied that I had any sources, but when he insisted I told him I would inquire. Cooky had in fact cursed me for saving some school books, especially those in mathematics. He hated math. "Is this what I risked my neck for?" he yelled when he saw them. There was one newer-looking geometry book among these that I smuggled into school for Mr. Edelstein. He was so delighted that he gave me a big hug. "Do you know what a treasure this is? Look! It's in Hebrew and was printed in Tel Aviv only a few years ago. Where on earth did you get it?"

We'd just put the textbooks in the corner and I never really looked at them. I told Cooky about a dream I'd had in which I'd let animals into the Ark, two by two, and Cooky thereafter called the school-books our alligators, snakes, and hyenas.

Mr. Edelstein, a rather shy man with big brown eyes and thinnish hair, had taught at the high school in Kaunas. He came from a small town where Lithuanian partisans locked the Jewish population into the synagogue, then set the building on fire. His whole family had been burned alive. Despite what he'd experienced, he still believed in noble ideals, and was convinced that good would eventually triumph over evil.

He had no relatives in the ghetto, and like nearly all single men he had "adopted" a family that no longer had a working male at its head.

The Jewish Council made such assignments in order to protect single women, children, and elderly people. S.A. Lieutenant Gustav Hermann, the German head of the labor office, apparently understood that his workers' morale depended upon keeping their families intact insofar as possible, so the Jewish Council created many fictitious families where none existed. Mr. Edelstein lived with a family of five.

Mr. Edelstein had grown very fond of his adopted family, and like others often traded with the Lithuanian guards to get them extra food. When I brought him the book he put it in a bag full of clothing he was carrying. That afternoon when I left school I passed him at the gate, where he had stopped to trade with the guard. Evidently Mr. Edelstein asked for more food than the guard was willing to give him. Suddenly the Lithuanian began shouting "What's this you got hidden there, Jew boy? A book? And in your heathen language too. You know I could shoot you for possessing books. How would you like that for special payment?"

I was only about ten yards away and turned to see what was happening. A German military car approaching the gate from the other side came to a stop, and an SS officer stepped out demanding to know what was going on. I felt the bottom drop out of my stomach.

Mr. Edelstein stood ashen-faced while the Lithuanian showed the book to the SS officer. The German turned the pages slowly, then demanded to know where Mr. Edelstein had gotten that book. I couldn't hear Mr. Edelstein's answer, but the German slapped him a few times and shouted, "Don't lie to me you filthy Jew! This book was printed in Palestine and is in some kind of code! Who is your contact? Where did you get this book? Tell me or I will kill you!"

I stood frozen in horror as he and the guard began beating my teacher. Any minute I expected Mr. Edelstein to point a finger at me, but instead he made a barely perceptible gesture for me to go.

With that I found my feet and started running. I was turning into a side street when I heard a shot. I looked back to see Mr. Edelstein fall to his knees. The German put his pistol to his head and fired again, and Mr. Edelstein fell over and lay still.

That night I had a terrible nightmare about the Ninth Fort. Cooky and I were falling into that mass grave, and I could see Lena far above me, falling. Suddenly she was on top of me and the hole in her throat kept getting larger and larger, pumping out a thick mass of blood that covered my face, my mouth, my nose. I was drowning. I woke up screaming, although the screams were only in my mind. For five minutes I just lay there trying to catch my breath. The reality I woke up to wasn't a great improvement. My teacher had been murdered, and it was my fault.

I stayed home from school and cried the whole day. Finally Cooky came over and tried to cheer me up, but I was inconsolable. Me and my stupid books. For the first time I fully realized the danger I had exposed everyone to with my foolishness. My mother was right. It was senseless to get killed on account of books. I wouldn't listen to her, and now Mr. Edelstein was dead. To this day I remember his feeble gesture waving me away from there. All he had to do was point in my direction to save himself, but he would not.

"Don't be stupid. You don't really believe that the German would have let him live if he had betrayed you! He obviously would have shot both of you and Mr. Edelstein realized it," Cooky tried to argue. "Besides, he should have been more careful." But no amount of logic was going to bring Mr. Edelstein back.

He was buried in the ghetto cemetery, only a short distance from where he was shot. Except for the family he lived with and a few of his pupils, including Cooky and myself, few attended his burial. He had no relatives, and violent death was such a common occurrence in the ghetto that nobody paid much attention.

There was no funeral, as all religious practices were forbidden by the Germans. Only the boys he shared a room with were crying as the burial party slipped him into the grave. I just stood there stunned, unable to utter a sound, until sprinkles of rain and a blackening sky sent everyone scurrying for shelter.

For the next ten days I didn't go to the trade school. I was too ashamed to face the other teachers and pupils who all probably blamed me for Mr. Edelstein's death. Instead, I once again became an "Angel" replacing Isaac Trotsky at the airport. The "Angel" system had become common practice in the ghetto: Boys my age replaced the ill and received food in exchange. I spent most of my time breaking the hard clay ground with a pickax. It was heavy, and you had to have real strength to wield one for any length of time. In their weakened conditions many adults could barely swing them. For this they were abused and given murderous beatings by the Ukrainian foremen.

I stuck it out both because Aunt Dora fed me and because she was the one person who could help when it came to my teeth. I spent many sleepless nights with terrible toothaches, which were sometimes so excruciating that I would run all the way to Dora crying like a baby. With her limited resources she could only help a little, but it was enough. It was partly out of gratitude that I agreed to replace Isaac at the airport, usually one day at a time. It took him ten days to recuperate from his most recent beating, however, and at the end I could barely stand on my feet. Somehow I staggered back to the ghetto that day, and more or less collapsed on Dora's step. I had not yet turned fourteen and was undernourished, and those ten days were too much.

Dora felt very guilty when she saw my state. She made me come every evening for a whole month afterwards to give me extra rations. By ghetto standards Dora was a wealthy woman, as her services were in demand, and she continued to receive food smuggled in by her old cook.

Those ten days were purgatory, but somehow they helped expunge my guilt over Edelstein. I gained a little perspective on the whole event, and with the extra rations and several days' rest I was ready to return to school. Much to my surprise, neither the teachers nor the pupils connected Edelstein's death to the book I had given him. He was simply caught trading and died, as so many people did.

Another surprise was the fact that Cooky went to our "library" almost every day. I had sworn I'd never go near the place again. Perhaps he kept going because he didn't actually see the murder of Mr. Edelstein. Perhaps he somehow became courageous when I got scared.

From time to time he would bring me a book or two, and after about a month I finally returned with him. In this evil place people not only lost faith in God, they lost faith in society and in mankind itself. Only in the books did I find consolation. Then one day my mother came back early from work and caught me reading. She was so upset that I promised myself I would not bring books home anymore.

Cooky and I spent more and more time up in our attic hideout, reading or discussing what we'd read, and one day Cooky took out an old Bible we had among the Hebrew books. I'm not sure what prompted me to salvage it, as my upbringing was secular; perhaps I thought that a library without a Bible wouldn't be a Jewish library.

"I think we should say Kaddish for Mr. Edelstein," Cooky said after some hesitation. I looked at him in astonishment. Whenever we discussed religion, Cooky dismissed it. Both his parents were agnostic, and Cooky was brought up by them to despise religion.

"I know what you are thinking, but I think we owe it to him. After all, he did get killed because of our book. I think perhaps he would have wanted someone to say Kaddish for him," Cooky explained with some embarrassment. And so I wrote down the words of the Kaddish on a slip of paper, and the next day after school we stopped at the cemetery and read the words at his unmarked grave. Strangely enough I felt better for it, and I continued to visit and tend Edelstein's grave in the months to come. When the weather warmed I planted some peas there. To my surprise they grew into bushes and eventually bore fruit, which Cooky and I shared. I knew Mr. Edelstein wouldn't mind.

Overall, 1942 was a period of relative prosperity. More and more "lucrative" working places came into being, where workers could trade with the Lithuanian population for food. Vacant land in the ghetto was tilled and vegetables were planted. Members of the Council negotiated with the Germans for better rations. Although we were hungry all the time, we were not starving anymore. Fanny, who continued to trade with Lithuanians at the railway station, became the family's main breadwinner.

Mother, however, had become a real source of worry. The "Book Action" only increased the depression she slipped into after losing her brother Jochil. She did the cooking for the household, since she was the best cook among us, and managed to make reasonably tasty meals with minimal resources. She had always taken pride in her cooking, so when the meals turned tasteless we realized that something was seriously wrong. As the days passed Mother stopped participating in conversations, and would hardly speak even when spoken to. The next time she caught me reading a book she showed no reaction at all, when only a short time before she had given me hell.

We were all very upset. We tried to cheer her with jokes or good news from the Russian front, to no avail. It was heartbreaking to see my mother reduced to this joyless, impassive person.

Aunt Anushka, meanwhile, had gone to work for the ghetto workshops. After some fits and starts they were operating at full capacity and starting to expand. The Germans began to realize the full potential of these workshops, not just for the Wehrmacht but for their own personal comfort and gain. Indeed the stream of quality goods from these small ghetto factories was what kept the ghetto at Slabodke intact long after other ghettos were liquidated.

S.A. Lieutenant Gustav Hermann, as head of the ghetto labor office, was one of the Council's main liaisons with the German authorities. He was interested in keeping the Wehrmacht supplied, not in torturing his workers, and relative to the other Germans who held power over us he was rational and almost humane. It was he who arranged to keep the workshops supplied with equipment and raw materials, and between his efforts and those of the Council the workshops rapidly expanded. They needed tailors, cobblers, knitters, lock and blacksmiths, carpenters, brush makers, and more. In the beginning the workshops employed only a few hundred workers, but this number eventually grew to three thousand.

Anushka soon took charge of a group of women who mended German army uniforms. The Germans were so pleased that they brought in a new batch of sewing machines and demanded greater output. Anushka's group needed at least ten more seamstresses, and she pressed Mother to volunteer for the job. New regulations required women from the age of fifteen to forty-six to report for work duty, and a ghetto workshop was a far better place to work than the airport or the peatfields at Palemonas. In her state of mind Mother didn't have much resistance to anything, and the next day she left for the workshop with Anushka. There she applied herself as if her life depended on it, working grimly from morning until evening and putting out more work than anyone else in her section. At first they resented it, but when the overseer praised their overall increase in output, they learned to appreciate her.

Anushka was also concerned about Mother's frantic pace, until one day she saw Mother smiling at a co-worker's joke. It was the first time Mother had smiled in a long time. A few weeks later her mood had noticeably lifted, and we all breathed a sigh of relief.

At the end of March the cold winter sun gradually began warming again. The snow began to melt, and here and there a clump of green sprouted in the muddy ground. Nature was waking from a very cold winter. We had been incarcerated for ten months, but we were still alive.

Spring always raised my spirits. I widened my circle of friends a bit.

There were Uri Chanoch and Chaim Konwitz, who worked for Gustav Hermann at the German labor office. I encountered the Gladzookes twins, Izia and Vova, at a trade school lecture. They were old school friends I hadn't seen since the invasion.

Hermann's labor office was situated inside the ghetto. He was in charge of registering all the able-bodied men and women for work detail, and regulated the flow of Jewish workers in and out of the ghetto. Uri and Chaim worked for him as runners. They found him to be a stickler for detail, but overall one of the better bosses to work for. Uri and Chaim were also members of the Zionist youth, and were in touch with the organization's underground. The developing resistance movement was divided into two main factions: the Zionists and their various subgroups, and the Communists. They had widely divergent political views, but in the face of a common enemy they cooperated.

It was of vital importance to obtain some kind of official documents that would allow the members of these organizations to move outside of the ghetto. Lieutenant Hermann was one of the few authorities who could issue permits. Permit forms and an official seal were kept locked up in his big desk. Uri and Chaim made many attempts to pry open the drawers, but there was no way to break into the desk without visibly damaging it.

Then one day when they were cleaning the office they tried to move the desk. Herman liked his office meticulously clean, and Uri and Chaim wanted to sweep the dust underneath. When they tried to lift it the whole top came off in their hands. At first they were frightened to death. If Hermann found out they had ruined his desk they were sure it would be the end of them. On closer inspection they discovered that the top was attached to the desk by four wooden pegs. For whatever reason these were loose, and they were able to lift the top off and replace it without anyone being the wiser. The official seal was right there in the top drawer. It was a great break. The passes they later provided helped many members of the underground contact Lithuanians who were organizing their own underground movement. Most of these were Communists who had not been discovered by the Nazi authorities.

One day Father brought news that the quarter of the ghetto where we kept our library was going to be given back to the Jews who had evacuated it. For the next few days we frantically transferred books to all kinds of hiding places. We hid some underneath our house and some in Cooky's attic. We gave quite a few to Izia and Vova, the Gladzookes twins. They were working as runners for the Jewish police and sometimes snuck out of the ghetto to pick up food. They were quite blond and Aryan-looking, and no one suspected they were Jews. One day Vova returned with a message from Petras. I had tried to make contact with Petras several times since the situation with the guards had cooled down, but he did not appear on any of the dates I suggested. Through the twins Petras sent a small parcel and a note, saying that he was sorry, but his family had moved to Kalautuvas, and he wouldn't be able to come anymore. I felt a great letdown. The food he brought was a great help, and we had left quite a lot of clothing and money with his family as payment.

Fanny began to expand her trading when Petras's family left. Although she was sometimes caught at the gate and had her contraband taken away, she was becoming ever more daring. She made contact with a Lithuanian railway worker who supplied her with larger quantities of flour. Mother baked buns with it and I sold them on Varniu Street so we could buy other necessities. I became a small entrepreneur, putting together trays with loops that went around the neck and organizing a couple of younger kids to help peddle the merchandise. There was a fair amount of money in the ghetto at that point.

With the money I made, and other articles of barter, Fanny and a co-worker smuggled more and more flour into the ghetto. Our business was expanding.

Then one evening I returned from selling buns to find Father in an uproar and Mother in tears. Fanny had been arrested by the Gestapo.

She and her new partner had been caught buying flour from a Lithuanian, and unfortunately, the Lithuanian was stealing it from the German army supply depot. They were all taken to the Gestapo prison.

Usually any Jew who fell into the hands of the Gestapo for even the smallest infraction was sent to the Ninth Fort for execution. Fanny's crime, trading in goods stolen from the German army, was of the severest kind. There was no hope for her at all. I was devastated, and Father simply fell apart. Fanny was his firstborn, his favorite, and she'd been practically a second mother to me. That whole night I couldn't stop crying. It was Miriam who sat and cried with me.

Father let go and felt helpless in this situation, but Mother suddenly came to life. Early in the morning she rose and pulled Father out of bed.

"First let us do our damnedest to save her, and then if we fail, you can wallow in your sorrow. Let's go to Lipzer," she told Father grimly.

Benno Lipzer was a curious character. He was in charge of the brigade that worked for the Gestapo in Kaunas and in contact with high Gestapo officials including the infamous murderer Schtitz. Schtitz had the blood of thousands of Jews on his hands, but it was convenient for him to have his own Jew, especially when he received so many expensive gifts from him.

In this position Lipzer frequently managed to free various Jews who fell into the hands of the Gestapo. As long as his palm was well greased, Schtitz didn't mind letting Lipzer have a few Jews from time to time. There were many more where those came from.

Lipzer earned the gratitude of many families by saving their loved ones from certain death. To them Lipzer was the all-powerful defender of the downtrodden, defenseless Jew who had no connections with the members of the Committee or the Jewish police and was therefore exposed to grave dangers. These people felt they were at risk whenever the Germans demanded Jews for the camps or some other unpleasant work. There were instances in the ghetto when people came to Lipzer with complaints that they were being discriminated against by the Jewish authorities. Lipzer, who fancied himself a protector of the common man, would intervene on their behalf. The Jewish Committee feared him, and would promptly carry out his orders, no matter how absurd.

Benno Lipzer didn't exactly circulate in our family's social circles before the war. He was an uneducated traveling salesman, and what he lacked in schooling he made up with an inflated ego and high ambitions. But he knew my brother Herman, for Lipzer was one of the many Jews Herman rescued from beatings by anti-Semitic thugs during the late 1930s. Lipzer swore that he would never forget that good deed, and would one day repay Herman.

"Our child's life is in danger. It is time to collect the debt," Mother told Father, who gave her a blank stare. He had completely forgotten the incident.

He thought of going to his friend Dr. Elkes and other influential Committee members, but he never considered Lipzer. He knew that we wouldn't be on Lipzer's list of unfortunates needing his special protection.

I quickly dressed to join them. In the beginning Father was against my coming, but Mother thought my presence might help: The little boy who comes to beg the mighty Lipzer for his sister's life.

Dawn was just breaking when we left the house. Lipzer's house was still dark when we arrived, and we lingered for about fifteen minutes waiting for signs of life. Even Mother, who was racked with impatience, didn't dare wake him. Finally a light came on upstairs, and Father had to restrain her from rushing to the door.

"Give him a few minutes to get out of bed. You don't want to get him angry, do you?" We waited another five minutes before the light went on downstairs. Mother bolted for the door. She knocked several times before Lipzer opened it.

He was still in his dressing gown and looked annoyed. Instinctively I moved closer to Mother and began to cry. I don't know how I did it; the tears just seemed to come naturally. Lipzer's expression softened. I guess we looked pathetic enough.

Without giving him a chance to ask any questions, Mother launched straight into the heart of the matter.

"Our son Herman Genkind once saved you from a severe beating, and you swore you would never forget it. Our daughter Fanny, Herman's sister, was caught trading with the Lithuanians and is now in the Gestapo prison. We were told that you are the only one who can help us. We appeal to you for her life." Mother enunciated carefully, as if trying to make sure this oaf understood.

For a moment his face darkened. Lipzer was a collector of debts, and didn't want to be reminded of any debts he owed to others. But then he relaxed and let us into the house.

"He is a brave man, your son. The boys called him Tarzan, didn't they?"

Mother nodded. "They killed him at the Seventh Fort in the beginning of the war."

"I am sorry to hear that. I liked your son. So many of our best boys were killed," Lipzer said softly. He looked genuinely sorrowful. Then he looked at his watch. "When was your daughter arrested, and why? Quickly, give me the details."

When Mother described the circumstances of her arrest to him, he whistled.

"I'm not sure I can help. Anyone who buys stolen German goods is beyond help. I will try my best, but I can't promise anything. Come to see me in the evening. You must prepare some gold or other valuables in case I'm able to bribe them."

We left his house with lowered heads. The situation seemed hopeless. Lipzer was pessimistic, and we had given up our valuables long ago.

"At least we tried," Father said, but Mother shook off his arm. "That's not good enough. We will have to do more than that. We must save her."

They then agreed to try their luck with Dr. Elkes. I left them and headed for the trade school, but my heart was elsewhere. I thought the day would never end. Cooky tried to cheer me up, and several of my teachers tried to console me. The news about Fanny's arrest had spread.

It was late in the day before my parents got home. Father looked exhausted, and without saying a word he went to bed. Mother sat down and had a cup of tea, telling Anushka about their day. It seemed they saw just about every important official in the ghetto, plus leaders of the Zionist organizations and everyone who had any connection with the Germans, including smugglers. No one offered any hope, although many offered their help for what it was worth. Mother said that one never knew where salvation might come from.

In the evening they went to see Lipzer with hope in their hearts, but Schtitz was out of town and Lipzer hadn't accomplished anything. He did find out that Fanny was still in prison and hadn't been sent to the Ninth Fort yet, and that was a good sign. He told them to return the next evening.

Later that night Anushka and Mother went outside, and Mother smoked one of Anushka's stinking cigarettes. She had never smoked before and I could hear her cough every time she took a puff. Then they disappeared, returning later with a small parcel that they carefully hid. I was sure it contained some kind of bribe, which came as a shock. In spite of all the terror we suffered they still had the guts to hide valuables from the Germans.

The next morning we got up early. It was a lovely sunny day. It was unthinkable that on a day like this my sister could be executed.

Father went to work and Mother and Anushka took the parcel to

Lipzer. Later they were going to see Moshe Kopelman,* the head of the Jewish police. Cooky came by on his way to the trade school, but I didn't feel like going. I stayed home and curled up in bed.

I felt miserable. I tried to read but I couldn't form images from the sentences. The words just danced around before my eyes without any meaning. I tried not to think of what the Gestapo was doing to my sister. Other victims had described the tortures they went through in the Gestapo's clutches. These people had remained alive to tell the tale. Perhaps Fanny would too. "I don't care if she comes back broken and disfigured," I thought, "as long as she comes back alive."

Another day passed and still no news. Usually when the Gestapo decided to release someone, they did it after a day or so. Lipzer told us that the chances of her release were slim. He had passed on the bribe to the Gestapo officer in charge of her interrogation. There was one ray of hope: although her partner had been sent to the Ninth Fort, she was still in the prison.

"Schtitz is still away and that is bad, because I have a good arrangement with him. On the other hand, perhaps it is good as far as you are concerned. He quite often executes not only the offender, but the whole family," Lipzer informed Mother.

Mother said nothing at the time. She didn't want to frighten us. But Father must have known about the possibility. He was well informed through his friends in the Committee. Some even advised us to hide, but if they wanted to arrest us they could have done it the first day.

Late one afternoon I went with Mother to stand before Lipzer's door and await his return from work. It was well past dark when his familiar figure finally approached. He swayed a little.

"Oh, it's you again! I am going to miss you tomorrow, now that I'm so used to you hanging around my door. Your daughter is coming back. You can thank your lucky stars that Schtitz was away. The interrogating officer took a liking to Miss Genkind and sent another woman to be shot in her place." All this in a jocular tone, as if he were passing along the latest gossip.

One sentence thrilled us, the next was devastating.

"What do mean, someone went in her place? Who was she?" Mother cried.

*No relationship to Cooky Kopelman's family.

"I don't think you want to know her name. She was caught exchanging her last shirt for a loaf of bread. She was put in the same cell with your daughter. Usually my intervention would get such a person off. Her offense is considered minor. But the officer in charge decided to make a switch and sent her to her death instead of your daughter.

"And," he added cruelly, "don't let your conscience be bothered by her two starving little children. They were picked up today and sent to the Ninth Fort. You see, God protects those who can afford bribes, and of course, pretty women like Fania Genkind. You see, the other woman was quite ugly. He, he, he," he giggled, pointing at Mother's fallen face. It was then that we realized he was drunk.

"I don't believe you," Mother whispered, holding her head between her hands.

"Believe what you want. But don't forget that Lipzer always pays his debts. He was a fine fellow, your Tarzan. Too bad they shot him. My regards to your charming sister Anushka. And now it is time for me to take a leak. Too much beer, you see. Bye now, bye . . . Your Fanny will be back tomorrow." He walked away swaying a little, whistling some popular tune.

It took a moment for Mother to compose herself. "Don't you say a word to your father about what that drunken swine said. You hear?"

Was it God's miracle that Fanny was coming back to us, or the devil's? I was happy and upset at the same time. It was ugly and inhuman the way these Germans played God with people's lives.

That night I dreamed I was the woman who was sent to be shot instead of my sister. I stood before an open grave and felt the bullets enter my body. I cried out in terror, and before I fell a large mirror appeared in front of me and I could see my face. No doubt, it was terribly ugly.

The next evening we all waited at the gate for Fanny's brigade to return. The Gestapo sent her back to the railroad station to do a day's work.

A fuse had blown somewhere, so it was dark by the gate when the brigade arrived. A lone emergency gas lamp cast long shadows on the people who passed through the gate. The Lithuanian guards didn't bother to check the workers for food and just passed them through. From a distance we saw Fanny's familiar figure. She was limping, and as she came nearer we could see her face was swollen and discolored.

But she walked through the gate with her head held high. I guess she wanted us to see that the Germans didn't break her spirit. Then we grabbed her and were all hugging and crying together.

We stood in awe as Fanny took off her backpack and began removing parcels of food. To take such a risk on the day of her release wasn't just reckless, it was sheer lunacy.

But then she explained. She was afraid that if she hadn't brought food that day she would never be able to take a risk again. "And I don't have to tell you that we need the food," she concluded. Both Mother and Father were furious at her recklessness, and made her swear she wouldn't take such risks again.

The beating she had taken looked pretty gruesome, but she didn't seem to have any serious injuries. Many of those who managed to return from the Gestapo prison were crippled for life.

"By the way, did Etke come by and bring regards from me? We were in the same cell and she was released a few days earlier."

So Lipzer didn't lie. There was a woman with her in the same cell and poor Fanny thought she was returned to the ghetto. Mother shot me a warning look.

"No, no one came by. She was probably busy with her children," Mother said.

"If she didn't come by how do you know that she has children?" Fanny asked, her suspicion aroused. At this point Mother became confused and started to stammer, which made Fanny even more suspicious.

"What's going on? What are you keeping from me?"

"I am sorry Fanny, but the woman never arrived in the ghetto. She was probably sent to the Ninth Fort," I said, louder than I intended. Everyone looked startled, especially Mother.

"Lipzer told Mother last night," I explained.

At this point Fanny finally broke down and started crying. She told us that she had been forced to watch the horrible torture of her partner, Dov. The Gestapo insisted that she tell them everything she knew. But what could she tell them? She knew nothing about the Lithuanian or the theft. After a terrible ordeal she was put back in her cell. As time passed she attracted the interest of a certain SS captain, who seemed to like her looks and manner. Herman's angel must have been looking over her, for the SS man was secretly engaged to a girl who was part Jewish and resembled Fanny. Even so the officer came very close to letting the Gestapo send Fanny to the Ninth Fort. Theft from the Germans was always punished by death.

Her story was so wrenching that I completely forgot about Etke until she reached the end. It became apparent that our bribe and the arrival of Etke as a scapegoat had tipped the balance in Fanny's favor. More than likely it was this SS captain who decided to send Etke in Fanny's place. I had the feeling that Mother was going to tell them what Lipzer said, now that I had revealed part of it, and I quickly intervened.

"Lipzer told us that Etke was sent to the fort because Schtitz had come back from Vilnius and gave the order to send her there. You came back because the captain asked Schtitz to spare your life," I said. Fanny gave me a long look, and I could see Mother breathing a sigh of relief. We never told Father or the others what Lipzer said. The only way Fanny would find out the truth was if Lipzer was spiteful enough to tell her.

That night as I lay in bed I thought of how lucky we were. I felt terribly guilty about Etke and her family, but what could I do? These things happened in the ghetto all the time. Those without connections were always in harm's way.

Before Fanny went to sleep I brought her two buckets of water from the well. Early in the spring the water was still icy cold, but Fanny didn't bother to heat it. She disappeared behind the curtain and washed and scrubbed her body for a long time.

She suffered badly for a few weeks before her buoyant spirits began to return. After a month or two she was almost back to her old self.

By May of 1942 the weather had turned quite warm. Summer was almost on our doorstep, and through Fima's underground connections we got word of what was taking place on the Russian front. One of the cells had a clandestine radio and was able to listen to the news. I brought back a small atlas from my library, and we studied the movements of both armies.

On the twelfth of May Fima came home with exciting news. Several Russian tank corps under Marshal Timoshenko had smashed through the lines held by General von Paulus, and were advancing to recapture the strategic town of Kharkov. A great joy gripped us all. We knew the Russians were not on the verge of collapse, as the Germans claimed. They had actually counterattacked and were inflicting heavy casualties on the Nazis!

That day we celebrated the Russian victory. Father even drank a toast to Stalin, whom he considered our biggest enemy after Hitler. The news spread through the ghetto and rekindled hope in all hearts.

I pestered Fima all the time to get me into the new underground movement. Finally one day he asked me to go to the workshops where Anushka and Mother worked. I was to retrieve a package that would be dropped over a fence, and put it in the little hiding place under the house.

"I was supposed to do the job, but tomorrow I have to work late, so it's up to you. Let's see how you carry it out. I don't know what is in that parcel, but I was told that this is a dangerous assignment, so be very, very careful," he warned.

The next evening I went to the fence as instructed. It was cool out, and I turned up my collar. The people who passed by hardly gave me a second glance, but my heart was beating fast. I don't know how long I stood there before I heard a low whistle. I whistled back and approached the fence. One of the boards slid aside and a bundle was pushed into the opening. As I pulled the bundle through I came face to face with Aunt Anushka, whose expression reflected the same astonishment I felt. Before I had time to say anything she shoved the board back into place and I took off as fast as my legs would carry me. I could hardly believe my aunt was involved in this!

Fima had strictly instructed me not to open the package, but as usual my curiosity got the better of me. Before I pushed it into the hiding place I opened it. That was when I got a real scare. It was the uniform of a German officer. What kind of dangerous game were these people playing? Apparently Anushka and Fima didn't even know that they were both collaborating. It seemed incredible, but I knew that the underground movement was divided into cells of three persons each, so that if one was caught and subjected to torture they wouldn't endanger the entire movement.

When Anushka came back from work she gave me a strange look, but didn't say anything. Later she whispered for me to meet her outside. At first she just stood there smoking. The burning end was almost down to her fingers when she finally said, "I don't know how you got involved in this thing, and I don't want to know. But I want you to promise me two things. One, that you will get out of this organization immediately, and two, that you never disclose to anyone that you saw me. I don't have to tell you how dangerous this is for us, and for the whole family." Then, unexpectedly, she smiled and gave me a kiss. "O.K.?"

"O.K." I answered solemnly.

Late that night when everyone was sleeping, I felt a sudden cold draft. When I looked up Fima was sneaking in. He came up to my bed and patted my head.

"You did well," he whispered.

I was dying to tell him what Anushka said, but I forced myself to keep quiet. It was quite a while before Fima approached me again with an assignment. He would go out in the evenings after work, and return long after curfew. I kept begging him to let me help, and finally dragged a promise out of him to let me know when they needed someone.

Our joy over the military situation on the eastern front turned out to be short-lived. On May 22, Wehrmacht Headquarters reported that von Paulus's Sixth Army, driving South, and Army group Kleist, driving north, had entrapped a major Russian deployment, capturing 250,000 soldiers and wiping out all their armor. Once again the Germans celebrated a great victory, and boasted that all Soviet forces would soon be defeated. It was a devastating blow to the Russians, and to our morale.

June brought better news. Father returned from work one day with a remarkable announcement: He had just been made the supply officer for the newly created ghetto orchestra. We all thought he was joking. An orchestra in the ghetto? But it turned out to be true. The musicians were made members of the Jewish police force. They performed regular police duties when they were not playing, and were entitled to the better rations and relative safety from German harassment that the Jewish police ordinarily enjoyed.

Since Father was in charge of supplying the orchestra, I became acquainted with most of the members. The conductor was the well-known musician Misha Hofmekler, a friend of Father's. Cooky's mother, Vera Shore, was one of the violinists. Then there was Abrasha Stupel, first violinist, the Bornstein brothers, Maya Gladstein, and many others. The drummer, whose name was Granat, had a boy about my age named David who was the "elbote" or runner for the orchestra. He would later become one of my best friends.

I remember the first rehearsal I heard. The orchestra was housed in the former Slabodker Yeshiva. I hadn't heard music in a long time. After Chaim's old gramophone was destroyed during the "Big Action," I thought I would never hear music again.

The orchestra was playing Tchaikovsky. It was the *1812 Overture,* and as the music swelled up from the pit I couldn't hold back my tears.

PART TWO

13

The Children's Action

T*he crippling of the U.S. fleet at Pearl Harbor was followed by Japanese conquests of other American outposts in the Pacific—on Wake Island, Guam, and in the Philippines. It would be a year before the U.S. defense industry could replace the material they lost in December of 1941.*

Through the following winter and early spring, Clarence Matsumura's parents continued to run the family grocery store in Hollywood. Despite the anti-Japanese sentiment rampant in much of the country, the Matsumuras were able to go quietly about their business in their neighborhood. Then on the evening of May 2, 1942, official notices went up. By Executive Order all persons of Japanese ancestry, whether alien or non-alien, would be evacuated from the West Coast. The Matsumura family had only six days to report to the Pomona, California, fairgrounds, where they were confined for two or three months while more permanent internment camps were constructed deeper inland.

Like most Japanese Americans relocated to these camps, Clarence's family lost everything they owned. Clarence's father had come to the United States in 1904. He was among the Japanese immigrants hired to complete the transcontinental railway lines over the Rockies. He settled in Wyoming, bringing his bride over from Japan and raising his family in various small railroad towns. He worked for the Union Pacific Railroad for thirty years, starting out as a water boy and rising to the position of section foreman. In the end he moved his family back to the West Coast because the rural schools didn't offer classes beyond the eighth grade. He wanted his seven children to be educated. He invested his entire life savings in the grocery store in Hollywood, and although he made hasty arrangements to sell it, he never

229

received a penny in payment from the new Caucasian owners.

That spring the Matsumuras, along with six thousand other detainees at Pomona, were sent by train to an isolated camp at Hart Mountain, Wyoming. Surrounded by barbed wire and armed guards, the camp comprised twenty blocks of wooden barracks that housed as many as twelve thousand inmates at a time. They were allowed out of the camp's confines for work, and were employed at farms or in defense plants in the area.

The next winter would be one of the coldest Wyoming had experienced in years. The inmates spent it in structures insulated by no more than tar paper. The Matsumuras, in a way, were lucky. They knew Wyoming, and were prepared for the harsh winters and the isolation, unlike many of the Nisei who had lived all their lives in southern California.

For nearly two years the U.S. War Department tried to decide what to do about military service for Japanese Americans. The Japanese American soldiers who joined the service or were drafted by lottery before Pearl Harbor were already serving in the armed forces, but the inmates of the camps were in limbo. No charges had been brought against them. There were no trials, no convictions, only incarceration.

Because Clarence had his radio license and was able to bring in some sound equipment from home, he was put in charge of the crew that provided entertainment for the camp. They ran movies in the mess hall, charging five cents admission for children and ten cents for adults. With these funds, the crew was able to pay for the camp entertainment, including classes for the children.

In January 1943 Questions 27 and 28 were circulated in the camps. They amounted to a loyalty oath. Question 27: If you are a citizen, are you willing to defend your country against its enemies? Question 28: Are you willing to take up arms to defend your country?

Issei, or first-generation immigrants, were denied citizenship, but were asked these questions as well. The Nisei, who were born in the United States, were automatically citizens, and many of them pointed out that as detainees they had been denied the protection accorded citizens under the Constitution. The government had no right to ask them to serve in the armed forces.

Those protesters who answered "no" to both questions of the loyalty oath were called the "no-no boys." Sixty-three of the "no-no boys" from Hart Mountain were tried in the courts of Cheyenne, and sentenced to three years at Fort Leavenworth.

Those Nisei who answered "yes" to both questions became eligible for the draft, but in fact many were eager to prove their loyalty to the United States. In

Hawaii, where the government asked for fifteen hundred volunteers, more than ten thousand came forward, including the National Guard, which was more than half Japanese, and the "Varsity Victory Volunteers."

Cal Matsumura wanted to continue his training in electronics, and volunteered for the air force. His paperwork, inexplicably, never came through. He went then to the navy, which also offered good training. His papers continued to be held up. It was some time before he finally learned of the exclusion laws that prevented Japanese Americans from serving in these branches of the service. The Nisei only had one choice: service in the army, in a segregated unit.

Clarence had no desire to volunteer for a segregated unit. He went to work for the Great Northern Railroad for six months, earning money to attend the University of Cincinnati, where he continued his studies in electronics. He was a university student when he was called up.

Unlike other Nisei who did their basic training at Camp Shelby, Mississippi, Clarence's group, all college boys, were trained at Fort Hood, Texas. Recruits from Fort Hood were shipped out to the Pacific, but Clarence's group was continuously passed over. They received additional training in anti-tank warfare, artillery, and machine gunnery as group after group was shipped out to the Pacific before them. Except for those Nisei who spoke Japanese and were enlisted into military intelligence, no Japanese Americans would be allowed to serve in the Pacific. It was not until the spring of 1944, when his group was sent to Camp Kilmer, New Jersey, the jumping-off place for the European theatre, that Clarence understood he would be joining the segregated 442nd Combat Team. He would be assigned to the team's artillery detachment, the 522nd Field Artillery, as a radio repairman.

By early 1943 the tide was turning on the eastern front in Europe. American material equipped the Soviet forces, who fought against the Germans with the grim determination of men defending their homes. The Russians reclaimed Stalingrad on February 2, 1943, a defeat the German authorities in Kaunas marked by shooting forty-five ghetto inmates at the Ninth Fort. By August 1943 the great German "March to the East" had ground to a complete halt. The prospect of retaliation by the now-advancing Soviets terrified Heinrich Himmler, the man in charge of the "final solution." By that time the infamous extermination camps at Bergen-Belsen, Sobibor, Auschwitz, Treblinka, and Maidanck had been completed. Faced with the possibility of a German defeat, the Nazis stepped up the pace, but now all evidence was to be destroyed. Himmler ordered all the bodies to be exhumed and burned, including those at the Ninth Fort. This dreadful chore fell to Jewish and Soviet prisoners, who were murdered and cremated after they had completed their work.

On January 27, 1944, the Russians finally broke the 880-day siege of Leningrad. During January and February the Germans in the east took 100,000 casualties, and by April the Soviets were bombing the German airfield at Alexotas.

Spurred on by news of the Soviets' advances and the massive exterminations in Poland, ghetto inmates began constructing hiding places. Most of them were underground dugouts, called malines. *Many children were hidden there, along with those sought by the Gestapo and others on their way to join the growing partisan movement now operating in the woods. Many boys worked as "elbote," or runners, within the ghetto—carrying messages for the ghetto institutions, the Council, the underground, and the Jewish police.*

The Jewish police dealt with thieves and common criminals, and carried out the orders of the Jewish Council as well as those the Germans transmitted through it. The Council of Elders continued to follow Rabbi Shapiro's advice—to obey the Nazis when necessary to save lives, even as it concealed and supported the activities of the ghetto underground. And no one in the ghetto was more deeply involved in the underground than the Jewish police force itself.

Compared to the bloody fall and winter of 1941, most of 1942 and 1943 were relatively quiet in the ghetto. Dr. Elkes and the Jewish Council continued to negotiate with the German military and civil authorities to keep the ghetto intact, arranging fresh bribes whenever new German officials and guards replaced the old, winning a few reprieves and clemencies for the inmates. Murders continued at the Ninth Fort, but at a slower pace.

Terrifying news reached us from outside the ghetto, however. We began to hear about Auschwitz and the gas chambers and killing grounds of Poland. In April of 1943 there was a terrible action at Ponar, about fifty miles from Kaunas. Some five thousand Jews were rounded up for transport from various hamlets around Vilna. They were told they were being transported to the Kaunas ghetto to join our workforce. Some seventy to eighty sealed freight cars crammed with these Jewish workers were brought to a halt in an open field. The cars were opened one by one, and those inside were pulled out and shot down by a gang of German and Lithuanian police. Hearing what lay in store, many of the Jews in cars toward the end of the train met their killers armed with the tools they brought with them—axes, shovels, even rocks, whatever they could get their hands on. A very few escaped. A number of Lithuanian police at Ponar refused to participate; they too were killed.

News of this atrocity, and of the extermination camps in Poland, trickled into the ghetto by way of witnesses and a few escapees who smuggled themselves into the ghetto and were hidden among us. Word of the uprising by the Jews of Warsaw came in the spring of 1943. Their tragic heroism further galvanized the will of the ghetto resistance groups.

March 27, 1944. I woke that morning well after sunrise, having stayed up late reading Thomas Mann's *Buddenbrooks*. I couldn't tear myself away from it, and stopped only when my candle guttered out.

As I lay in bed thinking about the gentle people who inhabited the book, it dawned on me that they too were Germans, perhaps of an earlier time, but Germans nevertheless.

My family left for work early, so I was alone in the house. I remembered someone trying to wake me before they left, but they must have given up. I was supposed to go to the trade school as usual, but it was already too late for that. Perhaps Cooky would be able to cover for me. Shimon, our instructor, threatened to throw me out of the course if I missed classes one more time, and then it would be work at the dreaded airport for me.

I was slowly pulling on my clothes when I heard loudspeakers blaring outside. A black private car with two speakers mounted on the roof was slowly moving through the street.

"*Achtung! Achtung!* You are all to remain in your homes. Anyone caught leaving his house will be shot!"

Behind the car were dozens of German Gestapo and Ukrainian soldiers from the notorious Vlasov Brigade. One of them was dragging along two little boys who lived down the street. They were in their nightgowns and their naked feet were caked with mud. Their grandmother was being pushed along by another guard.

My God, they were after the children and old people!

The previous November small children had been taken away from the ghetto of Siauliai and murdered. We all knew that if the Germans did it there, chances were they would do it everywhere, and many children were sent into hiding. As the months passed and no "action" took place, people began to relax. But now it was happening.

I threw on my coat and lowered myself from the back window just as the Germans broke in our front door.

I hid behind a clump of bushes growing in the back of the house. I had to figure out how to reach the garden toolshed.

During the summer of 1943 I had gone to work helping Gustav Hermann, the S.A. lieutenant in charge of the Labor office. He liked gardening, and cultivated a piece of land behind the *Kommandantur*, where he grew flowers and vegetables. My mouth always watered when I passed by and saw all the juicy tomatoes and cucumbers there. There was no way I could steal any, though. Not even the SS guards dared to take anything from Hermann's garden.

One summer day I watched as Hermann toiled there. He was perspiring heavily, and stopped from time to time to mop his brow. I approached him cautiously and asked him if he needed any help. He looked at me with surprise. No Jew dared address a German, especially not an officer, without being spoken to first. But Hermann had a reputation for being reasonable, and usually spoke civilly, even to Jews. He demanded only one thing: efficiency. When he gave orders he wanted them obeyed on the dot.

After a short but scary silence, he told me to grab a spade and start digging.

From that day on I worked in his garden twice a week. Just as Uri and Chaim had to keep his office spic and span, I had to keep his gardening tools sparkling. I would polish his spades and other implements until they gleamed. He showed his approval by presenting me with half a loaf of bread.

The toolshed, an old wooden structure, stood about two hundred meters away from the *Kommandantur*. Hermann kept his gardening implements there, with a padlock on the door. One evening, after a day of cultivating, I was cleaning his tools in the shed and noticed a loose plank in the floor. To my astonishment there was a big hole under the shack. It was a perfect hideout. Who would ever think of searching Hermann's own shack!

He had just left for town, so I carefully removed more earth from the hole, making a space large enough to hide in. Near the door a warped panel of siding was missing nails at the bottom. I pulled out two more at the top. In an emergency the bottom of the plank would move just enough for me to squeeze in. If I pushed some tools against the bottom of the board inside, it stayed in place.

I inspected my work. The wood had splintered a little at the top edge, but I didn't think anyone would notice. The whole building was old and rough. The main thing was that the shed was padlocked from the outside. Who would suspect?

I practiced a few times when no one was around, and it took less than a minute to slip into the shed, lower myself into the hole, and slip the floorboard back in place over my head.

Unfortunately, not long after that the SS took over command of the ghetto, and Hermann was replaced by an officer named Auer. Although he allowed me to continue working in the garden, he was a much worse boss than Hermann.

My problem now was how to reach that toolshed. Ukrainians were everywhere, breaking into houses and chasing children and old people out into the street. Once again I heard the cries of families being torn apart, the awful wailing screams of mothers whose children were torn away from them.

There was no way I could get past the guards unnoticed. My only hope was to join the others, and try to slip away from the crowd later. I had Hermann's old pass in my pocket, along with the armband of the "elbote." One never counted on passes, but sometimes they helped.

There was not much time for me to deliberate. If they found me hiding in the bushes, they would shoot me. I slipped from my hiding place and unhurriedly walked to the column. A Ukrainian kicked me in the butt for straggling, but allowed me to join the others.

As we approached the *Kommandantur*, I put on the armband. Everyone was being herded into the courtyard around it. The area was packed with children, women with babies in their arms, and a few who were elderly or sick. They were being loaded onto a large canvas-covered truck.

Mothers who wouldn't let go of their children were attacked by snarling Dobermans until they fell. Some were shot; others were thrown into the truck with their babies. The old and sick who couldn't move fast enough ended up crawling under a hail of kicks and blows, and were attacked by the dogs when they collapsed. The din was horrible—barking, curses, shrieks. I thought I would lose my mind. The dark opening at the back of the truck was like the maw of some prehistoric monster swallowing human sacrifices.

I closed my eyes and ears for a moment. Beneath my panic some other part of my brain kept thinking.

The truck before me was full. A minute or two passed while the guards latched the tailgate, then signaled the driver to leave. The truck rumbled away with its human cargo, and another moved up in its place.

I looked around. If only I could locate Auer, perhaps he would help me. I began pushing my way toward the *Kommandantur,* against a crowd that was being driven in the opposite direction. It seemed an eternity before I stood at the entrance. An elderly SS man was standing guard. He had been a friend of Gustav Hermann's.

"Sir, I'm the personal messenger of Hauptsturmbahnfuehrer Auer. He sent for me," I said, showing him my pass.

He raised his eyebrows at my perfect German.

"He's back in his garden," he said quite reasonably. "Go ahead, you'll find him there."

I turned for the door, fearing this was a trick, and waiting for a blow once my back was turned. It did not come. When the door of the *Kommandantur* shut safely behind me I faced a long corridor. The door out to the garden was at the far end. Before me dozens of Germans bustled in and out of their offices, and as I edged down the passageway I expected to be stopped any minute. I tried to make myself taller, straightening my spine and throwing my shoulders back, but the Germans weren't really paying attention. They saw my armband, and the fact that I was inside seemed to be sufficient proof that I had a right to be there. Behind me was the door to death. Before me was a door that perhaps meant safety. It seemed to be miles away. When I finally stood in front of it I was wet with perspiration. The tumult outside was dimmer here.

I cautiously pushed the door handle down and my heart stopped. It wouldn't open. For a while I stood frozen. Was it locked? In a panic I pressed the handle again and pushed against the door with my knee. It flew open and I found myself standing in the blinding sunlight.

It took a few seconds for my eyes to adjust. Auer had his sleeves rolled up and was turning over the soil for spring planting, as if the scene of depraved brutality taking place out front had nothing to do with him.

He kept digging, as if he hadn't noticed me. Then he called me over and asked what I was doing there. For a moment I was speechless, and racked my brain for something to say.

During the months that I helped him in the garden we found some common language. He even asked me once what our life was like in Heydekrug before the war. He said that he had passed the town once when he worked in Koenigsberg, a long time ago. Now my life depended on this tenuous relationship.

"I came to help you in the garden," I finally said, unable to think of anything else. I tried to smile.

He gave me a long look, and I could see death in it. I was doomed.

"All right," he said casually. "Just continue cultivating where I started." He rose and started for the building. He didn't want to have to deal with me himself.

As soon as the door closed behind him I took off across the freshly dug ground toward the toolshed, which sat hidden from view behind a low hill. I had reached the crest when two German guards burst through the door of the *Kommandantur.* They fired two shots and I felt something whistle past my cheek.

I made a quick decision. I lowered my head and started running away from the shed. When I thought I couldn't be seen below the hill I doubled back and ran as I have never run before. My blood was pounding in my ears when I finally reached the shed. To my horror, the outer panel I had loosened wouldn't budge.

"Someone must have fixed it," I thought in despair. I didn't dare look back. I threw myself on the ground and with both feet smashed the bottom of the panel, hoping that the din from the action would cover the sound. The panel gave way, and I squeezed myself through the narrow opening, scraping my back and ribs. I was in!

I shoved the bottom of the board back in place, and fearfully peered through a crack. The Germans were on top of the hill. I held my breath. When they ran off in the direction I first headed I almost whooped for joy. I'd fooled them!

I carefully lifted the floorboard and dropped down into the hole. My heart was still racing as I pulled the floorboard back into place over my head.

The emergency supplies I had left were still there. I had a tin of German army crackers, a tin of meat, two or three bottles of water, and some blankets. I received the food as payment from Hermann, and I was sorely tempted to eat it on several occasions. Thanks God I resisted.

Then I heard voices above, and a minute later someone was rattling the door. All my feelings of triumph instantly evaporated.

"It's padlocked. He couldn't be in there," someone said in German.

"He couldn't have disappeared into thin air," another voice said.

"So where is he?"

I heard them walk around the shed and then try the padlock again.

"Auer is going to have our hides. What are we going to tell him?"

"We'll tell him that we caught him and put him on a truck, that's what. Let him check the ashes at Auschwitz, if he wants to be sure."

The guards' voices grew fainter as they walked away from the shed. They had given up on me.

Auschwitz! I began shaking badly at this point, and rolled myself up in the blankets, which were musty and damp from being underground so long. Even under the shed I could hear the wailing of the children and the terrible screams of their mothers, and the sharp barking of the German's dogs. It seemed this would never end. I began to weep and couldn't stop. Eventually the sounds dimmed, and as the ghetto quieted I cried myself to sleep.

I woke up with a start. My clothes were damp with sweat, and the hairs on my neck and arms were standing on end. I held my breath, listening. And then I heard it, a sound that froze the blood in my veins. It was a dog trotting around the shed, sniffing. Then he growled and began digging into the ground at the base of the shed, right above the hole where I lay.

I stared at the spot where he scrabbled. The dog was snarling with impatience. I was utterly paralyzed.

Then bits of earth began dribbling down on me, and light appeared through a small opening. I watched as if hypnotized as the dog's paws appeared, then the snout. Now the whole head of a Doberman poked through the opening. His eyes glistened malevolently and his short, pointed ears were quivering as he strained to squeeze his lean body through. I squeezed my eyes shut.

I was drowning, caught in a whirlpool. I panicked, my lungs bursting for air. "Solly, listen to me. You must kick out with all your strength. Spread your arms and kick out. Do it," my brother Herman said.

"Wake up, wake up, or you are dead. . . . "

I opened my eyes. The Doberman's shoulders were through, his body heaving and his teeth snapping in anticipation. Hatred replaced the fear in my mind. I hated these dogs that ripped the flesh of Jews. I heaved against the loose plank above me and stood up in the shed, groping wildly until my hands closed on a spade handle. I pulled it to me and swung with all my might. All the pent up emotions of the day flooded over me as I swung the blade down on the Doberman's head.

My hands and arms recoiled from the contact. I felt a sharp pain in my shoulder blades. It felt delicious. The Doberman let out a howl of pain and fury, and so did I. I howled even louder than he did as I swung the spade again. His eyes expressed almost human surprise, and a dark stain of blood appeared on his head. He lunged at me, and I jumped to the side, bringing the blade down again and again with all my might. Never before or since have I felt such hatred and exhilaration at the same time.

The Doberman collapsed, his body twitching with convulsions and his eyes growing dim. Then he whimpered, a low, pitiful sound.

"Just like a puppy," I thought, and suddenly my hatred drained away. The poor beast was trained by his masters to attack human beings. It wasn't his fault. He was just a dog.

But I didn't have time to indulge in feelings of pity. I had survived so far, but I was not out of danger yet. Where there was a dog there must be a master, and I prayed no one had been near enough to hear our howling. I dropped down and tugged at the body until the hindquarters were all the way in, then I frantically began pushing dirt back up into the opening he'd dug, praying again that no one outside would notice the freshly turned earth at the base of the shed.

When I finished I pulled the board back into place over my head and lay down, panting. I avoided looking at the dog. My whole body was shaking, and I rolled myself in the blankets. It didn't help. My endurance had been stretched beyond the breaking point, and as much as I told myself I had to stay calm, I couldn't stop my sobs. A long fit of weeping left me limp.

I must have dozed off again, because I was awakened by voices and someone's whistle.

"Runzel! Runzel! Here boy! Here boy!" someone was calling in Lithuanian. Then there were voices right outside the shed.

"Where is that damned dog?"

"Shit, Heinz is going to have our hides."

"I hate these damn Dobermans. They are as unreliable as they are vicious."

Someone pulled at the padlock, and I held my breath in terror.

"What is this shack, anyway?"

"It belongs to that gardening maniac. He keeps his tools in there."

"You got a cigarette?"

I heard them trying to strike matches and cursing because they were wet. One of them started talking about an action the next day. The Germans were bringing in dynamite. "We are going to roast some little Jewish cockroaches in their hideouts," he said.

They continued to talk and laugh as they moved away. I was out of immediate danger, but I was utterly chilled. The Germans were not through with us yet.

I peered outside. It was almost dark. One of the guards switched on his flashlight.

I had to warn the underground about tomorrow's raid. I knew a little about the operations of Moshe Levin and his crew; from time to time they would entrust me with the delivery of parcels. They built one of the bigger hideouts in the ghetto. It had taken them six months to dig it, supporting it with beams and even concrete, and all of it done at night, in secrecy.

Others built hideouts anticipating the arrival of the Russian troops in Lithuania. Everyone believed that that moment would be the most dangerous time for us, and they hoped that the Germans would be too busy defending themselves to spend too much time searching for Jews. But now these plans were in jeopardy, and the Russians were still a long way off.

Clearly I had a duty to perform. This gave me a purpose and strengthened my spirit. First I had to get rid of the dead dog. Then I would have to warn the underground about the raid. After that I would go home to tell them I was alive and get some food. I couldn't think beyond that, and I didn't want to.

I moved the floorboard and lifted myself up into the shed. There was a piece of rope hanging on the wall among the tools and I tied it around the midriff of the dead beast.

His body seemed incredibly heavy. I had to use all my strength to get him up out of the hole. There was an abandoned dry well about fifty meters away from the shed; I would dump him there.

A blast of cold air greeted me when I crawled outside, dragging the body behind me. It was a moonless night and quite dark. The *Kommandantur*, which was usually dark after working hours, showed strips of light around the blackout curtains.

"They are probably planning tomorrow's raid," I thought grimly. In the ghetto the brigades must have returned from work, for I could hear shrieks and wailing as parents discovered their children were gone. I knew that my parents must be suffering the same torment.

In the sky the stars blinked merrily, as if nothing had happened, as if the murder of thousands of children and old people was a common occurrence.

But I had no time to think about that. I dragged the dog's body across the field, pried the wooden cover off the well, and shoved him in. Then I returned to the shed and smoothed the ground where the dog had dug, and scattered a few twigs and leaves there.

The ghetto was enveloped in darkness. All the way to the hideout I could hear doleful cries and laments emanating from the houses of the Jews.

The building above the hideout was dark, its windows covered by wooden shutters. Not a sound came from within. I sneaked around to the back entrance. It was pitch-dark inside, and I was trying to orient myself when I was grabbed from behind. A big hand was clamped over my mouth.

"Who are you and what are you doing here," a man's voice asked quietly in Yiddish. When he realized that he was grasping a boy, he added in a softer voice, "You can't hide here, you must leave immediately."

"No, no, I am an 'elbote' and I worked for Moshe Levin. I have an urgent message for him. Is he here?"

The man hesitated a second, then sighed.

"Moshe is gone and so are the others."

"Gone?"

"The Germans took all the policemen to the Ninth Fort."

I sucked in my breath in disbelief. "Moshe Levin? The Jewish police? They took them? My God, what are we going to do now?" I was horrified.

"I don't know. No one expected any of this. What is your urgent message, anyway?"

"Tomorrow they are coming with explosives to blast all the hideouts. I overheard it myself. We must warn everyone."

Then a horrible thought struck me, even as the man took me by the shoulders and began shaking me, demanding to know where I heard such information. I was putting two and two together. The Germans knew about the hiding places. They had taken the policemen, who were an integral part of the underground. They would no doubt be interrogated by the Gestapo.

My teeth were rattling in my head before I managed to shove my interrogator away. Then I repeated what I had overheard in the shed.

The man, whose name was Jakob, started crying. "Oh my God! My wife and children are down there." He was with the partisans, and was supposed to return to his group in the woods right away. "What am I going to do?" he kept crying. I was surprised and a little irritated that a resistance fighter would be so emotional. "We must go down and warn the others," I insisted.

Finally he quieted down. Moving to a corner behind a stove, he tapped out a signal. After a moment a small door, set low in the wall, swung open. We descended the wooden steps leading underground. The air below was damp and stale. In the dim light of a single bulb I saw what looked like a hundred elderly men, small children, and women with babies in their arms. They were sitting on the ground, tightly packed on wooden bunks built into the walls. The place was never meant to hold so many.

As we came down, all heads turned our way. Not a sound came from their lips. Only their eyes spoke.

When he told them my news a moan went up from the group. Some began to weep. One woman with a baby in her arms and a small boy clinging to her skirt came to Jakob and threw herself in his arms.

"What are we going to do? I don't want our children to die! Please, Jakob, take us with you to the forest. You can't leave us here to die!"

As Jakob tried to comfort her the little boy looked up at them with fear in his eyes. He was too terrified to cry. He hung on to his mother's dress, shaking his head from side to side, sighing and gulping.

"I won't leave you anymore," Jakob said firmly. "If we are to die, we'll die together, I promise."

As touching as this scene was, I felt an unbearable impatience. This man was supposed to be a partisan, a resistance fighter. He had to think about the cause. "Jakob, we must get the guns and ammunition," I said, my voice sounding harsh and strange in my own ears. "They mustn't fall into the Germans' hands."

"Yes, yes," he said absentmindedly.

I shook his arm again. "Jakob, you must think of all the Jewish partisans waiting for these weapons. Think of all the Germans that can be killed with them!"

He gently pushed his wife away and looked down at me. There was both sorrow and forbearance in his expression. "If by some miracle you live so long, you may have a family yourself some day," he said. Then he led me to a brick foundation toward the back of the dugout. He pulled out two or three bricks, and then a potato sack. From this he drew out two pistols and several boxes of ammunition. They felt heavy in my hands, and gave me an unexpected feeling of confidence.

Jakob replaced the bricks.

"Where are the rest?" I asked. I was waiting for the rifles, the submachine guns, the hand grenades.

He gave a short laugh. "There isn't anything else. These two pistols are a small fortune as it is. They may save the lives of two people. The partisans won't accept anyone without a gun."

I was shocked. I had imagined much more than this.

"Your contact man is Fima Shtrom," Jakob continued. "He lives at Gimbuto 20. You are to hand these over to him."

Now it was my turn to laugh. "That is where I live. Fima Shtrom is my cousin."

Jakob shook his head. "Small world. Well, he is a good man, so I will trust you with these. Don't try to load or handle them in any way. Just hand them over to Fima. Is that understood?"

I said yes.

"God bless you and be with you," Jakob said quietly, taking my hand in his own. It felt rough and warm. There was sadness in his voice.

"Good-bye, Jakob," I answered. I instinctively liked the big man. He and his family would probably be dead tomorrow.

The road was muddy where melting snow had collected in the ruts. As I approached Varniu Street I slowed down, my senses alert for danger. All seemed quiet, but not far away I spotted a tiny red point of light. A cigarette. I jumped for a ditch by the road and gasped as I landed in a puddle of ice water. Two guards passed by without seeing me. I made it home without any further incidents, but I was soaked and chilled to the bone. I hid the sack under the house and softly knocked on the door. I knocked again, and finally Fanny cautiously asked who it was.

When I answered she threw the door open and pulled me inside. Almost instantly the whole family was around me, crying with happiness and hugging me in my wet clothes. When we all settled down a little I washed up and changed. Mother heated some soup, which I practically downed in one gulp. Everyone in the room kept hugging and kissing me, asking one question after another about how I managed to escape the action. They were sure that I had been taken by the Germans.

I told them my story. When I got to the part about the Germans' plans to dynamite the hideouts the next day, there was a sudden silence in the room. The single candle sent shadows flickering over their horrified faces.

I couldn't understand how they could cry or feel shock or sorrow after all we had been through, especially after today. I felt an emptiness in me, as if some hand had reached into my soul and switched a light off. The only desire I felt was for revenge.

"I have to get back to my hideout before it gets light." I said.

"But darling, don't you want to stay and rest a little?" my mother asked.

"I have no time for sleeping," I said sharply. I didn't sound like their soft-spoken little darling anymore. Even to my own ears my voice sounded strange.

"But Solly . . ." Fanny said in a frightened voice.

I interrupted. "I promised Jakob that I would deliver the guns to Fima, and I intend to do that." I didn't tell them the guns were under our own house.

"But darling, you are only a boy! It is too dangerous!" Mother cried.

"Yes, Mother. It is too dangerous to be a boy. Unless I become a man quickly, I will die like the other boys in the ghetto." She looked shocked at my bluntness.

"I will make it," I added more softly, and gave her a kiss.

She took me in her arms and cried quietly, gently rocking me from side to side like she used to when I was small. "What are we going to do my darling, what is to become of us?" she whispered. A wave of weariness swept over me. How wonderful it would be just to fall asleep while she cradled me in her arms, fall asleep and never wake up.

It took all my willpower to pull myself away.

"I should go. It's not really safe for me here. I have a good hiding place," I smiled, trying to encourage her. "I've gotten through the day all right so far, haven't I? I can take care of myself."

I said good-bye to Father and Fanny. When I hugged Miriam I whispered, "Tell Fima that the ship has arrived. He will understand." She just nodded. I was sure that she too was involved in the resistance movement.

Fanny gave me a big chunk of bread and hugged me again.

There was a trace of pink in the east when I emerged from the house, and I broke into a run. Twice on the way I had to detour to evade patrols. When I finally reached the shed I was completely out of breath. I pulled the floorboard into place over my head, and almost as soon as I rolled up in my blankets I dropped off to sleep.

I dreamed again of Lena. We were walking through the woods picking wild strawberries. We saw a huge red one nestled among the leaves, but it flew up and attached itself to Lena's throat. I heard the sound of gunfire and Lena's laughter turned to screams. I woke up sweating.

The explosions I was hearing weren't a dream. They echoed throughout the ghetto, some of them quite near the shed. I cautiously pushed up the floorboard and peered through a crack in the shed wall. Fires glowed here and there around the ghetto. In the distance I could see a shadowy group of people being driven along the street by guards. Darting in and out among them were the dogs. Smoke floated gently through the air. Several more explosions echoed through the ghetto. They were blasting the hideouts.

I thought of Jakob and his family and all the people I saw in the cellar. I wondered if they had found a safe place. In my imagination I kept seeing their dismembered bodies flying through the air. I tried to shut the image out. The second day of the "Children's Action" passed. The monster's thirst for the blood of Jewish children seemed insatiable.

One of the policemen taken to the Ninth Fort shared a bunk with me a few months later. He told me what happened to the Jewish police on March 27, 1944.

"A day before the action started, our chief Moshe Levin was

ordered by Goecke of the Gestapo to assemble the whole police force at eight the next morning. Goecke said we were going to be instructed on air raid procedures. We were surprised, but we suspected nothing. Even after four years of lies, deceit, and murder, we still believed them!

"It was a beautiful spring morning, and that added to our good feeling. At eight o'clock sharp, a hundred and thirty of us, dressed in our best uniforms, stood at attention in the courtyard of the ghetto administration building.

"Goecke, resplendent in his gray leather coat and matching gloves, inspected our ranks carefully. He then smiled and ordered the policemen who were playing in the ghetto orchestra to step forward and enter the administration building.

"Suddenly I had doubts. Something was wrong here. But before anyone could say a word, a large group of SS men came running out from behind the building. They were armed and surrounded us from all sides.

"We were ordered to sit on the ground. Some of the policemen who were not fast enough were clubbed. Within seconds several large army trucks drove into the yard and we were ordered to crawl to them on all fours, the guards kicking and clubbing us all the way. The surprise was complete. There was no chance for us to resist, which we would have done had we had any inkling. Many of us were trained by the underground in hand to hand combat.

"We knew that our turn to die had come. One policeman, by the name of Levner, was absolutely paralyzed by fear and couldn't move. He was shot on the spot.

"As we neared the fort two of our officers, seeing that they had nothing to lose, decided to make a break for it. One was a lawyer named Zilberkweit and the other was someone called Levin. They didn't get very far. The Gestapo accompanying the convoy shot them down.

"At the fort they took everything away from us. They beat us systematically until we could barely stand. Later they locked us up in the fort's prison cells.

"Moshe Levin and his two lieutenants, Ika Grinberg and Judel Zupowitz, had been very active in the underground, and helped many young men to escape to the partisans' groups. The Gestapo and the SS had their informants, and probably knew to some extent what was going on. Thus when the 'Children's Action' started, they decided to get rid of Moshe Levin and his police force.

"Our chief and his two lieutenants were beaten so mercilessly that we barely recognized them. But we recognized Moshe's voice.

"'Listen, they are trying to extract information from us about the hiding places and the resistance movement in the Ghetto. Comrades, let us die with dignity! Not a word to the murderers!'

"Moshe Levin was a very strict boss, even a bastard sometimes, but when he spoke to us that day, I knew that I was standing before a hero.

"Sometime later the Germans and their Ukrainian helpers dragged us from our cells and lined us up in front of a pile of corpses that were stacked there for burning. They had been murdered a long time ago, and they smelled awful. They were stacked in many rows and on each row of corpses there was a row of kindling. Some of these stacks were almost two meters high.

"SS Obersturmbahnfuehrer Kitel was already waiting for us. Kitel was notorious for his sadism. He was an expert in extracting information from his victims by employing the most sophisticated methods of torture.

"Moshe Levin was the first to be interrogated while the remainder of us were forced to watch. No amount of torture brought a single word from him.

"Kitel kept on repeating the same questions: 'Where are the Ghetto hideouts? Who are the leaders of the partisans in the ghetto?'

"Then Kitel leaned too near, and Moshe spat a mouthful of blood and saliva into his face. The infuriated Kitel couldn't control himself. Drawing his revolver he shot Moshe dead.

"We all stood and trembled with fear. Not so much over our impending death—we knew that was inevitable—but whether we could withstand the torture the way our chief did, without divulging what the Germans wanted to know.

"I distinctly remember Kitel's cold eyes when it was my turn to be interrogated. It was as if he could penetrate my brain and extract information from me. I felt that he would know instinctively if I were lying. Fortunately, I had only worked for the police a few months and I really didn't know any secrets.

"After I was tortured and beaten for ten minutes, he looked at me again, and seemed to realize that I knew nothing.

"I remember how relieved I was. At least I could die in peace. You can imagine how surprised I was when they sent me and ninety others back to the ghetto. Unfortunately, there were several among us who couldn't withstand the torture. They told Kitel where many hiding places were. I'm not sure that I can blame them, really. I am still astonished that so few among the hundred and thirty broke down.

"Moshe's two lieutenants, Ika Grinberg and Judel Zupowitz, were also brought before us and tortured horribly. They, too, refused to speak, and met the same fate as Moshe, along with others who knew secrets and refused to divulge them. Kitel knew that they knew, yet they did not speak. They died in agony. All their bodies were thrown on top of a tall stack of corpses, and burned in the same pyre."

14

Evacuation of the Ghetto

After a day or two in the toolshed, I decided that it would be safer to return home than risk being discovered there by Auer. I couldn't really bear the hole much longer.

Cooky also survived the action of March 1944. It turned out that the boys at the trade school had been left out of the roundup. I returned to class, and steered clear of the *Kommandantur.*

During the early days of that month the Allies flew forty-two thousand sorties over Germany, striking Luftwaffe installations everywhere. By May the Russians had all but cleared the Germans from the Crimea, and as they turned toward the west the big question in everyone's mind was how we would get through the dangerous moment when the Russians finally arrived. The saying around the ghetto was that liberation was under our noses, but the knife was at our throats. After the last action no more than ten thousand of the ghetto's original thirty thousand inmates were still alive.

Many refused to wait it out. By the spring of 1944, my cousins Zunie and Milie had escaped to join the partisans. Dora and Isaac Trotsky, and Mara and Alek Shtrom had escaped and were hiding with Lithuanian Christians.

Fima, too, was scheduled to leave the ghetto with eleven other members of his group on April 14. At the last minute he fell ill, and was replaced by one of his comrades. The group was ambushed by Goecke and his Gestapo. The Lithuanian partisan driving the truck was a traitor. Eight out of twelve would-be partisans were shot down; Fima's friend was among only four who escaped. It was he

249

who got word back to Fima about the ambush.

Goecke, who had personally participated in the operation, tightened his grip on the ghetto after that. During the month of May there were several attempts to break out, but the Germans had doubled the watch around the fence and all attempts to escape failed. The Lithuanian partisans who were supposed to take our people to the forests were also a problem. Some of their group had been turned by the Gestapo.

Efforts to build hideouts were redoubled. There was no way we could dig one under our house, since it rested aboveground on pilings. My father believed them to be a folly in any event, especially after the disastrous bombings during the "Children's Action."

Many people in the ghetto thought otherwise. It was because of one such hideout that my little cousin Esterke Schuster escaped death. Her mother Frieda, one of Mother's cousins, was a vigorous, athletic woman who had been a table tennis champ before the war. She married a handsome man named Jacov Schuster, another athlete who had been a devoted soccer player in his youth. He was also a very kind man, but he came from a poorer, less educated family, and most of my family felt that Frieda had married beneath her. It was partly because of the family's resistance to their marriage that Frieda and Jacov left for Palestine a few years before the war. Life had been a struggle there, however. Listening to the family talk about their experiences in Palestine, where the very food in one's mouth had to be grubbed from the sand, made me wonder why anyone would want to go there. And so Jacov made the fatal mistake of bringing the family back to Kaunas, where he felt he could make a better living. Frieda was very angry that Jacov brought them back into the very teeth of the Nazis. One could hardly blame her, but I still liked the kindly Jacov better than I liked my bitter cousin.

I also adored Esterke. She had been born in Palestine, and was only three when everyone was forced into the ghetto. I occasionally sat with her while her parents were out working. By 1944 she was a lovely child of seven. When I read to her and taught her new words or numbers, her big blue eyes would grow wide with excitement. She seemed to enjoy the sound of my name, and while I was visiting she would trot around their little house repeating "Solly, Solly, Solly, Solly."

Frieda and Jacov were among many families who had built a hideout. It was not connected to the resistance network, and Frieda and Esterke made it through the "Children's Action" without being discovered.

On June 7, 1944, Fima brought us the exhilarating news that the Allies had landed in Normandy. The long awaited Second Front had become a reality. It concerned us mainly insofar as it would help the Russians. Only they were close enough to rescue us. Then on June 22, 1944, exactly three years after the Germans attacked the Soviet Union, the Russians swept down in vast numbers, taking Vitebsk, Bobruysk, and Mogilev. By June 29 they had liberated Minsk, and radio reports from both sides confirmed that they were concentrating forces along the Polish front.

Fima and his friends studied a map of the area and argued over the strategy the Russians would adopt next.

"There is no chance that the Germans could hold the Baltic States once the Russians start rolling through Poland," Fima argued. "I bet you ten to one that within a week the Germans will be moving all the divisions between here and Finland back to Germany to save the Fatherland from the Russian hordes."

Looking at the map, even I could see the logic in Fima's predictions. None of us knew that Hitler, not his generals, was now running the show, and Hitler's logic followed its own twisted path.

In fact, the German civilian authorities began to pack up and leave Kaunas by the score. The reaction of the population across the river was in marked contrast to ours in the ghetto. There was a great panic among the many who had collaborated with the Germans, for they knew the Russians were not likely to forget the Lithuanian attacks against their retreating troops in 1941. Thousands of Lithuanian families packed their belongings and retreated with the Germans.

The joy of the ghetto was almost complete. The loathsome Nazi beast was mortally wounded, wallowing in its own blood. But amidst the joy there was also apprehension. Would the Russians move fast enough to rout the Germans before they had a chance to wipe the ghetto out?

Fate had it otherwise. South of us the Russians advanced west of Bialystok, but in the north, for some reason, they stalled outside Vilnius, with disastrous results. The German evacuation slowed, and some Lithuanians even began to return to Kaunas, thinking that the Germans would push the Soviets back.

Jews were still sent out on work detail by the German ghetto command during all this time. More and more workers were running away, however, and finally Goecke brought a halt to all work activity outside the ghetto, and enforced the ghetto guard. Escape from the ghetto at that point was virtually impossible.

It was stifling hot the first week of July. Not a breeze stirred the air as Cooky, Fima, and I scoured every corner of the ghetto trying to find a likely escape route. There were none. We were trapped in the ghetto, and unless the Russians made a sudden breakthrough toward Kaunas, our fate was sealed.

"What are they going to do with us? Surely they aren't going to kill all ten thousand of us right under the Russians' noses?" my ever-optimistic father argued. "Then what? Evacuate us to Germany while hundreds of thousands of German troops remain trapped in the Baltic?" This was one of the arguments frequently voiced in the ghetto as tensions mounted.

On July 6 Dr. Elkes was called before Goecke, who informed him that all ghetto inhabitants were to be evacuated. This declaration was accompanied by the usual lies.

"The whole ghetto is going to be evacuated to a camp near Danzig. The workshops and other ghetto institutions will continue there in the same fashion. We will commence on July 8. Everyone will be evacuated within four days." Goecke said that since rail transportation was not available, transport would be by barge, down the Niemunas to the sea, and by sea to Danzig. He warned Dr. Elkes that every house in the ghetto would be thoroughly searched, and anyone found hiding would be shot on the spot.

The news that we were to be transported in barges fell on us like a pall, for rumors had been circulating that lately the Germans were taking Jews out in boats and drowning them at sea. It was a good reason not to obey these orders. But what else could we do?

That evening a number of family members discussed the situation. Fima and Miriam told us that they were going to hide with Zionist friends who had built a hideout.

"I would rather die here than be dragged to Germany where they will work us to death," Fima told us. Miriam agreed with him. Unfortunately, they didn't have enough space for the rest of us. Indeed, the existence of the hideouts placed many in a moral dilemma. Most of these dugouts were too small to hold more than a few people. Yet many felt that every Jew was morally bound to save other Jews, and some threatened their neighbors with exposure if they were not allowed in. Neither side in this quarrel could emerge without blemish.

Jacov and Frieda Schuster, however, offered us a place. They had worked on their hideout for the better part of the year, and urged the five of us to join them.

"We'll have to squeeze you in, but I am sure we won't be hiding for long. The Russians will be here within days, and we will be free men! Surely, Uncle, it is worthwhile taking the risk. Going to Germany is a death sentence." Jacov was a good-hearted man and was willing to face the wrath of the others in the hideout by taking us in.

Father went with him to look at the place and came back shaking his head. "It's a death trap, that's what it is," he declared. "A shallow earthen cellar that will surely be detected. Jacov is counting on the Germans not having enough time to search the whole ghetto."

It seemed that most inhabitants of the ghetto had decided to try to hide. Then the Gestapo spread another rumor—those who did not report for the barges would have to walk all the way to Danzig. This frightened the elderly, the ill, and those who still had small children, so on the first day several thousand Jews assembled and were marched off to the river, where open barges waited. Cooky and his parents were among them.

That morning Jacov Schuster appeared again to tell us that if we did not want to join them he would have to take in another family. Father was still against it, but Mother, Fanny, and Aunt Anushka had changed their minds. There were rumors that the Russians were moving again, and that the Germans were taking us out to sea just to drown us.

After some argument, Father reluctantly gave in.

That evening we gathered our last reserves of food and stole our way across the fields toward the Schusters'. The heat enveloped us like a blanket. The ghetto was like a ghost town. Most of those who decided to hide were long since underground. When we finally arrived at the house, Father gave a prearranged signal. After a few minutes Jacov opened the door.

The entrance to the cellar was below a small wood stove. Jacov was very handy, and had cleverly fastened the stove to a trapdoor, fashioning it all in such a way that the opening couldn't be detected. A few wooden steps led down to a small room. The low ceiling was supported by wooden beams, and wooden bunks were built along the walls. A tin pipe ran up to another stove above and then to the roof, to supply air. In one corner stood several large water bottles and two straw baskets full of food. Besides Jacov, cousin Frieda and Esterke, Jacov's uncle and aunt and two teenage daughters were there. They greeted us with unsmiling faces, barely nodding their heads. They were half undressed and wet with perspiration.

Small wonder that they received us with sour faces. The heat was suffocating, and our bodies only increased it.

Without saying anything Aunt Anushka, always practical, stripped to her underwear, and the rest of us followed suit. Jacov pointed out our bunks. We added our food to the two baskets for all to share. For better or worse, we were now committed, and we all lay down on our bunks and tried to stay as still as possible. We silently prayed that the Russians would come soon. Unless the weather changed we wouldn't last long in this place.

Thirst soon plagued us, and we begged Jacov to increase our ration of water. We soon finished almost half the supply. It remained quiet outside, and Jacov decided to sneak out and replenish our stores. I went with him.

The room above felt incredibly cool. Jacov located some additional empty bottles and cans, and we headed for the well. It felt like paradise outside, but it was so quiet we were afraid the entire ghetto could hear the squeaking crank as we hauled up buckets of water. But nothing stirred, and that evening the whole family slept upstairs, each of us taking turns on watch.

Jacov woke us at dawn. Not a sound could be heard anywhere, and we wondered if the Germans had run away. Later we found out that Goecke couldn't obtain transport that day. After some hesitation we decided to take no chances, and reluctantly descended once more to the hideout. It had cooled off a little in our absence, and each of us lay down in our assigned places and counted the hours. We had to hold out. Liberation was so near.

When the heat again grew unbearable and we still heard nothing above us, Jacov decided to see what was going on. He soon came back and told us that it was very quiet and we could come out again. We stayed indoors and kept a lookout.

On Monday, July 10, we woke to the sound of trucks entering the ghetto, and the barking of dogs. Dear God, they had brought the dogs with them. We were horrified. But Jacov, who had trained dogs when he was in Palestine, had cleverly prepared a concoction of spices and turpentine and spread it all around the house. He said it would keep the dogs from detecting our presence.

Then in the distance we heard the first explosions. We quickly descended the steps. Jacov carefully removed all signs of our presence and pulled the trapdoor shut over our heads.

As the sound of explosions drew nearer we lay quietly in our bunks and waited for death. No one moved, but each one of us knew what the other was thinking. Perhaps we should get out of this smothering hell and join the evacuation while there was still time. The Germans would leave no stone unturned to find us. Yet no one wanted to be the first to leave. Jacov and Frieda were concerned about Esterke. If they found a child that age still alive there was no doubt she would be killed, perhaps together with her parents. The other Schusters were also afraid for their teenage daughters. They were still not old enough to be classified as workers.

My family all looked anxiously at Father. We had a chance to survive, since we were all of working age. I was a borderline case, but I had just turned sixteen, and during the spring I had grown a fraction and my shoulders had widened a bit in spite of our meager rations. But once committed, Father was hard to move.

Suddenly the Germans were very close. We could hear their shouted orders and the barking dogs. We froze in our places, barely daring to breathe. In the heat an icy hand gripped my heart.

Two explosions rocked the foundations and lifted us out of our bunks. Sand and dust poured down on our heads, and we heard the furious barking of dogs and the rattling of submachine guns. Then we heard a baby cry and a woman shouting hysterically, "Don't shoot, we are coming out, we are coming out!"

We realized then that the Germans had discovered a neighbor's hideout, not ours.

"*Raus! Raus!* Out with you, you stinking Jews. Hands up! Up!" After a minute there were more explosions and the woman began screaming in Yiddish.

Little Esterke stood up in the middle of the room, her eyes glassy with fright. She was urinating and defecating. Methodically she began peeling off her clothes.

Frieda jumped up and began wiping her down with a rag, screaming at Jacov at the top of her lungs.

"You lazy bastard, you good for nothing lazy bastard. It was hard for you to build the roads of Palestine. You didn't think it proper that I should work as a maid in Palestine. Look at us now! Look at us now! Oh, my poor baby," she cried, taking Esterke into her arms.

Jacov jumped up and put his big hand over her mouth, his eyes searching the ceiling, listening for the sound of boots overhead. But all we heard was gunfire, and more explosions.

Apparently the Germans had followed their dogs to other hide-outs. For a moment it seemed that the danger was over, but smoke was now drifting down from the ventilator pipe and the smell in the hideout was becoming unbearable. Jacov's house was built of stone, but if the roof caught fire it would be fatal. All of us agreed to give ourselves up. Then Father suggested that he go up by himself to see what was happening. Jacov protested that this was his duty, but Frieda shut him up. Once more I had to admire my father's unexpected bravery. Perhaps I had always underestimated him. Mother also protested, but Father simply waved her off and climbed the steps. Jacov helped him lift the trapdoor, and Father disappeared from view. A rush of cool air, mixed with smoke, came down the hole. We could hear the crackling of burning wood, but the explosions and the dogs had moved a little farther away.

Within minutes Father was back, leaving the trapdoor open behind him. "They have skipped our house and are moving further down the street. Perhaps your concoction worked and misled the dogs. Fortunately, the house next door is not on fire, but the two beyond it are," he said.

With the fresh air coming down from above it became cooler and the smoke cleared. We decided to wait to see what developed. We believed that if we gave ourselves up we would be shot anyway. Why be in a hurry to die?

The ghetto quieted as evening fell, and we cautiously emerged to cool off a bit. Some of the neighboring houses were still burning, and we could see fires raging all over the ghetto.

"Oh God," Fanny moaned. "We won't survive this. Perhaps we could still give ourselves up. The evacuation is still officially on." Anushka, who was quietly smoking one of her smelly cigarettes, sided with my sister. Again Father suggested we wait until morning. Perhaps the Germans wouldn't return. Even as he said it, we knew he didn't quite believe it.

The next morning we were again awakened by explosions, this time quite nearby. It was Tuesday, July 11, and the Germans were back in full force, shouting obscenities, throwing grenades into houses, and letting their dogs run loose. We could hear screams, and twice the sound of heavy boots trampling over our heads. More than once I was ready to come out and let them shoot me. It was sweltering, and the stench of sweat, urine, excrement, and smoke made the air almost unbreathable.

How we survived that day I don't know, but we knew we couldn't stand another like it. When night fell we crawled out from that stinking hole, happy to be able to breathe.

Along the street many houses had been almost totally destroyed. One or two were burned to the ground, with only the chimneys left standing. Farther away the ghetto was illuminated by houses that were still ablaze.

Then Father had an idea, and he crept out to survey the area around us. After a while he came back, having found a cellar in one of the burned houses was still intact. He reasoned that the Germans wouldn't bother to check a burned house, and the chances that they would leave Jacov's house intact seemed remote. The trouble was that parts of the structure were still smoldering, and there was always the danger that pieces could come crashing down on our heads.

We decided to risk it. Father told Jacov and the others about our plan, and no one really objected. If anything, they seemed relieved at the prospect of having more space and air.

Before dawn all five of us sneaked to the other house, bringing some water and food with us. Before we left, Jacov and Frieda said a tearful good-bye to us, and Esterke clung to me. She didn't want us to go. We all knew that we probably wouldn't survive another day.

The other cellar was partly covered by the charred floor of the house. Burned boards, blackened furniture, and other debris had fallen through a gaping hole at the other end. We pushed a set of bedsprings against the back wall, under what remained of the floor, and piled other things around it to conceal ourselves.

Father suggested that we also smear our faces with ash as camouflage. I said that everyone looked much better in these masks, which provoked some laughter among the women, and Father gave me an approving look. Then we crawled behind the pile of debris to try to sleep. A moment after I lay down I leapt into the air in pain. Beneath me some live embers still smoldered under the ash, burning holes in my pants. After that we carefully raked over the ground before lying down again.

Although the place reeked of smoke, it was nothing like the terrible air in Jacov's cellar. I had no difficulty falling asleep.

We woke up at first light on Wednesday, hearing the voices of Jews. It was the last day of the transport, and many had decided to abandon their hideouts. Goecke had threatened to shoot anyone found hiding, and these people had decided to take their chances rather than perish in the flames of their homes.

The Germans arrived with their usual punctuality. Once again they were setting fires and blowing up houses, and they seemed to have sped up their pace. It was obvious they were not going to leave anyone alive. We were astonished that those who came out of hiding weren't shot on the spot, but the Germans seemed to be moving them on to the gate.

The wind had picked up, and here and there flames began to lick at the still-smoldering beams above us. Just then an explosion very near us shook the ground. We scrambled out from behind our pile just as a joist above our heads began to give way. We were climbing out of the cellar when a second explosion nearly threw us to the ground.

"Oh my God, my God, they are blowing them up!" Fanny cried as a wall of the Schuster's house caved in and the roof burst into flames.

At Fanny's outburst one of the Germans standing nearby turned and pointed his gun. We froze in our tracks. Our time had finally come. How many times in the past four years had I stood before a German gun waiting to die?

Then the German started laughing. He was very young and apparently found our ash-smeared faces funny.

At that moment Jacov Schuster emerged from the flames of their house, followed by Frieda carrying Esterke. Their hair had been burned off and their faces were blackened, but they were alive.

"Please, please, my baby is wounded. She needs help. She is a British subject. She was born in Palestine. She should be with prisoners of war, not here," Frieda shouted. Even as she was screaming her knees buckled.

For a moment the Germans just stared, as if stunned by this apparition and the wild things she was shouting. Then one of them
shouted, "Jude, der Weg nach Jerusalem ist Frei! Jude, der Weg nach
Jerusalem ist Frei!" ("Jew, the road to Jerusalem is free!") I thought
that he must have been crazy, too. Jacov was bending down to help
Frieda, and in the meantime Esterke had spotted us and gotten up.
She was crying, "Help me, Solly, help me. Solly, Solly, it hurts. Solly,
Solly, Solly help me it hurts." It was then that I saw the blood pouring
down her from the stump of her wrist. Her hand had been completely torn away.

"These won't be working for us anymore," one of the Germans said
calmly, and lifting his gun he sprayed them with bullets. Jacov and
Frieda were hit several times, and collapsed in a heap. But Esterke,
still alive, kept coming until one of the Germans pulled out his luger
and shot her through the head.

Without a second glance he turned and told us to report to the
gate on Varniu Street. As we turned to go several Latvian soldiers
bringing up the rear threw Esterke's body and those of her parents
into the flames of their house. Of the other four who had shared the
hideout, there was no sign.

I felt numb. With all the ways I had hardened myself, the brutality of
the Germans still shocked me. My God, what were they made of? It
seemed astonishing that they had arms and legs and faces, the same
as other human beings.

The walk to the Varniu gate revealed the total devastation of the
ghetto. Houses burned or gutted and corpses burned beyond recognition, many of them child-size. Some had lain in the sun for several
days and we had to hold our noses as we passed. The smell of burnt
flesh and burnt wood was everywhere.

Two thousand Jews gathered at the gate that day—whole families
with small children and even some older people. How had they all
survived the "Children's Action?" Their resigned faces were smeared
with soot and grime and their garments were torn and dirty. We sat
down on the ground with the rest. Around midday we shared the few
bits of food we had left. It was one of the rare times in the ghetto that
I wasn't hungry. I couldn't get the image of Esterke's death out of my
mind.

That afternoon we were ordered to line up in columns, a hundred in each group, each one accompanied by heavily armed guards. As we passed over the Vilijampole Bridge I took one last look at the ghetto. Flames and plumes of smoke rose in the sky, and we could still hear explosions. Ours was the last group to leave, we were told. Anyone found hiding after that would be shot.

We never saw Fima or Miriam again.

15

Arbeit Macht Frei

G oecke's threat to make us walk all the way to Danzig turned out to be an empty one. After about a two-hour march, during which there were many unsuccessful attempts to escape, we arrived at a small railroad junction. There we were loaded into cattle cars where we were packed in so closely that we had to sleep standing up. The cars had only a couple of small windows criss-crossed with barbed wire, and in the heat they were suffocating. We had only a single bucket for toilet facilities. I don't know how long we traveled in that heat and stench, but it seemed like days before we arrived at a station called Tiggenhoff. There the Germans opened the boxcar doors one by one, starting at the front of the train. All the women, children, and old people were ordered to get off.

We were in the last boxcar. Dr. Elkes arrived with our transport, one car ahead of ours. When the Germans opened the last two cars he stepped down with the women and children and approached the officer in charge. He told him that the commandant of the ghetto, Goecke, had promised that families would not be separated.

The SS officer gave him two resounding slaps that knocked him to the ground. "This is not the ghetto, you filthy Jew. Now get back into the train before I shoot you."

This scene deeply affected my father. Even butchers like Rauca and Goecke had treated Dr. Elkes with respect. It was obvious that this was a different world, and different rules prevailed here.

For some reason the men and women in our car were not separated. Our entire carload was taken off together, and we were loaded onto another waiting train. After a short trip we were taken off at Stutthoff.

The camp at Stutthoff looked huge. It was encircled by barbed wire and electric fencing, which was marked by white porcelain insulators. The fences were ringed with wooden guard towers manned by SS with machine guns.

Over the gate was a big sign that said "Arbeit Macht Frei."

As we stood in line waiting to enter, I watched a man in a striped prisoner's uniform and cap moving along the fence. He was holding a mess tin apparently filled with soup, walking ever so carefully and balancing the tin so as not to spill a single drop. He must have gotten too close to the fence, because a tower guard across the way turned his gun on him. I watched in horror. The guard seemed to take forever to aim. I wanted to scream a warning, but no sound escaped my lips. Finally the crack of a shot broke the afternoon stillness. The prisoner fell to his knees. Miraculously, in his outstretched hands the tin of soup remained upright. He quickly brought the tin to his lips and began to drink. A second shot rang out, but the man ignored it and continued drinking. Then a third shot went through his head, lifting his cap off, and the prisoner fell like a stone. Blood and brains spilled into the dust, but there was nothing to spill from the tin. He managed to down all of the soup between shots.

This was the harsh reality of a German concentration camp.

That night, when they allowed us to go to the latrine, I slipped my precious diary out from under my shirt and dropped it into a stinking hole full of excrement. I had written everything there, all that we had experienced, and kept it safe for almost four years, but it was simply too dangerous to try to hold on to it here. I felt as if I were throwing away a part of myself.

We slept in some kind of big storage room that held piles of old shoes. We were told that we would be processed the next day. Toward morning I awoke with my mother standing over me.

"We are going to be separated today, and I don't know when we'll see each other again. Here's a five ruble piece. You'll probably be able to exchange it for bread," she whispered, pressing the gold piece into my palm. We stood for a while hugging each other and crying. When Father, Fanny, and Aunt Anushka awakened we fell into each others' arms and cried with them.

"You are a strong boy," Mother whispered. "Take care of your father." Surprisingly, Fanny said the same thing to me. I didn't know whether they were simply trying to buck me up, but I promised them I would.

Then the big door in front was thrown open, and dozens of SS and men in striped uniforms streamed in, shouting orders and pushing us outside.

"Out, out, you lazy Jewish swine. Quickly, quickly. Women and children this way. Men here. Leave everything behind."

We hastily kissed each other good-bye once more before we were pushed out into the harsh morning sunlight. I looked back once to see Mother and Fanny walking the other way with the women and children. My mother looked back, too, and when our eyes met she held her head up and smiled. That last smile tore my heart.

Our group was pushed into a large white building where a tall prisoner who seemed to be in charge shouted, "Everyone strip and line up for inspection!" He wore a uniform with a black triangle on the arm. Others wearing the same triangle lashed those who did not undress quickly enough. We learned that this was the insignia worn by inmates who were common criminals. They ruled the camp at Stutthoff.

I added my clothes to the pile. We were ordered to leave everything behind. I left one last book and Lena's little portrait with my clothes—every last thing I owned, except the precious gold coin, which I concealed in my palm.

The inmate who searched me was a stocky red-faced man. He was very thorough. While he was peering into my mouth to see if anything was there, he whispered, "You have two choices. You can hand over whatever you're clutching so hard, or you can drop it on the floor and pray the SS doesn't notice. If they do, you're dead for sure."

Then he told me to bend over and inspected my rectum. When I turned I passed the coin to him, my heart beating like a drum.

Father was very anxious when we had to leave our clothing behind. I guessed that he had had a gold piece as well. Our next destination was the showers, and he was clearly distressed at the sight of them. There was a new anxiety and despair in Father's eyes. This was not the ghetto, where he had the support of friends in high places.

Water came out of the showers, and it was a relief to wash the accumulated dirt and sweat from my skin. We were issued striped uniforms and caps, and surprisingly enough we were given back our shoes. Father was greatly relieved. He had hidden a gold coin in one, and it was still there when he got them back.

We had hardly entered our assigned barracks before everyone was chased back outside. Hundreds of prisoners were sitting on the ground in a large, sandy square. To my delight my friend David Granat, who had been at a camp in Alexotas during our last months in the ghetto, was among them.

While we waited for roll call we told each other what had transpired since we last saw each other. I asked him if he had seen his mother since he reached camp. I knew that he was devoted to her. He pointed to a fence across the way.

"The women are over there. Sometimes in the afternoons, they allow them outside. I have seen my mother and sister twice already," he told me.

Twice a day we were assembled at the square and counted. This roll call was called the *appell*. We were lined up military fashion, each row straight as an arrow, and God help you if you didn't follow the orders of the capo quickly enough. Quite often he beat offenders senseless. When the SS man in charge appeared to count the rows, the capo would shout, "Muetzen ab! (Caps off!)" Every prisoner whipped his cap off and smacked it against his leg. This was to be done in unison, so that the slapping caps made a single sound. Those who were out of sync received a beating, and their whole block had to do push-ups as punishment.

The first few days we were drilled in this fashion until we were exhausted. The heat in the square was intense by midday. Many of the older men simply collapsed. The rest of us learned to do what was demanded of us, and within a few days we executed the orders with military precision.

Our Block *Aelteste* (leader) was a tall blond Pole named Peter, whom Father approached with a proposition. He told him he had sliced the bread rations for our ghetto and could be useful doing the same task here. Newcomers did not approach the *Aeltestes* so boldly, and Peter would have brought his stick down on Father's head had Father not slipped the gold coin to him as he spoke.

"You are a lucky old man," Peter said. "Let me see your expertise, then. If you are good, the job is yours." He brought a loaf of bread and a long sharp knife, and without missing a beat Father rapidly cut the bread into perfectly even slices. Peter was visibly impressed. I could understand why my father was known as an entrepreneur before the war. Despite everything, he had not quite lost that spirit.

And so my father was put in charge of dividing rations, under the supervision of the capos. The largest portion of bread was always at the end of the loaf. In Yiddish that piece is called the "Akraytchik." His brief position as a deputy minister after the 1917 Revolution was fairly well known in the Kaunas ghetto, and soon everyone in the camp was calling Father the "Akraytchik Minister."

David and I were supposed to stay in an upper bunk with two other boys. The space was only meant for one, and it was nearly impossible to fall asleep. Early on I made the mistake of sneaking out to the latrine in the middle of the night, and when I returned the other boys had completely taken over the space. There was no way I could fit myself in again.

A capo slept in the lower bunk, with the space entirely to himself. He was a big German Communist named Werner. He woke up as I stood there trying to figure out what to do, and offered to share his bunk.

I hesitated, and he said gruffly, "Don't worry, I am not that kind. You will be safe with me."

His bunk had a mattress and a soft blanket, and I was so tired that I dozed off almost immediately. I woke with a start when I felt his hand on my penis. I practically threw myself out of the bunk and scuttled off to the other end of the barracks.

Father was sleeping in a section for administrative workers, which was off-limits to the rest of us, but I didn't know where else to turn. When I woke him he was alarmed: one didn't take the harsh regulations of the camp lightly. But when I told him what happened he hid me under his blanket, where I spent the night.

The next day, after the morning *appell*, I was summoned to see the Block *Aelteste*. Peter came straight to the point. "Did that German Communist swine rape you?"

I realized that Father had spoken to him about the incident, and instinctively I knew that this was a mistake.

"No sir, he didn't," I said promptly. I was glad I didn't have to lie.

"You are telling the truth?" he asked severely.

"Yes, sir!"

He gave me a knowing look and then smiled. "You are a smart lad. Your father is a bit naive, but he cuts bread like the very devil!"

That afternoon I finally spotted Mother, Fanny, and Anushka. It saddened me to see them in those striped uniforms. Mother smiled and blew kisses, while Fanny took a few paces backward and threw something over the fence. It landed right at my feet. Fanny hadn't lost her athletic touch.

There was a portion of bread inside the parcel. I signaled that she was not to sacrifice her bread for me, and motioned that I was going to throw it back. The guard in the tower saw me and thought I might be one of the suicidal inmates who periodically electrocuted themselves on the fences. He swung his gun around, but I quickly sat down on the ground and he lowered it again.

David was with me. He had spotted his mother Alte, who called out to him from the crowd. Then the whole group of women at the fence started shouting greetings to the men on our side. In seconds a group of female capos rushed on them and began beating them with sticks. David and I watched and wept as our mothers were pushed back and disappeared in the milling crowd.

We had been in the camp for four days before those who had left the ghetto on the river barges arrived. David and I found several of our friends from Kaunas, including Abale Nauchowitz, who was one of David's best friends. As usual we spent most of the day sitting out in the *appell platz*, which we called the "torture field" because we had to sit there for hours in the beating sun. I kept scanning the crowd from where I sat. Late in the afternoon the guards allowed us to move around, and finally, far on the other side, I spotted that familiar, stooped figure. Cooky was thinner than ever, but his crooked smile was the same. The Germans on the boats had told everyone that the ghetto had been burned to the ground, and he thought we were dead. We had another tearful reunion. His mother was on the other side with mine; his father was dead.

That evening Father prepared four Akraytchiks for me and all my friends. Father said that if this kept up he would run out of Akraytchiks.

• • •

The camp was now crowded with Lithuanian Jews, and a day or two later Peter ordered all those under the age of eighteen out to the *appell platz*. Once again my heart hammered with fear. The same thought was on everyone's mind: Auschwitz.

We were ordered to take off our shirts and stand at attention. I stood next to Cooky, with David and Abale on the other side. All of us began flexing our muscles and pushing out our chests. A capo I vaguely recognized passed from row to row, writing down inmates' numbers. When he came to our row we stood smartly at attention, bellies in, chests out, muscles pumped up to the bursting point, as if our lives depended on it, which they did.

I stole a sideways look at Cooky and my heart sank. He was thin as a rail, and his white skin was almost transparent. He was trying to pump up his muscles as we did, but you can't make muscles where there aren't any.

David and Abale told the capo they were brothers. He looked them over and wrote down their numbers. He moved to me and gave me a brief once-over. To my relief he wrote my number down, too. Thank God I had my father's build.

But as I feared, he didn't even give Cooky a second glance. He just passed him by.

Life and death is on the tip of the tongue, as the scriptures say. "He is my brother, sir," I blurted out. "Can he stay with me?"

The capo gave me a brief look, and struck my number out. "He can't stay with you, but you sure can join him," he said, giving me a nasty grin. Then he looked at me once more. "Aren't you the son of Chaim, the breadcutter?" he asked.

I found myself completely tongue-tied. I couldn't say a word to save my life.

"Yes sir, he is," Cooky piped up. "And he is not my brother. We are good friends and he was just trying to save me," Cooky said calmly, and smiled at the capo.

The capo stared at him a second. I thought I saw a trace of respect in his eyes.

"What is your number again, boy?" he asked me. I found my voice and rattled off my number. I was gripped by terror, and wanted desperately to live.

"In the concentration camp," the capo said, "don't try to be a hero. There are no live heroes here, only dead ones. Thank your father for this, and the fact you didn't rat on Werner." Then he pinched my cheek like my Uncle Jacob used to do.

"Thank you sir, thank you," I gabbled, feeling enormous shame and relief at the same time. I didn't dare look at Cooky.

Out of a hundred boys, only about thirty had their numbers written down that day. The younger boys couldn't hold back their tears. The rest of us sat on the ground in a stupor. I could barely keep myself from weeping. Faced with death, I had been cowardly, while Cooky had nobly interfered on my behalf. I should have stuck by my friend. Cooky had shown his true strength, a strength I couldn't match.

Cooky himself had to calm me. Would I have saved him by sharing his fate? Hadn't Lena been foolish to choose death over life? Did I not speak up and claim we were brothers? Once again he used the arguments on me that he used when Mr. Edelstein was killed. Dearest Cooky, whom I had teased and been impatient with after he returned from the Ninth Fort. Now he humbled me once more.

Those of us who had been chosen were grieving, and the rest were gripped with terror. I calmed down enough to try to comfort the others. It was odd that they had left us all together. Always before they had marched the condemned ones away immediately after selections. We pointed this out to the younger ones, who calmed down a little. Who would not grasp at straws in the face of the gas chambers? In fact, none of us understood what was happening. Why were we still together? Perhaps we had merely been selected to join labor brigades, while the others would stay and work in the camp? As the day wore on even I began to put stock in this idea. When I presented this argument to Cooky, he just gave me a wan smile, but I thought I saw a flicker of hope there.

Toward evening Father appeared. He seemed to be in a daze. Tears were running down his face as he hugged me. He kept saying "We are saved, we are saved." For a minute I thought he had lost his wits.

He had just come from Peter, the Block *Aelteste*. Hitler had been assassinated by his own generals. They had planted a bomb and were sending out orders that henceforth there would be a new chain of command.

Suddenly the world stood still. A riotous vision filled my head, and I saw crowds of cheering Jews marching victoriously through the streets of Kaunas. Even the dead, all those killed in the small ghetto and at the Ninth Fort, were resurrected in my imagination. I saw our snarling captors in cages, pelted by mud and stones. A cheering tumult swept through the streets of Europe, floated over the Mediterranean, and filled the streets of Jerusalem.

The news of Hitler's death spread like wildfire, and euphoria swept through the camp. We hardly saw any capos or other functionaries that evening. They were all lying low while the rest of us gathered in groups, discussing what we would do when the gates of the camp sprang open and we were free. That night we hardly slept. Tomorrow would dawn on a new world.

The morning *appell* was a grim affront. It was especially long, and when some of the inmates showed signs of rebelling they were beaten by the capos with greater cruelty than usual.

Something was wrong here. When we finally heard the horrifying news that Hitler had only been slightly injured, the letdown was so enormous that many inmates threw themselves at the fences. They were either shot by the guards or died frozen to the wires, the current burning their hands black.

Those who had been selected for Auschwitz were the hardest hit. When that one-night reprieve evaporated Cooky was completely devastated. I did what I could to console him, falling back on hopeful arguments about the advance of the Allies and the Russians, but his spirit was utterly crushed.

The SS and the capos, however, were reinvigorated, and applied beatings and punishments with renewed enthusiasm.

After a few days life settled down to the usual gray routines. We boys were given jobs sweeping the yard and the barracks and cleaning the latrines. Sometimes we helped Father distribute bread.

A group from the women's camp was the first to be deported, Abale's mother and little brother among them. The women in my family, thanks God, were not.

Then on an especially hot day around the middle of August Father, David, Abale, Cooky, and I were all working inside the barracks. The capos came around and ordered everyone out for a special roll call. Some of us were to be transported to another camp.

Father called us over and we discussed what to do. The Russians were slowly pushing their way toward us, and conditions in the camp had settled a bit. We decided not to report and to take our chances here at Stutthoff.

The decision was short-lived. Peter crashed into the barracks and came after us with his stick. Even Father wasn't spared. "Are you crazy?" he yelled. "They have been calling your numbers for ten minutes already. Run or you are dead!"

Fortunately for us the capo with the list was one of the few decent ones in the camp. He called our numbers again, and sent us to join the column with a few swift kicks as punishment. Cooky tried to slip in with us, but he was immediately beaten and dragged back to the group whose numbers had not been called. Of the Lithuanian men in the camp, only the younger boys and the old men were left behind. We finally realized that Peter had saved us from a fatal blunder.

As we marched out the gate I turned and got one last look at Cooky, who slowly lifted his hand good-bye. There was a thin trickle of blood from his nose, but otherwise his pinched face was without color or expression.

16

Pigs

*T en days before the great Normandy invasion of June 1944, and after
more than three weeks at sea, the bulk of the 442nd Combat Team arrived
in Italy. There it participated in the heavy fighting of the Rome-Arno campaign. Clarence Matsumura's group shipped out later, in an armada of one
hundred ships bringing in reinforcements and resupply for the invasion forces.
Several attempts to land his troop ship were thwarted because so many harbors
had been devastated by bombs. It finally disembarked at a temporary dock built
by army engineers. The troops were then transported by rail, in train cars
called "forty and eights" because each could hold either forty men or eight
horses. It took Clarence's group nearly a week to reach Marseilles.*

From the camp at Stutthoff those of us with the lucky numbers were
marched to the railroad and loaded once again into cars meant for
cattle. After the Germans shut the doors, they kept us standing at the
station for hours. The car was stifling under the August sun. They
gave us decent rations for once, but our big problem was water. We
drank nearly all we had while we sweltered at the junction. I thought
we would suffocate. Finally several men started pounding on the
door, and the guards opened it. Air flowed in, and I fell asleep
standing up. When I awoke I found that Father and my friends had
made space for me on the floor, and the train was moving.

We passed through all kinds of little junctions with Polish names,
and then they changed to German. Frankfurt, Dresden, Zwickau,
Plauen, Bayreuth. We took turns standing at the tiny window to get
some air, and whoever was there would call out the names. Once we

271

crossed a road with a sign pointing to Berlin, but we seemed to be a long way from there.

About twenty of us in the car were from the Kaunas ghetto. Father's friend Jacob Portnov was with us, and David and Abale. The rest were from the ghetto at Siauliai. The entire transport was made up of Lithuanian Jews, which was a great advantage because we were supportive of each other.

At night the air turned chilly, and we bunched up together to gather heat from each others' bodies. Our thin uniforms left us shivering. We eked out our rations, since we had no idea where we were going or how long it would take us to get there.

As cultivated fields and small towns with German names rumbled by someone said we were traveling south through Thuringen toward Bavaria. One night the train stopped with a jerk. We heard the faint droning of engines somewhere above. They grew louder. Then the first tremendous explosion rocked our car, and bombs started exploding all around us. Germans were running from the train and diving into ditches.

No one bothered to let us out, and we were in grave danger of being killed. Yet suddenly, as if we were all struck by the same thought at once, the entire car broke out in a loud cheer. The Germans must have thought we were screaming in fright, otherwise they would have riddled the car with bullets.

I pushed up to a window to watch the tremendous spectacle. The planes were moving toward what looked like a very large town. Thousands of bombs fell one after the other, into the midst of houses, cathedrals, blocks of tall buildings. Their explosions lit up the whole city and seemed to stretch as far as the eye could see. We heard sirens and the sharp reports of antiaircraft guns, whose shells burst in the sky like firecrackers. Searchlights stabbed the darkness, crisscrossing the sky from one end to the other. Suddenly one caught a plane in its sights. The plane was clearly visible, like some giant white insect caught in a web.

In vain it maneuvered to escape into the darkness, but the lights clung tenaciously and the guns concentrated their fire. Suddenly it shuddered and one of its wings sheared off. It spun out of control and plummeted to the earth, hitting somewhere in the middle of town and erupting into a fireball. Someone in the car thought that the town was Nuremberg, where the infamous Nuremberg Laws were later concocted. We watched this destruction with the solemn satisfaction of those witnessing a terrible and exacting revenge.

Our progress was slower after that. We were continually shunted onto sidetracks as more important transports went through. We often detoured through small towns because so many of the tracks had been damaged by bombs. It seemed to take forever.

Finally, at a station called Kaufering, we were told to disembark. We were stiff and weak from hunger by then, and filthy, but as we lined up to be counted the countryside spread around us like a vision.

Everywhere were beautiful stretches of cultivated land dotted by small woods. There wasn't a piece of paper or other refuse to be seen anywhere. Even the railroad tracks seemed clean. We were in Germany, and at that moment it looked like paradise. All around us were lush green fields, neat farmhouses, and flower gardens. We were given larger rations, as well—bigger chunks of bread and more margarine and jam. I tried to eat slowly, but within seconds I had finished it all off. Then we were formed into columns and marched from the station.

It was a beautiful day, with a cool breeze blowing from a nearby lake we later found out was called Amersee. I almost forgot that we were Jewish prisoners condemned to extinction. How could so much evil dwell amidst so much beauty? I imagined Father and I as tourists at a hotel where we had a gorgeous lunch complete with soft white rolls that melted in our mouths.

When we reached a town called Utting we were again put on a local. Our destination was an outer camp of Dachau.

Dachau was the first slave labor camp the Germans built, but Lager Ten was one of its newest outposts. It was a small camp surrounded by the usual double rows of barbed wire and electrified fencing. Some prisoners were still stringing the wires, but slant-roofed towers had already been raised at each corner of the yard. Machine-gun barrels nosed out from under the eaves.

I had to keep my wits about me now. No more daydreaming about buttered white rolls: The first day in camp was crucial.

In the middle of the camp were some strange constructions that looked something like the huge beehives I had seen once in Lithuania. They were long gable roofs placed on the ground, about twenty meters long and less than five meters wide at the base.

"It looks as if they forgot to attach the barracks to these roofs," David said. And indeed there were no other barracks to be seen.

The Germans divided us up into groups of about fifty, and assigned each group to one of these hovels. Father, Jacob Portnov, and I were in the last row of our block, so David and Abale ended up in the next barracks. I was among the first to enter this dismal underground place. The few tiny windows let in little light, and it was almost dark inside. Several steps led down to a kind of trough which was the central passageway. On either side wooden bunks lined the walls. The walkway was covered with boards, and a few electrical bulbs hung from the ceiling. This was where we would sleep.

Halfway down a round iron stove stood in the walkway, its chimney poking up through the roof. It sent a chill down my spine. Surely we would not still be here in the winter of 1945, with the Allies pressing in from France and the Russians from the Baltics?

It was an incredible pleasure to shower. We all stank after God knows how many days on that train, and the filth washed from my skin in brown rivulets. From the showers they took us to a storeroom where we were issued new uniforms: a shirt, striped jacket and pants, and wooden clogs. We also received two army blankets and an aluminum mess tin and spoon.

Nothing fit, and we had to trade with each other to get something approximately the right size. Finding clogs in the right size was especially crucial. Father hung on to his boots, which were well worn but still in one piece.

After the *appell* we lined up for the evening meal. We were surprised and gratified that the soup was reasonably thick with potatoes, and we got a fairly large chunk of bread.

We were the only ones in the camp, and the capos and functionaries were chosen by the Germans who supervised our transport. Our camp administrator was a middle-aged, red-faced man named Burgin, who was from the Siauliai ghetto. He naturally picked his own people for administrative personnel.

Father tried to get an administrative job with him by telling him about his ghetto duties, but Burgin simply told him to get lost.

We feared what awaited him the next day. Father was now fifty-two years old, and had never done much physical labor. Three years of living in the ghetto had taken its toll. He had lost all his teeth and now wore ill-fitting dentures that caused him a lot of pain.

Worse yet were the deadening effects of his separation from Mother and Fanny. It was bad enough when Mother was out of reach just beyond a fence. Now she was hundreds of miles away. Watching her suffering and withdrawal after Herman disappeared had blinded me to her real strengths, and how much her very presence sustained my father. As much as Father and Fanny seemed to be our mainstays during those years, Mother had somehow always been at the center of the family. Only now did I realize how much Father and all of us had depended on her.

I tried to cheer him. The women were strong and in good health. Nothing would happen to them, I said. And our situation here was improved. Already the food was better and more substantial than in Stutthoff. Here the capos were our own Lithuanian Jews, who by and large didn't seem too bad, at least not in the beginning. We had been allowed to wash. We didn't stink anymore. We weren't starving. And so on. But when Father wasn't around, I often cried.

We slept well that night, spreading the blankets on the wooden planks of the bunk. We folded our uniforms into pillows and slept only in our shirts. We lay down with our heads toward the V made by the platform and the roof, and after we'd banged our heads against the roof a few times we learned not to sit up too quickly.

Appell was early the next morning. The sky was grayish, the landscape covered with a chill morning mist. We lined up straight as we had been taught at Stutthoff, and when the SS man appeared the chief capo shouted "Caps off!"

We did our best to impress the German by whipping off our caps in unison and smartly slapping them against our legs. He looked reasonably impressed. It was a fairly short *appell*. For breakfast we were given a piece of doughy gray bread, the usual margarine and jam, but also, incredibly, a piece of sausage. It was the first sausage I had seen in months.

David and Abale joined us, and we ate standing up, all of us trying to guess what kind of work lay in store. Obviously the Germans had not transported us all the way across Poland and Germany for some kind of cushy job, but whatever it was it must have been something important.

After being re-counted we were marched out of the gate and into the woods. I hadn't been so close to trees since our last summer at

Kalautuvas. There were white birch, pine, and other trees I didn't recognize, all of them majestic. The odor of balsam and fir was everywhere, and birds were singing. We even saw a hare run across the path ahead of us.

After a short walk we were brought to a halt in a large clearing and lined up in rows of three. I had a moment of alarm when I recalled all the killings in the woods in Lithuania, but the SS guards were joined by lightly-armed Germans in brown uniforms and a number of people in civilian clothing. One even wore lederhosen. After a short conference, our guards began dividing us up into various groups, which were marched off with one or more of the German civilians. Father and I were at the back of our column, and as we waited I was mulling over another one of my crazy ideas. What if I simply wasn't in any of these assigned groups? If I hid in the woods no one would know where I belonged. But what if the guards tallied the total again, and found a prisoner missing?

I decided I would take that chance, and when none of the Germans was looking I slipped behind a tree. I could see Father go rigid, but he restrained himself from looking back. As quickly and silently as I could I inched back into some undergrowth, my heart thumping with excitement as much as with fear. I lay still as the last of the columns was given orders and marched away. After a few minutes all was quiet.

The forest embraced me like a long-lost child. If some wizard had offered to turn me into a squirrel or bird that day, I would have gladly accepted. Memories and daydreams filled my head. The contrast between this world and the purgatory we lived in was so poignant that I was overwhelmed with self-pity and cried myself to sleep.

When I awoke the low rays of the sun indicated it was late in the afternoon. I ate a bit of bread and sausage I had saved from breakfast and thought about my situation. I was loathe to leave this place, but I had to find a way to rejoin the workers returning to camp. I knew that my father would be terribly worried. Cautiously I peered out of the bushes. No one was in the clearing, and I began to make my way toward camp, slipping from tree to tree until the guard towers came into view. Only one road led to the gate. I found a big tree near a bend in the road and crouched behind it.

It was getting dark before I heard the workers returning. I recognized the strange clicking sounds their wooden clogs made. The first columns marched in rows of four and were surrounded by a lot of guards. There was no way I could join them unseen.

I looked for Father or David and Abale. It seemed safer to slip in with them than with strangers. Many of the men were covered with a gray dust. They were dragging their feet and seemed completely exhausted. My worries about Father increased tenfold.

I finally got my chance among the groups bringing up the rear. Here the exhausted prisoners were stumbling in disorderly ranks, and when a guard fell back to roust the worst stragglers I darted into the column. Many of them were older men and all were in a weary stupor. No one paid the least attention to my sudden appearance.

At the gate an SS guard split us into rows to be counted. My plan had worked. The tally coming in would be the same as the tally going out.

I didn't know how I could put my "freedom" to use yet, but my plan was to join a brigade that had access to food.

I found Father in our barracks, deep asleep on his bunk. My heart twisted in my chest. His face was so thick with pale dust it looked like a death mask, and his ill-fitting dentures protruded from his mouth.

I remembered a beautiful day in Kalautuvas, when he came from town to join us for the weekend. He completely surprised us when he drove up in a brand new convertible. We all rushed out to greet him and I remember how tall and proud he looked. He put his arms around Mother and gave her a hug that lifted her off the ground. How handsome he was! How his eyes shone! Now he was reduced to this pitiful creature. His dentures wobbled in his mouth with every breath.

Jacob too was stretched out on the bunk and covered with dust, as were most of the people in the barracks. I felt like a freak with my clean face and uniform.

Then our sub *aelteste*, Leizer, entered. It was time for the evening *appell*. Leizer was short and meek-looking and seemed like a decent sort. He was shaking the men, trying to wake them, but he couldn't get anyone up. Obviously he was not entirely suited to this job.

I thought of how Peter used his stick on us at Stutthoff. Leizer had a stick too, but he didn't seem up to using it. I knew we would all be in for it if we were late for the *appell*, and I felt sorry for Leizer. Besides, ingratiating yourself with the functionaries could be a useful thing to do.

So imitating Peter's voice as best I could, I began shouting in German. "All out for the *appell*. Everyone up! Quickly! Quickly!"

This had an immediate effect. The inmates jumped up from their bunks and rushed out to the platz. Leizer looked very relieved and thanked me.

Father rose wearily from his bunk, and when he spotted me at the entrance he started to cry. When we hugged each other I could smell the strange mineral smell of all that dust.

Father and Jacob, who had also seen my disappearing act, bombarded me with questions on the way to the *appell*. When I explained, Father was angry with me. "The war will soon be over," he insisted. "Why take such risks now?" I could only look at him. "We will need extra food if we are to survive this place," I answered.

The *appell* lasted forever. The SS sergeant didn't like the way we took off our caps. He didn't hear that unified slap.

"So, you lazy Jew bastards, you shit-heads, you assholes. One day of honest work and you become sloppy! If I don't hear that tzack tzack you can stand here till doomsday!

"All right now! Caps off! Tzack tzack! Again! Caps off! Tzack Tzack! Again!" This went on for nearly an hour, until we were exhausted and he finally grew bored.

The evening soup was once again fairly thick, and Father regained a little color. That night he and Jacob told me about their day.

They were working for a firm called Dickerhof und Wydman, which made all sorts of concrete products. Jacob and Father's brigade had to unload a freight train carrying the raw materials. Jacob had to carry fifty-kilogram bags of cement, while Father shoveled sand and gravel. All of it was loaded onto a small-gauge trolley which ran to the cement works. They even had to lay trolley tracks, and the heaviest work was carrying the iron railings.

The German supervisors belonged to an organization called "Organization Todt," and some of them were worse than the SS. They cursed and beat anyone who slacked off for as much as a minute.

"One of them was particularly vicious," Father said. "He wore a little green Bavarian hat with a white feather in it. We called him 'The Feather.' He walks around beating people up for no reason at all."

This was worse than the airport job at Alexotas, and Father himself admitted that he didn't think he would last long in this job.

I was glum. I had promised Mother I would take care of Father.

Somehow I had to convince Burgin to give him a better job, but how?

David and Abale were in the neighboring barracks, and I went to see how they had fared. To my surprise they both looked clean and seemed to be in good shape. They had had a wonderful stroke of luck.

They, too, had initially been assigned to Dickerhof und Wydman. "But then, like an angel from heaven, a German in a brown uniform appeared and took us and a third boy to the kitchen where they cook for the Organization Todt. They call it the O.T. kitchen. We were assigned to take a cart to Utting and haul back the foodstuffs! We even managed to steal a loaf of bread on the way back," David told me excitedly. He opened his jacket and showed me what remained of a loaf under his arm. "They steal like crazy here," he explained. Then without another word he broke a piece off and gave it to me. "We didn't forget what the 'Akraytchik Minister' did for us in Stutthoff," Abale said.

I told them what had happened to Father, and how I planned to speak with Burgin somehow. They didn't know Burgin either, but those from Siauliai who did said he was a real bastard. The one ray of hope was that Leizer was related to him.

When I told them what I had done that day they shook their heads in amazement. Then I began asking them how far it was to Utting from the O.T. kitchen, and how heavy the cart was.

David just looked at me. "You don't have to beat around the bush, Solly. I've been thinking the same thing myself. But what will the guard say when he sees a fourth person? He is bound to ask questions."

"We'll just have to play it by ear," Abale announced. "We'll think of something."

This brought tears to my eyes. My friends would risk their own jobs to help me, and here the job could mean life instead of death. But what they offered might save my father, as well as me.

The next morning I joined David and Abale and we marched out of camp together. The other boy, whose name was Zelig, was from Siauliai. At first he didn't want anything to do with me, and I couldn't really blame him. He was afraid for his own job, but we convinced him to keep his mouth shut, and in the end we became friends.

The big test came when all four of us reported to the O.T. kitchen and waited for our guard to escort us to Utting. My heart was beating fast when he approached. The other three looked nervous too.

The SS guard was a tall, thin man of about fifty with a sallow face and tired eyes. He looked us over and then signed a paper that he had taken over our custody, which he turned in to the kitchen.

"Let's go," he said when he re-emerged. He hadn't given us so much as a second look. It was another terrific stroke of luck. "He isn't the same guard we had yesterday," David whispered. I wanted to jump into the air and let out a whoop, but instead I grabbed a harness and pulled with all my strength. The cart held only empty milk cans and wooden crates, and we took off at a smart pace.

I'll never forget that walk through the Bavarian countryside. There were neat green fields everywhere, and lining the road were trees laden with ripening apples. Utting itself looked like one of those little towns in Grimms' Fairy Tales. Tidy vegetable gardens, quaint Bavarian houses, window boxes full of flowers. How could we come to harm in a place like this?

The guard led us to a small inn and restaurant where we were to pick up the provisions. We pulled up into a small cobblestone court-yard behind the inn. While the supplies were being readied for loading, the guard went inside for a beer, telling us to wait outside.

A cigarette butt was at my feet, and looking quickly around I snatched it up and put it in my pocket. I spent the next few minutes scanning the ground and found three or four more.

At the back of the courtyard a big pink pig lay in a wooden enclosure full of muddy straw. I was fascinated. I hadn't seen a pig since before the war. As I approached the animal, its tiny eyes stared right back at me. Even German pigs seemed cleaner than the ones I remembered. Then my eyes really popped. There was a huge yellow potato lying in a corner of the pen. Part of the skin had sloughed off. It had surely been boiled and was ready to eat. My mouth filled with saliva.

Before I had a chance to think about the consequences I jumped down into the sty. My clogs promptly sank into the soft mud under the straw. The pig was apparently frightened by my sudden proximity and let out an ear-piercing squeal. I froze in fright, certain that all the Germans in the inn would come running out to save the pig from the attacking Jew. David thought I had lost my mind, and told me to get the hell out of that pigsty before the guard came running.

"What do you intend to do, eat the pig alive?" he shouted. Although

I laughed at that later, at the moment I was too frightened to laugh. I was completely stuck in the mud, confronting an enormous sow that had risen to her little feet, and David was cracking jokes.

I tried desperately to free my own feet, but they seemed stuck like glue. I had to pull them out of my wooden clogs and dig the clogs out with my hands. Throwing them up to David, I ran barefoot around the pig and grabbed the potato. The pig squealed again as if it were being slaughtered, and came after me. I kicked it in the snout and scrambled up over the low fence into the courtyard.

I was covered with mud, but I had the potato firmly in my grasp. I washed myself and the potato in a wooden trough at the edge of the courtyard, keeping an eye out for the guard. I was sure I would pay dearly had I been caught mugging a German pig.

I offered to divide the potato among us, but David said no. "You vanquished that pink monster single-handedly," he declared. "To the victor go the spoils."

We all laughed, but the way everyone eyed that potato I had to share it. It was absolutely delicious. After that we decided that whatever food we got in the future would be shared among us.

I thought I would faint looking at the things they finally began bringing out of the inn. There were slabs of butter and big round cheeses, eggs, whole smoked hams, and even fresh rolls. There were tomatoes, cucumbers, onions, carrots, and more. I wanted to jump into the cart and eat myself to death, but two Germans stood at the door watching us.

After we finished loading the cart, with the smell of the food driving us crazy, the owner of the inn brought us a loaf of bread. She was a slim woman with dark hair and kind eyes, and she looked at us with pity. "Tomorrow I will have some soup for you boys," she said. We thanked her profusely, and Zelig even grabbed her hand and kissed it.

I was disgusted with his performance, and told him so, but he explained to me that she reminded him of his mother. "Besides," he said sadly, "this is the first time a Christian woman has been kind to me since before the war." I had to admit that I, too, was touched by that simple act of kindness. We were as starved for affection as we were starved for food.

The guard appeared while we were dividing the bread into four portions. His face was flushed with drink and he looked mean. All of us cowered at the sight of him. The woman must have noticed what was going on because she came out again. "It's all right," she said to him. "They didn't steal it. I gave it to them."

"You shouldn't do that, Marian," he replied. "It's against the law." But he didn't punish us, and he even let us keep the bread.

The loaded cart was much harder to pull going back, but we did our best. We didn't want to provoke this man.

When we had delivered the groceries we had to clean the O.T. building—the showers, toilets, and kitchen. After the German workers ate their dinner, the mess hall attendant threw the scraps into a barrel. When he saw us looking hungrily at the last plates of leftovers, he told us to come and help ourselves. The bits and scraps weren't much, but they helped.

I saved the quarter loaf of bread for my father. I had felt guilty the entire day. Here I was, young and fairly strong, and I had this easy job and extra food, while he had to load cement.

I found him in worse shape than I expected when we got back to camp. Again he was lying asleep on his bunk. His stubbled cheeks were gray with cement dust and he smelled of sour sweat. He had removed his false teeth, and his whole face looked caved in. When I woke him for the *appell* he looked at me in confusion at first, as if he didn't recognize me. Then he tried to smile, but his face merely contorted and tears began trickling down his cheeks. I put my arms around him and we both cried. This was almost worse than outright killing. It was torturing a man to death by backbreaking labor and starvation, and it was happening to my own father. If I could have killed every German in the world at that moment, I would have done it without thinking twice.

17

Scheherazade

That evening I stripped the cigarette butts I'd gathered at the inn and presented Leizer with a tiny pile of tobacco. I told him about my father's condition, and asked for his help with Burgin.

"He's in bad shape, all right," Leizer admitted. "I'll try to talk to Burgin, but I can't promise anything. You'd better save the tobacco for him. He's an avid smoker. If you can get him some actual cigarettes it would be better."

I thanked him profusely, but he told me not to get my hopes up.

"There are many people from Siauliai who are in as bad shape as your father, and if Burgin can, he'll help them first."

Almost as if it were an afterthought, Leizer asked why Father was called the "Akraytchik Minister." I told him about Father's job at Stutthoff, and also about his Menshevik history. The latter struck a note. It turned out that Burgin was addicted to stories about the Revolution, and was a great admirer of Leon Trotsky. I left Leizer feeling hopeful, despite his warnings.

The next morning, against his protests, I gave Father my bread ration and half of my soup. He didn't want to take it until I showed him the bread I'd gotten at the inn. I bade him good-bye with a heavy heart. He was deteriorating so quickly.

When the four of us got to the O.T. kitchen the German guard from the first day had returned. He was a much older man than the one who had accompanied us yesterday. This one sauntered out of the mess smoking a pipe and was about to sign the release form for us when he said, "Just a minute. The first day there were only three of you. Who is this other prisoner?"

My heart stopped. I had completely forgotten about this particular problem. My mind raced.

"Well?" he demanded.

"Sir. I was sent here because the cart is much too heavy for three boys to handle. You need the food here on time, and with additional help it will be much faster."

"But where were you the first day? Did you run away from a brigade? You'd better tell the truth or I'll have your hide!"

"No sir! I was assigned to this work the first day, but because of some confusion I went to work elsewhere. Yesterday they sent me back here."

I was grabbing at straws, but yesterday's list saved me. When he saw four of us on it his expression changed.

"Nevertheless, I am going to check," he grumbled. "If anyone is missing from a brigade you are going to get it good and proper. Now get going. We have wasted enough time."

The lady innkeeper was true to her promise and gave us each a bowl of soup that day. Thick with meat and potatoes, it was the most delicious and nourishing meal I'd had since the invasion. I wished I could bring some to Father.

After we finished eating I took the four bowls back to her. I was terribly frightened of what I was about to do, but I had to do it.

"Dear lady, you are so nice to us. God will repay you for your kindness. But you could do something else that might save my father's life." I quickly told her what was happening, and begged for some cigarettes in order to save him. She looked at me as if I had proposed something indecent.

"A likely story," she said, but when she saw the tears in my eyes she realized that I was telling the truth. Suddenly she exclaimed, "My God, what are they doing to you in that camp? I understood it was a working camp, and everyone was treated decently."

This time it was my turn to be astonished. With all that was going on around them, how could the German people still believe government propaganda?

"It is a working camp, and they work you to death. We do hard labor twelve hours a day, on practically empty stomachs. They are starving us. Even the youngest and strongest will perish within a few months," I said, looking her straight in the eye.

She recoiled as if I had personally insulted her. I suddenly realized I had exposed myself to terrible danger. If she was a Nazi, which was likely, I was doomed. I broke out in a cold sweat. She must have noticed my alarm, because she told me not to worry, but added that I shouldn't go around saying things like that if I wanted to continue living. Then she disappeared inside.

When we finished loading the cart, she came out and gave us another loaf of bread, and slipped a small parcel into my hand.

On the way back to the camp I was almost jubilant. Wrapped up in newspaper was a pack of twenty German cigarettes, a veritable treasure.

After the *appell* Leizer appeared to tell me that Burgin wanted to see me. Leizer's eyes popped when he saw the cigarettes. He told me it was lucky he didn't smoke; otherwise he would demand half the cigarettes for arranging this meeting. "But I tell you what. I am dying for some fruit. You could bring me some. An apple, perhaps."

I promised him I would do my best. I had told Father nothing of my plan. I didn't want to disappoint him if nothing came of it.

Burgin lived in a small mobile barracks. I was astonished at his quarters. He had a bed with a mattress, a night table, and a lamp with a flowered shade that filled the place with a cozy light. I didn't realize the Germans gave their top capos such luxuries.

This was the first time I'd seen Burgin up close. He looked well fed. His full face was even redder than I thought, and so was his thick neck. He had graying curly hair and cruel eyes that looked at you through thick lenses.

"Did you bring me the cigarettes?" he asked, impatiently extending his hand. I quickly took the pack out from under my arm and handed it over. He ripped the cellophane off, stuffed a cigarette into his mouth and got it lit practically all in one motion. Then he took several deep drags in succession, emitting deep sighs of pleasure.

"So," he said, "I hear that your father fought in the Revolution, and actually knew Trotsky. Is it true?"

I told him a little about Father's revolutionary days. Burgin was skeptical of my story, saying that many claimed to know the great Trotsky. Finally I played my last ace, and told him how Lev Bronstein had changed his name to Leon Trotsky while he was in hiding in

Kaunas, and that he took the name from a member of my family. "There are people here from Kaunas who can tell you about the Trotskys of Kaunas," I said.

This hooked him, and he decided that Father should come and tell him the story himself. Then I told him about Father's condition, and about his administrative positions at Stutthoff and in Kaunas. "I have administrators galore," Burgin said, "but I do have an opening for a foreman. Here," he said, writing something out on a slip of paper, "tell him to report to Abrasha in the morning, and give him this. And you keep on bringing me cigarettes."

Before I left his pleasant barracks he said to me, "You are a bright young man and I'm sure that you will go places. But the most important thing for you to do now is to keep clean. Cleanliness is the key to survival here."

At the time it seemed like an absurd statement. The first key to survival was food, the second was food, and the third was tolerable working conditions.

When I returned to the barracks the lights were out, and Father was already asleep, but I was so excited that I woke him up.

"Dad, you're saved! You're saved! I have a Jordan Pass for you," I whispered to him. For a moment he was silent.

"What is this, some kind of cruel joke?" he asked, but then I explained. I could feel his hands tremble as he took the paper from me. He began to cry softly. We fell asleep that night holding hands.

In the morning, before we went to work, I found the piece of newspaper the cigarettes were wrapped in in my pocket. It told how the "heroic Panzer divisions" had broken out of an encirclement by the British, Canadians, and Americans in Normandy. The date was August 17, 1944. Up until then all we had heard was snatches of conversation suggesting that the Germans had the Allies hopelessly pinned down on the beaches. Now it was clear that the German army was actually on the defensive.

When my father returned to the barracks that evening the look in his eyes told me everything. Some of his natural optimism had returned, along with a bit of color in his face. He had been transferred to a new brigade that also loaded sand and gravel, but he was now a foreman and he only did heavy labor when he went to the aid of his workers.

That night the entire camp was buzzing with the news from

Normandy. It was the most exciting news we had heard in a long time, and it spread around the camp like wildfire. Everyone wanted to see my clipping, and by the time I got it back the print was almost completely smeared off.

Hope was rekindled. Once again we numbered the days until our rescue. As the summer of 1944 turned to fall, the camp inmates coined a new blessing: "May you have a boil on your ass in 1945."

After the evening *appell* Leizer told Father to report to Burgin. We had expected that invitation, but we didn't know it would come so soon. "So now I am going to become the Court Jester," Father said ruefully, but I could tell he was actually excited, and a little nervous about the appointment. He immediately went to the wash house and scrubbed himself down. He even managed to beat some of the cement dust out of his striped prison garb. The war was coming to an end, and until then survival could depend on people like Burgin.

By the time Father returned from Burgin's that night I was already asleep. He woke me anyway, and pushed half a sandwich into my mouth. I couldn't believe my taste buds. It was soft white bread with real butter and cheese.

Burgin kept Father there for hours, demanding that he begin at the very beginning, and so far Father had only scratched the surface of his story.

"I'm to appear before His Majesty again tomorrow night," Father laughed. "I feel like I'm in the middle of *A Thousand and One Nights.*"

The second night Father took me with him to Burgin's barracks. When Burgin objected, Father pointed out that I was young and perhaps would survive the war. The younger generations should know these stories, Father said, so that they might continue to be passed down. Burgin relented.

And so Father once again plunged into his story. He was a wonderful storyteller, and it was nearly midnight when Burgin's alarm clock jolted us back into our grim reality. It was time for us to return to the barracks.

"Your talent at storytelling shouldn't be wasted," Burgin said. "I have an idea for you. After lights-out, you should tell stories in the barracks. You could go to a different barracks each evening. Since there is no other entertainment in the camp I'm sure you would be a great success. As a reward you would get an extra bowl of soup."

Father looked at him in surprise.

"I am not the monster everyone thinks I am," Burgin said. "Someone has to do my job. Would you have preferred one of the murderers from Stutthoff to me?"

He was right. As bad as Burgin was, we were lucky to have him. At least he was one of ours, and overall he was more helpful than dangerous.

"You must go now," he said, "but before you do, may I see the finger marks you claim Rebecca left on your ankle?"

Without hesitation Father rolled up his pant leg, and there were the four unmistakable imprints. Burgin looked at Father with new respect.

"Until tomorrow, then," he said, and he gave Father another sandwich wrapped in paper. We devoured it before we were halfway back to the barracks.

The next day disaster struck my kitchen detail. We arrived at the O.T. kitchen to discover that the cart's axle was broken, and we couldn't make the trip for provisions. The mechanic told Erhard, our guard, that it would take at least a day to fix it. A senior O.T. supervisor was lingering around the mess, and when Erhard ordered us to clean the latrines, he interrupted.

"You are coming with me," the supervisor announced. "Today you're going to do some honest work, you lazy swine." With that we were marched off to haul cement. And when Zelig didn't move fast enough to suit him, he lay into him with his stick, beating him unmercifully while Zelig curled on the ground, trying to protect his head with his arms. When the German finally grew tired, he ordered us to march out. Zelig's hands and face were puffed and bleeding, and one eye was swollen shut. He could barely stand on his legs, and we had to support him all the way to the railyard.

At the yard a swarm of inmates was unloading sacks of cement from the train to a spot about a hundred meters away. Their bodies sagged under the weight of the sacks and their legs trembled. Once they shed the load they were prodded to run back to the train for the next sack, and those who didn't run fast enough were clubbed.

When they put the first fifty-kilo sack of cement on my back I had the shock of my life. I could not imagine how I would last the day.

No breeze stirred in the heat, adding to our misery. Time seemed to stand still. It took enormous effort not to give up, to just fall under the load and leave this miserable life. Only two things sustained me. One was the thought of the green village of Utting, the apple trees and the inn where Marian would give us a bowl of her wonderful soup. The other was the sight of Zelig, who shamed me for my whining self-pity. His face swollen and discolored, his hands battered, he stoically carried one sack after another, all day long. I couldn't imagine how he stayed on his feet.

Before the day was over one of the older men in the brigade collapsed. The sadistic German foreman beat him with his stick until he lay completely still. Later we found out that they buried him right in the yard. He never regained consciousness.

Now it was Father who was shocked at my state when we returned to camp. I had to restrain him from running to Burgin. I had no permanent injuries, and it seemed wise not to solicit Burgin except in real emergencies. Zelig was in such bad shape the next morning that the doctor reported him sick and kept him in camp, something that was almost never allowed.

When we reported to the kitchen we were dismayed to discover that the axle still had not been repaired. I feared the worst until the cook threatened the mechanic with army rations unless he got the job done immediately. The mechanic went into his shed and returned saying it would take an hour. Erhard, noticing our immense relief, barked, "All right you lazy lot. Go and clean the latrine until the cart is ready." We ran all the way to the latrine practically jumping for joy.

It wasn't until we were loading the milk cans onto the cart that Erhard noticed one of us was missing. "Where is Zelig?" he demanded. It was gratifying to hear that he knew our names, not just our numbers. Somehow it made a difference. When we told him what had happened to Zelig he just snorted, but I got the feeling he felt sorry for him. He was such a quiet, kind boy it was hard not to like him.

As we set out on the road to Utting we encountered the German supervisor who had beaten Zelig the day before.

When he saw us with the cart he signaled for us to stop. Ignoring Erhard altogether he began swearing and demanded to know who gave us permission to leave the loading yard. Without waiting for an answer he began laying into us with his stick. In the beginning Erhard just stood there in confusion, then suddenly he grabbed the supervisor's arm. The civilian was astonished, and began to shout at our guard.

"Silence!" Erhard thundered. "Who do you think you are, beating on my prisoners? I am in charge of them and they are coming with me to Utting to bring food for the O.T. kitchen. Or do you want to eat emergency rations today?" He was using the cook's argument on this man.

The astonished supervisor began to protest, but Erhard silenced him again. Pointing to a military ribbon on his tunic, he hissed, "You see that ribbon? That's for valor on the Russian front. While you were growing fat and lazy at home I was fighting for three bloody years there, bleeding and freezing my butt off. Don't open your big mouth at me, you hear?!" And without giving the foreman another glance, he gave us a sign to move on.

An angel in the unlikely guise of an aging SS corporal had rescued us from a day in hell. That day the road to Utting looked more beautiful than ever, and Utting itself like something from a fairy tale.

18

Moll

Paris was liberated by the Allies on August 25, 1944, but German forces in eastern France continued to put up fierce resistance. In October the 100th/442nd and 522nd Field Artillery was shifted from Italy to the French Front, to help clear the way to the German border.* In slow, bloody fighting over rugged terrain, the Nisei liberated Bruyeres and several other small towns, suffering hundreds of casualties before they finally captured Biffontaine on October 23. Three days later they received orders to help rescue the "Lost Battalion," troops from the 36th Texas Division who had been cut off by strong enemy forces in the Vosges Mountains just west of the German border. The situation of the "Lost Battalion" had become dire. It took four days of intense fighting before the Nisei were able to reach the crest where the Texans were pinned down. All units suffered terrible casualties. Sergeant George Oiye, a forward observer for the 522nd, led one of the field artillery units that had to advance through undergrowth laced with tripwires and murderous "Bouncing Betty" mines. Under constant enemy fire, they took what cover they could in ditches and behind trees. Oiye and other field artillery personnel were issued M-1 rifles, and joined combat troops in fixed-bayonet advances that progressed slowly, tree by tree, up the forested slope. I and K Companies and elements of the "One Puka Puka" (the 100th) were the first to reach the stranded Texans, who had spent seven days in the trenches, five of those days with no rations and very little water.

*The 100th was the first all-Nisei unit to see action. It was originally composed entirely of Hawaiian volunteers; they served bravely with Mark Clark in Italy, suffering heavy casualties, before the 442nd and 522nd FA, Nisei recruited from Hawaii and the mainland, joined them in June of 1944, and the Combat Team was formed.

When it was all over the slopes had been virtually deforested, and the Combat Team had lost another eight hundred men. K Company had been reduced to seventeen soldiers. B Company of one of the "One Puka Puka" was down to eleven. I Company had been reduced from two hundred riflemen to eight.

After the operation, when the troops were assembled for review, only a few hundred men turned out. They were all that was left. Many of their officers broke down and wept.

Among others decorated for bravery in this bloody battle, Barney Hajiro, Fujiyo Miyamoto, and Jim Tazoi of the 442nd all received Distinguished Service Crosses. Oiye, Sus Ito, Toru Hirano, and Captain Jack Andrews of the 522nd were awarded the Bronze Star; Yuki Minaga the Silver. By the end of the war the Nisei would claim 1,000 decorations for gallantry, 3,600 Purple Hearts, and a Presidential Citation for the entire unit, but the cost in blood was devastating.

A few weeks after the Vosges campaign, what remained of the 100th/442nd and 522nd FABN was shipped back to the Franco-Italian border, where newer recruits like Clarence Matsumura replaced some of those who had fallen. The team would remain in that sector for nearly four months.

By October 1944 we realized that the war was not going to end that year, as we had all hoped. The Germans trumpeted the great defeat of the Allies at Arnhem, and even assuming they were exaggerating, the Allies were clearly still far away. As the days passed, starvation and hard labor cut down more and more of the inmates. Many just collapsed while working; others were beaten to death by the German O.T. supervisor. More and more just refused to get up from their beds, and eventually died in their own filth. The Germans would eventually lose the war, but we wouldn't be around to see it.

Lice became an enormous problem in the camp. In the beginning most of the inmates tried to keep themselves reasonably clean, although the sanitary facilities were almost nonexistent. The only thing you could do was search the seams of your clothing and smash the lice between your thumbnails one by one. It was not a very efficient method, and just when you thought that you'd finally licked them, they came crawling over from your neighbor who was either too tired or too apathetic to care. All many of the inmates could do after returning from work was eat their meager rations, collapse on their bunks, and sleep until morning.

Others still struggled to hold on. That month five new prisoners were transferred to Lager Ten from some other camp. One was a tall young man about twenty years of age, beardless, well fed, in a brand new striped uniform and shiny black leather boots. His name was Max. He was a capo at his previous camp, and now he was assigned to Lager Ten. He came in swinging, determined to show who was boss, and beat up on people for no reason at all.

He soon found himself surrounded by a hostile camp. Our inmates were mostly from Lithuania, and he had no support from any of our capos. After Max beat up an older man, a group of young inmates, mostly from Siauliai, decided to take action. That evening, when Max was on his way to his quarters, ten of them ambushed him. Throwing a blanket over his head, they pushed him to the ground and beat him until he promised to behave himself. They warned him that if he said a word to the Germans they would kill him. Max had been in Auschwitz, Mathausen, and a string of other concentration camps before coming to Lager Ten, and he knew the rules of the game. He fell into line. After that, he did more shouting than hitting, and when he had to wield his club because some SS were around, he did it so expertly that his victims suffered little damage.

In the meantime Father began telling his story to the inmates in the barracks, as Burgin had suggested. When he finished with his own tales, he told other stories. Many inmates were too far gone to listen, but among those who had a little strength many were fascinated by his storytelling. Some would follow him from barracks to barracks, listening to the same stories several times over. To many, he was a lifesaver. Not only did he temporarily remove them from the insane world we were living in, he aroused hope in them, hope for an end to the madness of Hitler's Germany. He even managed to rouse a *musselman*, one of the living dead who had lain down in his bunk and given up. Like my father, he too had worked for the Revolution in his youth, and had been full of hope and high ideals. He said that Father had instilled in him something he hadn't felt in a long time: shame. Shame that he had let himself be overwhelmed by despair, shame that he had given up on life. His name was Shmuel. That night Father and I helped him wash, and after that Shmuel went back to the business of living, which meant scrounging for food and trying to keep clean.

Other educated men among the inmates also began to give

lectures on various subjects. One of them, whose name I think was Gans, was called "The Strategist." The whole camp would gather information for him either by eavesdropping on the Germans or, more importantly, by stealing their newspapers. "The Strategist" would then take these scraps of information and give us an overall picture of what was happening on the eastern and western fronts. Unfortunately, many of his predictions turned out to be far too optimistic, and we were continually disappointed.

The weather added to our misery. It began to rain more frequently, and the nights turned cold. Winter was on its way. The arrival of bad weather was a serious threat to our cushy job ferrying food from Utting to the O.T. kitchen. Several times, driving rain made us late delivering the provisions, and the chief cook, a cruel, foul-tempered creature who was drunk half the time, cursed and beat us. One day it was raining so hard that Erhard, our guard, decided to stay in Utting until the weather cleared. While he sat in the tavern drinking beer, we hid in the pigsty. We dared not think of the consequences of this delay.

By the time the rain stopped and Erhard had sobered up a bit we were four hours late. The cook was waiting for us with a big wooden stick. He was thoroughly drunk and beat each of us in turn. If Erhard hadn't stopped him he would probably have killed us. The worst of it was that we knew the cook would resort to other means of transport if this situation kept up, and we would be loading cement again.

We returned to camp that night covered with bruises, and I had a big black shiner. For all my resourcefulness and maneuvering, I knew I could no longer escape the fate that awaited me in the cement yard. My only hope was Father and his connection with Burgin, whose respect for Father redoubled when he heard about Shmuel's return from the dead.

It continued to rain heavily after we returned from the O.T. kitchen, and the water penetrated our barracks. When we got up in the morning the floor was ankle-deep in water. Some woke up soaking wet from lying under the leaky roof.

We went to work scared of facing the cook and even more frightened of losing our jobs. To our great relief the drunken lout had been replaced by an elderly man who told us that our nemesis had been sent to the Russian front. We were jubilant, and wished him a slow death by a Russian bullet. But we rejoiced too soon. Erhard appeared and told us we were to report to the loading yard.

My heart fell. The four of us marched off feeling utterly dejected. We were about fifty meters down the path when the new cook came running after us.

"Erhard, bring them back quickly. The damn storage cellar is completely flooded. Look at my brand new shoes. They are soaked!" He started cursing so violently that, to our great surprise and amusement, his upper denture popped out of his mouth and dropped to the ground.

We had to hide our smiles as the cook became even more agitated. He quickly found three metal buckets and sent us down to bail out the cellar. We soon found ourselves up to our ankles in ice water, and we stopped laughing. We removed our wooden clogs and went to work.

The four of us lined up with one standing in the water, one on the steps, and two emptying the buckets in a gully by the trees. We soon got into the rhythm of swinging the bucket up and out. We changed places with the one in the cellar when his feet grew numb standing in the icy water. From time to time the cook would poke his head in and swear at us. When it was my turn to go below I took a look around. Tall wooden shelves laden with provisions lined the walls, reaching all the way to the ceiling. I grabbed four tubes of something that looked like toothpaste but was actually cheese, and dropped them into the bucket. They immediately sank to the bottom. David, who was on the steps next to me, noticed what I was doing. Abke was at the door, and Zelig was emptying water into the ravine. I hissed at David to warn the others. David quickly passed the bucket to Abke and the cheese was out! I dropped some packets of margarine into the next bucket and started to pass it to David, but to my horror they floated to the surface. I shoved a big can of vegetables over them just as the cook's head appeared again. I thought he had seen me, and my heart almost popped out of my chest, but he merely yelled at us to speed it up. I felt as if death had just appeared before my eyes, but a minute later I was liberating four cans of sardines. I was treading the thin line between necessary risk and suicide. One minute you were cowering, the next you risked your life again for food.

When my feet grew numb David took my place, and he continued the harvest of supplies. We worked like crazy, and by the time we were done we were completely exhausted. In spite of his swearing and verbal abuse, the new cook was not a bad fellow, and rewarded us with a large bowl of thick soup, a virtual feast. We prayed that he didn't take inventory every day. If he discovered the missing food we would get twenty-five lashes at the very least. But it seemed worth the risk. We had amassed an incredible treasure—tubes of cheese and liver paste, sardines, margarine, sausage, and cans of sweetened milk labeled with a Red Cross sign.

The next problem was how to get the supplies into camp. During the last few days the guards had subjected returning workers to frequent and thorough searches because many of them were stealing empty cement sacks. They lined their clogs with the paper or put it underneath their uniforms to protect themselves from the cold. We were also afraid that the food would be stolen once we got it into camp. There were many starving people there, and theft was rampant among the prisoners.

When we had a moment to ourselves we huddled behind the latrine and devoured some of the cheese and sweetened milk. We decided to take only a few items with us; the rest we buried a short distance behind the latrine. Even fathers and sons were known to steal from each other in camp, but the four of us trusted each other implicitly.

We hoped and prayed that the cook would keep us working at the O.T. kitchen, now that the carting job was done for.

When the whistle blew ending the shift, David and Abke went on ahead while Zelig and I dawdled on the road. I would come to regret that tardiness many times.

Zelig was a quiet boy. He came from a small town where his entire family was murdered at the beginning of the war. He was the only one to escape, eventually finding his way to the ghetto of Siauliai. He talked about his Uncle Moshe sometimes, but otherwise all he ever said was, "Where are the Allies?"

"Where are the Allies, where are the Allies?" he would say out of the blue, and he said it so often we nicknamed him, "Where are the Allies?"

Erhard emerged from the kitchen, smelling of beer as usual, and called after us. "You two come with me," he said. I was terrified that they had discovered the missing food and were going to search us. Instead Erhard led Zelig and me to a waiting truck. We were to help deliver a load of potatoes to another O.T. kitchen. It served a site where the Germans were building some kind of underground factory, and we had heard terrible stories about it. Among the prisoners it was known simply as Moll.

We traveled for what seemed like an hour along a tree-lined dirt road. Darkness had fallen, and in the distance we could hear the low grinding roar of heavy machinery. The din increased just before we emerged into a huge clearing lit by the glare of floodlights. The road dropped into a vast excavation, and from it rose an enormous concrete vault, bristling with vertical reinforcing rods so that it looked like some monstrous hedgehog. Narrow railroad tracks curved toward the opening.

The installation was a half-cylinder of concrete, 1,300 feet long and spanning more than 275 feet at the base. It rose some 95 feet into the air at the top of the arch. Under the glaring lights, cranes and bulldozers moved into and around its mouth. Scores of tractors, trucks, and small locomotives pulling open cars of material. Cement mixers and other heavy equipment created an ear-shattering roar. The concrete shell was nearly ten feet thick in places, but great patches of it had not yet been poured. Along the sides, scores of prisoners stood on platforms handling huge flexible hoses that spewed wet cement into the spiked gridwork, while others moved about with shovels and buckets. Everywhere we looked we saw what looked like thousands of men in striped uniforms moving about the compound, carrying lumber, iron rods and sacks of cement. It was like an enormous, evil hive.

Those who moved too slowly were assaulted by well-fed capos or SS men, their curses mingling with the din of the machines. Men who fell to the ground under the beatings were trampled under their torturer's boots.

Even as we watched we heard inhuman screams coming from above. The men who were maneuvering the huge hose had lost their grip, and the pipe began writhing about, spewing concrete in all directions. The men desperately tried to seize it, but it whipped and flailed and knocked several men off their feet. One after another they fell screaming onto the spikes, while the hose poured hundreds of pounds of concrete on top of them.

Zelig and I looked on in horrified silence. Now we understood how hundreds of prisoners were dying here every day, and why our camp was considered the best in the area.

We moved on to a warehouse where Zelig and I unloaded a dozen bags of potatoes. Then we piled back into the truck and the driver drove straight up to the mouth of the factory.

From this vantage point the place was even more frightening. Below us bulldozers and steam shovels continued excavations underneath the vault. Here, too, hundreds of prisoners were moving about, hauling materials, digging, being beaten by the capos and Germans. The whole scene filled me with horror. I longed to be back under the low roof of our barracks in Lager Ten. Our capos and even our German guards seemed like paragons of kindness compared to these inhuman beasts.

We were to deliver some machine part, and Erhard directed Zelig and me to carry it to a hut. It didn't weigh more than ten pounds. I was praying to God that we would get away from this place immediately, but Erhard and the driver decided to stay and have a bite at the German canteen. I couldn't understand why anyone would want to linger in this place. It looked like the very maw of hell. But Erhard told us to climb aboard the truck and stay there until they returned. It was getting quite late, and the temperature was dropping rapidly. We crawled under a tarpaulin, trying to keep warm, but there was no way I could sleep. The place filled me with dread. I don't know how long we huddled there, with me silently cursing Erhard. I was certain he was lounging about swilling beer, and had completely forgotten about us.

After a long, cold wait we were startled by a German voice quite nearby. The man was swearing loudly.

"So you're trying to hide, you lazy swine, you good for nothing lousy Jew. I'll teach you to hide from work!" We heard repeated blows and someone crying out in pain.

"Please, please, I'll never do it again. It was so terribly cold. I was freezing," someone begged in Yiddish.

Suddenly Zelig was scooting out from under the tarp, shouting, "Uncle Moshe, Uncle Moshe!" He had reached the tailgate before I had the presence of mind to grab for his ankle, but he slipped from my grasp and jumped to the ground, still shouting, "Uncle Moshe!"

I froze with fright under the tarpaulin. Should I follow him and try to save him from the beating he was sure to get? But what could I do? It was too late, anyway.

"So you are hiding too, and in a military truck, no less. I will have your hide for that!" the German screamed, and began hitting Zelig.

"No sir, no sir, I wasn't hiding," Zelig cried, trying to explain between blows. "I am from Lager Ten . . . We brought some machine part . . . Our guard told me to wait here . . . He is at the canteen . . . Sir, sir!" Every blow that descended on Zelig cut me like a knife.

The German stopped a moment, then demanded to know if the other man was Zelig's uncle.

Zelig was quiet for a second, then he began stammering.

"N-nooo sir. I am sorry, Sir . . . I made a . . . mistake. He sounded exactly like my uncle. . . . My uncle is here in this camp, that is why I thought. . . ."

"Well, now you will have the honor of joining this worthless piece of shit of an uncle up top," the German said, completely ignoring what Zelig had told him. "You see that cement hose there? That is where you are going."

Moshe was Zelig's only living relative. Was this man really him, or was it just someone who sounded like him, as he claimed? "*Schnell, Schnell!* Move your asses!" the German was screaming.

"But Sir, I am not from this camp! I am from Lager Ten! I have to go back there," Zelig cried.

"I don't care if you are Jesus Christ going to his last supper! You will go where I tell you to go!"

I huddled under the tarp praying fervently that Erhard and the driver would show up and stop this. After a minute or two I couldn't bear it. I had to see what was happening to Zelig. I cautiously stuck my head out and saw him, the other prisoner, and the German guard climbing the wooden walkway over the concrete vault. Above them a group of prisoners grappled again with the monster pipe. I could hear the German supervisor swearing. The planks were still slick from the previous spill, and prisoners grabbed at each other when anyone slipped.

With growing dread I watched Zelig making his way toward the group with the hose. The one he called "Uncle Moshe" was a skeleton of a man, barely able to walk, and he hung on to Zelig for dear life. The German followed them, lashing out at "Moshe" with a stick. Then something startling happened. "Moshe," who had cowered so before the brutal guard, suddenly turned on him, and screaming at the top of his lungs grabbed the man about the waist and flung himself over the side, taking the German down with him onto the iron spikes below. Zelig reached out for "Moshe," trying to stop their fall, and he too lost his balance. Without uttering a single cry he fell headlong after them.

The whole thing happened so fast that few seemed to understand what had taken place, but with the screams of "Moshe" and the German all hell broke loose. Many of the men on the walkway simply froze, with the pipe still spewing cement, and scores of Germans ran shouting toward the site, lashing out at every prisoner in the way. Floodlights were directed toward the spot where they fell, but all that could be seen was a shred or two of fabric caught on the spikes, if indeed it wasn't flesh. The three had been immersed in fresh concrete almost as soon as they tumbled in. Two Jews and a German had joined the others who had fallen to their deaths, to be entombed in that gigantic mausoleum forever.

That scene froze in my mind. I tried to shut it out, but the more I tried the more sharply it etched itself into my brain. I saw it from Zelig's eyes too, those horrible stakes and the suffocating cement rushing up to meet him as he fell. Suddenly I felt someone slugging me in the ribs. Erhard was shouting, "What is going on? Why are you screaming at the top of your lungs?"

At that moment this boozy old SS guard pummeling me in the side might as well have been a knight in shining armor. I had a hard time holding back sobs as I told him what had happened. Even Erhard blanched a little.

"So that is what the commotion is all about," he said gruffly. "Couldn't you have stopped that idiot? He is a friend of yours! Why did you let him go?" he shouted, giving me another cuff. But it wasn't very hard. I could see he was dismayed.

"Shit, now I have one prisoner missing. I will have to get a certificate of death," he said to the driver. "I can't go back with a prisoner missing."

Telling the driver to wait there, he hauled me down off the truck. "You will have to be my witness. Come along."

Then he stopped and gave me a suspicious look. "Wait a minute. For all I know the boy has run away and you are covering for him. How do I know you're telling the truth? Those men who fell may all be local workers. For all I know your friend is on his way to Switzerland." I looked at him in astonishment. How did one get to Switzerland from here? Seeing my baffled expression, he said, "All right," and gave me a shove forward. "Let's get to the commandant.

You better explain this correctly or I will have your hide. You understand?"

We made our way to a small temporary building marked with the SS logo. Erhard entered, telling me to wait outside. A thin layer of frost had formed on the ground, and I swung my arms and stamped my feet trying to keep from freezing.

A long, shrill whistle announced the end of the night shift, and hundreds of prisoners began moving toward the road, most of them barely shuffling along. The ever-present capos used their clubs on the stragglers, trying to hurry them along. Many of them were *musselmen,* walking skeletons, their eyes large and luminous in their cadaverous faces. They carried on through sheer will, afraid to be shipped to a sick camp.

These people looked much worse than the prisoners in our camp. Some who passed close by looked at me with hostility. They must have thought I was a capo, because here only capos looked as well fed as I.

Finally Erhard opened the door and motioned me inside. Then he knocked on a door marked "Commandant."

"Come!" a gruff voice answered. Erhard pushed me in and yelled, "Muetzen ab!" I stood at full attention, and in one swift move removed my cap and slapped it down smartly against my right leg.

The commandant, an SS captain, grimaced at Erhard's shout and gave me a curious look. I guess he wasn't used to quick reactions from his starved prisoners.

"Do you speak German, boy?" he asked sharply.

"Yes sir. I do."

"Very well. Describe to me what happened. Since there are no German witnesses who can verify that one of the dead prisoners was from Lager Ten, you will have to do. But be careful not to tell me any lies or I will hang you. You understand?" A pair of cold gray eyes measured me carefully. I knew my fate lay in that gaze.

I described the events of the evening as clearly as possible, pronouncing each word in correct German. I had decided to omit the fact that "Uncle Moshe" committed suicide and took the German with him. The murder of a German could have tragic consequences for others, as well as for myself. Instead I said that the O.T. foreman slipped and fell against "Uncle Moshe." I ended by telling him that Zelig tried to save the two and fell in himself.

Again those cold gray eyes bore into me. My heart contracted with fear. I was sure he sensed my lies, and I almost shut my eyes under that stare. I had to force myself to stand steady.

"What was his number?" he asked.

"I won! I won!" I almost shouted aloud. But then it dawned on me. It would never have occurred to this German that a cowardly Jew would do what "Uncle Moshe" had done. He probably wouldn't believe me if I did tell the truth. A great weight was lifted off my shoulders.

I quickly told him Zelig's number and he drew out a tablet of forms and began scribbling with a pen. I wondered at the infinite trouble these people took to determine the identity of one dead prisoner, when scores of them obviously died here every day. But this was the Nazi way: order, punctuality, and efficiency. To them we were just numbers, and the numbers had to add up. Whether the people behind the numbers were dead or alive didn't really matter, as long as the books balanced. Quite often we stood in rain and snow at an *appell* while they counted us over and over because the numbers wouldn't come out right. Several people would collapse and die while this was going on, and then we had to be counted all over again.

I continued to stand at attention while I waited for this man with the scratching pen to determine my fate. When he finished he gave me an ironic smile.

"Since you were the only actual witness who can identify the dead prisoner, you'll have to sign this document."

Was this some kind of joke? This "number" was to sign an official German document? I feared the worst.

"But, sir, these prisoners have no legal rights," Erhard nervously interjected. "They are officially *untermenschen* (subhumans). Won't that make the document illegal?

"Besides, Sir, I believe that he's under eighteen," he added meekly.

"Listen, you dumb ox! If you hadn't been cooling your heels in the canteen none of this would have happened. I'm trying to help you out of a difficult situation and you're giving me this legalistic prattle. I doubt your commandant will even look at this document once he sees my signature, but I must have verification from a witness." Without another word he handed me his pen and showed me where to sign. He also had Erhard sign a statement.

I carefully signed my name, making it as neat and precise as I could. The captain apprised Erhard's form, and then mine, and then he sighed. "I wish some of my Bavarian subordinates had such penmanship. I wish they too could give me such a precise report, in German that I could half understand."

Erhard reddened and gave me a nasty look.

"All right. You're dismissed," the captain said, and before Erhard had a chance to scream, "Muetzen auf!" (Caps on!) he said "Put on your cap, boy." I hesitated, looking at Erhard.

Again Erhard blushed and said to me in a normal voice: "The captain gave you an order. So do it." I quickly put on my cap and almost saluted. Fortunately, I caught myself in time, or it would have meant lashes.

When we left the office Erhard gave me a kick, but otherwise left me alone. It was nearly time for breakfast and we were both exhausted. Neither of us had slept for twenty-four hours. The sky was pink in the east, the sun reddening a line of great snowy peaks in the distance. I had never seen them from camp. Switzerland?

I was still baffled by the behavior of the SS captain. In the midst of his inhuman efficiency he seemed to notice I was a human being. Perhaps he was surprised that this "number" had an education. Perhaps, on the other hand, getting a "subhuman" to sign an official document was a perverse bit of humor on his part. The whole thing made me uneasy.

On the way back I mourned my friend Zelig and recited Kaddish for him in my head. Also for the man he called his uncle, who had died a hero's death. His tormentor never expected to be set upon by such a frail, sorrowful creature. I could still hear that vicious German's screams as "Moshe" carried him to his death. It disturbed me, though, that Zelig and Moshe were entombed next to that swine. The good and the evil together.

Hundreds of prisoners died constructing the huge underground installation known as Moll, one of several major slave-labor projects around Kaufering and Dachau. This bomb-proof factory was to produce one of Hitler's secret weapons, a project code-named "Ringeltaube." While the Allies were shooting the Luftwaffe out of the sky, the Germans were furiously building the first combat jets—the Messerschmitt ME 262. A few of these jet fighters got off the ground early in 1945, but by then the air superiority of the Allies was overwhelming.

19

The Present Is a Mighty Goddess

It took nearly an hour to get back to Lager Ten from Moll, and the whole place was in an uproar. The SS sergeant in charge was supposed to have informed the camp administration that Erhard had taken the two of us to Lager One. He forgot to do it, and we were declared missing. All the inmates had been forced to stand for *appell* half the night as the Germans counted and re-counted them. David and Abke thought we had returned to camp shortly after they did, and my father thought I was up to my old tricks again. He was worried sick, and it took him a long time to gather the courage to tell Burgin that I was one of the missing.

When we arrived at the gate that morning the guard rang the camp commandant. Erhard was to report to his office immediately, bringing me along.

The commandant was an elderly SS major with a ruddy complexion and small pig's eyes. It was rumored that in Poland and the Ukraine he had been responsible for the deaths of thousands of Jews, but we had no idea whether this was true or not. We hardly ever saw him in our camp. Perhaps he was losing his enthusiasm as the war dragged on and the Nazi armies continued to lose ground. Perhaps he saw the writing on the wall. In any event, when we came before him I quickly realized that he was drunk.

The title of this chapter is a translation of *Die Gegenwart ist eine mächtige Göttin* by Goethe.

Erhard walked in first, smartly saluted, then handed over the death certificate. I stood at attention by the door, my cap off.

"A fine mess you've made here, corporal. Why didn't you report that you took these two prisoners to Moll?"

Erhard looked astonished. "But I did, Sir. Here's the signature of the sergeant on duty," he replied, handing over a document.

The major looked at it and picked up the phone. After a minute he banged down the receiver and started swearing. "The asshole left on a week's furlough. Apparently he forgot to report it," he growled.

"What exactly happened to the other prisoner?" he demanded. "I understand he dragged a German O.T. man to his death?"

"I wasn't present, sir, but this prisoner saw it all as it happened," Erhard answered, pointing at me.

The commandant squinted at me and I quickly lowered my eyes. My heart was beating like a drum. In one sentence this old man had demolished my theory that the Germans would not believe a prisoner capable of killing. He knew the truth! Or was he just trying to test me?

I decided to stick to the original version of my story, come what may.

"Come here boy, and tell me what happened," the commandant said calmly. He didn't raise his voice or make threats, but I felt his menace.

"Sir, I saw the O.T. foreman slip. He fell against the prisoner from Lager One. Zelig, the other prisoner from Lager Ten, tried to save them and fell in as well." I could hear the blood rushing in my head like a waterfall.

"Look at me when you speak!" he said sharply. Then I knew that all was lost. I was a goner. I raised my eyes and looked at him and his eyes reminded me of the pig's whose potato I stole.

But the commandant then turned to Erhard. "Who was the witness who signed this document?" he yelled.

Erhard looked very uncomfortable. He swiped at his neck with a handkerchief and kept looking in my direction. My heart sank.

"I asked you a question, corporal!"

"It was this prisoner here, Sir. I told the captain at Moll that it would make the document illegal, but he insisted. The prisoner was the only witness to what happened, sir."

"What! Has he lost his mind? I will have him sent immediately to the Russian front! And you too, you stupid asshole!" he screamed at Erhard.

Suddenly he rose from his seat, his face crimson with rage. He looked wildly around his office as if he didn't recognize it, as if he thought he were somewhere else. Then he screamed, "Take that Jew out and hang him!" This man was as crazy as he was drunk, but his command was irrevocable. I was as good as dead. Yet I stood there with all my functions intact. I was breathing. I felt tired and hungry. If only I could freeze time, I could go on living. There must be some mathematical formula for it. I didn't think about the rope around my neck, I thought about how to solve this time problem, while another part of me was screaming, "How can you think of such nonsense at a time like this! Do something! Do something!"

Erhard turned white as a sheet, and stood there with his mouth open, unable to respond. Finally he said stupidly, "How am I to hang the prisoner when we have no gallows?"

I hoped that he would say something in my defense, that it wasn't my fault, that the captain forced me to do it, but all he could think of was that the camp had no gallows. No doubt the commandant would tell Erhard to make use of a tree. There were plenty of them around. Instead he returned Erhard's stupid look. He looked at me, then back at Erhard.

"Very well then. Let him have twenty-five lashes," he said mildly. One minute I was dead, the next minute I was saved. I fainted on the spot.

The lashes were to be administered after the evening *appell,* and I was locked up in a small room until the appointed hour. I was so exhausted that I dozed off on the cement floor. I cannot describe the dread that engulfed me when I was awakened by a sharp kick in the ribs. "Wakie, wakie, prepare your assie!" Max sang out, sounding like a retarded child. He stood over me, chillingly blond and grinning, slapping a coil of black rubber hose against his thigh. In that moment I understood the men at Stutthoff who electrocuted themselves on the fences. Just an hour ago I had fainted with relief at my fate. Now the idiotic Max, with his ruddy face and fair hair, towered over me like some mindless golem.

With me in the same room was a boy we called "Yisheshe," who was also from Kaunas. He was about my age, delicate in nature, with narrow shoulders and a slight stoop. He was a very bright boy, and like my father was one of the camp storytellers. During the "Children's Action" in the ghetto, he hid in an open field, and his ears froze during the night. They were discolored and shriveled looking, and he always wore some kind of rag around his head to cover them. Yisheshe had been caught hiding from work and was also to receive twenty-five lashes. I did not know if he could stand them.

"Wakie, wakie, prepare your assie!" Looking into Max's childish, brutal face, I felt as if a veil had been lifted from my eyes. I saw the bare depths of the world we lived in, with no scrim of daydreams or futile hope. It wasn't the Allies who would liberate me from the abomination of this camp. It was death. So why wait? Why prolong the torment? *Where are the Allies? Where are the Allies?* Zelig's words echoed in my mind. He was the staunchest believer in our liberation, and now he lay entombed in the concrete vaulting of a Nazi underground factory.

With no further ceremony Max dragged us out to the middle of the *appell platz.*

All the inmates were lined up in a square to witness the execution of the sentence. In the middle stood a rounded wooden rack. We had to lie over this to receive our lashes. Yisheshe, whimpering with fright and buckling at the knees, went first.

Max pushed him onto the rack and waited for the commandant's signal to begin. But the commandant hadn't come out from his quarters. All was quiet on the platz. No one a spoke a word. A thin mist rose from the ground, enveloping the camp. It made eerie haloes around the lights of the yard and blurred the inmates' faces.

It was an hour before the commandant emerged, swaying slightly. When he arrived Burgin shouted, "Muetzen ab" and we all snapped off our caps.

The commandant then signaled Max, and Max swung the rubber hose. When it came down on Yisheshe's ass a cloud of dust rose from his pants. Yisheshe screamed, but somehow it sounded false. When Max hit him again, another cloud of dust rose into the air. This time the commandant saw it too.

"Just a minute! What has he got under his pants? Take them off!" he screamed at Max.

Max grabbed Yisheshe by the scruff of his neck and yanked down his pants. There for all to see was an obviously dusty but neatly folded blanket. Yisheshe started crying and pleaded with the commandant to spare him. I feared the commandant would decide to hang him, but all he said to Max was "Proceed."

Max seemed to fear that he had compromised himself, and laid into Yisheshe good and proper. This time Yisheshe really screamed in agony. As the lashes came down in quick succession Yisheshe's screams grew fainter. By the time Max reached twenty, he had collapsed on the rack. Max stopped and looked at the commandant.

"Carry out the full punishment!" the commandant shouted. Max counted another five lashes, and Yisheshe was carried away unconscious.

With Yisheshe's first cry I had decided not to give them the satisfaction of hearing me scream. I would simply clench my teeth and bear it all in silence. It is all very well to make decisions ahead of time, of course. The first lash stunned me, the second was so excruciating that it immediately overpowered my vocal cords. I heard myself scream as I had never screamed before. I knew that I would never be able to survive twenty-five lashes. With every stroke I wished that death would relieve me of the pain that emanated from my bottom and flooded my senses.

When Max brought the hose down the sixth time I heard a great wailing sound and the lights went out. At first I thought that I had simply gone blind from pain, and was hearing my own wailing from a distance. Then from far away I heard shouting. "Licht auss! Flieger Alarm!" Moments later I heard the steady droning of oncoming planes.

The Allies were here, and had come to liberate me personally.

Then in the darkness I heard the commandant's voice. "Proceed with the punishment." The rubber hose swished viciously but barely touched my ass. Anticipating its sear I howled in agony, and was caught by surprise when it hardly hurt. I could only gasp with the next lash, then I gathered my wits and howled again. I kept howling until Max counted twenty-one lashes. Then I feigned a collapse, and after Max finished another four strokes I fell to the ground and lay still.

All the inmates remained where they were, waiting for dismissal, but the signal didn't come. In the darkness the commandant had taken off for the air raid shelter and left the whole camp standing exposed in the square.

I lay on the ground and carefully felt my ass. It was terribly painful and swollen. I wondered what had happened to poor Yisheshe, who got the benefit of the full twenty-five strokes.

Max bent down and asked quietly, "Are you O.K.?"

"Thank you Max," I answered. "You saved my ass." When I heard him laugh I realized that I had unwittingly made a pun.

Somehow I felt better. The black clouds of my despair had parted a little. Pain was more tolerable than dread, and even the amoral Max seemed to harbor some particle of humanity. Suddenly the planes were directly overhead. It sounded as if there were thousands of them, the vibrations of their engines making the ground shiver and filling us with longing.

When would the incredible hour arrive? I don't believe that anyone in history desired anything more than we desired liberation. The most fervent believer could not have desired paradise more than we desired liberation.

We watched the fireworks in the sky as the heavy planes plowed through hundreds of floodlights directed at them from the ground. Then came the bursting flames of ack-ack as the German antiaircraft guns opened fire. The planes returned streams of tracer bullets. They were red, orange, and green. It was a magnificent display of power, and it thrilled our souls. We knew that many of us would die before the blessed day came, but we knew that when it came many of our tormentors would die too.

It took a half an hour for the planes to pass over us. Our hearts ached as some of them burst into flames and spiraled to the ground. Occasionally we heard heavy explosions as bombs hit somewhere close. Some must have tried to lighten their loads by dropping their payloads onto empty fields.

Finally we heard the all clear sirens coming from Utting. A few minutes later the commandant sent a corporal to dismiss the *appell.*

Father was so overjoyed that I was still alive that he stayed up half the night telling stories. Yisheshe lay in a coma with a very weak pulse, and the doctor feared he would never regain consciousness. I felt very bad for him. If I had been first in line I might have been the one lying in a coma. Everyone talked about Yisheshe and the cloud of dust that rose from his bottom, and agreed that if he been less lazy and beaten the blanket first, he might have gotten away with it.

Life goes on. My last thought before I went to sleep was about Zelig's portion of the food we stole from the O.T. kitchen. Who would get it, now that Zelig was dead?

20

Christmas 1944

D espite the welts on my ass I slept like a log. The next morning I found out that Father had gotten me a temporary job in camp, where the work was usually much easier. He thought it was advisable, as he feared that Erhard would vent his anger on me. Yisheshe was still in a coma.

Shmuel was now in charge of the burial of the dead, and I was to help him. Since his "reawakening" after listening to Father's stories, he believed that he owed my father his life, and he was specially considerate of me.

The cemetery was about five hundred yards from the camp, through a small back gate. We had a two-wheel cart for transporting the bodies. In the beginning the cart had been open, and the corpses were simply piled on top of it, but some German women who worked in the vicinity complained about the gruesome sight, and the camp's carpenter was ordered to enclose it. Now the cart was essentially a big wooden box on wheels, with double doors at one end.

That morning there were three corpses to be taken out. They lay outside the barracks, little more than skeletons in striped uniforms.

I was surprised that no one had stripped them, as the extra pieces of clothing were life-savers in the ever-increasing cold. Then I found out why. These uniforms were crawling with lice. Although I was more or less used to the vermin by then, seeing them in broad daylight, crawling about in the thousands, was nauseating. But we had to get their uniforms off.

Although Shmuel had become expert at this process, we couldn't entirely avoid contamination, and inevitably some of the lice crawled onto us. After the Nazis and their helpers, the lice were our number-two tormentors.

Shmuel transferred the uniforms into a bucket with a hooked stick, then he led me to a storage room that had the same kind of iron stove the barracks had. It was red-hot and spread a pleasant heat. Shmuel told me to take off my uniform and got undressed himself. Taking up one garment at a time, he spread them out like a tore-ador's cape, and shouting "Ole!" he swacked them against the stove. The lice infesting the garments were immediately incinerated, while nothing happened to the fabric. He did the same with his shirt and pants. This indeed was a completely new Shmuel! Only a short time ago he was like one of the skeletons we had just undressed.

"Listen, listen," he said as he picked up my shirt and swung it. When I leaned in close I could hear a faint popping sound. The lice were exploding as they came in contact with the red-hot stove. A most disgusting and most satisfying sound!

Shmuel had had an ingenious idea, and from that day every night before I went to sleep I gave my uniform this treatment. Soon I got the nickname "Lice Popper." Everyone who was still able to stand on their feet after a day's work tried it too, quite a few burning holes in their uniforms. This was a job for someone with good coordination.

As we passed through the gate to the cemetery that day, trundling the cart of corpses behind us, Shmuel handed the guard a list of the dead, their names and numbers. The guard looked inside the box, counted the bodies, and told us to proceed on our own. The guards knew we had nowhere to go, and most of us could move about the perimeter more or less at will, as long as we stayed within easy shooting distance of the towers.

The cemetery had large mass graves prepared by a tractor so we didn't have to dig into the frozen ground. We laid the corpses in a row and poured disinfectant over them. I couldn't bear their glassy stares, however, and I quickly pushed their eyelids down and put pebbles on them before we covered them with earth. Shmuel looked at me and nodded. "The first time is always the most difficult," he said.

Actually I felt very little, considering the circumstances. The spirit had left these bodies, and what remained was just something to be recycled by nature. More ominous was the size of the grave. There was room for at least fifty more corpses.

At the gate the guard waved us in with barely a glance. That immediately gave me an idea. I had been racking my brain trying to figure out how to smuggle our stolen food into camp. Since they started searching all the returning workers we were unwilling to smuggle anything on our persons. It was too risky. David was almost caught with a tube of cheese, but had the presence of mind to push it under his cap, where the guard didn't bother to look. If one of us had been caught the commandant would certainly have hung us, even if he had to build gallows himself.

Now I had the perfect solution. The next time we had bodies to bury we would bring back the supplies in this rolling coffin. It was a little ghoulish, but I couldn't afford to be squeamish.

Whether we liked it or not we would have to share the cache with Shmuel, but we had Zelig's share, so why begrudge him? That evening I approached David and Abke with the proposition. Only David was still working at the O.T. kitchen. Abke had been sent to the cement works, where fortunately one of the foremen took a liking to him. He ran one of the small locomotives that ferried sand and gravel to the workplaces.

So it was up to David to unearth the cache and bring it to the cemetery, which was about a kilometer from the O.T. kitchen.

With David and Abke's assent I told Shmuel about the plan. When he heard we were going to share the food with him he was very enthusiastic.

Two days later a large transport of Jewish prisoners arrived from Auschwitz. Some were from the Lodz ghetto. They were all terribly thin, just an inch away from being *musselmen*, and very frightened. They had the most gruesome stories to tell about Auschwitz. We had heard terrible tales second- and thirdhand, but this was the first time we heard them from people who had been there. It turned out that many were already undressed for the gas chambers when their captors told them to put their clothes back on, and the next thing they knew they were on a train headed for Kaufering. With these unfortunates came several well-fed capos. It wasn't long before they started throwing their weight around at Lager Ten. At one point I saw Max standing around with them, laughing. The newcomers upset the balance of power, and Max's behavior quickly changed for the worse.

That night four of the newcomers died. In the morning I informed David that this was the day, and we arranged to meet at the cemetery during the lunch break. Shmuel and I found busywork to do until then. Near noon we took the cart around to the four corpses. They lay naked outside the barracks. Lice or no lice, the inmates from Auschwitz had taken every stitch of their clothing.

The transfer went without a hitch. We dropped the corpses and brought in six tubes of cheese, six tubes of liver paste, four cans of sardines, four packs of margarine, three small sausages, and four cans of sweetened milk. We put the food in a hiding place Shmuel had devised in a small storage room where he kept his cleaning tools. That evening we divided the supplies into four equal portions. The problem was where to hide them. More and more thefts occurred during the night, especially since the newcomers had arrived. Shmuel offered to continue hiding the food in his spot, and we agreed. We had no choice but to trust him.

That night we had a feast. Father and I shared a tube of cheese and drank half a can of sweetened milk. It was one bright moment in an increasingly grim situation. More and more prisoners were joining the ranks of the *musselmen*.

Even Jacob Portnov, father's friend, had succumbed. In the beginning Jacob had borne the conditions in the camp better than most. He worked in Father's brigade, and was always ready to lend a hand to those who couldn't keep up. Father became very friendly with him, and in the evenings they would discuss many topics. It was strange seeing the two of them searching their garments for lice while discussing the role of the Christian churches in the present genocide of the Jews, or the future of Zionism after the coming collapse of the Nazis. Jacob was a brilliant analyst, and many of his predictions later came true. He was only a few years older than my brother Herman, and Father somehow saw in him his murdered son.

In the beginning of December, however, Jacob was badly beaten by an O.T. foreman known for his cruelty. We called him "Die weisse Hitale"—"Little White Hat," because he wore one all the time. There seemed to be no reason for him to beat Jacob, as he was a good worker, and after that day Jacob's health steadily deteriorated. The beating itself was not severe enough to cause his health problems; I think he simply lost hope. Both Father and I tried to rally him, sharing our stolen food, but he sank deeper and deeper into depression. He would come back from work, plop himself down on his bunk, and pass out like the other prisoners on their way out. Soon he was infested with lice. At first Father and I would get him out of his clothes so that I could give them the stove treatment, but after a while he began to resist and told us just to leave him alone. He scratched at the lice so much that his skin became covered with raw patches and the lice swarmed around the sores, sucking his blood away. Father talked to him for hours without success. Jacob seemed beyond our reach, and among the fifty or so prisoners in our barracks more and more dropped out like Jacob and became infested by lice. Under such circumstances no matter how much we fought to delouse ourselves, we were always reinfested. The situation became so bad that even the Germans realized that they had to do something about it, lest they lose all their slave labor.

I don't know whether it was deliberate sadism, or whether some SS man discovered a louse on his person and flew off the handle, but around the middle of December we were all rousted from our bunks in the middle of the night. The SS guards and our capos came into the barracks shouting for everyone to undress. Clubs and whips descended on those who didn't react fast enough. Our clothing was taken away to be disinfected, while we, completely naked, were chased through the snow into the showers. I will never forget the feeling of the snow on my naked feet. It was like someone grabbed them in a vice. A freezing wind was blowing, penetrating our very bones. And then, God help us, we had to shower in cold water. The SS guards were shouting, "You lousy Jews! You filthy beasts! Move it, move it, move it!" as many of the older men and a great many *musselmen* collapsed on the cement floor. The guards were sore as hell that they had to get out of their warm beds in the middle of a snow storm to delouse the Jews. I looked at these men bundled in their greatcoats, with their caps and scarves and gloves, and wondered again if they were human at all. When the ordeal was over we had to drag those who had collapsed back to the barracks through driving snow. I thanked God that Father had the presence of mind to add some wood to the stove before we were chased out of the barracks. We all crowded around it trying to get some warmth into our frozen limbs. Our clothing and blankets were still being disinfected, and it was another two hours before we got them back.

We tried to support Jacob through this ordeal, and in fact I was surprised he survived it. If anything, it seemed to bring him out of his lethargy for a while. Father, however, came down with a severe cold, as did many others. Some caught pneumonia and were dead within days.

We continued to receive more inmates from Auschwitz, who continued to tell stories about Mengele, about the graves at Birkenau, about the crematoria. For the first time we realized the full scope of the calamity that had befallen the Jews. We thought we were at the bottom of the pit, but there were far deeper levels of horror. As far as European Jewry was concerned, it seemed Hitler had already won the war, with the last remnants of the Jews dying by the thousands here in the camps of Kaufering and Landsberg.

December 25 was my father's birthday. Christmas Day, for the Germans. We got the day off and were permitted to stay in camp. It had snowed all night, and in the morning the camp and the woods were covered with a beautiful thick white blanket.

We received some extra coal and wood that day, and inside our underground barracks it was nice and warm. More surprises came our way. Each one of us received a Red Cross parcel! Inside we found a whole kilo of lump sugar, sweetened condensed milk, a dry sausage, and a pack of cigarettes. It was an incredible treasure. For most inmates it meant an additional week or two of survival.

The last gift was the most astonishing. We were all given winter coats. They were civilian coats, old and threadbare with a large white X painted on the back, but they were coats and would keep us warm. Someone said he wished that it were Christmas every day. Father laughed, saying that Christmas was a cursed day. From that day forward, he said, the Jews never had a minute of peace.

Christmas or not it was Father's birthday all the same, and I decided to surprise him with a celebration. I got some of our closest friends together, and even got Jacob Portnov to cooperate. The disinfection campaign worked for a while, and Jacob was making a modest effort to take care of himself.

Shmuel, ever Father's admirer, even contributed some food. He must have spread the word about Father's birthday, for soon about twenty inmates showed up wanting to congratulate Father and drink to his health. We crowded into the barracks when Father went out to wash up, and when he returned we held up our tins of sweetened milk and sang Happy Birthday.

Father stood at the entrance with his mouth open, totally surprised. Who remembered birthdays under these conditions? He was so touched that he started crying, and soon all the guests cried too, not exactly appropriate conduct for a birthday party.

Later some of my friends even ventured out and threw snowballs at each other. It had been a long time since any of us had done that, not since we were children. Now we were old, old men at sixteen years of age.

For lunch we received a bowl of thick soup full of potatoes. There were even some pieces of meat in it. We had to wade through two feet of snow to get to the kitchen, but the wind had died down and the sun was out. It was a sparkling day, and I was glad to be alive, even in a Nazi concentration camp. Jacob calculated that the day's booty would prolong our lives for at least two weeks.

That afternoon most of the inmates took naps. I had been asleep for about an hour when I was awakened by Father, who suddenly cried out in his sleep. He bolted upright in the bunk and said, "Your mother just died."

Then he began to weep. His face was ashen and he kept repeating "Rebecca." I tried to calm him and told him it was just a nightmare. He shook his head.

"You don't understand. I was there standing by the bunk. I saw Fanny applying a cold compress to her head. Then I heard Fanny cry out and I knew that she was dead. My life's companion, my sweet Rebecca is no more."

By the expression on his face I saw that he actually believed this. My heart filled with sorrow for him. I scarcely believed in such supernatural phenomena, but I felt a certain uneasiness all the same.

Later, he told me that when he was young he was a traveling salesman for a time. He was somewhere in East Prussia when he had a dream that his father had died. He saw him lying on a large white pillow with the whole family surrounding his bed. He even remembered where each of his brothers and sisters was standing.

At that time he thought that it was just a dream, but when he returned home, he found out that his father had died the same night he had the dream, with his sisters and brothers around the bed just as he had seen them.

"I was there. Don't ask me how. And I was with your mother today."

Then he said, "We might as well say Kaddish, son," and started chanting the ancient prayer for the dead.

"Ithgadal Veihitgadash . . . Shmei Rabo . . ."

"Stop it! Stop it!" I shouted, aghast. "Don't do it, Father! Don't bury her before she is dead! It was just a dream, for God's sake!" I started crying and shaking him, but he paid no attention to me and continued his chanting. Unable to bear it, I ran outside.

It was quiet outdoors. Very few inmates were about, but in the distance I could hear the drunken voices of the guards singing Christmas carols. I looked up into the brilliant blue sky and I prayed once more to a cruel, merciless God. Grant me only one request, I begged, and I will never bother you again. Please, let Father's dream be just a dream.

The next morning, as if to compensate for the day before, we were awakened earlier than usual. It was still dark outside as we lined up for roll call. The sergeant who counted us had a hangover, and kept us out in the bitter cold for more than an hour, trying to get the numbers straight. Even the winter coats didn't help much. We slapped our arms trying to keep warm, which infuriated the guard. He thought we were trying to make his life difficult and delivered many kicks and blows. When a few of the newcomers collapsed in the snow he told us to leave them there. Finally another sergeant came to his aid and they got the numbers right. I kept glancing over at Father. He had withdrawn deep inside himself, and hardly answered me when I talked to him.

Finally he turned around and looked at me for a long time. His gaze was clear and steady. "Don't worry about me, son. No one in the world can take away the wonderful years I spent with your mother. Nor the beauty of her person. I know she is gone, but she will live within me forever. That is how one has to look at it and that is how one can live with it," he said quietly. I was still bewildered by his conviction that Mother was dead, and now it sounded to me like he was trying to rationalize something that couldn't be rationalized. But if that gave him strength to deal with the situation, who was I to argue with him? Father was made of stronger stuff than I had realized.

My mother died of typhoid fever in Stutthoff on December 25, 1944. My sister Fanny, who survived the war, was applying cold compresses to her brow when she died.

I hate things that I can't explain rationally. This remains one of the unexplained mysteries of my life.

21

Vernichtung Durch Arbeit

E arly in March the 442nd Combat Team and the 522nd Field Artillery
parted ways. The Combat Team was reassigned to the Fifth Army in Italy,
but field commanders requested that the 522nd, known for its pinpoint accu-
racy in supporting fire, remain attached to the Seventh Army. On March 9,
the 522nd headed for the Siegfried Line, and was in position near
Kleinblittersdorf by March 12. From there it participated in a multi-pronged
armored assault brilliantly coordinated with Patton's Third Army. The combined forces of the Seventh and the Third crushed the remains of the German
army west of the Rhine River, and by March 21 the Allies held the western
bank from Holland to Switzerland. East of the river sixty German divisions
were poised to defend their homeland, but they were short of fuel, weapons, and
ammunition. By March 25 seven Allied armies, with the greatest concentration of tanks ever assembled, had crossed over the Rhine.

At the beginning of January 1945, I lost my job with Shmuel. One of
the new Polish capos told me that my place would be taken by one of
their men, a professional undertaker, he declared. The Pole was a
short but powerfully built man, and he kept hitting his club against
the palm of his left hand, the very picture of a troublemaker. I could
see that he was a bit nervous though, since I was taller than he and
did not look like one of his starved *musselmen*. The Poles also knew
that the Lithuanians were well-organized and we'd give them trouble
if we were pushed too far.

Since I had accomplished my purpose—smuggling in our stolen
food—I saw no reason to stay with the job, especially since there were

more and more corpses to bury every day. David was still at the O.T. kitchen, and because his workload had increased he thought perhaps the cook would allow me to return. I hoped that by now Erhard had forgotten about the incident at Lager One, but fortunately, he had been replaced by another guard. The cook didn't mind when I showed up, and sent the two of us to scrub the O.T. washroom.

Our stores of stolen food, which once seemed so vast, were shrinking, and I wanted to get back into that storage cellar again. David told me that the chances were almost nil. For one thing, the Germans had installed a sump pump in the cellar after the first flooding, and whenever any water collected it was immediately pumped out.

Even the Germans were beginning to feel the pinch in their rations. In the mess they were really cleaning their plates now. The only scraps we managed to get were from the barrel of pig slop the cook kept for some local farmer. We took some of the stinking stuff home and tried to cook the bacteria out, but it still gave most of us diarrhea. We resorted to the barrel only when we got desperate.

Early in the month the cook greeted us with a big smile. He and the new guard had been drinking and were quite happy about something.

"Ha, you Jews! If you thought that you were soon going to be liberated, forget about it! We have smashed the American army and are on our way to recapture France!" To confirm his words he showed us his newspaper. A banner headline read, "The glorious German army is advancing on Antwerp!" We had heard some rumors about a German offensive in the Ardennes, but this news, in bold black and white, came as a shock. Even if we discounted the propaganda, the Allies were clearly experiencing a setback. If the war was prolonged it could mean death for all of us.

My morale plummeted. I felt lower than I had even in 1942, when the Germans were near Moscow and the Nazis were about to conquer the world. We didn't really have any expectations then, but when every passing day seemed to bring the Allies nearer, our hopes mounted. Now I felt completely deflated.

When we returned to the camp that night, I did exactly what the *musselmen* did. I curled up in a fetal position on my bunk, hoping to drift off to a painless death. The idea that my mother might be dead contributed a lot to my depression. I didn't even bother to delouse my uniform. Everything seemed pointless.

When Father came back from work he knew immediately that something was wrong. At first he attributed it wholly to his dream. He was sorry that he had told me about it, sorry that he had said Kaddish for Mother. When I finally told him what the O.T. cook said he was silent. I could see how shocked he was. He too was losing hope, and seemed to be groping for something to renew it.

"Look, let's find out what's really happening. We need to get our information-gathering team together and have the Strategist analyze what we find. We must figure out what the situation really is, even if the news is bad. In the meantime let's not sink into despair," he said.

Then for some reason he began telling me about his life with Mother when I was just a boy in Heydekrug. He made me remember my birthdays, the carousel ride I took in Memel, the trip back to Kaunas on the paddle wheel ferry. Down to the smallest detail he painted a picture of our family surrounded by love and affection: my grandparents, aunts, uncles, and cousins. Most of them were dead. I couldn't understand why he was talking about such things; it was tearing me apart. I started crying and was unable to stop for hours. When I finally calmed down I felt drained, but somehow relieved. Father had managed to reawaken some fortitude in me. Somehow he made me see that those we loved still lived in our hearts and minds. As long as we continued to live they would stay alive in us, and that alone was a good reason to go on. Now I understood what he meant when he said that no one could take Mother away from him.

I got up, stripped, and fried the lice on my clothes. Then I took a few sips of sweetened milk, which gave me a needed shot of energy. Perhaps the German attack on the Allies wasn't as disastrous as I supposed.

The news of the Allied setback in the Ardennes slowly seeped through the camp. Many reacted the way I had, and fell into despair. Our old news-gathering network had disintegrated. Some of the original members were dead, others had fallen into apathy. The Strategist himself had even lost hope, and was in bad shape. Father had to talk to him for an hour before he finally agreed to cooperate, on two conditions. We were to give him a slice of bread, and we had to supply him with a certain minimum of information before he would attempt an analysis.

Father agreed and we went to work. There were a number of prisoners who worked as shoemakers or tailors or otherwise provided direct services to the Germans. They were in a position to overhear conversations and see newspapers. The rest of us did our best to steal papers and find out whatever we could.

In the meantime more and more of our people were dying and being replaced by evacuees from Poland, Hungary, and Czechoslovakia.

No one was able to report any earth-shaking news. Those who managed to see newspapers reported that the Germans were still fighting in central Belgium, but there was no further mention of Antwerp. From this the Strategist concluded that the German advance had been stopped and was probably being pushed back.

Then, around the third week of January, we got news from a different quarter. One of the capos from Auschwitz was originally from Holland. In the beginning he was a bastard, but soon changed under our influence. He was in an O.T. foreman's office when the foreman was called out, leaving the capo alone there with a radio. He quickly tuned it to a Dutch station in a liberated town. Before the foreman came back he managed to hear that the Russians had commenced a massive offensive, and were rolling over Poland toward eastern Germany and Berlin!

That evening we sat in the Strategist's barracks and listened to his lecture. He looked much better than when I last saw him. Someone had brought him an empty cement sack and a pencil, and he drew us a map that showed both the eastern and western fronts.

Using a stick he pointed out the various routes of attack the Russians and Americans were taking. I looked longingly at the map. Only two fingers separated us from our liberators.

"There is no doubt that we are now in the final phase of the war," the Strategist said. "The Russian army is now unstoppable, especially since Hitler has probably squandered precious divisions trying to stop the western allies, instead of concentrating these divisions against the Soviets.

"To be honest, when I first heard about the German attack on Antwerp I despaired. But I'm beginning to believe it was madness, and may well hasten the devil's downfall! He'll probably try to stem the Russian flood toward Berlin by switching some divisions from the western front. Once that happens, the western allies will arrive here quickly. This is my conclusion from the information you have gathered for me. Thank you."

The Strategist took pride in the calm rationality of his lectures, so we were all surprised when he stood up and shouted "Brothers, the *Geule* (deliverance) is near. Hold out! Hold out! Soon we will be free!" His excitement was so great that he burst into tears.

We too were greatly affected by this speech, and left the lecture in a state of excitement. Even Jacob, who was barely holding on, was moved and showed signs of renewed hope.

The situation had varying effects on the Germans. Some redoubled their beating of prisoners. Others began to treat us more humanely, as if they could see the writing on the wall.

Hope was important to us, but it wasn't enough by itself to keep us alive. Father and I were now down to our last reserves of stolen food, which we shared in dwindling portions. Once again we were hungry all the time, as if the desire to eat were some terrible disease that always threatened us with a relapse. We still had a few cigarettes for emergencies, and occasionally exchanged one with the kitchen crew for a potato.

Father approached Burgin a couple of times and asked if he'd like to hear more of his Trotsky story, but Burgin seemed to have lost interest. He was now engaged in a power struggle with a ruthless Pole who had been promoted to the position of head capo. Burgin was now irritable all the time, and told Father in no uncertain terms to get lost.

Disaster struck late in February. One of Father's boots completely fell apart. He tried to reattach the sole to the top with a piece of wire, but it didn't work. The loss of boots in camp almost inevitably ended in death. Some of the Polish Jews who arrived from Auschwitz wore old shoes that fell apart in the snow, and when they went to work barefoot their feet simply froze. There was nothing one could do about it. The condition was extremely painful, and once gangrene set in death was slow and agonizing. One of these unfortunates couldn't stand the pain any longer and sneaked to the railroad tracks near camp, where trains from Munich passed twice a day. When the train approached he threw himself under its wheels, no doubt hoping for a quick death. But the wheels cut his legs off, and he screamed for a long time.

With Burgin in such a foul mood the only person I could turn to was Shmuel. Among the corpses he ferried there must be some that had boots or at least wooden clogs, even with their neighbors robbing most of the dying of all their possessions. It was our only hope. The problem was that we didn't have much to trade with.

Two-thirds of the dead and dying were Poles from Auschwitz, so when I came to Shmuel with Father's plight he immediately began inquiring among the Poles about a possible trade.

That evening, as if to increase Father's misery, the German commandant kept us at the *appell* for a long time. The cement sack Father had tied around his foot completely disintegrated in the snow, and when we got back to the barracks we had to massage his foot for a long time before the feeling returned. We were anxiously awaiting news from Shmuel. When he finally showed up he looked very discouraged. There weren't any boots available, but for two packs of cigarettes he could get Father a pair of wooden clogs. Father had no choice but to accept the deal, even though he had tried my clogs and found them too uncomfortable to wear. We did manage to bargain the Pole down to one pack of cigarettes.

After Shmuel left Father walked around the barracks in the clogs trying to get used to them, but it didn't look good. Someone advised him to cut pieces from his blanket and wrap them around his feet, but several inmates had been hanged for that. The scraps often peeked out of the clogs, and the destruction of German property, including blankets, was punishable by death. The next day Father's clogs rubbed his feet raw. Unable to bear it, he worked in the mud and snow in his bare feet. The second day the German supervisor, who usually got along well with Father, dismissed him from his foreman's job, and Father had to go back to shoveling sand and gravel into the tilt wagons. In two days Father had lost his boots and his job. Both were terrible blows. Another day of working a twelve-hour shift barefoot, and then having to march back to camp, would surely cripple him.

In most cases, prisoners who lost their foot gear were soon shipped to Lager Four. The Germans called it the "Kranken Lager"—the "Convalescent Lager," but in fact it was a death camp as much as Auschwitz was, though without the gas chambers. At Lager Four the men were simply left naked on their bunks. Their rations were drastically reduced, and most simply starved. As far as we knew, no one returned from Lager Four.

In desperation I ran again to Shmuel and explained what happened. I had little hope of success, but later that night Shmuel came to me all excited. He had located a pair of boots. They were two sizes too big, but that was far better than too small. The trouble was the price. The owner of the boots, a Polish Jew from the ghetto of Lodz, inherited them from his brother who had passed away. He wanted four packs of cigarettes, two loaves of bread, margarine, and a can of condensed milk. All we had was a pack of cigarettes, a can of milk, and half a box of sugar cubes.

I went with Shmuel to talk to this Pole. Like many of his countrymen, he was short and emaciated-looking. His protruding eyes studied me shrewdly. He knew that I worked in the German O.T. kitchen and figured I must be loaded with food. When I offered him all that we had, he gave me a contemptuous look.

"You Litvaks think we are all fools. I gave you my price, take it or leave it," he said, and spat on the floor.

I simply could not leave without the boots. Father's life depended on it. For a minute I was tempted to appeal to his conscience, but looking into his cunning eyes I was convinced this would have the opposite effect. If I had had a gun I would have killed him for those boots, but I had no weapon, not even a knife.

"Look," I said in desperation. "I don't have all the items on your list at the moment. But you know that I work in the O.T. kitchen. I can bring you a few items every day. Since I can't give it to you all at once I will add some cheese and liver conserves," I said, in as confident a tone as I could muster. "But I am afraid that the bread is out. I have no way of obtaining bread."

In response he just spat again. There was nothing more I could do at the moment, and I turned to leave. Shmuel stopped me.

"You know that his father is the Storyteller, don't you? If he dies, who is going to tell the world what had happened to us here? He is the only one for the job, and you know it," Shmuel said, looking steadily at the Pole.

The Pole gave Shmuel a startled look. I had no idea that Father's reputation was known even among the newcomers, and thought that Shmuel had lost his marbles appealing to the Pole in this fashion. How could such an abstract idea appeal to someone who was starving? But I was wrong. The fact that this scrawny fellow even considered the proposition made him stand a little taller in my eyes. I was certain he could get what he asked for somewhere else. I'm not sure that I myself would have had the stamina to give up so much food on behalf of an idea.

Grabbing the Pole's hand, I told him that I had access to the food cellar at the German kitchen and that I would bring him food every day, that he wouldn't get a better offer from anyone in the camp.

Shmuel suddenly said, "I will add a can of condensed milk and a pack of cigarettes of my own."

The man gave us a long and searching look. "How do I know that you will keep your word?" he said doubtfully.

"I always keep my word, no matter what," I said earnestly.

I could see him struggling with himself, his face contorting with the effort. Suddenly he stood up. He seemed to have made up his mind. I could hear my heart beating as I stood waiting for the verdict.

"I'll give you the boots on three conditions. One, that you swear on the Bible to bring me the food you promised. Two, that I deliver the boots to the Storyteller myself. Three, that he mention the name of my brother when he tells the world what happened to us here."

A surge of happiness filled my heart. My father was saved! Before I knew what I was doing, I grabbed him and gave him a big hug. The tears in my eyes were tears of both happiness and shame. I was ashamed not just because moments before I had been ready to murder this man, but also because I'd regarded him with such condescension. I had no inkling that so much humanity could reside in such a wasted creature.

I would get that food for him even if it killed me.

He disappeared for a moment to retrieve the boots. They were worn and patched but still sturdy-looking. "My name is Metek," he said, shaking my hand. Then the three of us marched solemnly toward our block, with Metek cradling the boots in his arms.

Father knew nothing of this. I was afraid that if the deal fell through it would have come as a terrible blow. He was asleep when we came in.

Father was so excited by the boots that he hardly uttered a word. The boots were indeed too big, but Father didn't give a damn and recklessly cut off two pieces of his blanket to wrap his feet in. When he stuck his feet in the boots he let out a long sigh of relief—the most satisfying sound I'd heard in a long time.

● ● ●

The next day I was utterly dismayed to discover a big padlock on the door to the food cellar. There was nothing in the world I could do to get in there. I felt terrible. What was I going to tell Metek? How would I look him in the eye?

Father returned that evening with good news, however. He had gotten back his foreman's job, because the O.T. supervisor wasn't satisfied with his replacement. The fact that Father wore boots again made a difference. He and I agreed to give our bread rations to Metek.

I found Metek lying in his bunk. Telling him what had happened, I begged his forgiveness and offered him the two portions of bread. Metek lay there, not saying a word. Then he emerged from the shadows of his bunk. His nose was broken, both eyes were turning black, and he was cradling his left arm in his right. I was aghast.

"'Weisse Hitale' did this to me. I think he broke my arm. This is what I get for my good deeds." He tried to smile, but both of us knew he was as good as dead.

I gave him the two portions of bread and said fiercely, "Tomorrow I am going to break that lock and bring you the food I promised and I don't care if they hang me for it!"

He gave me a long look and then sighed. "Too bad I didn't get to know you before. But don't risk your life for me. The way I am, they are probably going to send me to Lager Four."

I had a hard time sleeping that night. I somehow felt as if I had taken advantage of Metek, as if he had been sacrificed in my father's place, at my instigation. I thought about Lena. I thought about the things that she and Miriam said to me about sacrificing my humanity. I thought about Mr. Edelstein. I thought about Cooky. I was a survivor, and I felt as if I had blood on my hands.

The next day at the O.T. kitchen I walked around like a man obsessed. I had to get into that food cellar somehow. I knew perfectly well it would take more than food to save Metek, but that had no effect on my burning desire to bring him some of the promised payment.

We were having a warm spell, and the snow was melting in places, creating slushy puddles of water and ice. Here and there small rivulets of water ran through the woods.

"Too bad the water isn't running into the cellar," I thought, and then: "What if I somehow flooded the damn thing?" If I erased my tracks they would surely think it was the thaw that did it. The very thought of doing this frightened me to death. It was the most insane idea I'd had yet, but I was obsessed with my promise to Metek. I had to get him something good to eat, especially now that he was virtually sentenced to death. Was it pride that moved me this way? Up until now I'd taken only calculated risks, when necessity seemed to demand it. Now I was about to do something that made no sense at all.

Two voices battled it out in my head, even as I circled the kitchen looking for a means of achieving my goal. With the end of the Nazis so near at hand I was going to throw my life away on a stupid promise, when the man I'd made the promise to had even released me from it.

At the back of the kitchen there was a small window at ground level. I knew there was no window in the storage cellar, but this room was next to it. If I could flood it I was sure that the storage room would flood as well.

Then I discovered a faucet, with a length of old hose still attached, behind a neat stack of cordwood. It seemed too near a miracle to resist. "So you do this, and then what?" I said to myself. "They have installed an electric pump which does the job without any bucket brigade." I felt as if there were two people dwelling within me, one quite mad and the other trying to control the madman. I dragged the hose to the window and then opened the faucet. My heart was beating so wildly I thought I would have a heart attack. What was I trying to prove to that dead man, anyway? If the Germans caught me in an act of sabotage, they would hang not only me but my father and who knows how many other innocent people. At that moment I must have truly been insane. I have no other explanation for it.

I let the water run as long as I could endure the fear of exposure, then closed the faucet and hid the hose in the woodpile again. I was practically breathless at that point, hardly able to believe I wasn't caught red-handed.

I hadn't dared tell David about my plan, and he kept giving me curious looks, not understanding why I was so agitated most of the day. We did our usual chores, cleaning and scrubbing the wash room and the mess hall. The workday was drawing to a close. I began to think that the sump pump had done its work, and all my effort and risk had been in vain.

Then the old cook started screaming and cursing and all hell broke lose. His assistant came out searching for us. "Quickly, quickly, there is water in the cellar!" he shouted.

We found the cook ankle-deep in water, yelling at the mechanic who was repeatedly trying to start the sump pump, to no avail. I hadn't dared dream of such a lucky break. I had simply flooded the place with no idea what might happen next. I was beginning to have faith in God again. Perhaps God really did protect madmen, and I had surely been a madman that day.

We grabbed two buckets and began emptying the water outside. We had two problems this time, however. One was the German mechanic tinkering with the water pump. The other was that there were only the two of us bailing, when last time there were four. That brought to mind poor Zelig, now entombed in the concrete roof at Moll.

But there was no time to waste mourning the dead. I grabbed a few tubes of cheese, liver paste, and sardines and shoved them into a bucket of water the instant I had a chance. I avoided the packets of margarine. I sank two or three more small loads in the next few buckets, keeping an eye on the mechanic all the while. I had just liberated some condensed milk and a sausage when the electrician turned around and almost caught me in the act. Fortunately he was just searching out the switch on the opposite wall. He ran to it, threw the lever, and the hum of the pump made him laugh out loud. It had the opposite effect on David and me, but we couldn't really complain. We had managed to steal a fair quantity in a short time.

Because of the ever-increasing numbers of lice on the prisoners, the guards at the gate had discontinued body searches for the most part, and David and I decided to risk carrying our booty under our uniforms. The stuff wasn't terribly bulky, and could be hidden pretty well under the rags and old cement sacks most of us used to pad ourselves against the cold.

We passed through without a hitch, and I immediately took off for Metek's barracks.

As if possessed I burst in shouting "Metek, Metek, I made it! Look what I got for you!" Waving a tube of cheese in the air I ran to his bunk, but it was empty. Bewildered, I asked his neighbor where he was.

He gave me a sad look and said: "They sent him to the Kranken Lager." His words hit me like a thunderbolt. They had already taken Metek to Lager Four! Suddenly all the tension that had built up in the last few days—the loss of Father's boots, our dicey negotiations with Metek, my obsession with keeping my promise, and my frightening act of sabotage—all of it burst like an enormous balloon. I had taken huge risks, all for nothing. It was a terrible letdown. I felt I had been cheated of something important, and I sat down on Metek's empty bunk, buried my head in my arms, and cried.

"Did you know him well?" a deep voice asked. It sounded exactly like my brother Herman's. Startled, I looked up and saw a tall, wide shouldered man standing by the bunk. He even resembled my late brother, with his straight dark hair and high cheekbones.

"You look as if you've seen a ghost," the man said. "Why? And why are you mourning Metek? He came with us from Auschwitz and he hasn't been here long." His voice was gentle, but curious.

Wiping my face on my sleeve, I said, "In answer to your first question, you sound just like my brother." He asked Herman's name, and I told him. "But his friends called him Tarzan," I added. "The Nazis killed him at the beginning of the war."

"My name is Bertholt," the man said, then gave a short laugh when he saw my face.

"I know, I know. Only my mother was Jewish, and my father insisted on this stupid name. I must be the only Bertholt in the camp. I also have a nickname. They call me 'The Judge' because I studied law before the war broke out, and the inmates here come to me when they have a dispute.

"Now why were you crying so bitterly when you heard that Metek was sent away?"

I suppose it did seem unnatural to grieve for a perfect stranger, where very few grieved at all except over a lost bread ration or a spilled bowl of soup. I tried to explain, and ended up even telling him a little about Lena and her accusations.

"If you can still entertain such fancy moral principals, you are still human all right. Obviously you were never in Auschwitz. I understand that at the Kaunas ghetto you lived a rather sheltered life."

This was a startling idea, given all the horrors we witnessed there. I thought of the people of our ghetto as morally motivated. Even our ghetto police were exceptionally moral, and the best of them ended up tortured and murdered at the Ninth Fort.

Perhaps it is easier to be morally motivated when you're better fed than they were at Auschwitz. Who knows. Without stopping to consider I extended the cheese to Bertholt. Perhaps I was trying to prove a point about the exceptional nature of the place I came from.

Bertholt's eyes narrowed. I could see that he was struggling with himself. Then he smiled, and took the cheese.

"You almost infected me with your morality. But I think Metek would have liked me to have this," he said, half-apologetically. This made me smile, too.

A week or two later David and I lost our jobs at the O.T. kitchen. The chief supervisor announced that all prisoners would now work full-time at the cement works. A great urgency seemed to have overcome the Germans, and as deadly as the pace had been that winter it was redoubled in March. Father managed to get David and me into his brigade, loading the wagons, which was better than carrying bags of cement, but our rations continued to deteriorate. The bread was often completely green with mold, and I didn't see how we could last long without nourishment. The small quantity of food we'd brought from the O.T. cellar didn't go far among the four of us. We had to give some to Shmuel in exchange for hiding it.

The Germans and Polish capos were also beating prisoners more frequently. As more and more of the Lithuanians were shipped off to Lager Four, they were replaced in the brigades by new arrivals from Poland, Hungary, and Czechoslovakia. The capos who arrived with the Poles were strong and well-fed compared to us, and growing in numbers. The original Polish capos now took revenge on the Litvaks for the hard time they gave them earlier on. Max, in particular, became vicious again.

Early in March, David and Abke came to say good-bye. A group of prisoners was being transferred to Lager One, and they had volunteered to go. Both their fathers were interned in that camp, and they wanted to join them.

They had become close friends, and parting with them was wrenching. "Who knows if we will ever see each other again," David said, barely holding back his tears. "Next time we meet we will either be free, or we will meet on the Other Side."

Father also suffered a loss when Jacob Portnov left the camp. Jacob's physical condition deteriorated until he finally couldn't work anymore. He stayed in the barracks for a few days, and we nursed him as well as we could, sharing what bits of food we could spare and trying to keep him deloused, but he showed no improvement. One day when we returned from work he was gone. He and several other *musselmen* had been shipped off to Lager Four.

The lice problem was escalating. Around the same time that Jacob disappeared a boy named Yankale Bergman, from Kaunas, came down with a high fever and a rash. His was the first case of typhus, and within a couple of weeks ten more cases were reported. One morning after roll call Burgin appeared and announced that we had an epidemic on our hands, and until further notice the camp was under quarantine.

I was reminded of when they burned down the hospital in the ghetto. Being cooped up in camp with an epidemic raging was frightening enough, but we also feared that they would simply burn the camp down, with us in it.

There was, however, one advantage. No more backbreaking work in the cement yards.

We were now shut off from the world, and for all we knew, the Allies were still in France and the Russians in Poland. The one message that got through came in the form of bombers and ever-increasing numbers of fighter planes flying low overhead. They machine-gunned everything that moved on the roads around Utting. At least our tormentors and their families were now getting a taste of their own medicine. Even more satisfying was the fact that we never saw a single Nazi plane challenging the Allied aircraft.

Every morning there were more corpses lying outside the barracks awaiting burial. What a terrible shame to see the lights of liberation so near, yet die at the last minute in this darkness.

With David and Abke gone I began to spend time with Bertholt. He was five years older than me, but I felt strangely drawn to him, probably because he reminded me of Herman. He was well educated, and impressed by the number of books I'd read in the ghetto with Cooky and Chaim. During the month of quarantine we spent many hours together, discussing the books we'd both read.

One time a capo wouldn't accept one of Bertholt's "judgments," and tried to hit him with his club. Bertholt gracefully ducked and with a quick chop to his neck laid him out on the floor. It was the first time I'd ever seen a karate chop. Bertholt had huge hands which he exercised regularly. He let me feel the edges of his palms, and they were hard as rocks. Like my brother, he too got into fights with anti-

Semites when he was in school. After he had been beaten several times by his Polish classmates he took karate lessons, and became so good at it that the Poles gave him a wide berth. I felt safe when I was around Bertholt.

The last weeks of March were quite warm, and when the snow melted and the ground dried a little we started sitting outside in the sun. One day Bertholt surprised me with a copybook and a pencil. God knows where he got them. I'd told him how much I missed the diary I'd had to throw away in Stutthoff.

I wanted to rewrite the events of the war while my memory was still fresh, and was surprised to discover how hard it was to hold a pencil. Starvation and lassitude were taking their toll. Nevertheless I was determined, and I settled in a corner of the yard where the SS in the watchtowers couldn't see me. I started with the arrival of the Soviets in Kaunas, and continued from there. I was surprised at how much I remembered, perhaps because I had already recorded these things once before in the ghetto. I stuck to the main events, however, having neither the strength nor the paper to include all the details. Whenever I forgot a date or name I asked my father or someone else who had been in the ghetto. The one person who helped more than anyone else was Yisheshe. The same Yisheshe who'd gotten the twenty-five lashes and whom I'd given up for dead. He almost died among the *musselmen* at Lager Four, but he ended up impressing one of the capos with his storytelling skills and received enough rations to recuperate. He was transferred to a barracks for the "healthy and privileged," and after several months transferred back to Lager Ten.

I introduced Yisheshe to Bertholt, and they immediately took to each other. Yisheshe, with his phenomenal memory, intrigued Bertholt, and the three of us would pass the days of quarantine discussing politics, philosophy, literature, the past, and the future. It helped to take our minds off the hunger that gnawed at our guts twenty-four hours a day.

Bertholt's family, like ours, nearly made it to the United States. The American consul in Poland told him it would be no problem. Then he discovered that Bertholt's mother was Jewish and that his father was a member of the liberal Socialist party in Poland. "We don't need any Reds in our country," he said, "and we don't need millions of you Jews flooding in, either. We have enough Yids as it is." With that

Bertholt's father, who was not a violent man, lunged for the consul and knocked him out cold.

"That was the end of our immigration to the U.S.A.," Bertholt said. "As a consequence, my mother and little brother ended up in the gas chambers at Auschwitz, and my father was killed in the Warsaw uprising."

What an extraordinary difference between this anti-Semitic American diplomat and our consul from Japan!

The days passed, until finally no new cases of the deadly typhus were reported. A few days later the quarantine was lifted.

April was upon us. The day they sent us back to work the sky was cloudless, the sun warm. The fields on the road to Utting were beginning to bloom with early wildflowers. The O.T. foreman declared that everyone had to work in the cement yard, but I went straight to the O.T. kitchen anyway. We had been on starvation rations for a month, and I was determined to get some food.

Without asking anyone I slipped into the washroom and started scrubbing. The place was filthy. When the cook discovered me he allowed me to stay, and even gave me a piece of fresh bread. It tasted like some exotic cake.

"I'm relieved that you are back," he said, sounding not at all like the grumpy cook I remembered. "My last worker was a lazy bastard, and last week he took off and never came back. I've been without any help at all.

"Don't worry," he added, "I won't let the O.T. foreman take away my one good worker."

Later that day a squadron of American fighter planes came roaring over the roof, descending toward the railroad tracks. I could hear their cannons rattling, followed by loud explosions. It was an incredible sight, and my heart leapt for joy. The cook panicked when they came so close, and ran for the cellar. "Get out, get out, get out!" he screamed when I tried to follow him. "I saw you. You were gloating! Just stay out there and let your pals up there shoot you down!"

Getting this man angry with me was a big mistake. I needed this job. I didn't want to die in the cement yard or starve to death at the eleventh hour, with the Allies so close. When the air raid was over I begged his forgiveness. I insisted that I was just as frightened as he. When he relented I was so relieved that I ran to the mess hall and raised a cloud of dust with my broom.

One of the Germans who worked with the O.T. was sitting there reading the paper. "What are you trying to do, get it all clean before the war is over?" he laughed. Then he folded the paper and stood up. I managed to read only a headline: "Heavy Fighting in the Ruhr."

"Oh, sure, the war will soon be over," the German said, coming up quite close and grinning into my face. "It will be the end of us, but the end of you, too. You think the SS will let you stay alive? It only takes a second to put a bullet through your head," he said, pointing his index finger between my eyes like a gun. "Poof!"

I watched him as he sauntered out the door and into the bright sunlight. He was still laughing.

22

The Death March

B y the middle of April 1945, German troops were withdrawing so fast that the Allied ground troops could hardly keep up. Motorized units began ferrying the infantry east, toward Munich. The Allies wanted to give the Germans no opportunity to regroup and entrench themselves.

By this time the 522nd had been attached to so many different battalions it was famous. Its artillery provided accurate supporting fire for assaults on Mannheim, Heidelberg, Rothenburg, and Morlbach. Its forward observers and scouts acted as the eyes and ears for the advancing Third and Seventh armies. Driving over the remains of Hitler's autobahn, often at highway speeds, they zig-zagged over the German countryside, going for weeks with very little sleep. Clarence Matsumura, Norm Funamura, Herb Kumabi, Yosh Arai, Mas Fujimoto, and David Sugimoto were patrolling in a radio equipment weapons transport when they approached the outskirts of Munich.

"When we first crossed over into Germany nearly everything had been bombed flat. It wasn't until we reached Bavaria and the area around Munich that I suddenly noticed birds singing. For weeks, every night there had been gunfire and bombs going off and my ears were always ringing. After two or three days the ringing went away, and that's when I started hearing birds sing. I hadn't heard any birds in two months. Then I started hearing this strange sound which turned out to be rabbits. Rabbits crying for their mates. . . .

"Near the end of April we entered a really peaceful-looking town called Dachau. I had never heard of it before."

April 24, 1945, was our last day of work. A great urgency was in the air—confusion among the Germans, excitement mixed with fear

335

among the prisoners. That morning I was led out from the O.T. kitchen to dig a pit, and for a while I thought I was digging my own grave. It turned out to be a trench for an anti-tank gun.

Early that afternoon the Germans brought everyone back to camp. All the prisoners, including the sick and the dying, were told to report to the *appell platz* for a special roll call. It was an anxious moment for us, but we also sensed confusion and insecurity among the Germans. I thought of the "Big Action" in the ghetto in 1941, and remembered an arrogant Rauca standing there in his glossy boots, determining who would live and who would die with a casual wave of his hand. The Nazis were the masters of the world then.

One thing hadn't changed: the Germans' insistence on order. They counted us endless times. God forbid that anyone should be missing. There were only six hundred of us in the camp, but it was late afternoon before they were satisfied with the count. We were then given some meager rations and told we would be evacuated the next morning.

No one could sleep. I crept outside several times to make sure that the Germans hadn't run away, but the tower guards were still there, and there were extra patrols at the fence.

Early the next morning we were given our usual watery *kaffee ersatz* plus a little extra bread. The Commandant made one of his few appearances, looking haggard. He told us we were going to march to Dachau and had nothing to worry about, so long as we were orderly. Anyone who broke ranks would be shot.

It was a beautiful day when we marched out, escorted by a new SS squad. In the beginning they tried to keep us in formation, but no amount of cursing or kicking could keep the starved prisoners marching in proper fashion. Soon we were a disorderly mob shuffling toward Munich, and the SS stopped trying to order the ranks. Their great efficient engine of destruction was falling apart. It was a messy business now.

Father, Bertholt, Yisheshe, and I all managed to stay together. I was surprised that Father and I could keep up as well as we did, but we carried little with us. All I had was two blankets and my precious diary. Yisheshe was the one who tired easily. Apparently his twenty-five lashes had done some permanent damage to his legs. After four hours of marching he simply sat down. We struggled with him, trying to drag him along because the guards were beating those who stopped altogether, but he begged us to leave him alone.

We were surprised a short while later when a truck moved along the line picking up those who could no longer walk. We helped Yisheshe and a few others climb aboard. I was sure that they were going to be taken somewhere and shot. They just didn't want to do it out in broad daylight, where German civilians might see. I watched the truck pull away, with Yisheshe waving from the back. He even tried to smile, which completely broke my heart.

There were several air raids the first day, but they were low-flying bombers attacking trains and military convoys. At one point the planes attacked a train moving along in the distance. The locomotive received a direct hit, leaping off the tracks and blowing up in a cloud of steam. The Nazi beast was disintegrating before our very eyes.

The next day, as we passed through a suburb, we could see the furtive parting of curtains as German civilians peered out at us. To our surprise a few of them came out and tried to offer us bread, but the result was disastrous. Hundreds of starving inmates would descend on the benefactor, often knocking him or her down. The bread was immediately torn to pieces, and the guards set upon the mob. Each time this happened several more bodies were left by the side of the road.

As hungry as we were, we stayed away from these mad rushes. I have to admit it was not only compassionate, but daring for these civilians to venture out offering bread. This was the first time we'd seen German civilians up close, outside of one or two in Utting and those in the Organization Todt, and the latter were as callous as the SS. I always wondered how a whole nation could be evil. Apparently this one was not.

In the late afternoon we stopped for a rest, and to our great relief a truck came by giving out bread rations. The guards said they would shoot anyone who became disorderly, but there was still an anxious crush in the bread line. Father, Bertholt, and I all got portions. We ate every crumb.

Despite the losses along the way, our numbers were increasing. Prisoners from camps all over the area were now joining our ranks. We were converging on Dachau.

It was late in the afternoon before we arrived at the gate, which was inscribed with the cynical phrase "Arbeit Macht Frei." The watchtowers at Lager Ten were puny in comparison to the formidable towers here.

It was the first concentration camp the Germans built, and it had seen so many months and years of brutality that one could almost feel pain emanating from its walls. You could feel the evil in the place, as if Lucifer himself was in residence. I felt a wave of fear and loathing pass over me when we went in.

They led us straight to the opposite end of the camp and told us to undress. They said that we were going to shower and then they would issue us new uniforms. I clutched my diary. I was going to lose it again, after all my painstaking work at Lager Ten. Father and Bertholt were giving each other nervous looks when suddenly the capos were on us, shouting and swinging their sticks.

The gas chambers. The transition from life to imminent death was so fast I barely had time to contemplate it. Some of the Poles who had worked at Auschwitz told us that the victims of the gas chamber suffered terribly before they died. That when they opened the door afterward there was a pyramid of people piled up in the middle. The gas spread from the floor up, so the victims climbed on top of each other trying to get one last breath of air. I thought of Cooky in Auschwitz. I thought of the suffocating pit at the Ninth Fort. Father was squeezing my hand so hard he almost broke it, and Bertholt had gone almost rigid with fear. My gut tightened into a huge knot, and I closed my eyes.

Then I heard my father laughing. I was certain that he had lost his wits. "Look, look!" he shouted. "Open windows! We're going to have a shower after all!"

Relief flooded over me even as streams of lukewarm water began flowing from the nozzles along the wall. I even began humming a tune as the water washed down the crust of dirt that covered my body.

They gave us reasonable portions of bread and margarine that evening, and then led us to an empty barracks. It was aboveground, and the spring air moving through the windows was chilly but fresh. I plopped down on the first available bunk, filled with an unreasoning happiness. I barely had time to wonder what force of nature made us cling so hard to a miserable life before I dropped into a deep and dreamless sleep.

When the capos woke us the next morning I opened my eyes to discover a mob of new prisoners. They were everywhere, crammed two and three to a bunk and sleeping on the floor. We discovered that we had been among the first to enter the camp. Those who arrived in the middle of the night got neither a shower nor clean uniforms, and the place reeked.

When we first arrived the camp was clean and orderly, with capos and SS enforcing their usual iron discipline. Overnight the situation had changed completely. Thousands of inmates from the eleven satellite camps in Landsberg and Kaufering were now being held here, and it was pandemonium. We emerged from the stinking barracks and hardly recognized the place. Torn clothing, old shoes, and all kinds of rubbish filled the yard. The system was utterly breaking down. There were rumors that we would be exchanged with German prisoners of war, and that Red Cross representatives were due in the camp any minute. Others said that we would march to the Swiss border for the exchange. Whatever course destiny would take, we knew that the end was near.

Soon afterward we lined up to receive our rations for the march. To our astonishment we received a whole loaf of bread, a tin of meat weighing a kilo, margarine, and jam.

And among the new crowd in the yard I met two friends we thought were dead. One of them was Yisheshe. He was so happy to see us that he fell into our arms and began to cry. The other was Jacob Portnov.

Like Yisheshe, he found someone in power at Lager Four who knew him and got him an administrative job. The easy work, the extra food, and the better conditions soon brought him around. Although he was still thin as a rail, he didn't look like a *musselman* anymore. Father cried when he discovered Jacob alive.

The sky turned darker as we lined up in rows of five, and as we marched out of the gate, leaving Dachau and all it meant behind, it started to drizzle. On the road the marchers became a long column that disappeared into the murk ahead. Beside Jews, there were Russians, Ukrainians, and prisoners from other east European countries.

Yisheshe had decided to stay back in camp with those too ill to march. He knew he wouldn't be able to get very far. I was afraid of what they might do to the sick who stayed behind, a fear that Father, Jacob, and Bertholt shared. Except for that moment of bliss after our showers, the place filled me with foreboding. It was in terrible disorder now, but there were still enough SS surrounding the camp to kill every inmate there. At least on the march we'd be on public roads.

I also felt that with so much food we could easily make it to the Swiss border. Strangely enough I believed this story. If they wanted to kill us, they would have done it a long time ago. Why would they waste so much precious food on us at the end of the war? What we didn't know was that the Nazis had one last, mad plan to hole up in the mountains of Tyrol and put up a last-ditch defense. We were the slave labor who would build the fortifications. The Allies even got wind of the plan.

Almost from the beginning it was an arduous march. The drizzle quickly penetrated our thin garb, and the temperature began to drop. Father, who had somehow gotten himself a coat at Dachau, dropped it on the road the first day. It got too wet and heavy to support.

We emerged from the suburbs of Dachau and headed south. With the arrival of cold weather we ate much more of our rations than we intended. The guards were increasingly nervous, beating and cursing the stragglers. Many of the guards had dogs on leashes, big German shepherds and some especially vicious Dobermans. The dogs barked and snapped constantly, and often lunged at prisoners who strayed too close.

The first night we camped in a wooded area, putting some of our blankets on the ground and the others over us. They were almost as damp as our uniforms, and we huddled together trying to retain a little body heat. The cold was a particular affront. It was almost the end of April.

During the night some of the Russian prisoners tried to get at our food, but we chased them away. In spite of our weariness none of us really slept. The cold rain completely penetrated our blankets and clothes, and throughout the night we could hear the dogs barking and the intermittent sound of rifle fire. Either prisoners were trying to escape, or the SS were taking potshots at the clumps of sleepers.

The next day we marched out early. The drizzle stopped, but the sky remained dark and lowering. There must have been many thousands in our column alone, because on one long, straight stretch the mass of people moving behind and ahead of us reached as far as I could see. A biting wind kicked up, adding to our misery. I asked the prisoners around us, most of them from Lager Ten and Lager One, if they knew whether David and Abke were on the march. No one knew, although a few knew David's father Melechke, and said he was somewhere in the crowd.

The little food we had left we hid under our clothes. The Russians in the column were becoming more daring, and would actually attack other prisoners for their food.

When we stopped for a break I took out the tin of meat they'd given us at Dachau. Out of the corner of my eye I saw a Russian prisoner running straight for me. I clutched my tin and quickly stuck out my foot. He went flying. He was cursing when he rose from the ground, ready to jump me, but Bertholt had also risen to his feet. He hit the Russian flat in the face with his open hand, and my attacker fell over as if he'd run into a brick wall. He staggered back up with fear in his eyes, then ran. Bertholt grinned and said that apparently he hadn't yet lost his touch. For a while the Russians in our group steered clear.

We passed a road sign that said we were twenty kilometers from a place called Wolfratshausen, wherever that was. Many of the weaker inmates were now falling by the wayside, and we heard shots behind us. There were no more trucks to pick up sick prisoners. The SS were taking care of them with guns and dogs. It was a bad omen, and demolished my theory that the Germans wouldn't shoot prisoners where the civilian population might witness it.

Jacob was growing weaker by the minute, so we took turns supporting him, two on either side. By the time we stopped for the second night we were exhausted. Once again we marched into a wooded area, and we just dropped where we were standing. It wasn't raining, but a cold wind had kicked up and quickly penetrated our sodden blankets. We huddled together, teeth chattering.

Again we spent a miserable, sleepless night. I began to think that Yisheshe was right to stay behind. Joining this march had been a horrible mistake.

The next morning the Germans lined us up again and led us out to the road, then suddenly chased us back into the woods. In a minute we heard the roar of planes over our heads, and long bursts of cannon fire ripped through the trees. Our attacker seemed to think we were German troops. Fortunately, no one in our immediate group was hit, although other inmates around us took casualties.

We remained in the woods that day, trying to recover our strength. From a distance we could hear faint explosions, and as they continued and the volume increased we realized they weren't bombs. Then one of the Russians came crashing past, laughing and singing like a madman.

"What is it, comrade? What's happening?" my father shouted after him.

"That's field artillery! The front is upon us! It's the Americans!" he shouted back, throwing his hat in the air.

My heart was racing. Had the unbelievable hour come?

Father, Bertholt, Jacob, and I threw ourselves on each other, laughing and crying all at the same time. We were hugging and clapping each other on the back when Jacob fell back against a tree. He had a funny smile on his face, as if he were drunk. Then he slid to the ground. Suddenly we all stopped laughing.

"What is it Jacob? What's the matter with you?" Father cried. Jacob just kept smiling foolishly and said nothing. I looked into his eyes and saw them moving about erratically, as if he were unable to focus. There was a strange brilliance in those eyes. I had seen it before. It was the radiance of a soul about to leave a tortured body.

"Oh no! Don't die now Jacob! The Americans are here! They're coming! They're coming!" I screamed.

Suddenly Father grabbed him in his arms and started sobbing.

"Don't die Herman. Don't leave me now, my son! I won't let you! You will not die, you hear me?!"

I stared at Father, my heart twisting in my chest. This time his mind had definitely snapped.

Father clutched Jacob to him, rocking him and calling out Herman's name. But Jacob's eyes had turned glassy. Nothing was behind them anymore.

The rest of us fell into a numb silence. Then Sugihara's last words floated into my head. *"Vaya con Dios,* Jacob," I whispered. *"Vaya con Dios."*

We left him sitting underneath the tree, the smile still on his lips. Perhaps he saw a better world on the other side, I don't know. I closed his eyes. I didn't want him looking at this miserable world anymore.

Father wept for a long time, and then turned mute. He didn't say a word the rest of the day.

That evening, as we sat eating our last rations, a Russian prisoner came running from out of nowhere and snatched Father's tin of meat from his hands. Father didn't move a muscle. Bertholt and I chased after the thief, but a dozen of his comrades rose up and blocked our path. It was senseless to try to fight all of them. The short distance we ran made us realize how weak we were.

The artillery fire we heard that morning died away. Either it wasn't field artillery, or they had moved on, and once again we were plunged into a dark world ruled by Dobermans and SS.

After nightfall the guards marched us out once again. We started to think that they had no idea what they were doing. Someone had given them an order that no longer had any relevance, and they were mindlessly following it. And so our column marched through the picturesque Bavarian countryside, littering the roads with the bodies of the some of the last Lithuanian Jews in Europe.

23

Liberation

The next day it began to snow.

At a certain point my senses began to dim, I suppose from hunger and exhaustion and the endless numb repetition of putting one foot in front of the other. A dreamy quiet seemed to have settled over the ranks, and even the occasional rifle shot toward the rear of the column seemed very far away. Father, Bertholt, and I moved along in silence, among a large body of prisoners. We were like a column of gray ghosts shuffling along, heads down.

I don't know exactly when Father dropped away. It could have been an hour before I looked over at the man walking beside me, and discovered he was a stranger.

The last one to leave me was Bertholt.

When my father disappeared I turned in my tracks, confused. The others in the column parted and moved around me. I wanted only to lie down on the ground and drift away. Death held no horrors now. There were too many others who had gone before me. We must have lost a thousand people that morning alone, the guards shooting them where they fell. At the rate it was going they would soon run out of ammunition.

But the dogs were tireless, and I did fear the dogs.

"Hold on," Bertholt said. "You have to fight to stay alive. Liberation is on its way. You know it and I know it. What would your father say if he saw you giving up? You've got more strength than you know. Stand up. Keep moving."

One of the curious things about starvation is how the largest, strongest men among us were more susceptible than those who were slight of build. It simply took more calories to move a bigger frame. It was hardly an hour after Bertholt spoke to me that he suddenly stumbled on something and fell. He couldn't get up. I bent toward him, and dizziness overcame me. I stood there helpless.

At first Bertholt's face registered surprise, then fear. He was simply unable to rise to his feet. Then something passed over his face, a kind of resignation.

"Go on, Solly. Go. It's no good."

I stood over him, trying to clear my swimming head. Then, as if out of nowhere, a huge Doberman leapt on Bertholt and went straight for his throat. There was a horrible noise and then blood everywhere on the wet ground. I stumbled away, my own blood pounding in my ears.

After that my mind cleared a little. We passed through a little town called Koenigsdorf. On either side of the road the buildings were completely dark. Blackout curtains. Except for our column of ghosts not a soul was in sight. Even the SS guards were exhausted. Nearly all of them were older conscripts, and we had gone a long time without rest. Occasionally I could hear one of them cursing his superior officers and the elements. It was the first day of May, and a soft blanket of snow was starting to collect on the Germans' beds of daffodils and tulips.

There was a gap in the blackout curtains of one sagging old building we passed by. Through it I saw an old man dozing in his chair, a big book open in his lap. A small fire in the fireplace sent flickering lights and shadows over the walls. It was warm and painfully ordinary and it was the closest thing to paradise I could imagine.

Finally the order came to stop at a small clump of woods. I found a spot under a tall pine and wrapped myself in my wet blanket. I was alone now, the last of my group. Out of all of those who were better and braver and smarter than I, I was alive. Why me, God?

The snow continued to fall, covering everything, including me. I fell asleep. During the night I could hear shots. The guards must have been firing at the sleeping prisoners. No one had the strength to try to escape now. I was too exhausted to care.

I awoke with a start. It was well past dawn, and the sun had emerged from the clouds, glittering on the white fields around me. There was something else, something strange that immediately alerted my senses. It was the silence. There wasn't a sound anywhere, no shouted orders or barking dogs. It was as if I were the only one left in the world. Not a soul was in sight.

I must be free, I thought with mild surprise. *Watch it, Solly,* a voice in my head replied. *Don't lose your sanity now.*

Still nothing moved. I could see huddles of prisoners covered with snow all around me, but nothing stirred.

Up on a rise I could see an overturned cart, the horse in the harness lying dead in the road. As I got closer I saw the body of a dead civilian. There was an old folding chair, some kindling, and an aluminum canteen full of potato peelings in the cart. In the German's pockets I found a knife and a cigarette lighter. It was everything I needed.

I moved to the horse and cut strips of meat from his belly, then pulled some splintered boards off the wagon. I had to stop every few minutes and rest. Finally I retreated to the woods with my booty. It seemed to take forever to build a fire. When it was finally lit I cooked soup. I thought of nothing but the soup. I became an extension of the soup. I couldn't think or feel anything else.

Below me, on the road, a tank appeared. Then what looked like a jeep. I closed my eyes, waiting for a bullet to put me out of my misery. Then I heard someone speaking English. When I opened my eyes, four men in khaki uniforms were approaching. They looked unshaven and tired. Their oriental features astonished me. They looked like Sugihara and his family. I stared at them, unable to grasp the situation. Japanese? I continued to sit and stir my soup. My throat constricted. I dared not think, and could not speak.

One of the men came up and knelt in front of me. He gently touched me on the shoulder and said, "You are free, boy. You're free now," he said, and then smiled. That smile has been with me ever since. It wreathed his whole face and made his eyes nearly disappear.

When all I did was stare he removed a chocolate bar from his pocket. "That's for you," he said kindly.

I was groping for my English, actually wanting only to fall on my knees and kiss his feet. "Who . . . are you?" I whispered.

Now he was surprised. "Hey," he called back to the others, "he speaks English."

"Who? . . ." I said again.

"Americans. Americans," the angel said. "Nisei. Japanese Americans. My name is Clarence," he added. "What's yours?"

I almost gave him my camp number, as I always did to the authorities. But I am free now, I thought. The realization filled me with a kind of panic.

"Solly," I managed to say, and took another swallow of soup. There was a big chunk of tough horsemeat in it. I chewed on it. It felt good to chew. I continued to eat my soup, while somewhere inside me a small boy named Solly from Kaunas, Lithuania, was slowly going insane with joy.

The soldiers had a smoke and patiently waited for me to finish. I put the chocolate bar into the knapsack. You just don't eat treasures.

"That's good," Clarence said. "You probably shouldn't eat that yet. We'll take you to our unit and they'll take care of you there. Understand?"

The soldiers helped me to my feet and led me to the jeep. A sergeant named Fujimoto was driving. Clarence sat beside me and kept smiling reassuringly. "You'll be all right. You'll be all right. Just hang on."

Then we were in a camp, and there were American soldiers and MPs and prisoners in striped uniforms. My legs turned to rubber as we headed for the field kitchen. The men set me down, and Clarence brought me a bowl of soup. "Better than horse soup," he said.

Then he squatted beside me, lit a cigarette, and told me that he and his buddies would be moving out soon. To Berchtesgaden. They were going after Hitler.

I was taken to a barn and given a German army blanket. The soldiers kept moving in and out, bringing in more and more prisoners from the road.

Toward evening Clarence appeared again and knelt down at my side. "We have to go now," he said, clasping both my hands in his.

"Thank you, thank you," I whispered, clinging to his hands. Then he was gone.

It was one of the ironies of freedom that many prisoners died within one day of their rescue. Many had lost their teeth from scurvy, and they were perhaps the luckier for it. Many of those who could still chew overate, and the richness of the American rations killed some of them outright. Some had a kind of toxic reaction even to moderate quantities of food. Others developed intestinal problems. Some simply choked to death. The lucky ones were nursed back to health with broth and soft, simple foods like pancakes and mashed potatoes. We were like newborns.

The next day we were fed again. I was already regaining some strength, and I set out to explore the place, to see if I could locate anyone I knew from the camps.

We were in a small town called Waakirchen. The Americans were everywhere, and American tanks and artillery continued to move east on the main road through town, pursuing the last remnants of the German army. The soldiers showered the civilians along the way with cigarettes, chocolates, chewing gum, packets of crackers. I remember watching one soldier leaning out of a tank turret eating an orange. I hadn't seen one in years. He pulled out a section, stuck it in his mouth and sucked out the juice, then spat. The pulp landed on a bush not five feet away from me. I was stupefied at the waste of such precious fruit, and without thinking twice I scooped it up and popped it into my mouth. It was delicious. It makes me squeamish to think of it now, but these Americans were not ordinary human beings. They were like gods.

It was in Bad Toelz, just outside Waakirchen, that I spotted a familiar figure eating something out of a can. It was David Granat. I hadn't seen him since he left for Lager One outside Dachau, trying to get back with his father. We fell into each other's arms and cried our eyes out. Then we laughed. The last time we cried together we were cleaning the washroom of the Organization Todt.

We sat on a small bench outside a building, letting the sun warm our bones. Spring had resumed again, as if there had never been snow on the first of May. It was too late, of course, for those who had frozen to death on the march. Another of God's cruelties, I thought.

David had seen Yisheshe, and told me that he was well, although he still couldn't walk. Abke and David Pozeitser had survived. So had Meishke Olitzky, a boy we called "Bumpa." I told him about Bertholt, and about Father.

He looked at me aghast. "For God's sake, Solly. Your father is alive! I saw him only an hour ago, and he looked very much alive to me!"

I stared back, disbelief and joy flooding over me. Then I realized that this had been the missing piece, the cloud that had darkened my joy at our long-awaited liberation. David grabbed my arm and hauled me from my seat. We started running.

David led me to what had been a German army hospital. When the Allies arrived the beds were full of wounded German soldiers, mostly officers. The Americans put the Germans on the floor, and gave the beds to the concentration camp victims.

I spotted my father in a corner, and was rushing to his bed when an army doctor stopped me. He told me in broken German that I must not wake him. "But that is my father, sir! I thought he was dead!"

The American looked pleased. "You know English? Good. Stick around, all right? Half the time I don't know what these people are saying. You can translate.

"But let your father rest. He was vomiting his food so I had to give him an injection."

For the remainder of the day I stayed on the doctor's heels, translating the Yiddish that most of the patients spoke. I kept tiptoeing back to look at my father, just to make sure he was still breathing. Finally, toward evening, he began to stir, and I sat down by his bed. When he opened his eyes he just stared at me, his eyes filling with tears. Then he took my hands in his and held them. I don't know how long we sat there, not speaking, just holding hands and weeping together. Like the broths and bland foods that slowly brought us back from the threshold of death, the idea of life outside the camps, life without the Germans, had to be slowly and carefully digested.

Now that I'd found Father I could cautiously crack the door and peek into the future. All I could see there was the blinding light of freedom.

A REMEMBRANCE

It is not possible in one volume to tell the stories of all those whose lives touched mine in the ghetto and the camps of Germany. Only a few survived, but the many who perished live on in memory.

George Shtrom, who tried to help my father with the Russian authorities in 1941, was murdered at the Lietukis garage massacre that same year. George Shtrom's wife Jennia perished in an outcamp of Stutthoff, two weeks before the liberation.

Uncle Itzhak Shtrom made it across the Russian border during the *schrecklichkeit* of 1941. He spent the remainder of the war in a village in Siberia, returning to Kaunas after the war. He died there, of a heart attack, in 1946. His daughter Frieda died of meningitis in the ghetto. His wife Sonia and daughter Miriam were worked to death in an outer camp of Stutthoff. His son Arik was killed by Lithuanian partisans in 1941, as was my mother's cousin Sonia Weiss. Sonia Weiss's daughter, Irena Weiss, survived the war and is a professor at the University of Vilnius.

Itzhak's sons Zunie and Milie managed to escape from the ghetto in 1943, joining the partisan movement and fighting against the Germans. Both survived the war and emigrated to Israel in 1972. Milie died there a few years later. My cousin Zunie still lives in Hulon.

Uncle Jochil and Aunt Dobbe died in a camp near Riga. Fima and Miriam perished in their ghetto hideout in July 1944.

Aviva's grandfather Chaim died in his bed in the ghetto at the beginning of 1944.

Rose Gutman was the person who gave me my first lessons in English in the ghetto. She and her granddaughter Ruth were both killed during the "Children's Action" in March 1944.

Cooky Kopelman's father was sent to Auschwitz during the "Children's Action." Cooky died there a few months later. His mother, Vera Shore, died in Stutthoff.

My friends Izia and Vova Glass (Gladzookes) perished in a camp in Estonia.

Little Ronnie Temkin was discovered hiding at Maria's cottage. He was taken to Auschwitz. Maria was caught smuggling weapons to the anti-Nazi partisans and was shot by the Gestapo. Jasha Temkin died in an attempt to escape during the last days of the ghetto.

My mother's cousin Dora Trotsky, her husband Isaac, and son

Mulie were hidden by a Lithuanian family before the Germans evacuated the ghetto. While trying to escape from the Soviets in 1946, they were caught and sent to various camps in Russia. Mulie, who was fourteen years old, was sent to Siberia. For eight years he managed to survive terrible conditions there. He spent a total of twelve years in concentration camps. He emigrated to Israel in 1972, where he died twenty years later.

My sister Fanny and my Aunt Anushka both survived the war. Anushka was liberated from an outer camp of Stutthoff and returned to Lithuania, where she died in 1969. My sister Fanny was shipped out of Stutthoff by the SS and put on a barge, presumably to be drowned in the Baltic Sea. When the barges were inadvertently bombed by the British, most of the women were killed or drowned. Fanny's swimming skills saved her. She was picked up by a German navy patrol and brought to British-occupied Kiel. She married Sam Skutelsky from Riga and moved to the United States. Both died in the early 1980s. Their son Robert, my only living nephew, lives in Boulder, Colorado.

My mother's cousin Pola Ginsburg was drowned in the Baltic, thrown overboard by the SS. Her son Vova survived the war and was liberated from Kaufering in May 1945. He and his wife Ibbi emigrated to England where they live to this day.

My cousin Margaret Shtrom-Kagan and her brother Dr. Alexander Shtromas were hidden by Lithuanians prior to the return of the Russians in 1944. She and her husband Joseph Kagan escaped Lithuania in 1945, and emigrated to England, where Joseph was eventually knighted and then given the title Lord for his contributions to the British economy. He died recently in London. Margaret Kagan now lives near Boston. Her brother Alexander teaches peace studies all over the world.

Those from the ghetto and camps who were liberated with me in 1945 remain my closest friends. Uri Chanoch, Aba Naor (Abke Nauchowitz), Chaim Konwitz, Arie Ivtsan, and Zwi Katz all emigrated to Israel. David Grant and Israel and Efraim Gruzin all live in Baltimore, Maryland. Miriam Rogol Pfefer lives in Paris; Izke Rom in Munich. Mike Oliver (Meishke Olitzky—"Bumpa") lives in Carson City, Nevada, and David Levine (Pozeitzer), Abke's cousin, lives in Cincinnati, Ohio.

My brother Herman, who disappeared behind the walls of the Seventh Fort in 1941, was seen by a friend a year later, marching with a group of Russian prisoners of war. That was the last we heard of him.

My father died peacefully in Tel Aviv in 1966. He survived the war, thanks, in part, to the boots we got from Metek Joskowitz. Metek's brother's name was Chaim.

ABOUT SOLLY GANOR

After his liberation from the Nazis in 1945, Solly Ganor decided not to accompany his father to Canada; he chose instead to go to Palestine and join the fight for the independence of Israel. Upon victory and honorable discharge from the army in 1949, he joined the Merchant Marine and fulfilled his desire to see the world. He spent twelve enjoyable years on ships, and by the time he left to marry his wife Pola, he had attained the rank of chief officer.

Solly Ganor next spent three years at London University studying Russian, German, and English literature, as well as Slavic languages. Completing his studies, he and Pola went back to Israel, and he managed a textile factory owned by his wife's family. After fifteen successful years in the textile business, Solly and Pola then decided to make another change. They sold their shares in the company and moved to La Jolla, California in 1977. They lived there until 1984, and since then have divided their time between the United States and Israel.